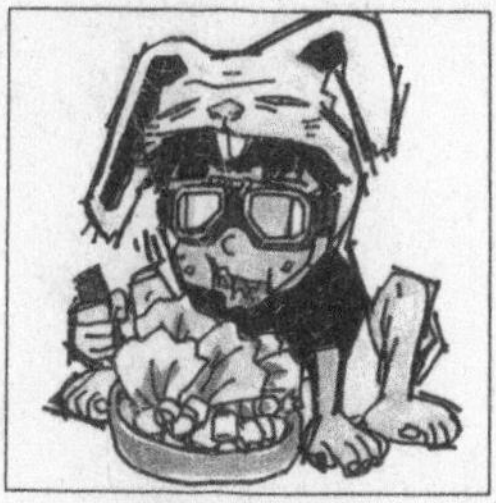

岸本斉史

One day I got a phone call from a relative of mine and got seriously chewed out. Why? The reason was the art I drew of myself in volume one. My aunt saw the picture of me eating ramen, and said "Is he only eating ramen *again?!* Every time you came over to my house, you demanded instant noodles instead of the home-cooked meal I had ready for you! You'd better be getting your vegetables!" Don't worry, auntie—I *am* eating my vegetables. (P.S. They just came out with instant noodles in "Cheese Curry Flavor." It's really tasty.)

—Masashi Kishimoto, 2000

Author/artist Masashi Kishimoto was born in 1974 in rural Okayama Prefecture, Japan. After spending time in art college, he won the Hop Step Award for new manga artists with his manga **Karakuri** ("mechanism"). Kishimoto decided to base his next story on traditional Japanese culture. His first version of **Naruto**, drawn in 1997, was a one-shot story about fox spirits; his final version, which debuted in **Weekly Shonen Jump** in 1999, quickly became the most popular ninja manga in Japan.

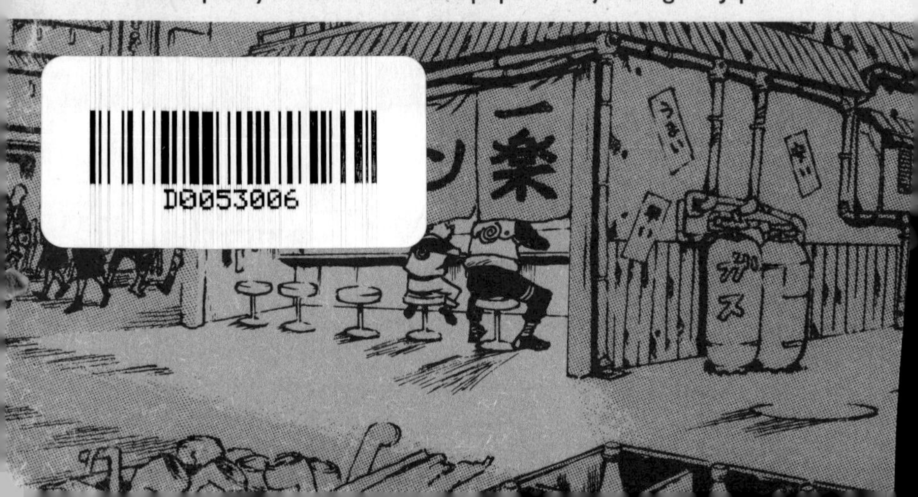
一楽

NARUTO VOL. 2
SHONEN JUMP Manga Edition

This graphic novel contains material that was originally published in English in **SHONEN JUMP** #6–10.

STORY AND ART BY
MASASHI KISHIMOTO

English Adaptation/Jo Duffy
Translation/Katy Bridges, Mari Morimoto
Touch-Up Art & Lettering/Heidi Szykowny
Cover Design/Sean Lee
Graphics & Layout/Sean Lee
Editor/Jason Thompson
Series Editor/Joel Enos

Printed in the U.S.A.

Published by VIZ Media, LLC
P.O. Box 77010
San Francisco, CA 94107

22
First printing, November 2003
Twenty-second printing, February 2016

www.viz.com

SHONEN JUMP MANGA EDITION

NARUTO

VOL. 2

THE WORST CLIENT

STORY AND ART BY
MASASHI KISHIMOTO

SAKURA サクラ
Naruto and Sasuke's classmate. She has a crush on Sasuke, who ignores her. In return, she picks on Naruto, who has a crush on *her*.

NARUTO ナルト
Shunned by the older villagers because of the fox spirit dwelling inside him, Naruto grew up to be an attention-seeking troublemaker. His goal is to become the best ninja ever, and be recognized as the next *Hokage*.

SASUKE サスケ
The top student in Naruto's class, and a member of the prestigious Uchiha clan. His goal is to get revenge against a mysterious person who wronged him in the past.

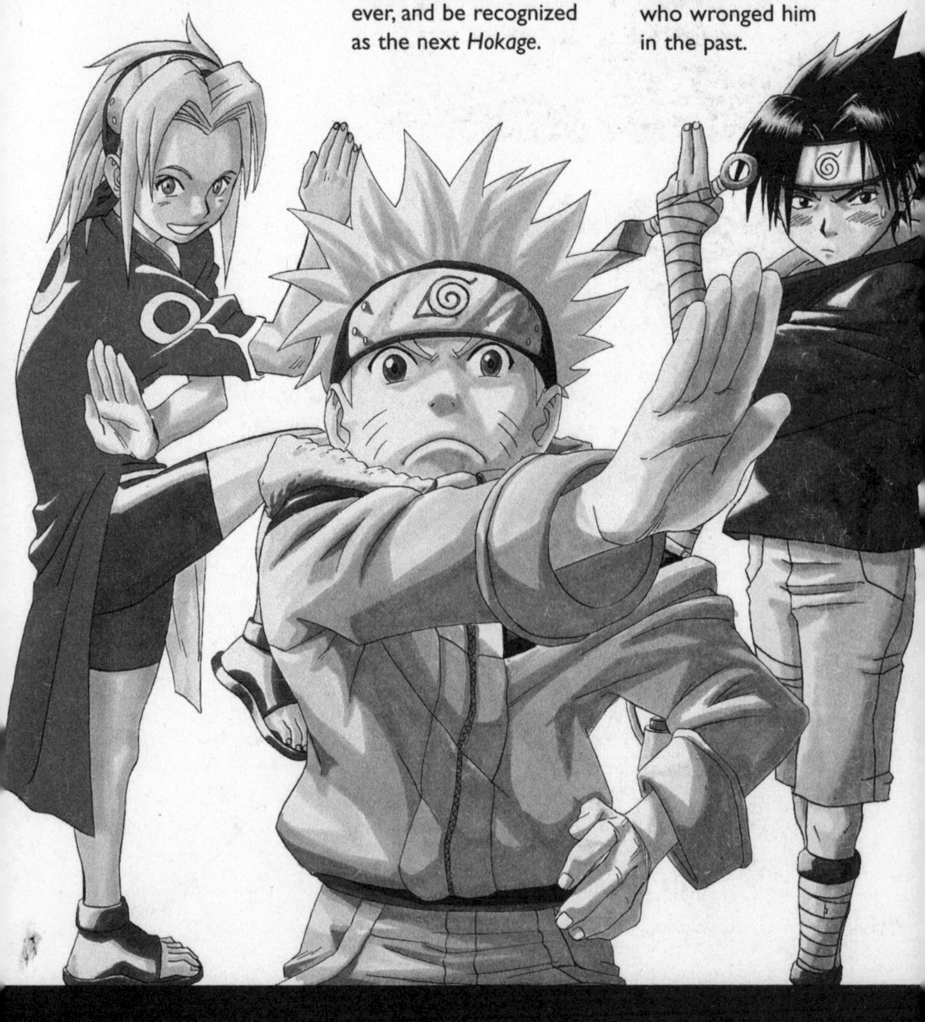

KAKASHI カカシ

An upper-level ninja assigned to train our heroes. Although he seems easy-going, he is a master of *ninjutsu*.

THE THIRD HOKAGE 三代目火影

The most respected person in the village, ever since the fourth *Hokage* died fighting the demon fox. His name means "Fire Shadow."

イルカ IRUKA

Naruto's old teacher at the Ninja Academy. His parents were killed by the demon fox, but he doesn't blame Naruto for it.

THE STORY SO FAR...

Twelve years ago, a giant fox demon attacked the ninja village of Konohagakure, until the *Hokage*, the village champion, managed to defeat it by sealing its soul into the body of a baby boy. Now that boy, Uzumaki Naruto, has grown up and become a ninja-in-training, like his classmates Sasuke and Sakura. Forced to work as a team, the three ninjas received a strange assignment: steal a bell from the belt of their teacher Kakashi. But they failed...and now Kakashi has told them *to give up their hopes of ever being ninja!*

NARUTO

VOL. 2
THE WORST CLIENT

CONTENTS

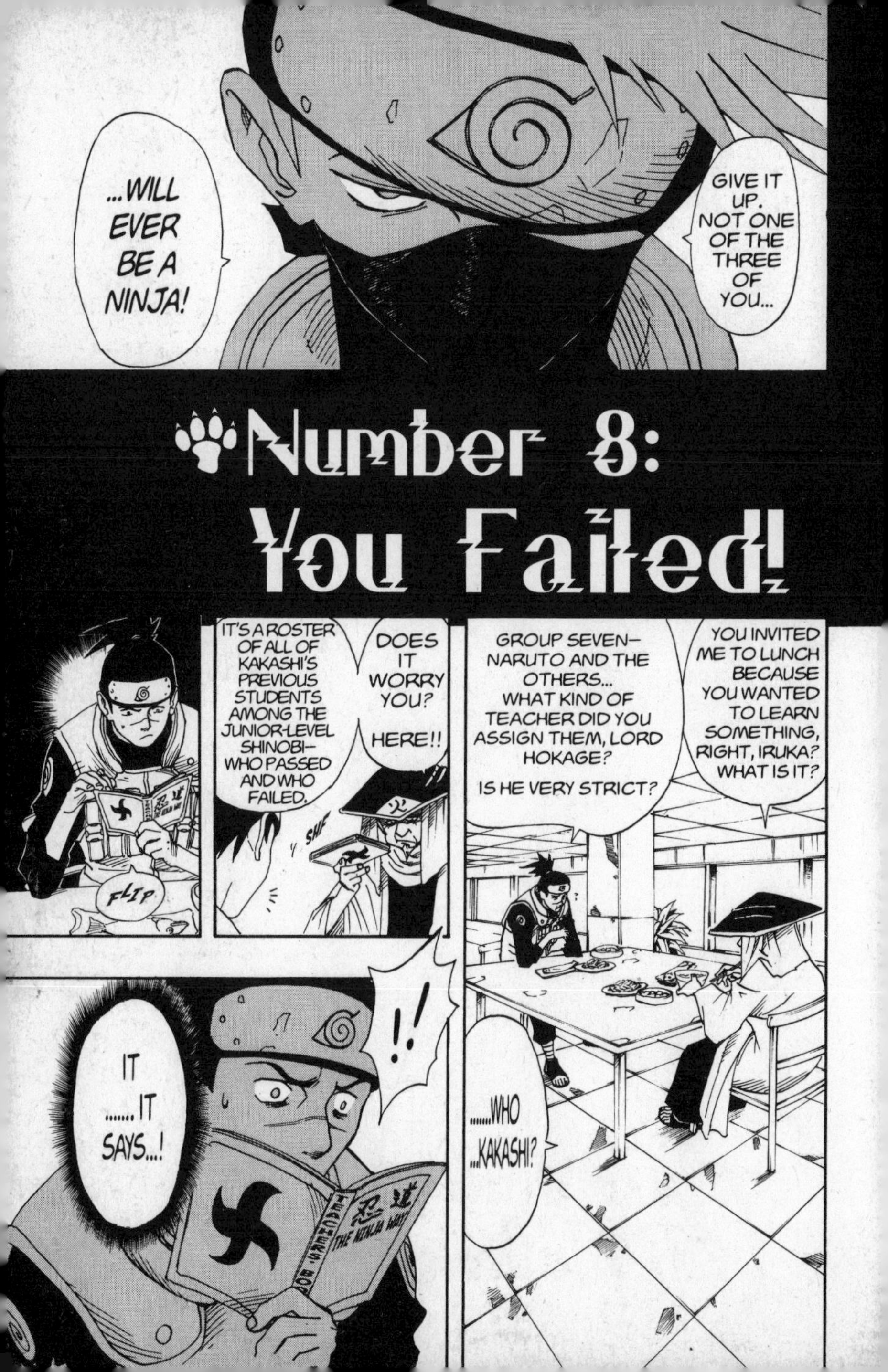
GIVE IT UP. NOT ONE OF THE THREE OF YOU...
...WILL EVER BE A NINJA!
Number 8: You Failed!
YOU INVITED ME TO LUNCH BECAUSE YOU WANTED TO LEARN SOMETHING, RIGHT, IRUKA? WHAT IS IT?
GROUP SEVEN- NARUTO AND THE OTHERS... WHAT KIND OF TEACHER DID YOU ASSIGN THEM, LORD HOKAGE?
IS HE VERY STRICT?
......WHO ...KAKASHI?
DOES IT WORRY YOU?
HERE!!
SHF
IT'S A ROSTER OF ALL OF KAKASHI'S PREVIOUS STUDENTS AMONG THE JUNIOR-LEVEL SHINOBI- WHO PASSED AND WHO FAILED.
FLIP
!!
IT ......IT SAYS...!
THE NINJA WAY

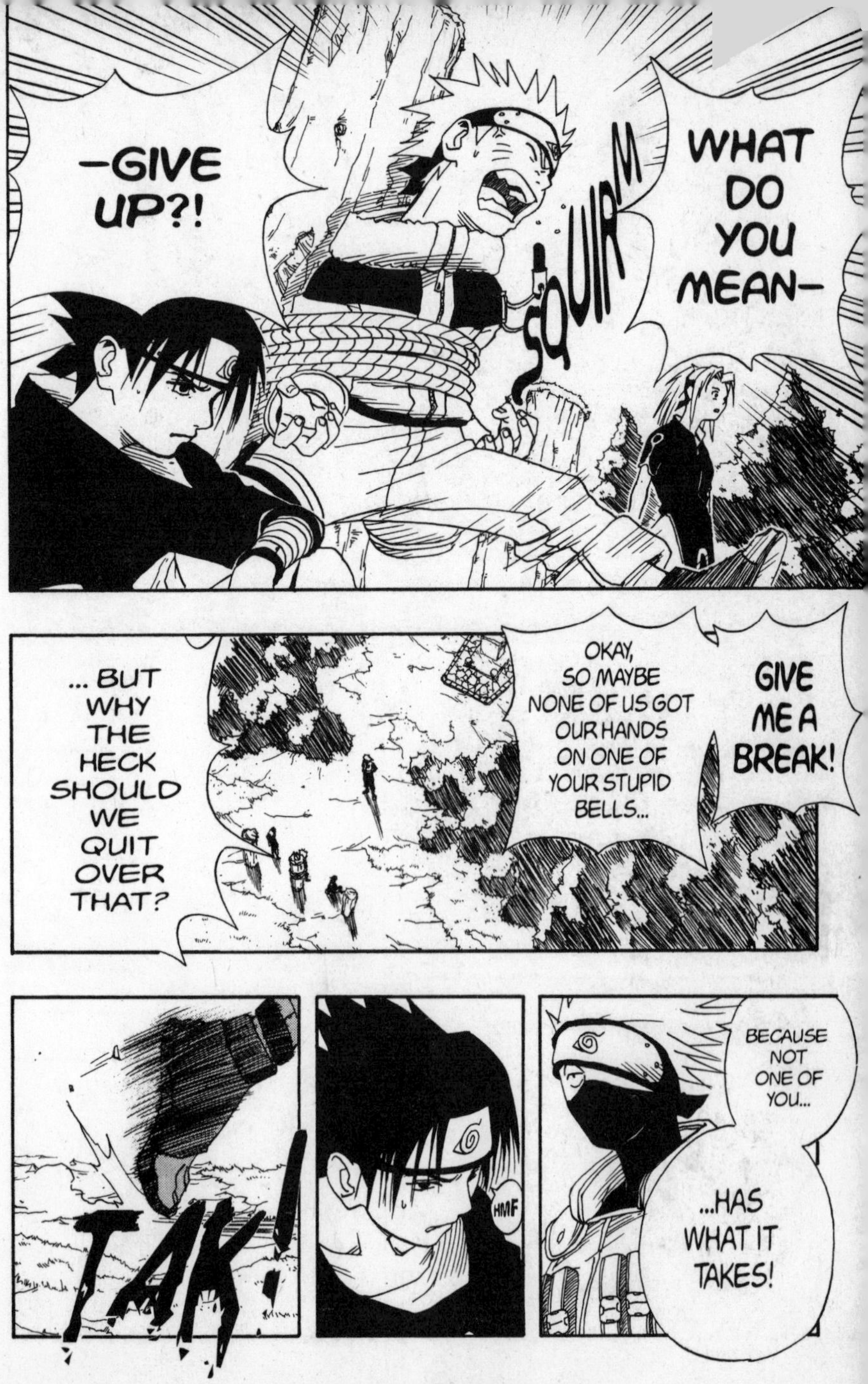
WHAT DO YOU MEAN–
–GIVE UP?!
SQUIRM
GIVE ME A BREAK!
OKAY, SO MAYBE NONE OF US GOT OUR HANDS ON ONE OF YOUR STUPID BELLS...
... BUT WHY THE HECK SHOULD WE QUIT OVER THAT?
BECAUSE NOT ONE OF YOU...
...HAS WHAT IT TAKES!
HMF
TAK!

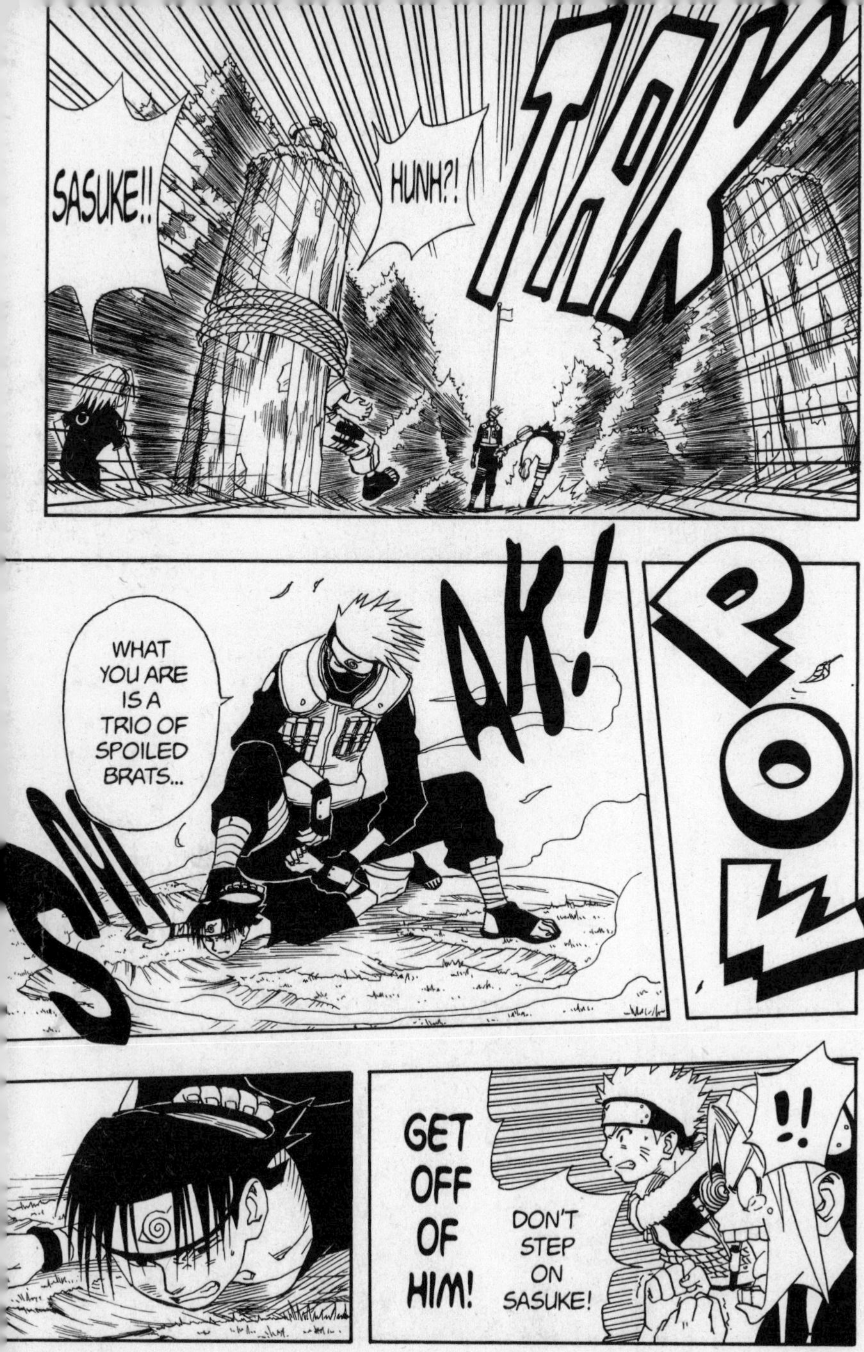
TAK
HUNH?!
SASUKE!!
POW
SMAK!
WHAT YOU ARE IS A TRIO OF SPOILED BRATS...
!!
DON'T STEP ON SASUKE!
GET OFF OF HIM!

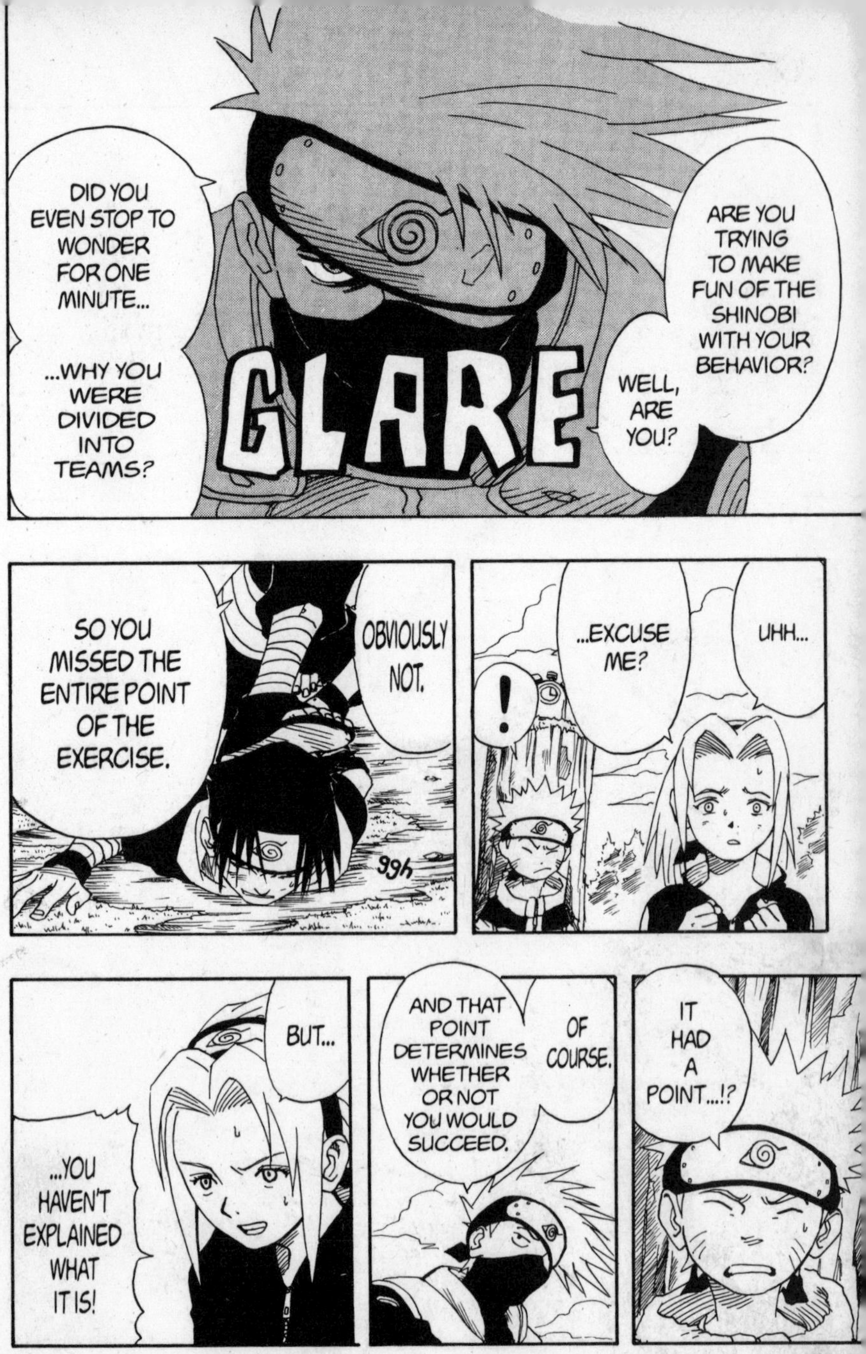
ARE YOU TRYING TO MAKE FUN OF THE SHINOBI WITH YOUR BEHAVIOR?
WELL, ARE YOU?
GLARE
DID YOU EVEN STOP TO WONDER FOR ONE MINUTE...
...WHY YOU WERE DIVIDED INTO TEAMS?
UHH...
...EXCUSE ME?
!
OBVIOUSLY NOT.
SO YOU MISSED THE ENTIRE POINT OF THE EXERCISE.
ggh
IT HAD A POINT...!?
OF COURSE.
AND THAT POINT DETERMINES WHETHER OR NOT YOU WOULD SUCCEED.
BUT...
...YOU HAVEN'T EXPLAINED WHAT IT IS!

READ THIS WAY

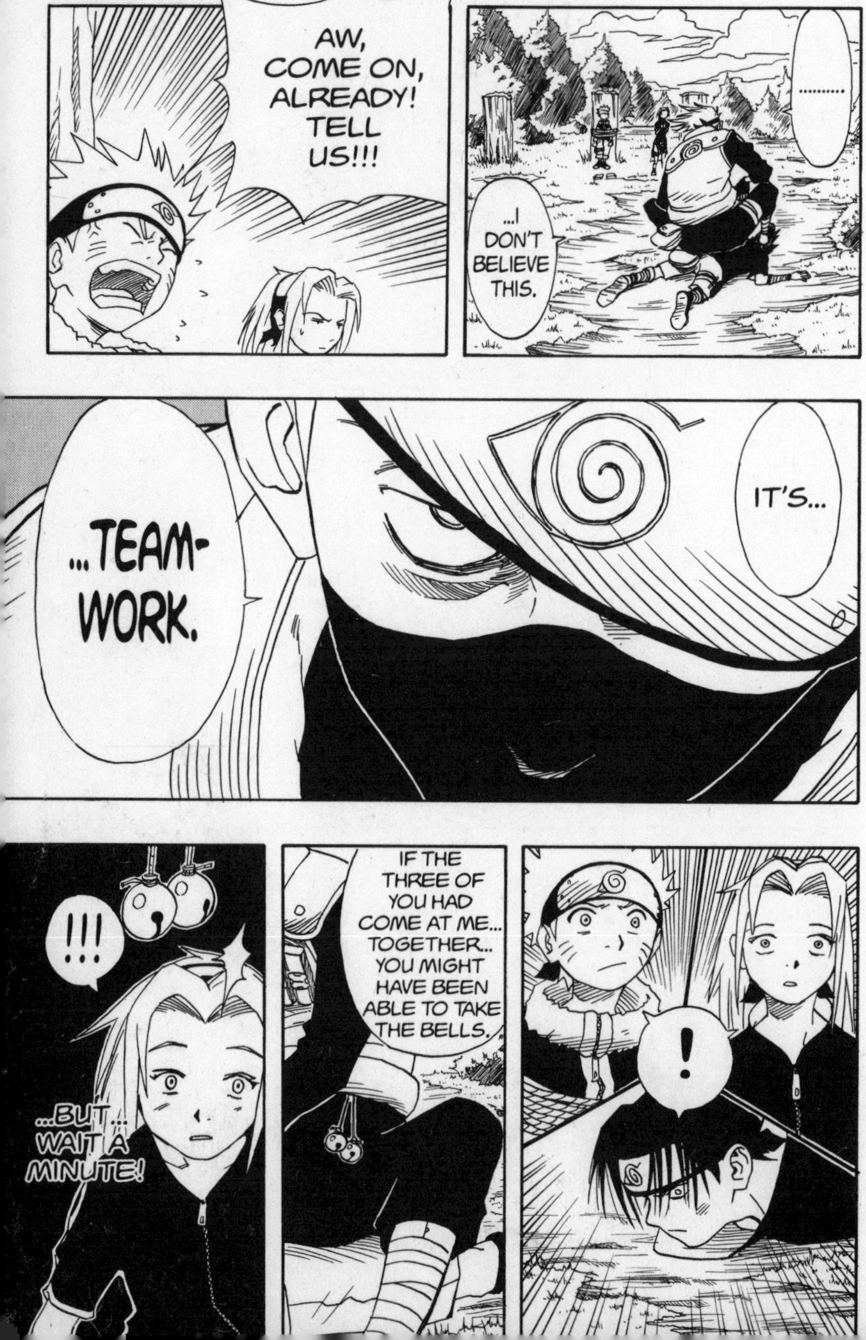

....
...I DON'T BELIEVE THIS.
AW, COME ON, ALREADY! TELL US!!!
IT'S...
...TEAM-WORK.
!
IF THE THREE OF YOU HAD COME AT ME... TOGETHER... YOU MIGHT HAVE BEEN ABLE TO TAKE THE BELLS.
!!!
...BUT... WAIT A MINUTE!

READ THIS WAY

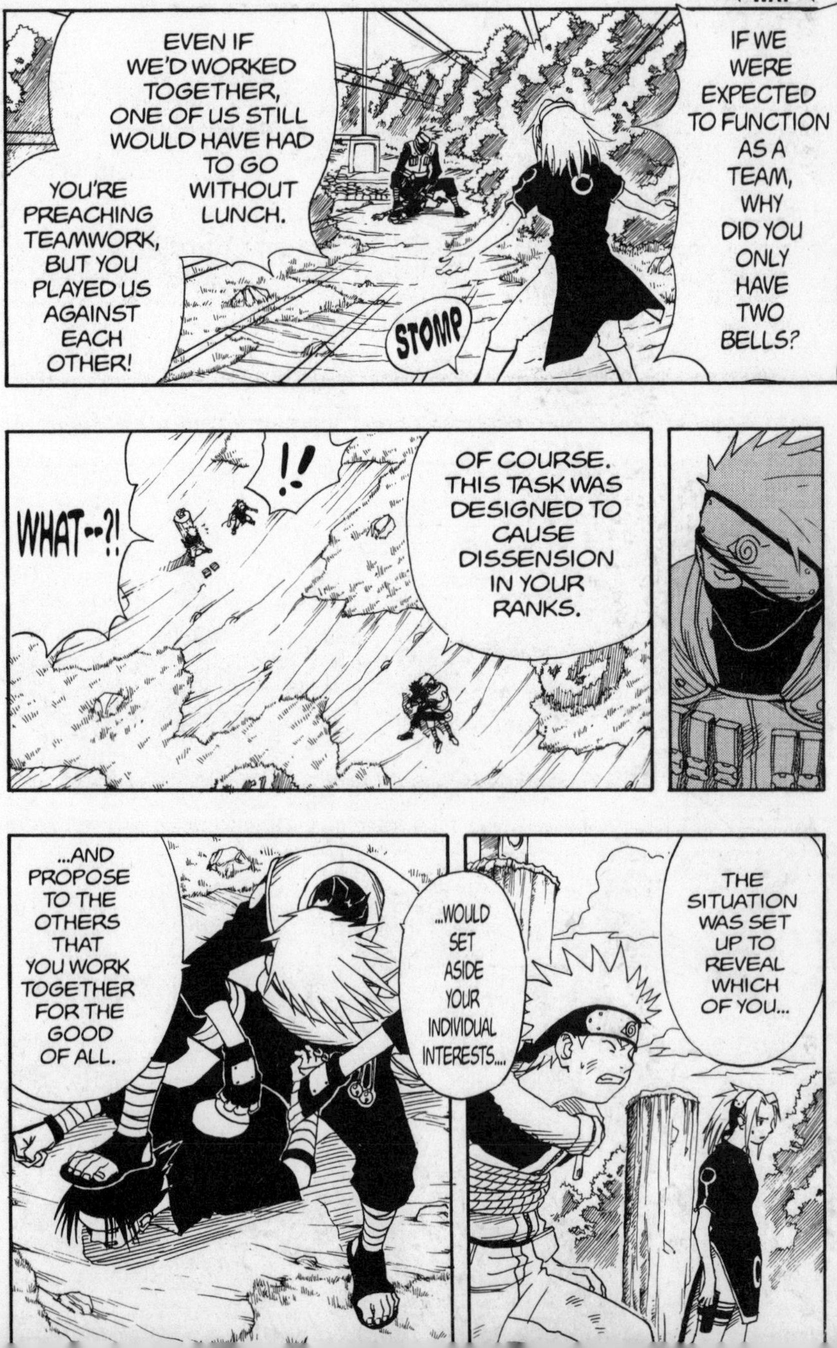
IF WE WERE EXPECTED TO FUNCTION AS A TEAM, WHY DID YOU ONLY HAVE TWO BELLS?
EVEN IF WE'D WORKED TOGETHER, ONE OF US STILL WOULD HAVE HAD TO GO WITHOUT LUNCH.
STOMP
YOU'RE PREACHING TEAMWORK, BUT YOU PLAYED US AGAINST EACH OTHER!
OF COURSE. THIS TASK WAS DESIGNED TO CAUSE DISSENSION IN YOUR RANKS.
!!
WHAT--?!
THE SITUATION WAS SET UP TO REVEAL WHICH OF YOU...
...WOULD SET ASIDE YOUR INDIVIDUAL INTERESTS....
...AND PROPOSE TO THE OTHERS THAT YOU WORK TOGETHER FOR THE GOOD OF ALL.

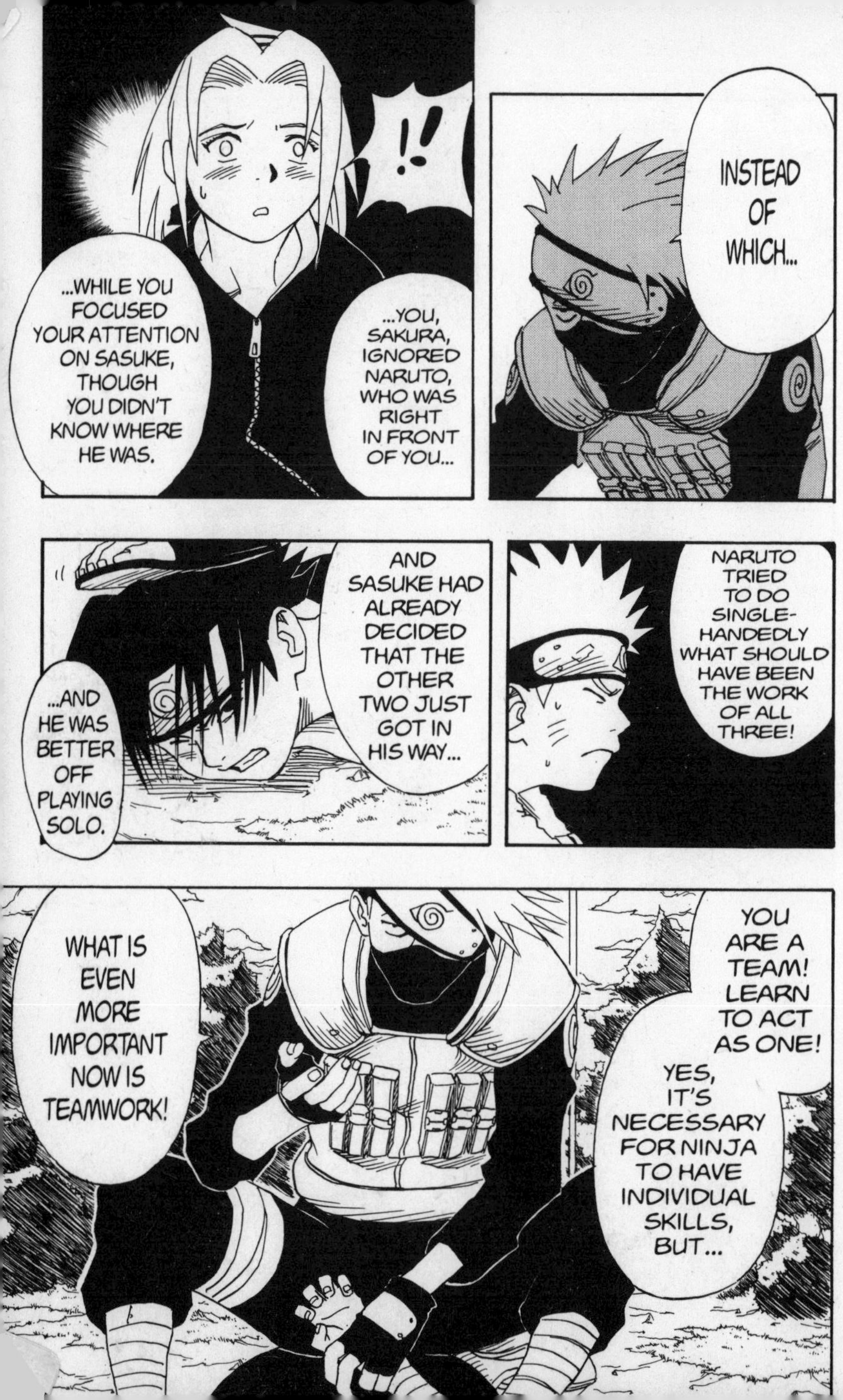

INSTEAD OF WHICH...
!!
...YOU, SAKURA, IGNORED NARUTO, WHO WAS RIGHT IN FRONT OF YOU...
...WHILE YOU FOCUSED YOUR ATTENTION ON SASUKE, THOUGH YOU DIDN'T KNOW WHERE HE WAS.
NARUTO TRIED TO DO SINGLE-HANDEDLY WHAT SHOULD HAVE BEEN THE WORK OF ALL THREE!
AND SASUKE HAD ALREADY DECIDED THAT THE OTHER TWO JUST GOT IN HIS WAY...
...AND HE WAS BETTER OFF PLAYING SOLO.
YES, IT'S NECESSARY FOR NINJA TO HAVE INDIVIDUAL SKILLS, BUT...
WHAT IS EVEN MORE IMPORTANT NOW IS TEAMWORK!
YOU ARE A TEAM! LEARN TO ACT AS ONE!

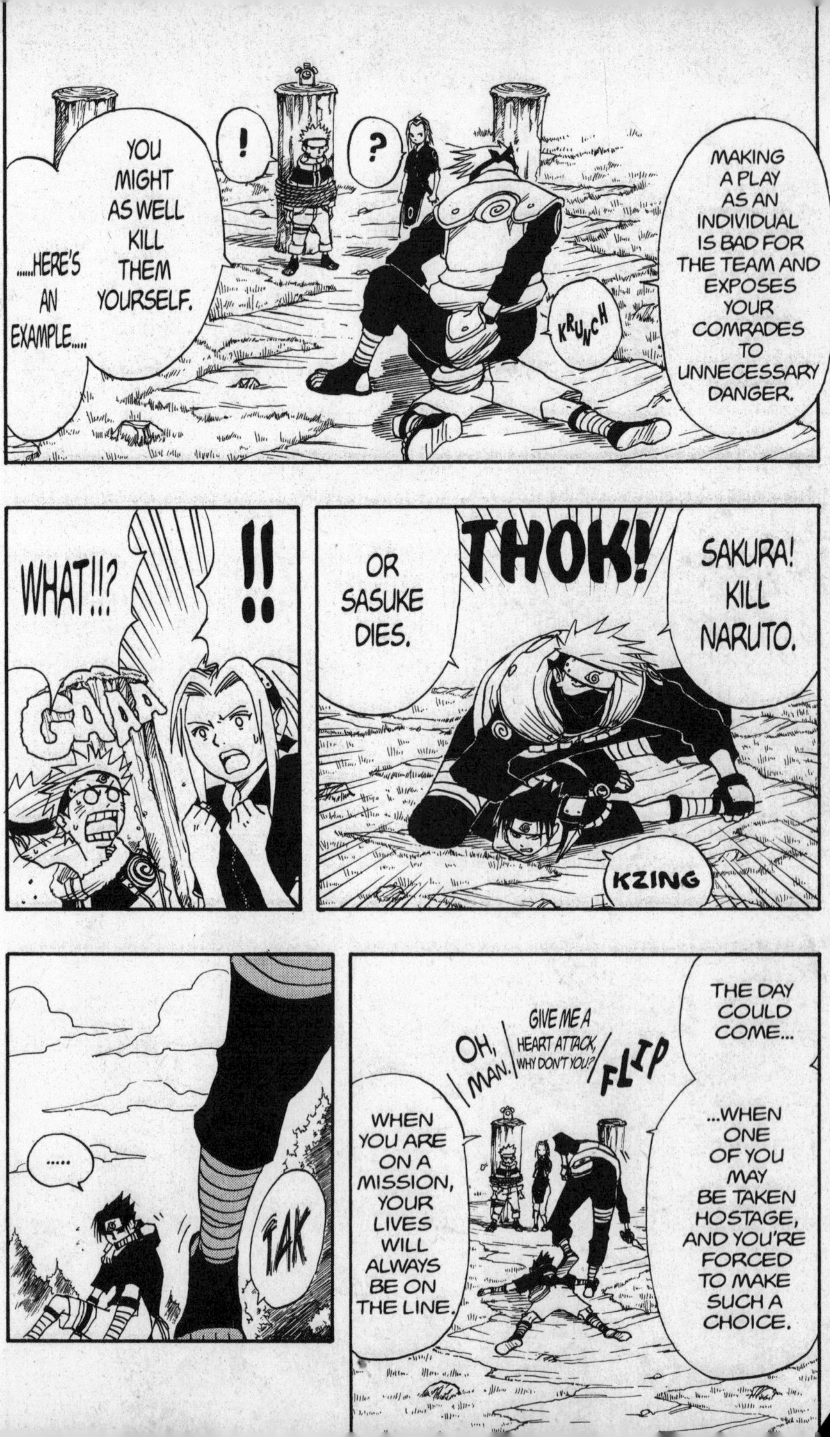
MAKING A PLAY AS AN INDIVIDUAL IS BAD FOR THE TEAM AND EXPOSES YOUR COMRADES TO UNNECESSARY DANGER.
KRUNCH
?
!
YOU MIGHT AS WELL KILL THEM YOURSELF.
.....HERE'S AN EXAMPLE.....
SAKURA! KILL NARUTO.
THOK!
OR SASUKE DIES.
KZING
!!
WHAT!!?
GAAA
THE DAY COULD COME...
...WHEN ONE OF YOU MAY BE TAKEN HOSTAGE, AND YOU'RE FORCED TO MAKE SUCH A CHOICE.
FLIP
GIVE ME A HEART ATTACK, WHY DON'T YOU!?
OH, MAN.
WHEN YOU ARE ON A MISSION, YOUR LIVES WILL ALWAYS BE ON THE LINE.
TAK
.....

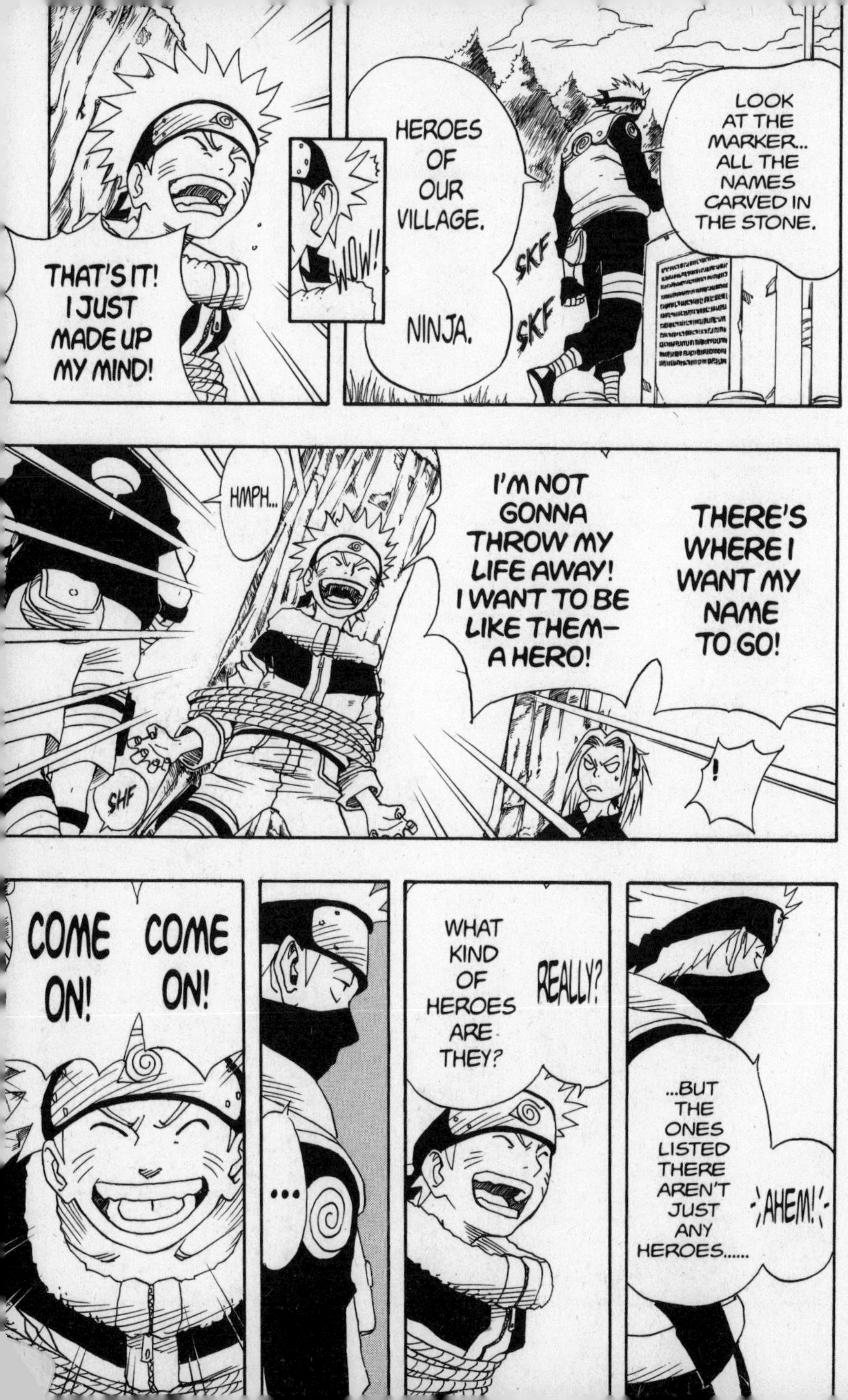
LOOK AT THE MARKER... ALL THE NAMES CARVED IN THE STONE.
SKF
SKF
HEROES OF OUR VILLAGE.
NINJA.
WOW!
THAT'S IT! I JUST MADE UP MY MIND!
THERE'S WHERE I WANT MY NAME TO GO!
I'M NOT GONNA THROW MY LIFE AWAY! I WANT TO BE LIKE THEM—A HERO!
!
HMPH...
SHF
...BUT THE ONES LISTED THERE AREN'T JUST ANY HEROES......
AHEM!
REALLY?
WHAT KIND OF HEROES ARE THEY?
...
COME ON! COME ON!

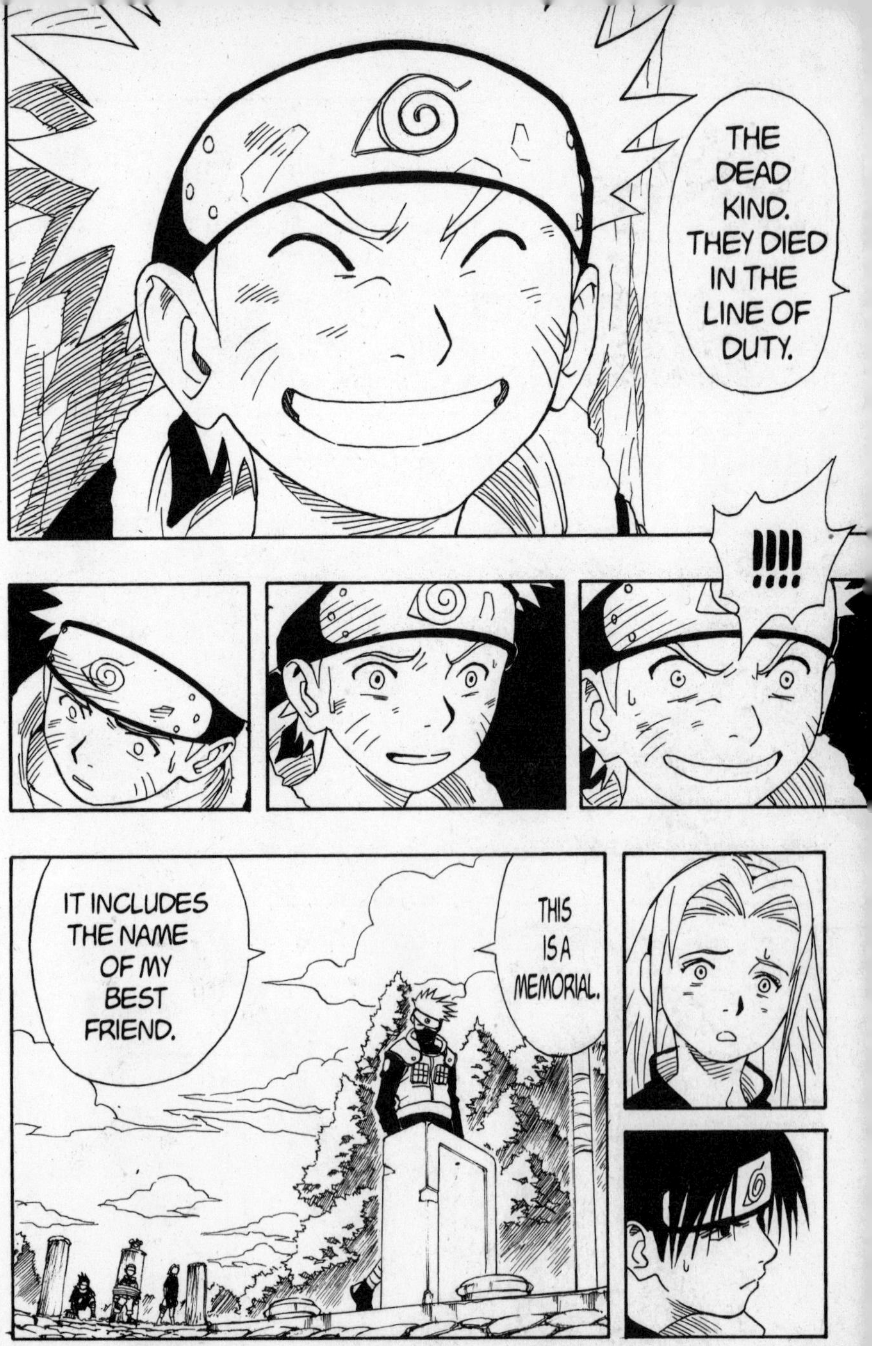
THE DEAD KIND. THEY DIED IN THE LINE OF DUTY.
!!!!
THIS IS A MEMORIAL.
IT INCLUDES THE NAME OF MY BEST FRIEND.

READ THIS WAY

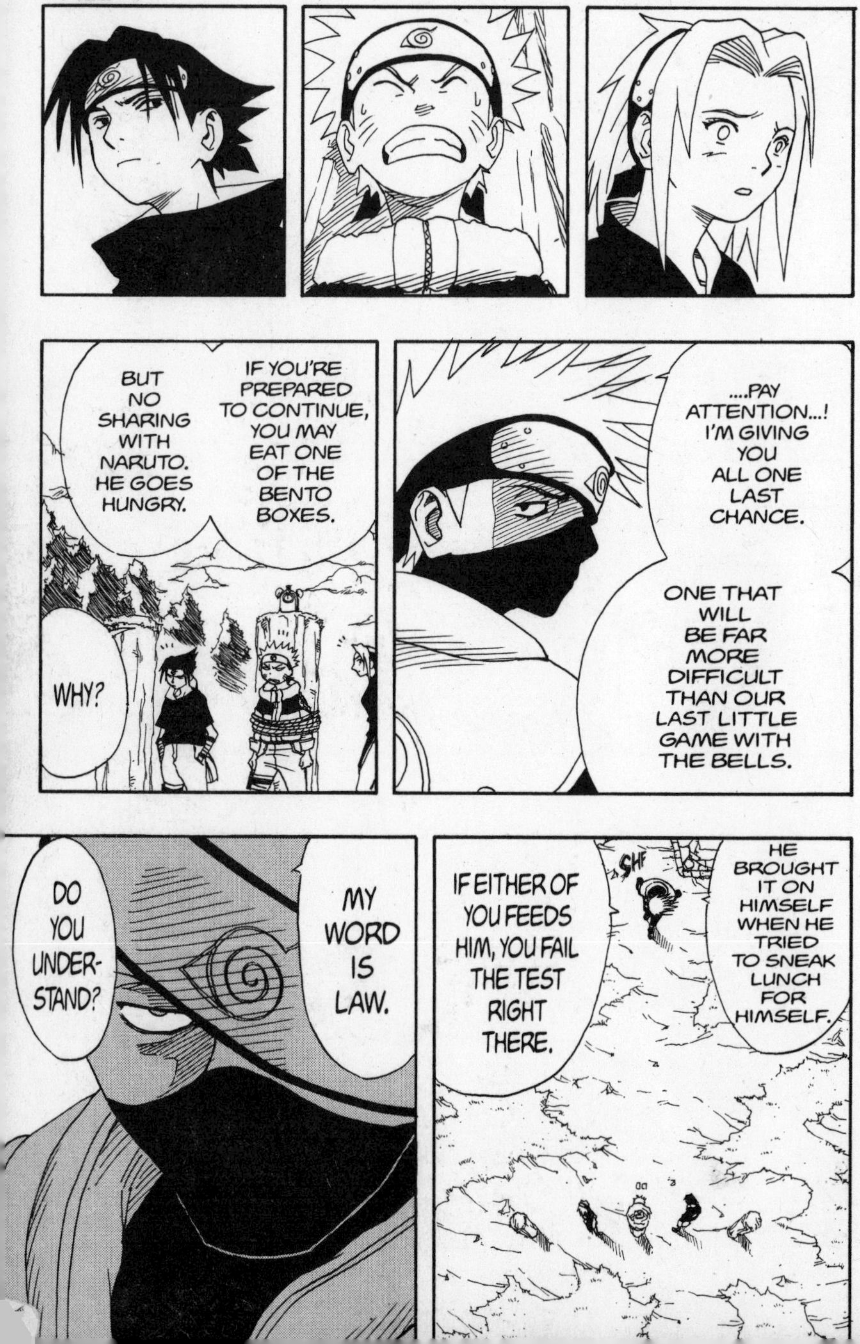
....PAY ATTENTION...! I'M GIVING YOU ALL ONE LAST CHANCE.
ONE THAT WILL BE FAR MORE DIFFICULT THAN OUR LAST LITTLE GAME WITH THE BELLS.
IF YOU'RE PREPARED TO CONTINUE, YOU MAY EAT ONE OF THE BENTO BOXES.
BUT NO SHARING WITH NARUTO. HE GOES HUNGRY.
WHY?
HE BROUGHT IT ON HIMSELF WHEN HE TRIED TO SNEAK LUNCH FOR HIMSELF.
SHF
IF EITHER OF YOU FEEDS HIM, YOU FAIL THE TEST RIGHT THERE.
MY WORD IS LAW.
DO YOU UNDER-STAND?

READ THIS WAY

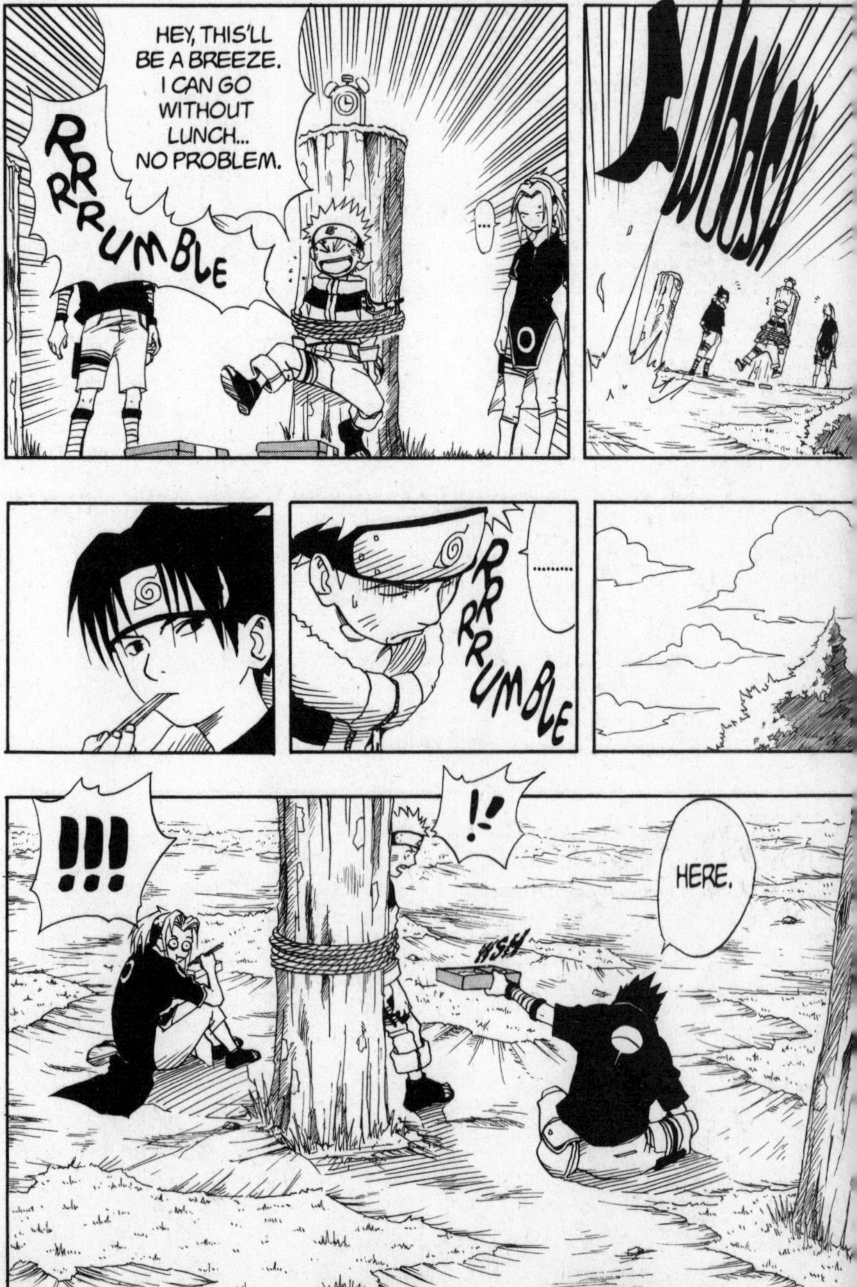
WHOOSH
HEY, THIS'LL BE A BREEZE. I CAN GO WITHOUT LUNCH... NO PROBLEM.
...
RRRRUMBLE
....
RRRRUMBLE
HERE.
WSH
!!
!!!

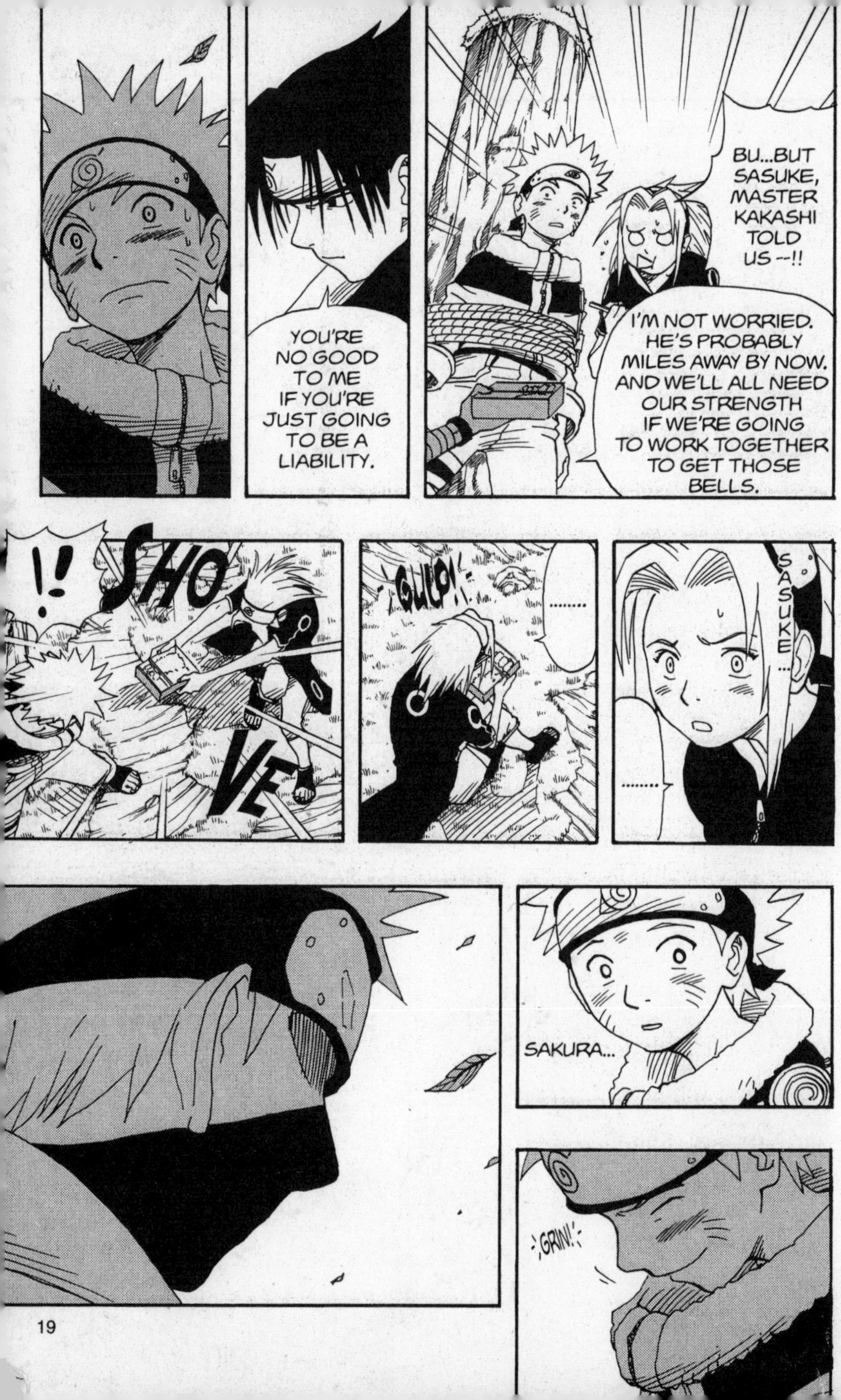
BU...BUT SASUKE, MASTER KAKASHI TOLD US --!!
I'M NOT WORRIED. HE'S PROBABLY MILES AWAY BY NOW. AND WE'LL ALL NEED OUR STRENGTH IF WE'RE GOING TO WORK TOGETHER TO GET THOSE BELLS.
YOU'RE NO GOOD TO ME IF YOU'RE JUST GOING TO BE A LIABILITY.
SASUKE...
....
....
GULP!
!!
SHOVE
SAKURA...
GRIN!

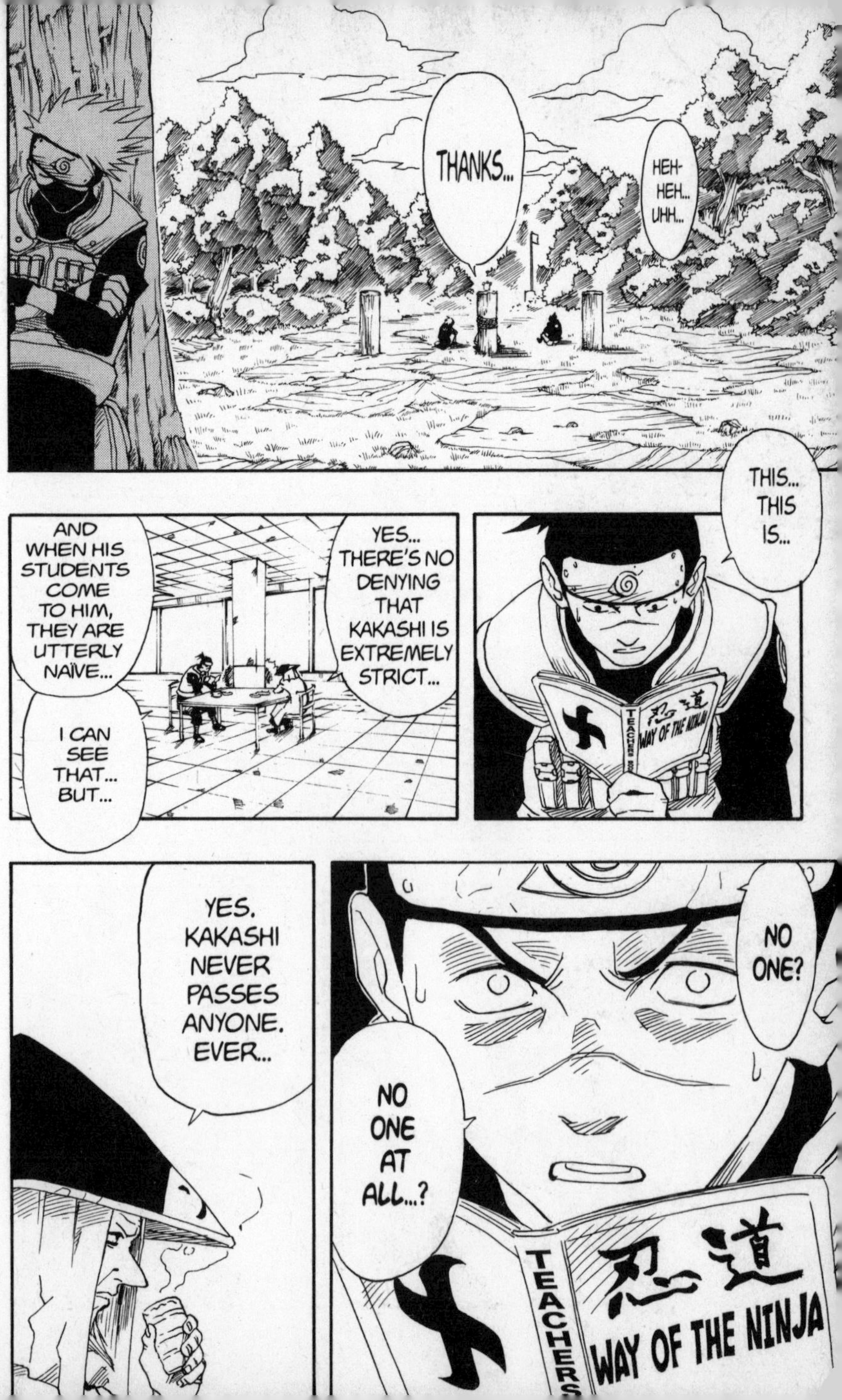
HEH-HEH... UHH...
THANKS...
THIS... THIS IS...
忍道
TEACHERS
WAY OF THE NINJA
YES... THERE'S NO DENYING THAT KAKASHI IS EXTREMELY STRICT...
AND WHEN HIS STUDENTS COME TO HIM, THEY ARE UTTERLY NAÏVE...
I CAN SEE THAT... BUT...
NO ONE?
NO ONE AT ALL...?
忍道
TEACHERS
WAY OF THE NINJA
YES. KAKASHI NEVER PASSES ANYONE. EVER...

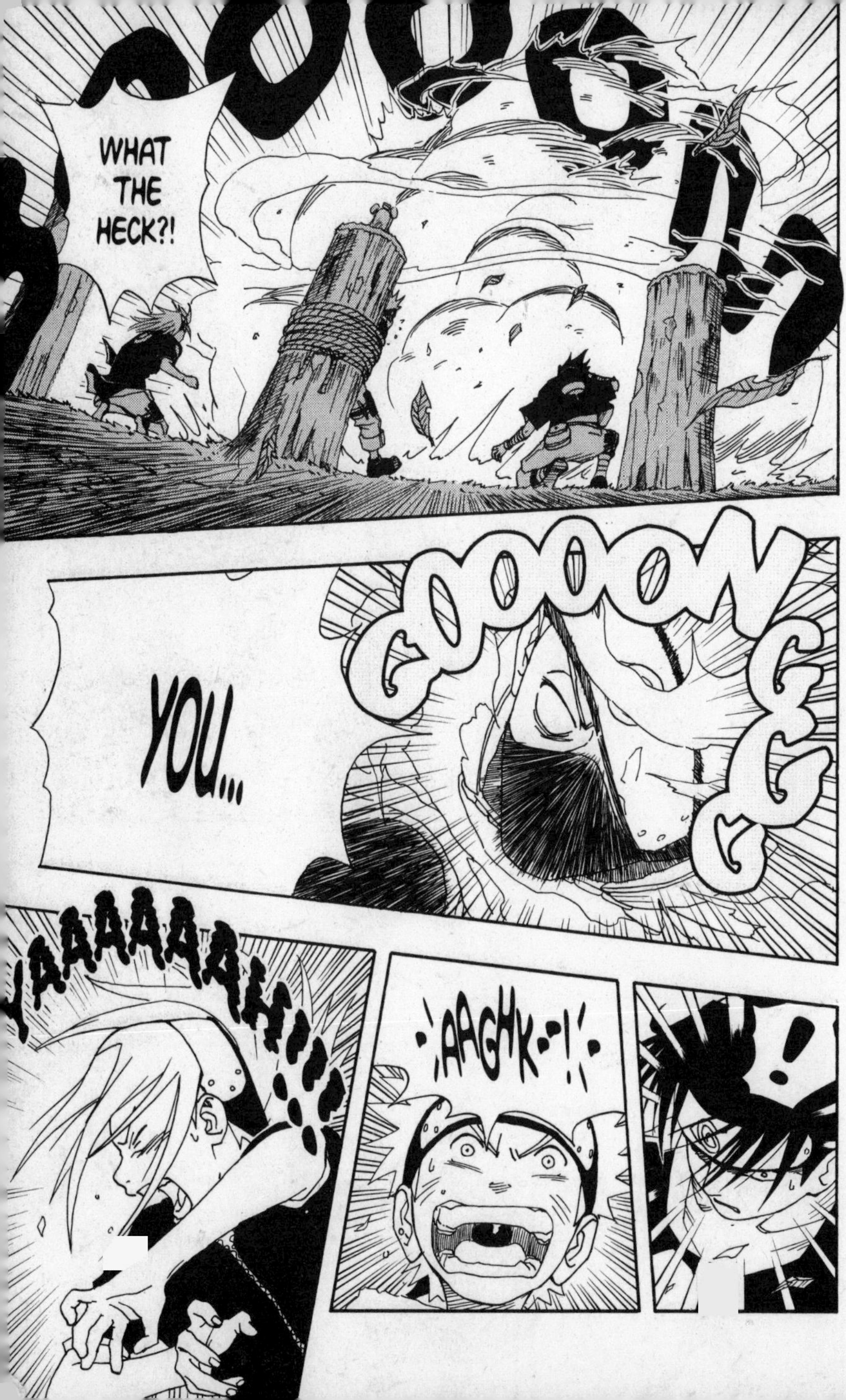
WHAT THE HECK?!
YOU...
!
AAGHK--!

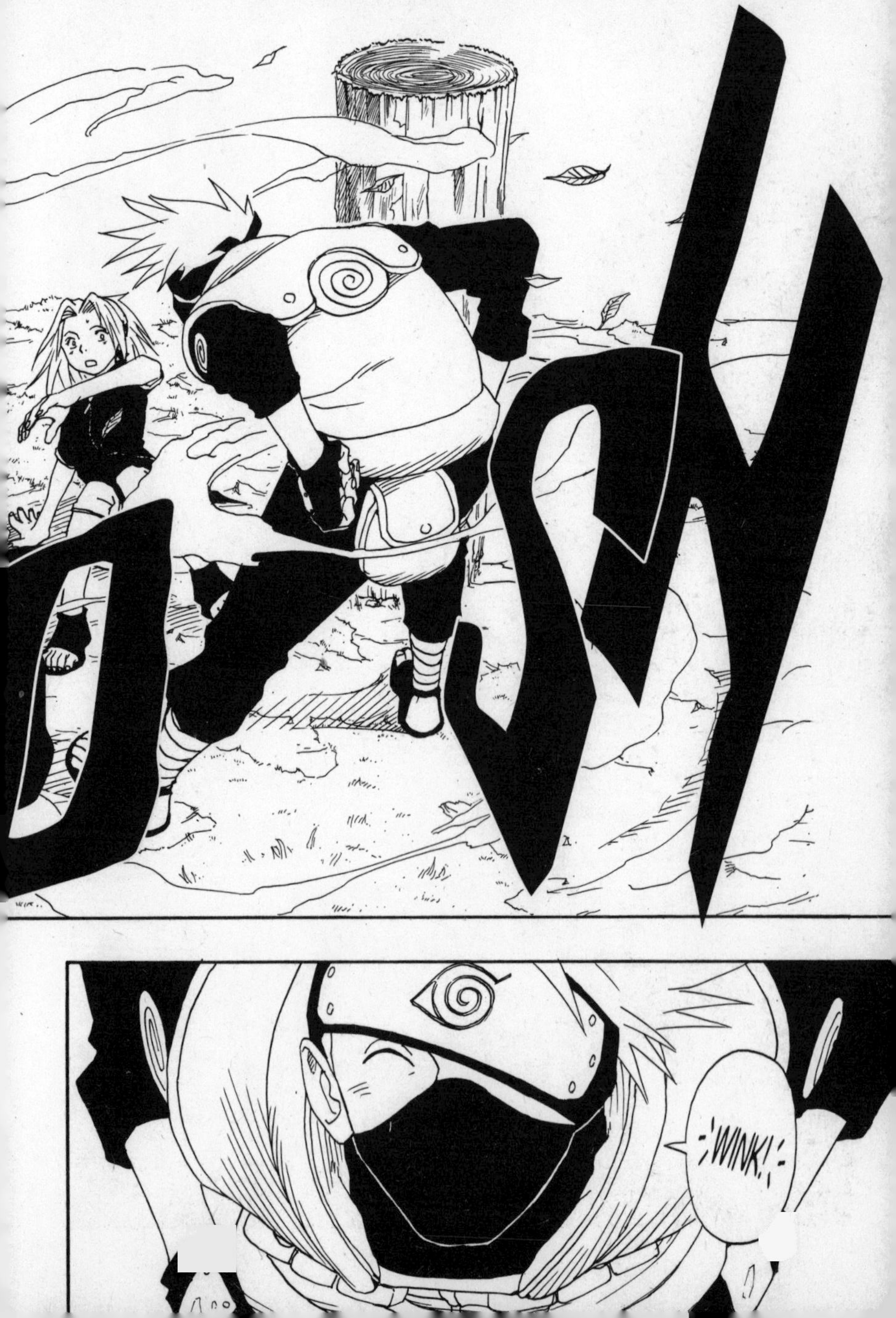
WINK!

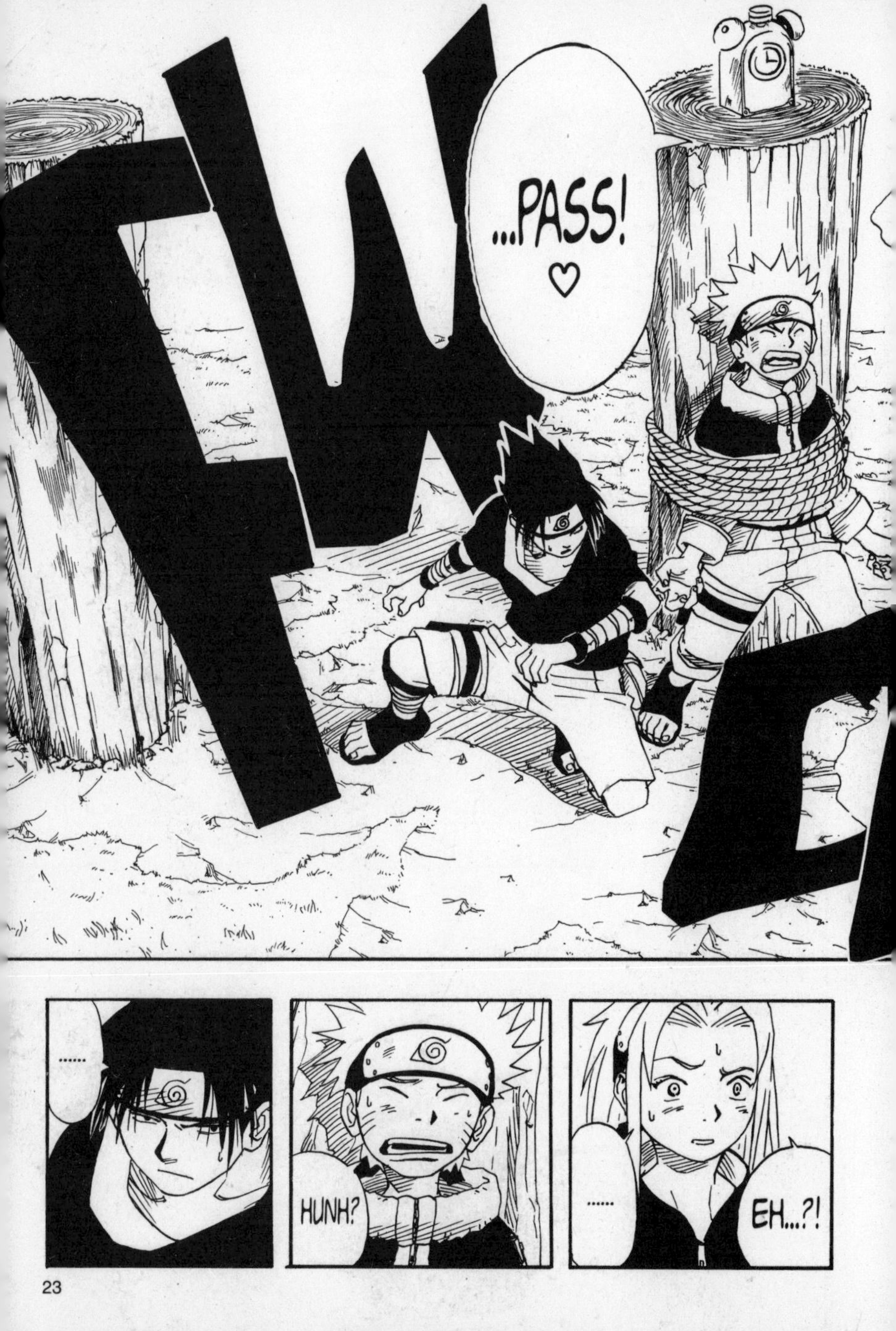
...PASS! ♡
EH...?!
......
HUNH?
......

READ THIS WAY

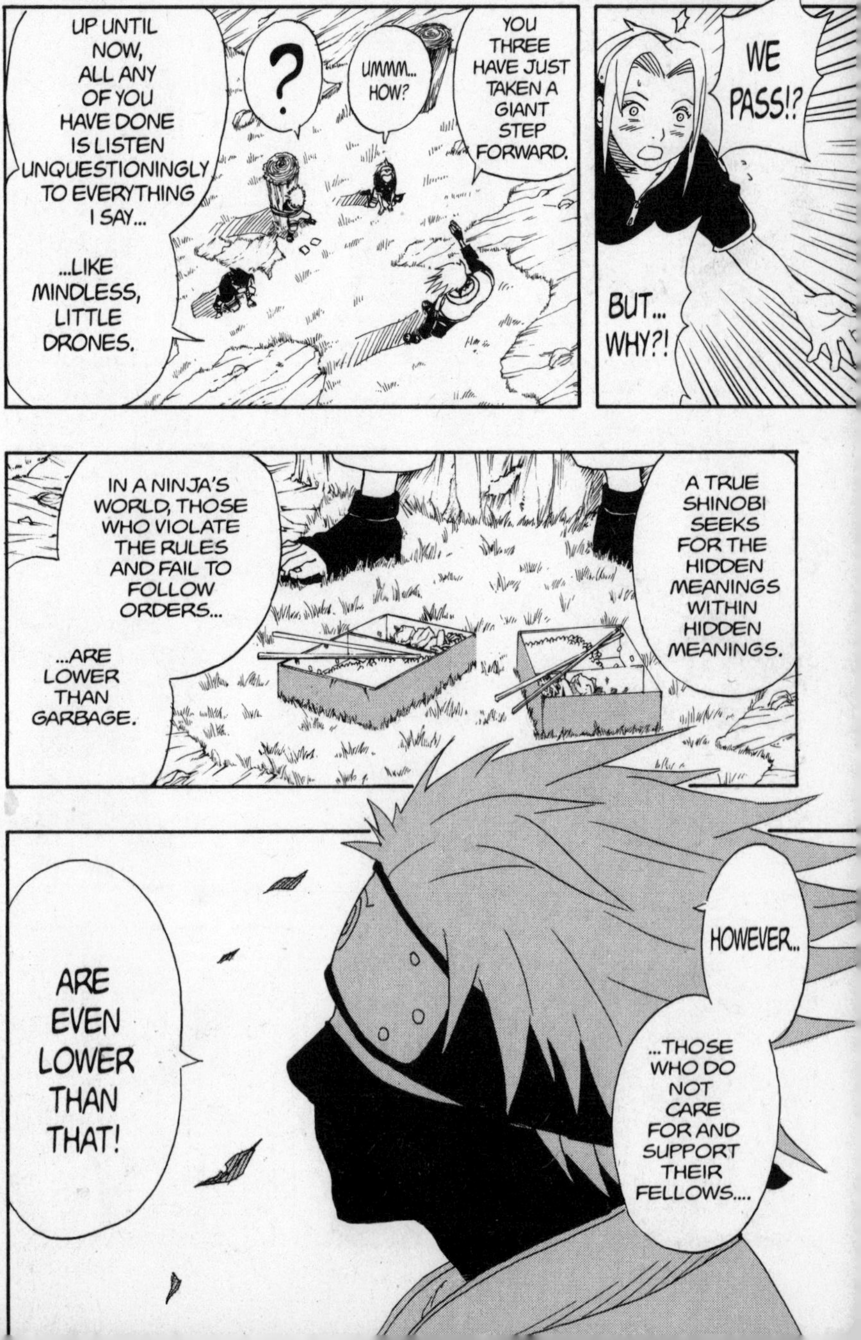
WE PASS!?
BUT... WHY?!
YOU THREE HAVE JUST TAKEN A GIANT STEP FORWARD.
UMMM... HOW?
?
UP UNTIL NOW, ALL ANY OF YOU HAVE DONE IS LISTEN UNQUESTIONINGLY TO EVERYTHING I SAY...
...LIKE MINDLESS, LITTLE DRONES.
A TRUE SHINOBI SEEKS FOR THE HIDDEN MEANINGS WITHIN HIDDEN MEANINGS.
IN A NINJA'S WORLD, THOSE WHO VIOLATE THE RULES AND FAIL TO FOLLOW ORDERS...
...ARE LOWER THAN GARBAGE.
HOWEVER...
...THOSE WHO DO NOT CARE FOR AND SUPPORT THEIR FELLOWS....
ARE EVEN LOWER THAN THAT!

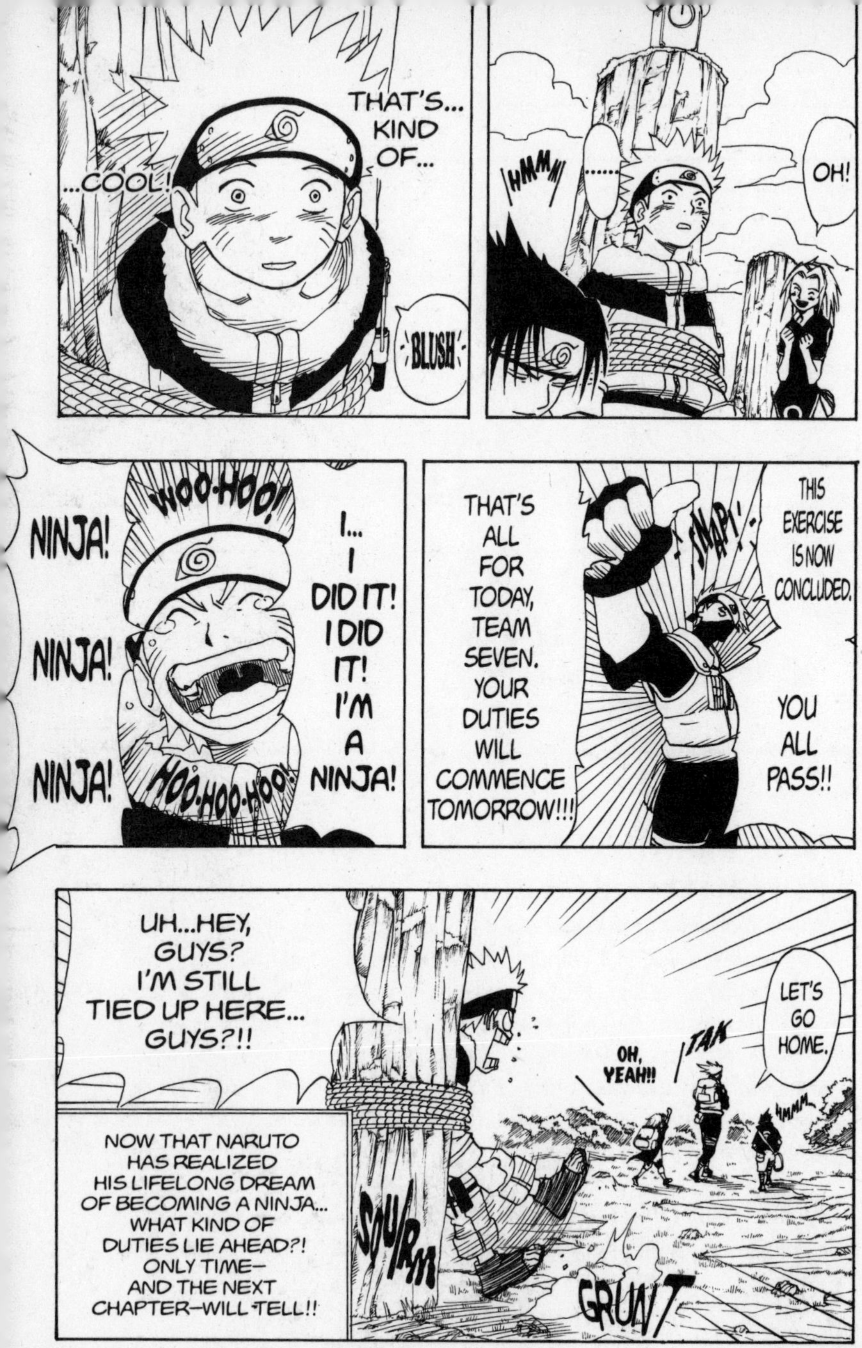
OH!
......
HMMM
THAT'S... KIND OF...
...COOL!
BLUSH
THIS EXERCISE IS NOW CONCLUDED.
YOU ALL PASS!!
SNAP!
THAT'S ALL FOR TODAY, TEAM SEVEN. YOUR DUTIES WILL COMMENCE TOMORROW!!!
I... I DID IT! I DID IT! I'M A NINJA!
WOO-HOO!
HOO-HOO-HOO!
NINJA! NINJA! NINJA!
LET'S GO HOME.
HMMM
TAK
OH, YEAH!!
UH...HEY, GUYS? I'M STILL TIED UP HERE... GUYS?!!
GRUNT
SQUIRM
NOW THAT NARUTO HAS REALIZED HIS LIFELONG DREAM OF BECOMING A NINJA... WHAT KIND OF DUTIES LIE AHEAD?! ONLY TIME—AND THE NEXT CHAPTER—WILL TELL!!

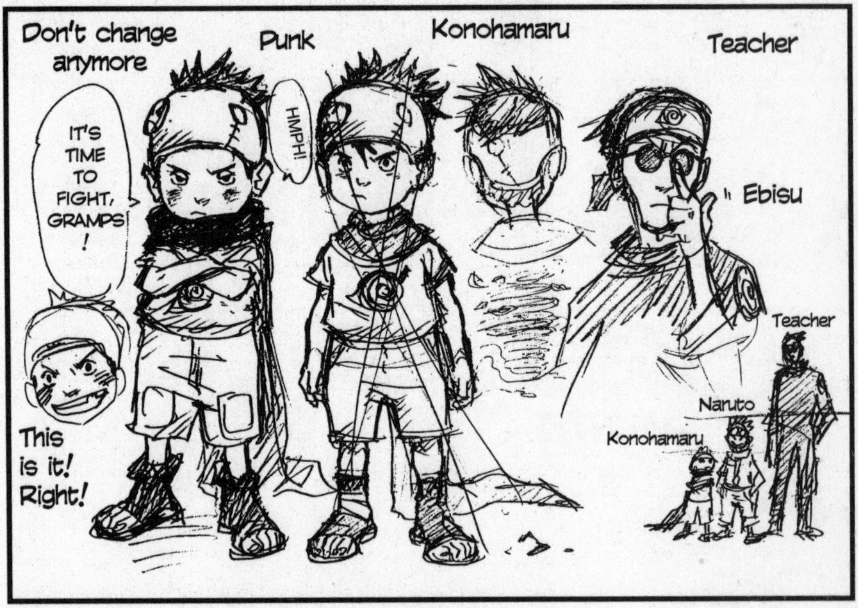
Don't change anymore
Punk
Konohamaru
Teacher
IT'S TIME TO FIGHT, GRAMPS!
HMPH!
Ebisu
Teacher
Naruto
Konohamaru
This is it! Right!

THE MAKING OF NARUTO:
KONOHAMARU & EBISU

These were my first sketches of Konohamaru and his teacher, Ebisu (see **Naruto** Vol. 1). I remember really struggling with Konohamaru's design. He was supposed to be a little punk, smaller than Naruto, but he kept coming out looking like Naruto no matter what I tried. I tried drawing a big-eyed kid, but this didn't work either. It always turned out like a face I'd seen somewhere before. Eventually, I drew an angry-looking face with small eyes, and somehow I knew I'd found it!

At that point I decided that Ebisu would look like the sketch above. I like Ebisu's design because he's like me, somehow…

Number 9: The Worst Client

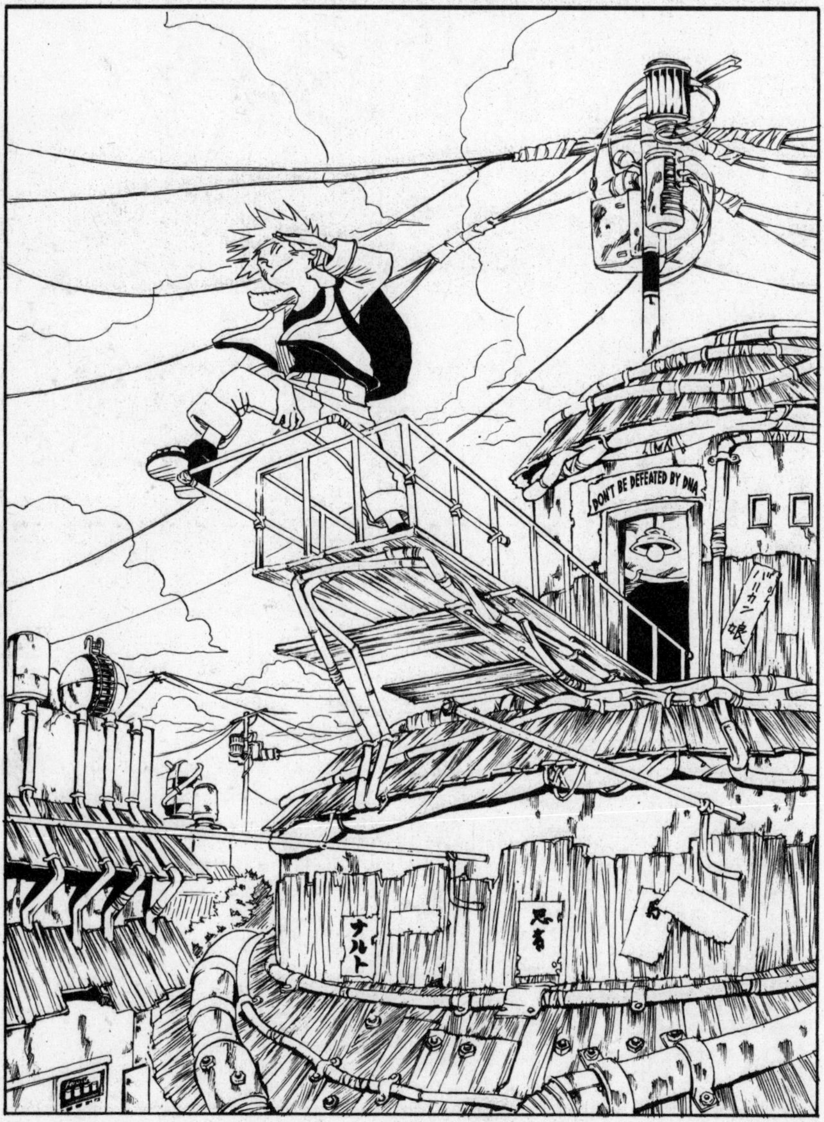
DON'T BE DEFEATED BY DNA
バリカン娘
ナルト

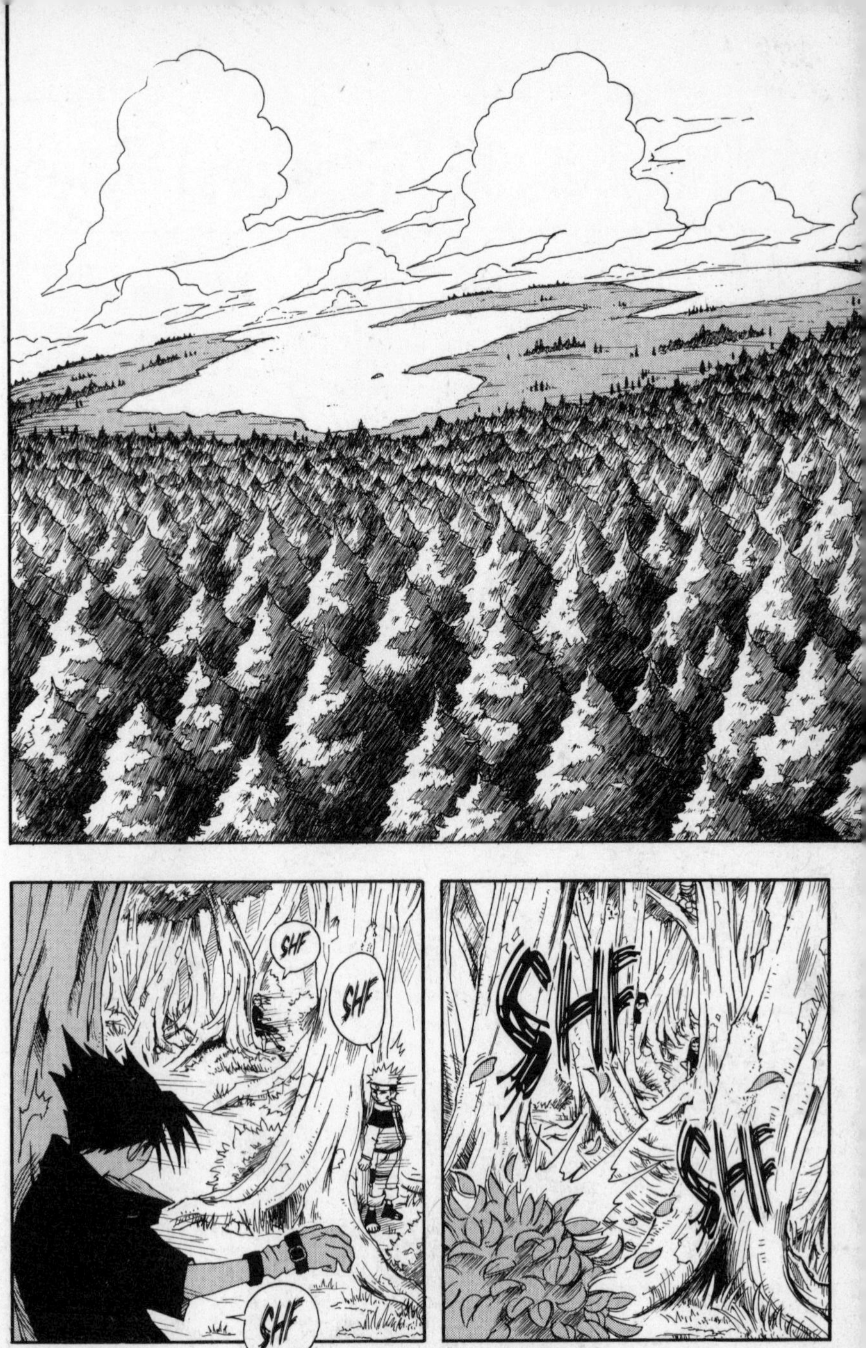
SHF
SHF
SHF
SHF
SHF

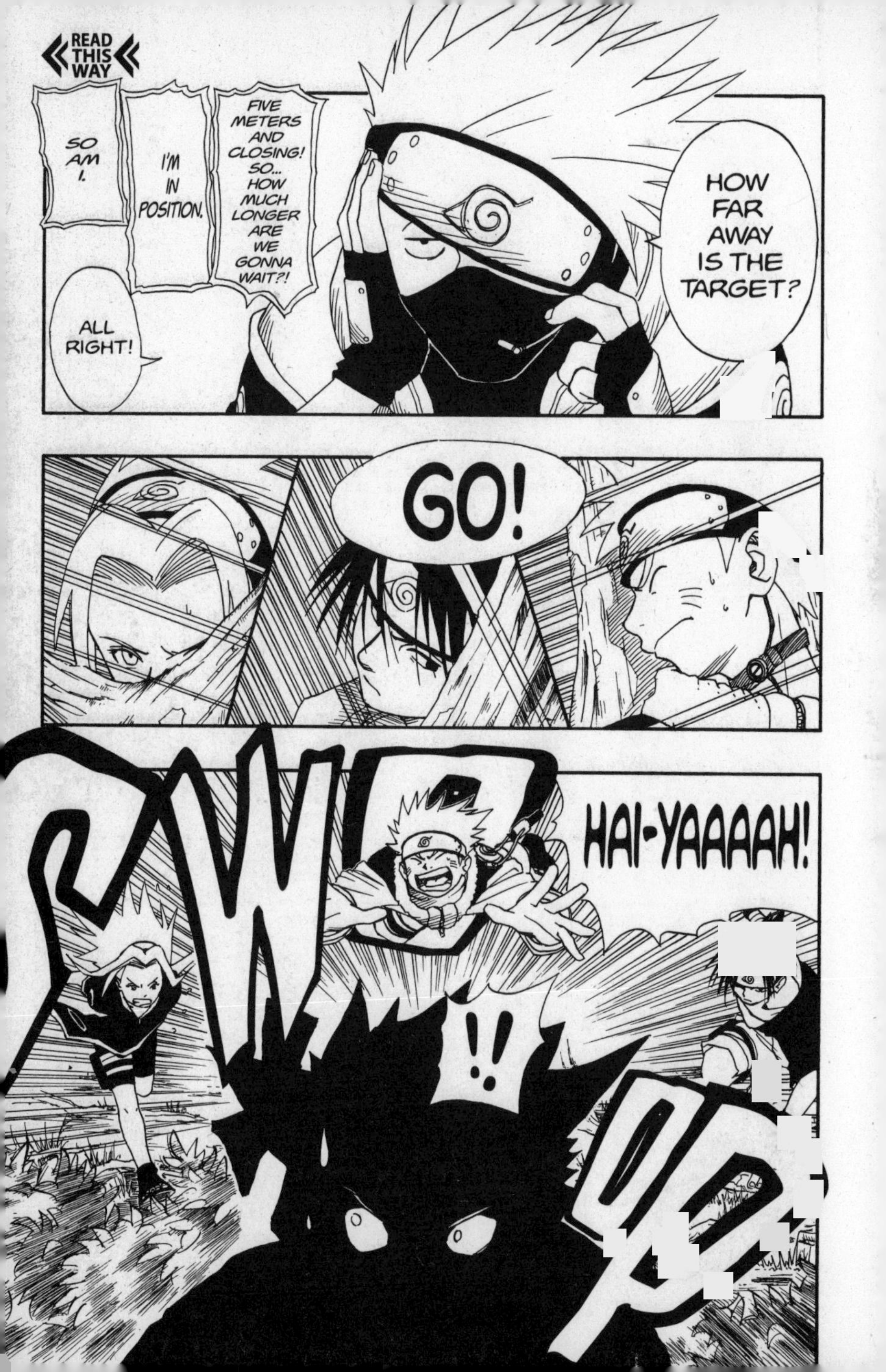
READ THIS WAY
HOW FAR AWAY IS THE TARGET?
FIVE METERS AND CLOSING! SO... HOW MUCH LONGER ARE WE GONNA WAIT?!
I'M IN POSITION.
SO AM I.
ALL RIGHT!
GO!
HAI-YAAAAH!
!!

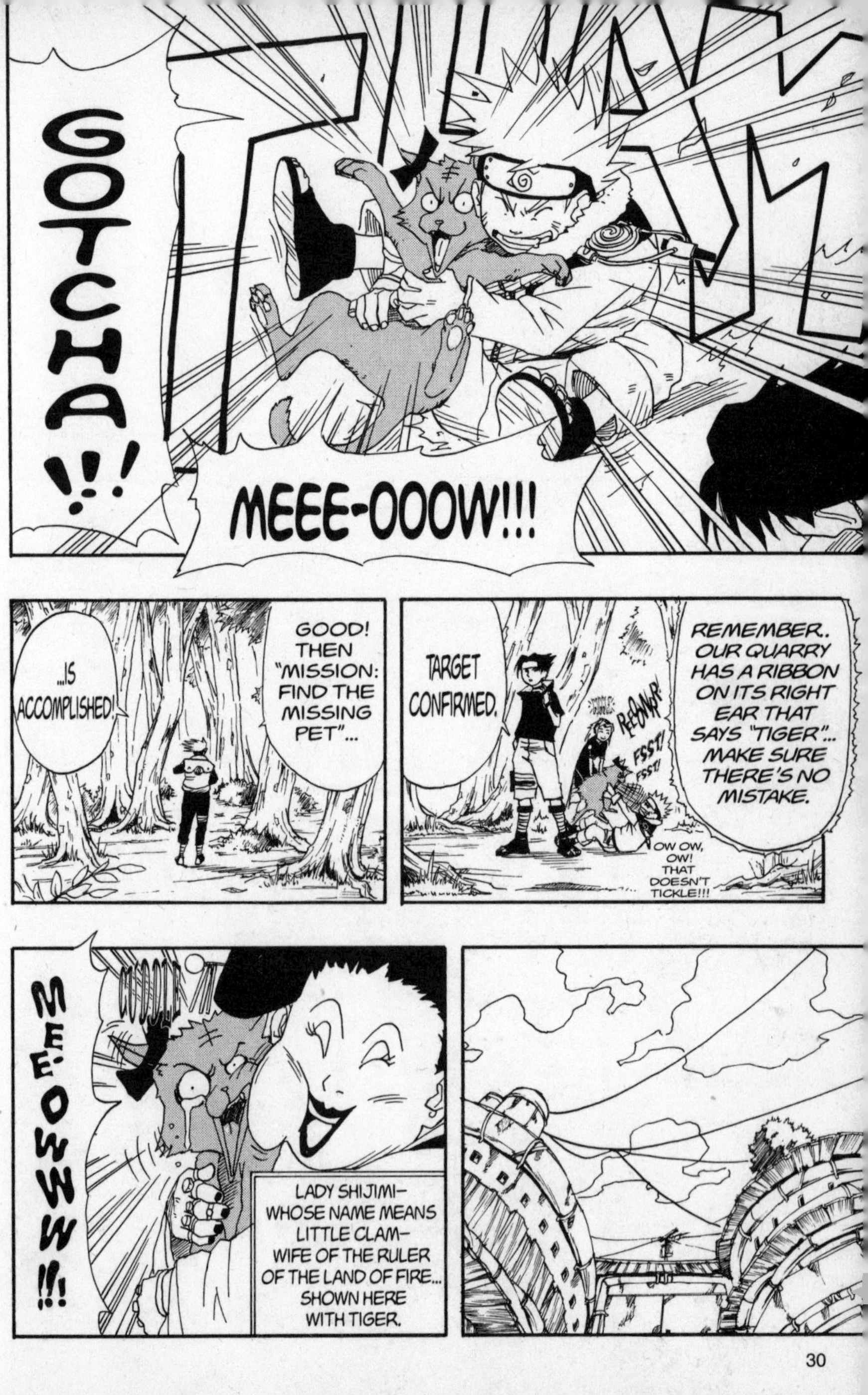
GOTCHA!!!
MEEE-OOOW!!!
REMEMBER.. OUR QUARRY HAS A RIBBON ON ITS RIGHT EAR THAT SAYS "TIGER"... MAKE SURE THERE'S NO MISTAKE.
FSST! FSST!
OW OW, OW! THAT DOESN'T TICKLE!!!
TARGET CONFIRMED.
GOOD! THEN "MISSION: FIND THE MISSING PET"...
...IS ACCOMPLISHED!
MEEOWWW!!!
LADY SHIJIMI—WHOSE NAME MEANS LITTLE CLAM—WIFE OF THE RULER OF THE LAND OF FIRE... SHOWN HERE WITH TIGER.

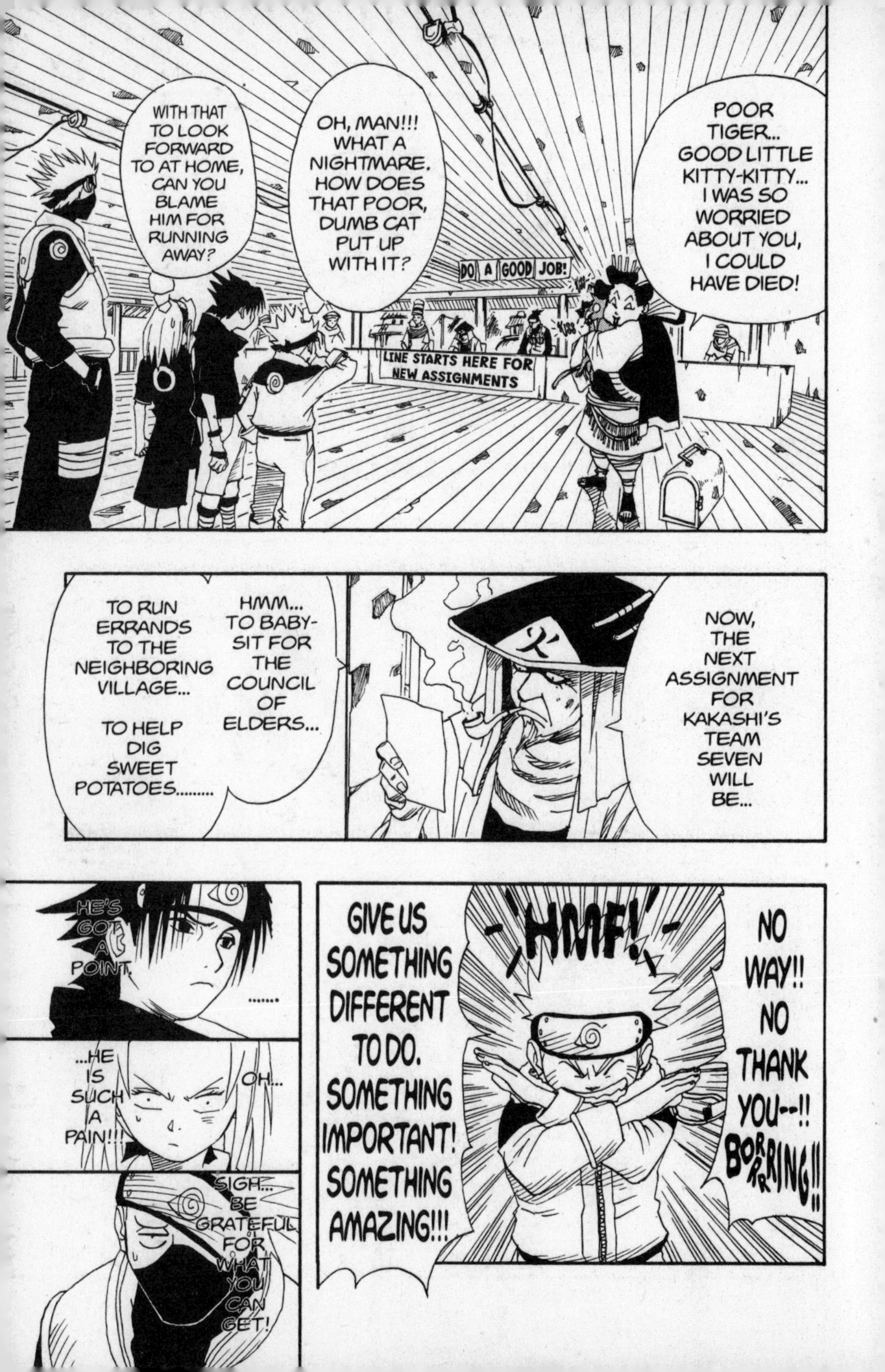
POOR TIGER... GOOD LITTLE KITTY-KITTY... I WAS SO WORRIED ABOUT YOU, I COULD HAVE DIED!
DO A GOOD JOB!
OH, MAN!!! WHAT A NIGHTMARE. HOW DOES THAT POOR, DUMB CAT PUT UP WITH IT?
WITH THAT TO LOOK FORWARD TO AT HOME, CAN YOU BLAME HIM FOR RUNNING AWAY?
LINE STARTS HERE FOR NEW ASSIGNMENTS
NOW, THE NEXT ASSIGNMENT FOR KAKASHI'S TEAM SEVEN WILL BE...
HMM... TO BABY-SIT FOR THE COUNCIL OF ELDERS...
TO RUN ERRANDS TO THE NEIGHBORING VILLAGE...
TO HELP DIG SWEET POTATOES........
NO WAY!! NO THANK YOU--!! BORRRING!!
HMF!
GIVE US SOMETHING DIFFERENT TO DO. SOMETHING IMPORTANT! SOMETHING AMAZING!!!
HE'S GOT A POINT.
......
OH...
...HE IS SUCH A PAIN!!!
SIGH... BE GRATEFUL FOR WHAT YOU CAN GET!

READ THIS WAY

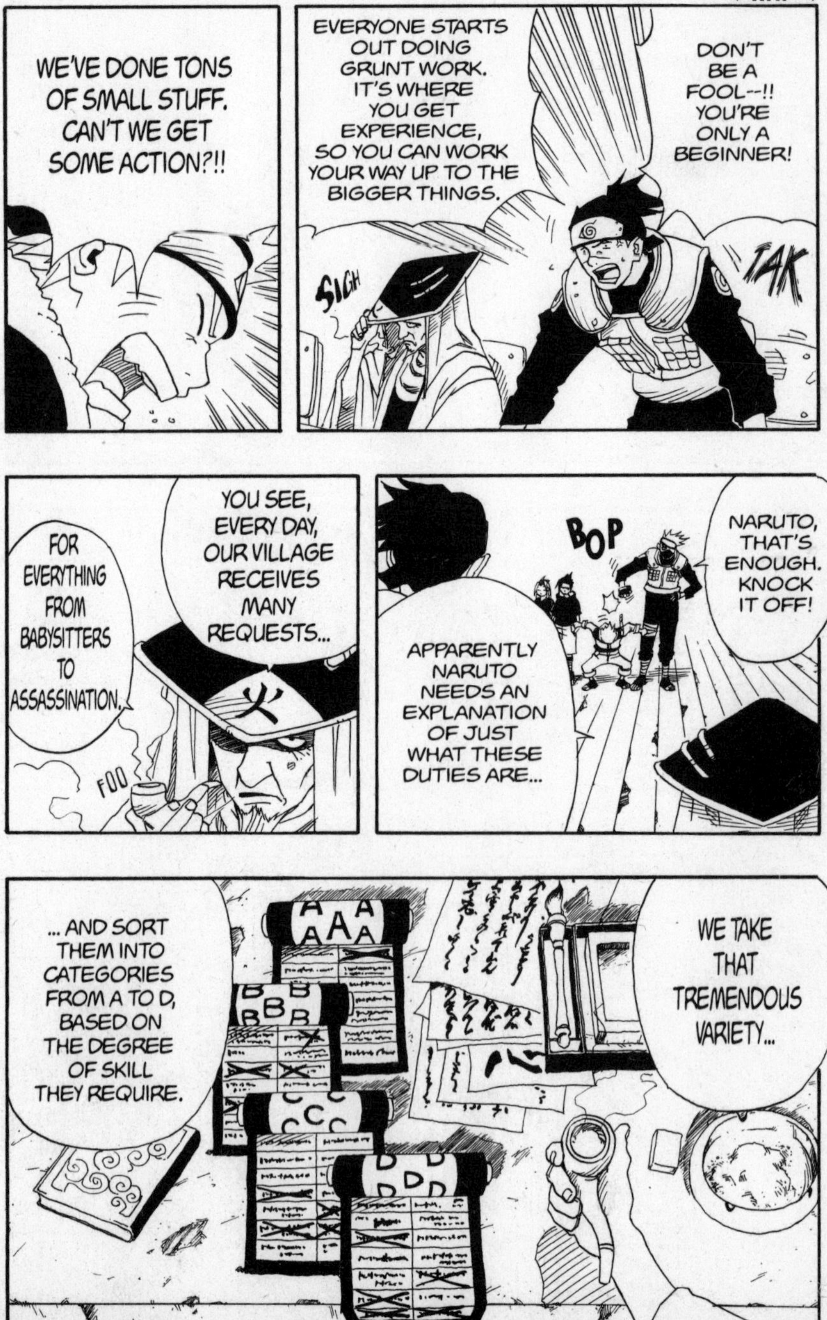
DON'T BE A FOOL--!! YOU'RE ONLY A BEGINNER!
TAK
EVERYONE STARTS OUT DOING GRUNT WORK. IT'S WHERE YOU GET EXPERIENCE, SO YOU CAN WORK YOUR WAY UP TO THE BIGGER THINGS.
SIGH
WE'VE DONE TONS OF SMALL STUFF. CAN'T WE GET SOME ACTION?!!
NARUTO, THAT'S ENOUGH. KNOCK IT OFF!
BOP
APPARENTLY NARUTO NEEDS AN EXPLANATION OF JUST WHAT THESE DUTIES ARE...
YOU SEE, EVERY DAY, OUR VILLAGE RECEIVES MANY REQUESTS...
FOR EVERYTHING FROM BABYSITTERS TO ASSASSINATION.
FOO
WE TAKE THAT TREMENDOUS VARIETY...
... AND SORT THEM INTO CATEGORIES FROM A TO D, BASED ON THE DEGREE OF SKILL THEY REQUIRE.

READ THIS WAY

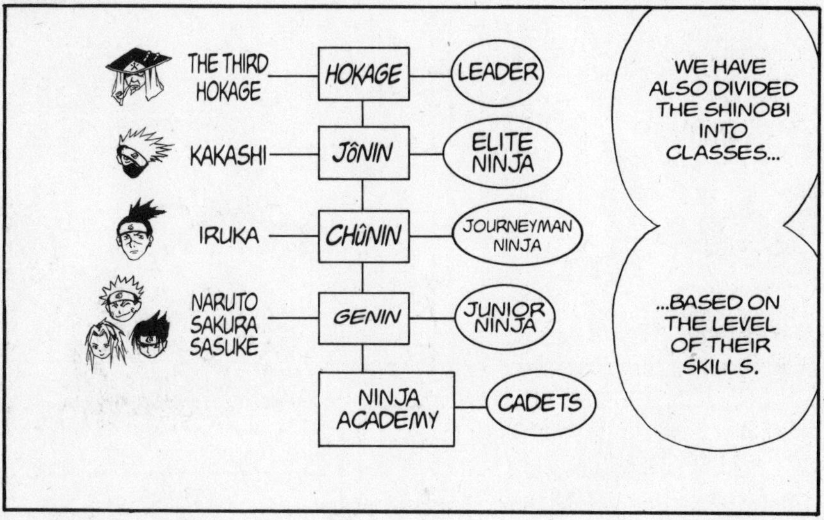

WE HAVE ALSO DIVIDED THE SHINOBI INTO CLASSES...
...BASED ON THE LEVEL OF THEIR SKILLS.
THE THIRD HOKAGE
HOKAGE
LEADER
KAKASHI
JÔNIN
ELITE NINJA
IRUKA
CHÛNIN
JOURNEYMAN NINJA
NARUTO SAKURA SASUKE
GENIN
JUNIOR NINJA
NINJA ACADEMY
CADETS

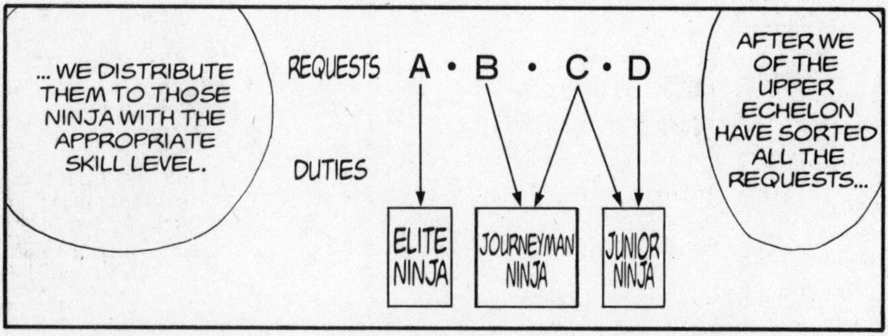

AFTER WE OF THE UPPER ECHELON HAVE SORTED ALL THE REQUESTS...
REQUESTS
A • B • C • D
DUTIES
ELITE NINJA
JOURNEYMAN NINJA
JUNIOR NINJA
... WE DISTRIBUTE THEM TO THOSE NINJA WITH THE APPROPRIATE SKILL LEVEL.

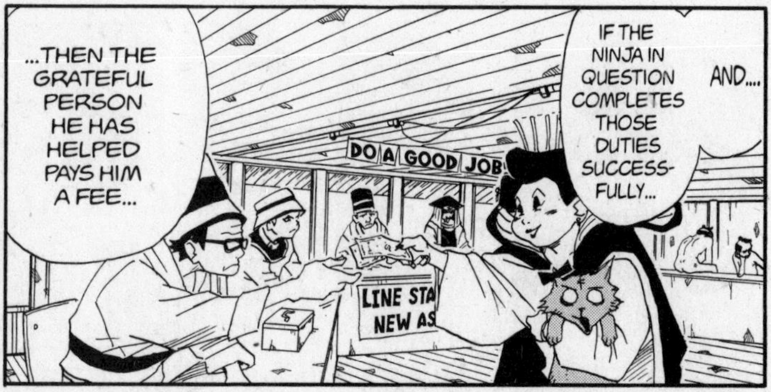

AND....
IF THE NINJA IN QUESTION COMPLETES THOSE DUTIES SUCCESS-FULLY...
DO A GOOD JOB
LINE STA
NEW AS
...THEN THE GRATEFUL PERSON HE HAS HELPED PAYS HIM A FEE...

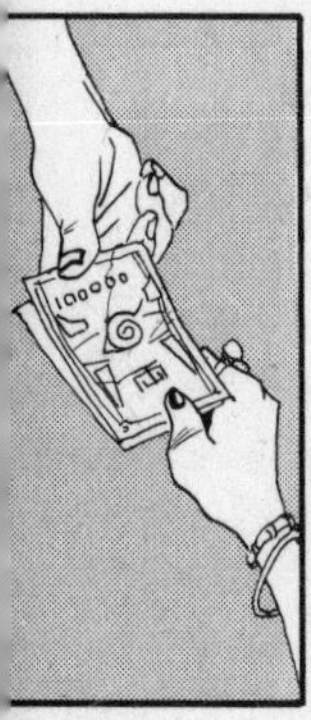

READ THIS WAY

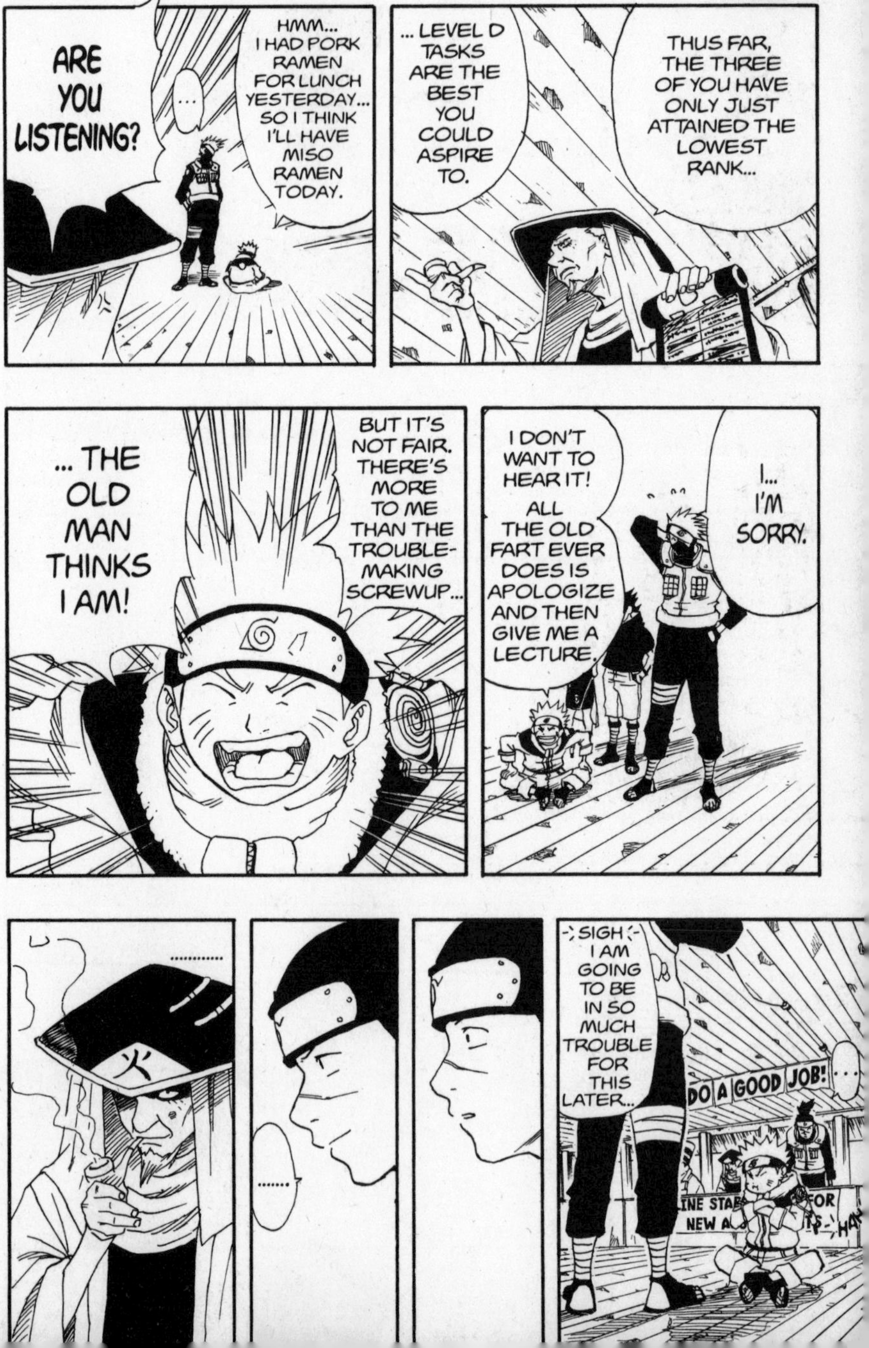
THUS FAR, THE THREE OF YOU HAVE ONLY JUST ATTAINED THE LOWEST RANK...
... LEVEL D TASKS ARE THE BEST YOU COULD ASPIRE TO.
HMM... I HAD PORK RAMEN FOR LUNCH YESTERDAY... SO I THINK I'LL HAVE MISO RAMEN TODAY.
...
ARE YOU LISTENING?
I... I'M SORRY.
I DON'T WANT TO HEAR IT!
ALL THE OLD FART EVER DOES IS APOLOGIZE AND THEN GIVE ME A LECTURE.
BUT IT'S NOT FAIR. THERE'S MORE TO ME THAN THE TROUBLE-MAKING SCREWUP...
... THE OLD MAN THINKS I AM!
-SIGH- I AM GOING TO BE IN SO MUCH TROUBLE FOR THIS LATER...
DO A GOOD JOB!
...
....
....

READ THIS WAY

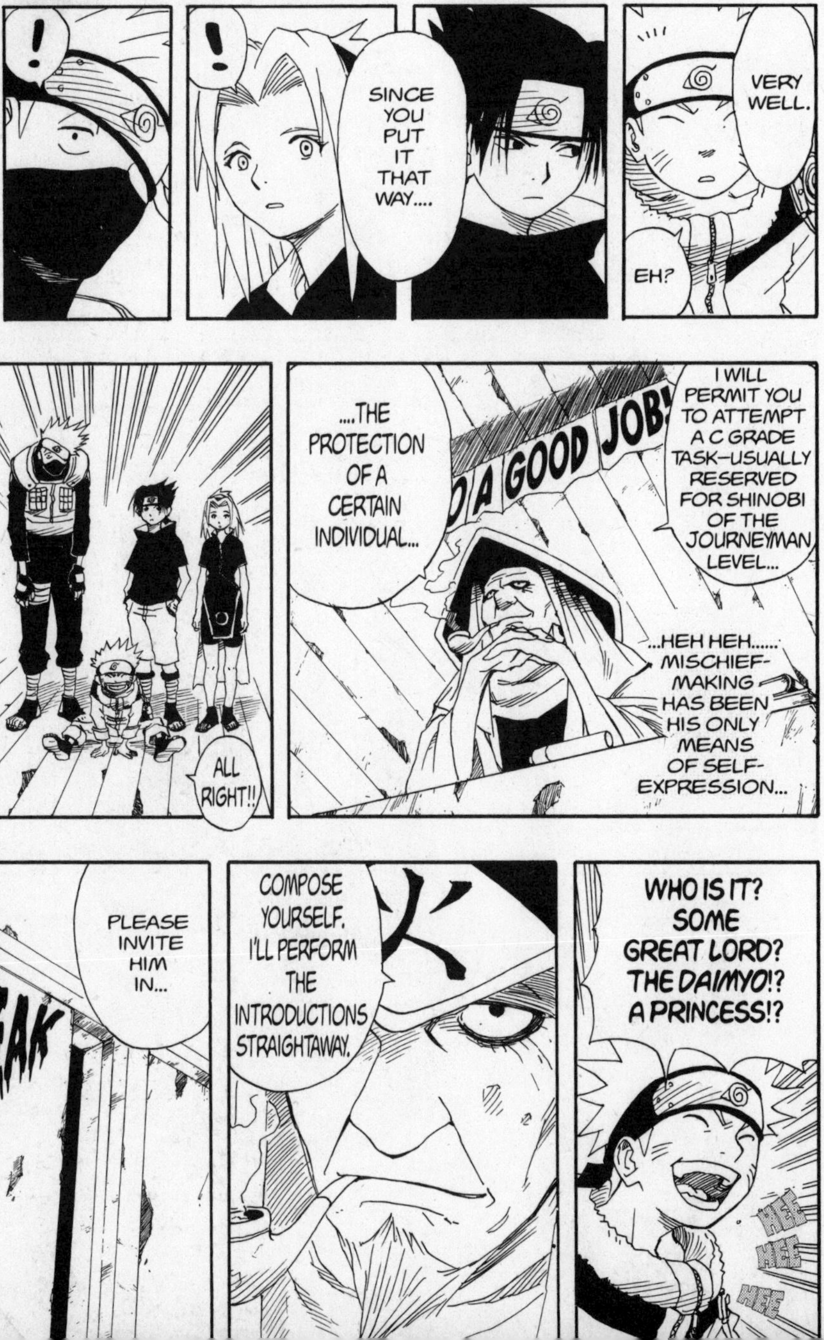

VERY WELL.
EH?
SINCE YOU PUT IT THAT WAY....
!
!
I WILL PERMIT YOU TO ATTEMPT A C GRADE TASK—USUALLY RESERVED FOR SHINOBI OF THE JOURNEYMAN LEVEL...
A GOOD JOB!
....THE PROTECTION OF A CERTAIN INDIVIDUAL...
...HEH HEH...... MISCHIEF-MAKING HAS BEEN HIS ONLY MEANS OF SELF-EXPRESSION...
ALL RIGHT!!
WHO IS IT? SOME GREAT LORD? THE DAIMYO!? A PRINCESS!?
HEE
HEE
HEE
COMPOSE YOURSELF. I'LL PERFORM THE INTRODUCTIONS STRAIGHTAWAY.
PLEASE INVITE HIM IN...
EEEAK

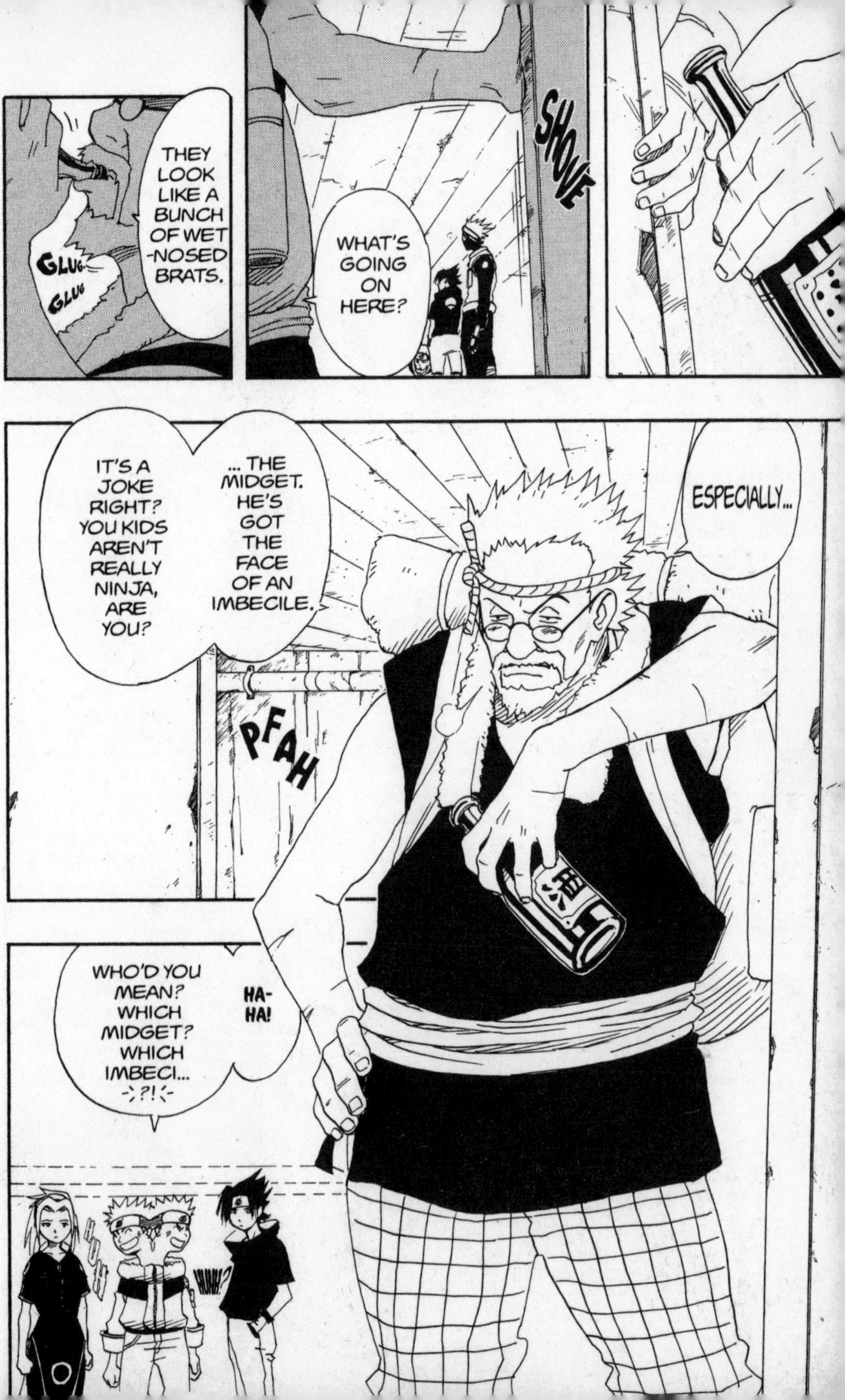
SHOVE
WHAT'S GOING ON HERE?
THEY LOOK LIKE A BUNCH OF WET-NOSED BRATS.
GLUG GLUG
ESPECIALLY...
... THE MIDGET. HE'S GOT THE FACE OF AN IMBECILE.
IT'S A JOKE RIGHT? YOU KIDS AREN'T REALLY NINJA, ARE YOU?
PFAH
HA-HA!
WHO'D YOU MEAN? WHICH MIDGET? WHICH IMBECI... ?!
HUH!?

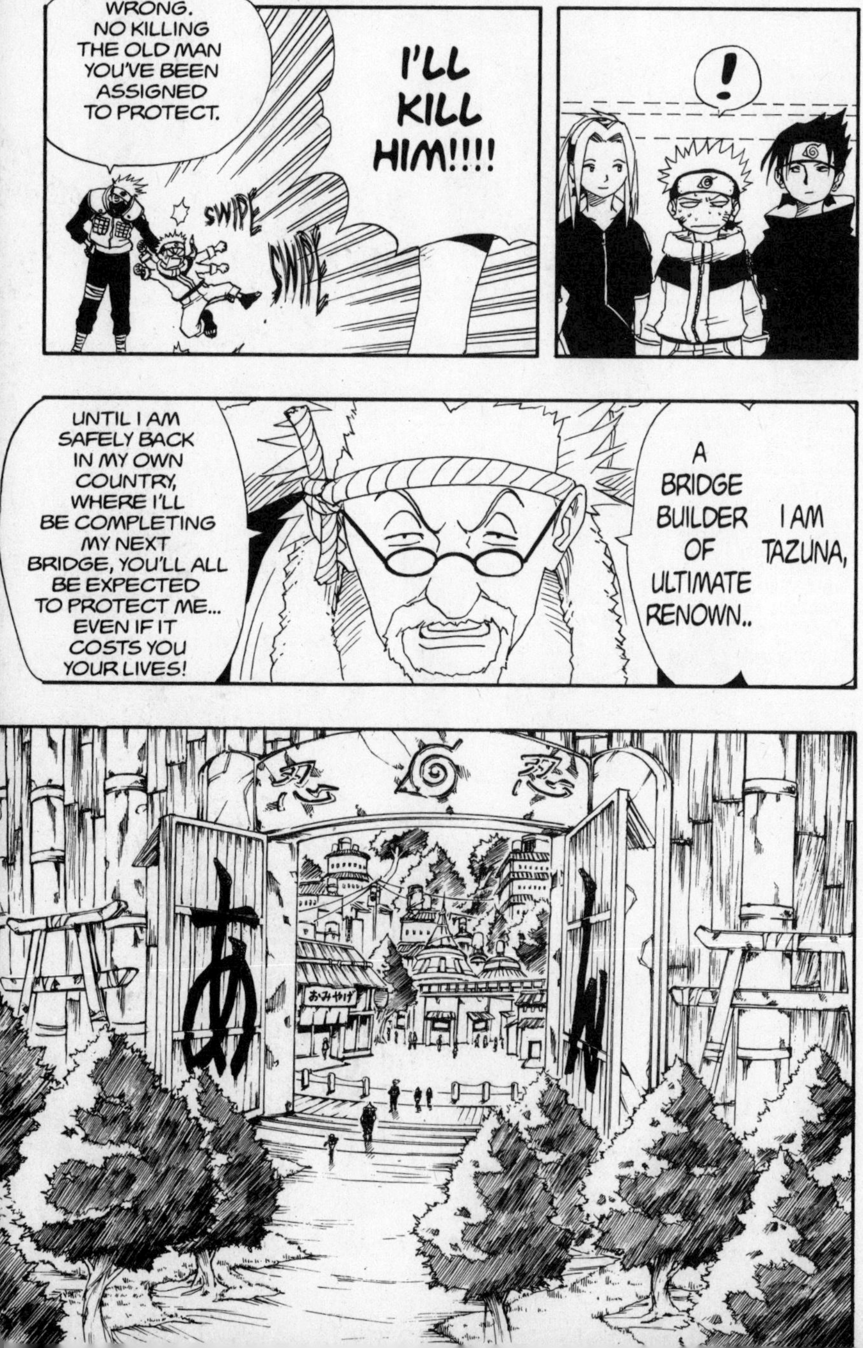
!
I'LL KILL HIM!!!!
WRONG. NO KILLING THE OLD MAN YOU'VE BEEN ASSIGNED TO PROTECT.
SWIPE
SWIPE
I AM TAZUNA,
A BRIDGE BUILDER OF ULTIMATE RENOWN..
UNTIL I AM SAFELY BACK IN MY OWN COUNTRY, WHERE I'LL BE COMPLETING MY NEXT BRIDGE, YOU'LL ALL BE EXPECTED TO PROTECT ME... EVEN IF IT COSTS YOU YOUR LIVES!
忍 忍
あ ん
おみやげ

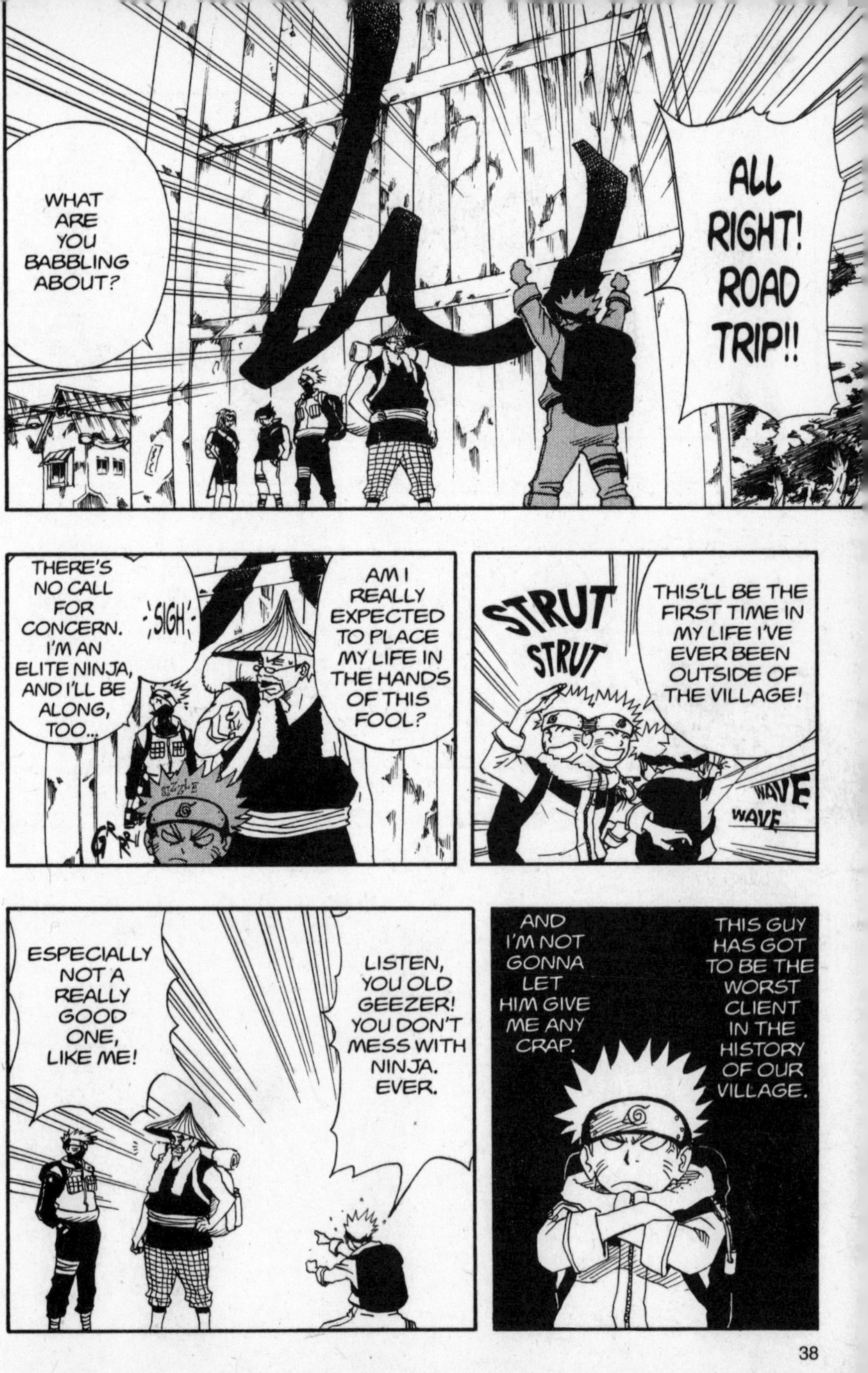
ALL RIGHT! ROAD TRIP!!
WHAT ARE YOU BABBLING ABOUT?
STRUT
STRUT
THIS'LL BE THE FIRST TIME IN MY LIFE I'VE EVER BEEN OUTSIDE OF THE VILLAGE!
WAVE
WAVE
AM I REALLY EXPECTED TO PLACE MY LIFE IN THE HANDS OF THIS FOOL?
SIGH
THERE'S NO CALL FOR CONCERN. I'M AN ELITE NINJA, AND I'LL BE ALONG, TOO...
GRRR
THIS GUY HAS GOT TO BE THE WORST CLIENT IN THE HISTORY OF OUR VILLAGE.
AND I'M NOT GONNA LET HIM GIVE ME ANY CRAP.
LISTEN, YOU OLD GEEZER! YOU DON'T MESS WITH NINJA. EVER.
ESPECIALLY NOT A REALLY GOOD ONE, LIKE ME!

READ THIS WAY

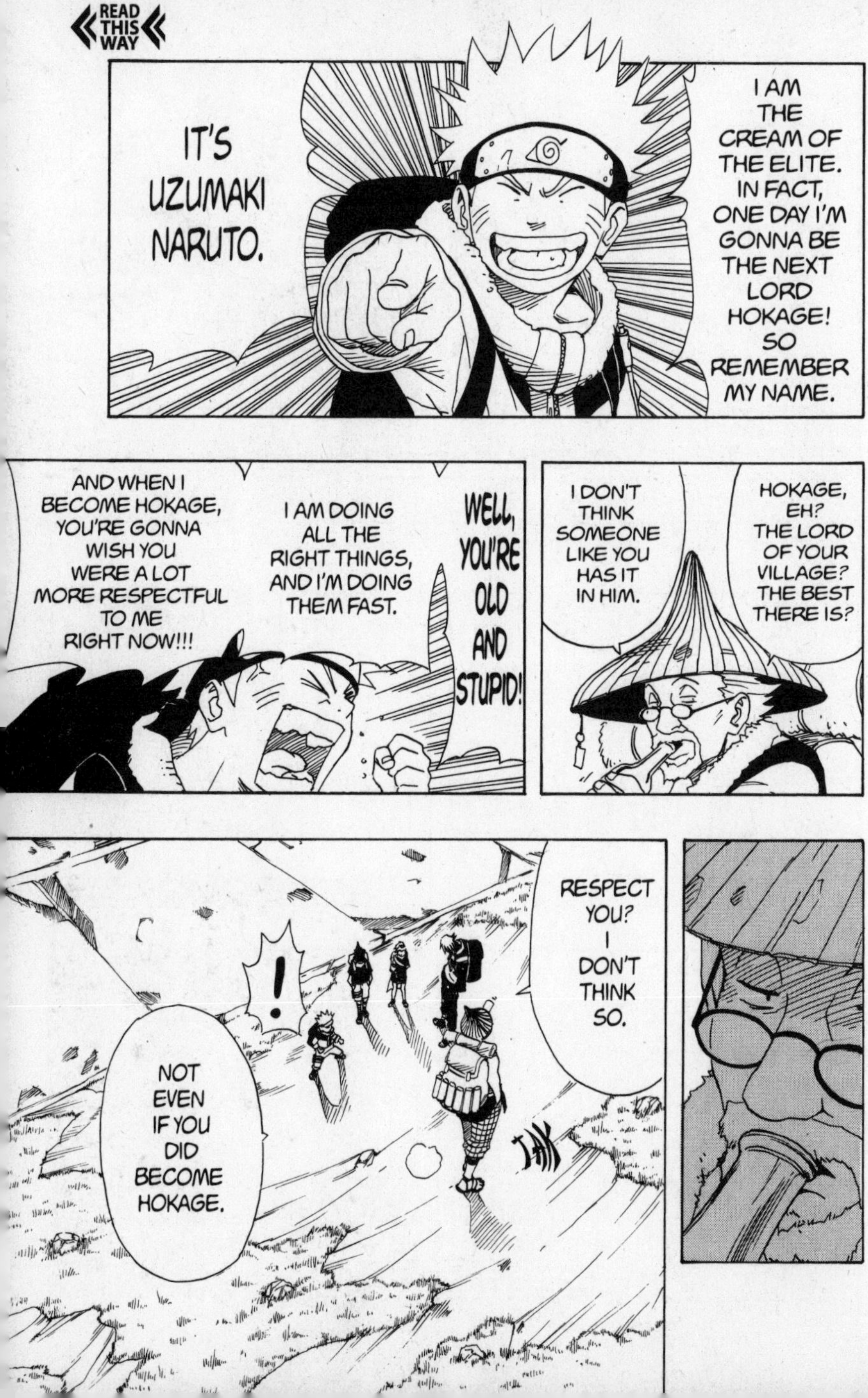
I AM THE CREAM OF THE ELITE. IN FACT, ONE DAY I'M GONNA BE THE NEXT LORD HOKAGE! SO REMEMBER MY NAME.
IT'S UZUMAKI NARUTO.
HOKAGE, EH? THE LORD OF YOUR VILLAGE? THE BEST THERE IS?
I DON'T THINK SOMEONE LIKE YOU HAS IT IN HIM.
WELL, YOU'RE OLD AND STUPID!
I AM DOING ALL THE RIGHT THINGS, AND I'M DOING THEM FAST.
AND WHEN I BECOME HOKAGE, YOU'RE GONNA WISH YOU WERE A LOT MORE RESPECTFUL TO ME RIGHT NOW!!!
RESPECT YOU? I DON'T THINK SO.
!
NOT EVEN IF YOU DID BECOME HOKAGE.
TAK

READ THIS WAY

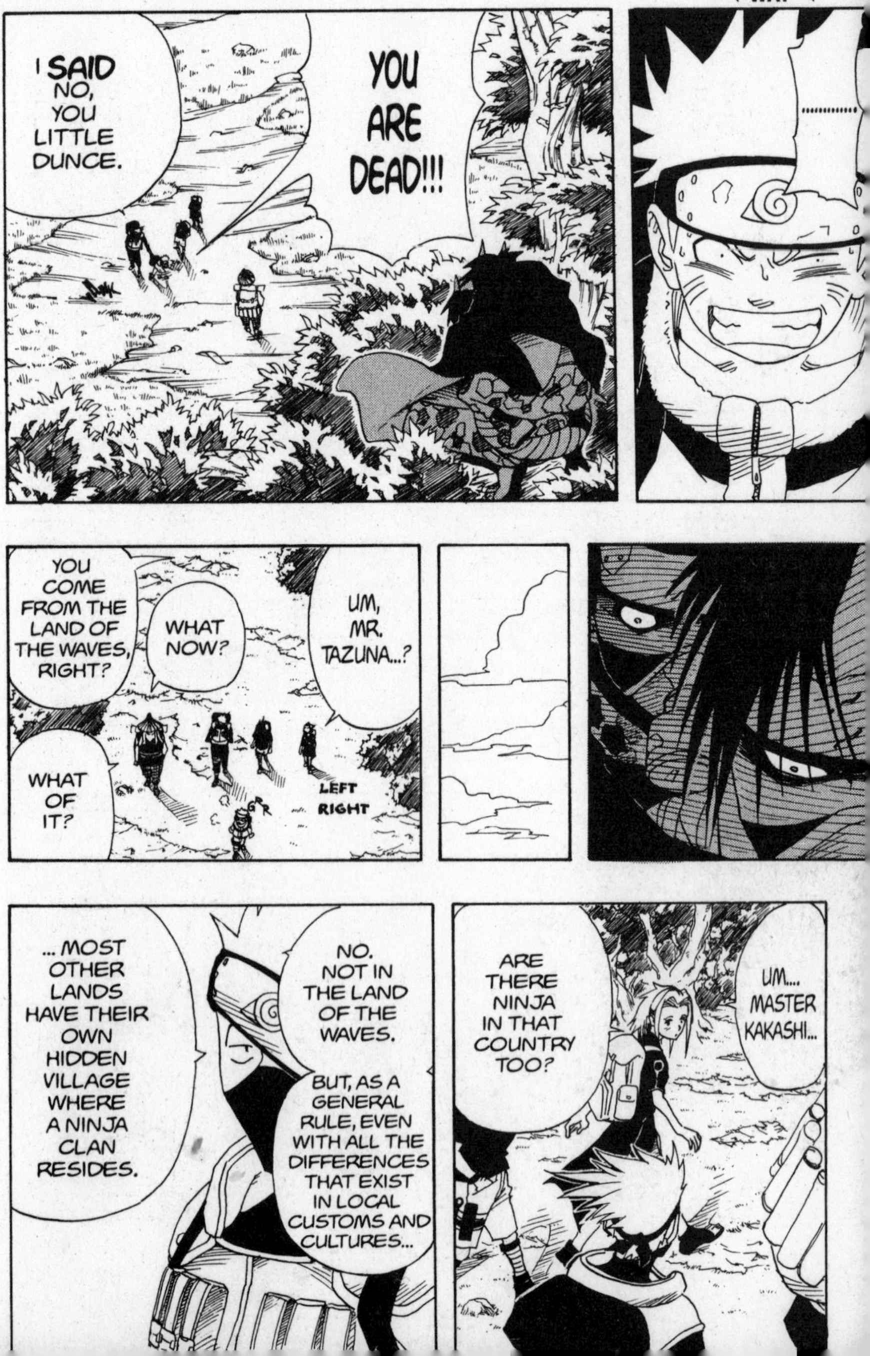
....
YOU ARE DEAD!!!
I SAID NO, YOU LITTLE DUNCE.
UM, MR. TAZUNA...?
WHAT NOW?
YOU COME FROM THE LAND OF THE WAVES, RIGHT?
WHAT OF IT?
LEFT RIGHT
UM.... MASTER KAKASHI...
ARE THERE NINJA IN THAT COUNTRY TOO?
NO. NOT IN THE LAND OF THE WAVES.
BUT, AS A GENERAL RULE, EVEN WITH ALL THE DIFFERENCES THAT EXIST IN LOCAL CUSTOMS AND CULTURES...
... MOST OTHER LANDS HAVE THEIR OWN HIDDEN VILLAGE WHERE A NINJA CLAN RESIDES.

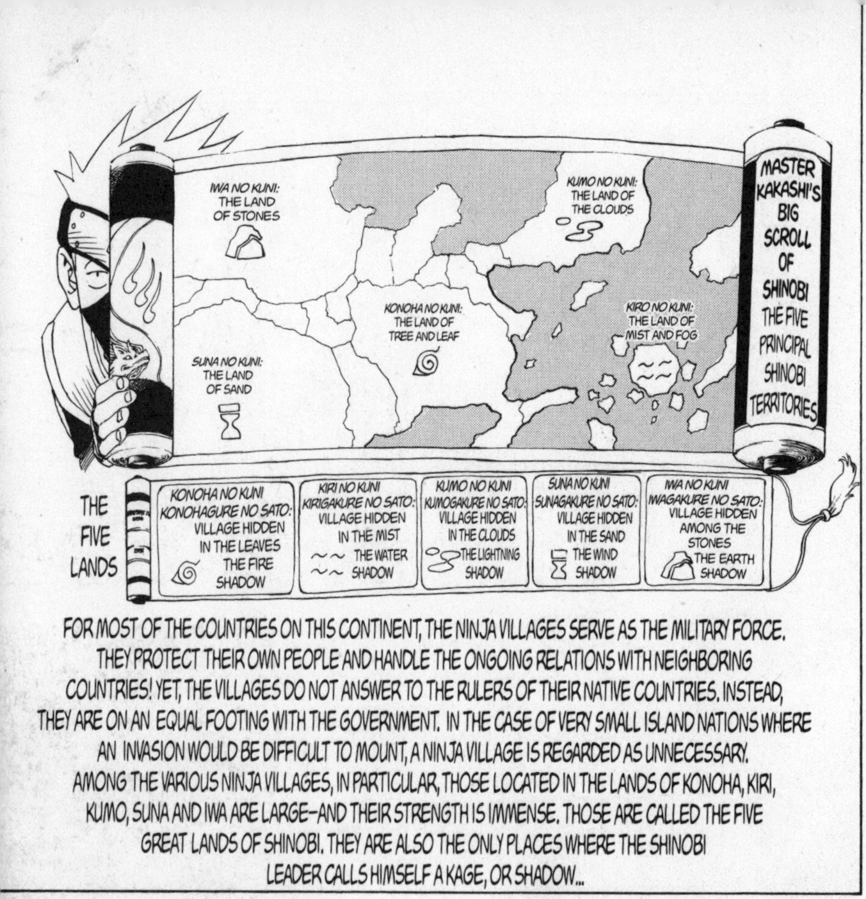
MASTER KAKASHI'S BIG SCROLL OF SHINOBI THE FIVE PRINCIPAL SHINOBI TERRITORIES
KUMO NO KUNI: THE LAND OF THE CLOUDS
KIRO NO KUNI: THE LAND OF MIST AND FOG
KONOHA NO KUNI: THE LAND OF TREE AND LEAF
IWA NO KUNI: THE LAND OF STONES
SUNA NO KUNI: THE LAND OF SAND
THE FIVE LANDS
KONOHA NO KUNI KONOHAGURE NO SATO: VILLAGE HIDDEN IN THE LEAVES THE FIRE SHADOW
KIRI NO KUNI KIRIGAKURE NO SATO: VILLAGE HIDDEN IN THE MIST THE WATER SHADOW
KUMO NO KUNI KUMOGAKURE NO SATO: VILLAGE HIDDEN IN THE CLOUDS THE LIGHTNING SHADOW
SUNA NO KUNI SUNAGAKURE NO SATO: VILLAGE HIDDEN IN THE SAND THE WIND SHADOW
IWA NO KUNI IWAGAKURE NO SATO: VILLAGE HIDDEN AMONG THE STONES THE EARTH SHADOW
FOR MOST OF THE COUNTRIES ON THIS CONTINENT, THE NINJA VILLAGES SERVE AS THE MILITARY FORCE. THEY PROTECT THEIR OWN PEOPLE AND HANDLE THE ONGOING RELATIONS WITH NEIGHBORING COUNTRIES! YET, THE VILLAGES DO NOT ANSWER TO THE RULERS OF THEIR NATIVE COUNTRIES. INSTEAD, THEY ARE ON AN EQUAL FOOTING WITH THE GOVERNMENT. IN THE CASE OF VERY SMALL ISLAND NATIONS WHERE AN INVASION WOULD BE DIFFICULT TO MOUNT, A NINJA VILLAGE IS REGARDED AS UNNECESSARY. AMONG THE VARIOUS NINJA VILLAGES, IN PARTICULAR, THOSE LOCATED IN THE LANDS OF KONOHA, KIRI, KUMO, SUNA AND IWA ARE LARGE–AND THEIR STRENGTH IS IMMENSE. THOSE ARE CALLED THE FIVE GREAT LANDS OF SHINOBI. THEY ARE ALSO THE ONLY PLACES WHERE THE SHINOBI LEADER CALLS HIMSELF A KAGE, OR SHADOW...

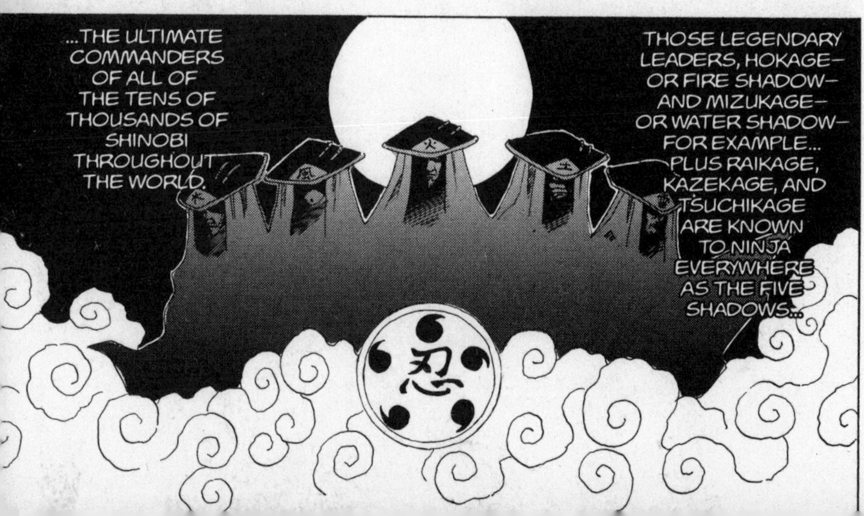
...THE ULTIMATE COMMANDERS OF ALL OF THE TENS OF THOUSANDS OF SHINOBI THROUGHOUT THE WORLD.
THOSE LEGENDARY LEADERS, HOKAGE– OR FIRE SHADOW– AND MIZUKAGE– OR WATER SHADOW– FOR EXAMPLE... PLUS RAIKAGE, KAZEKAGE, AND TSUCHIKAGE ARE KNOWN TO NINJA EVERYWHERE AS THE FIVE SHADOWS...

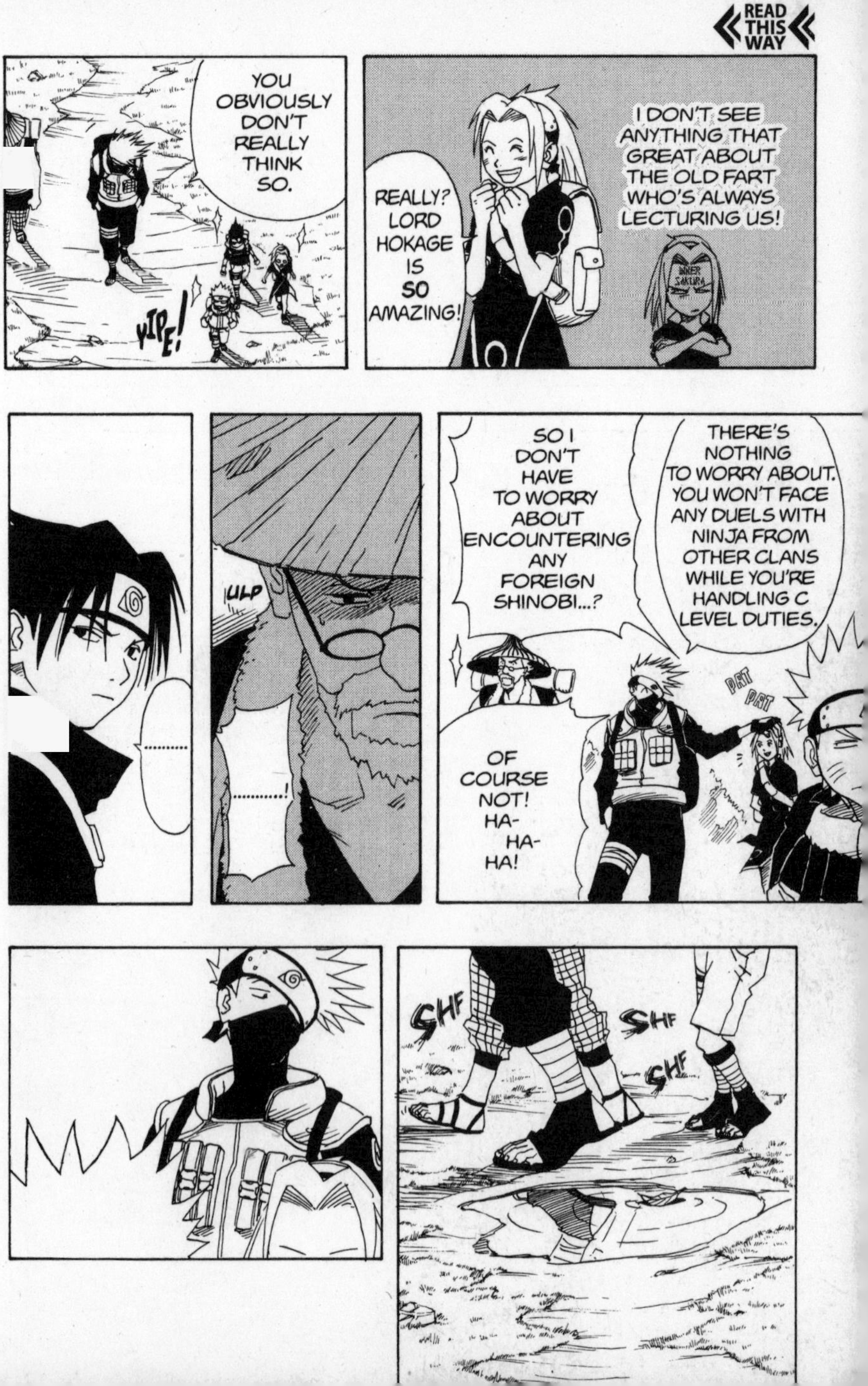
READ THIS WAY
I DON'T SEE ANYTHING THAT GREAT ABOUT THE OLD FART WHO'S ALWAYS LECTURING US!
REALLY? LORD HOKAGE IS SO AMAZING!
INNER SAKURA
YOU OBVIOUSLY DON'T REALLY THINK SO.
YIPE!
THERE'S NOTHING TO WORRY ABOUT. YOU WON'T FACE ANY DUELS WITH NINJA FROM OTHER CLANS WHILE YOU'RE HANDLING C LEVEL DUTIES.
SO I DON'T HAVE TO WORRY ABOUT ENCOUNTERING ANY FOREIGN SHINOBI...?
PAT
PAT
OF COURSE NOT! HA-HA-HA!
ULP
..........!
....
SHF
SHF
SHF

READ THIS WAY

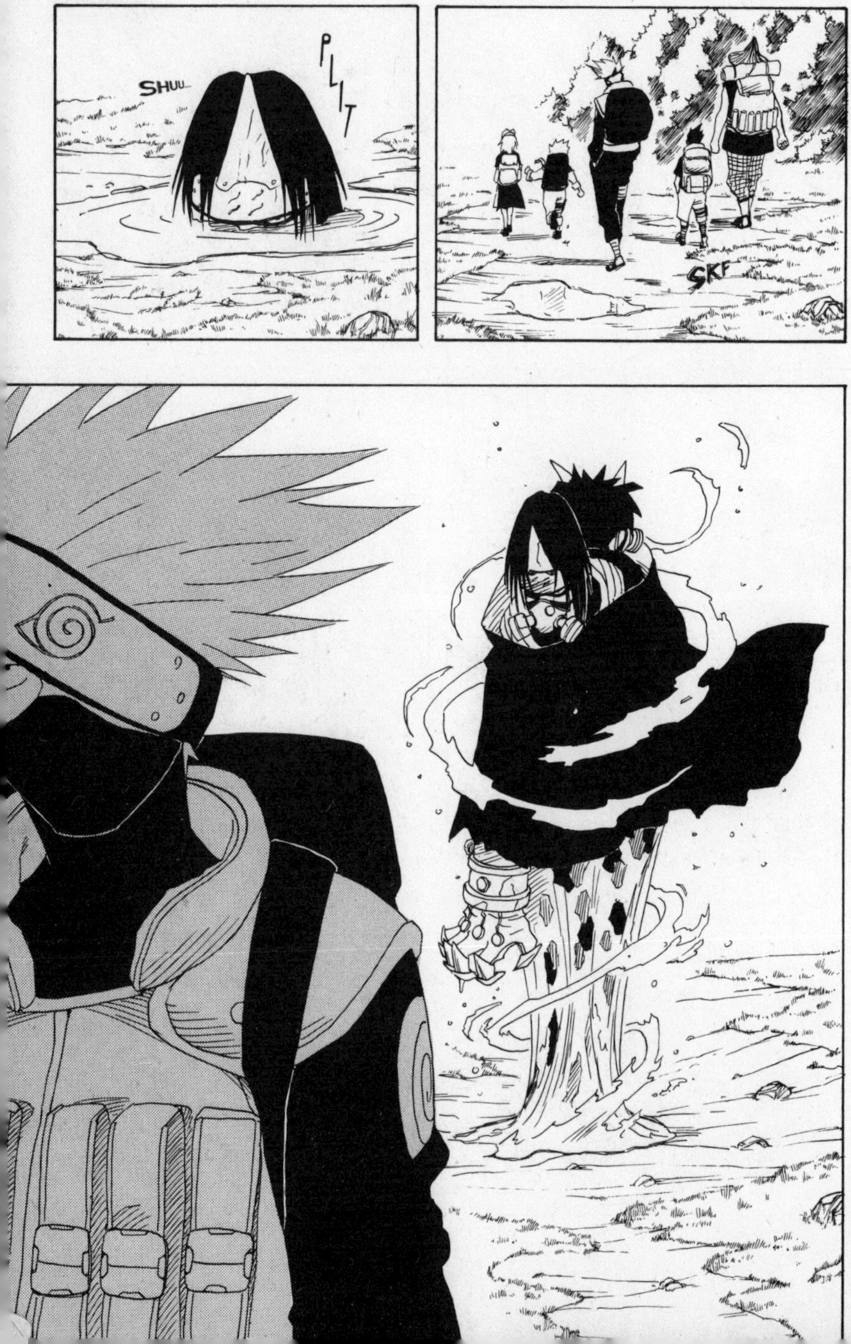
SKF
SHUU...
PLIT

READ THIS WAY

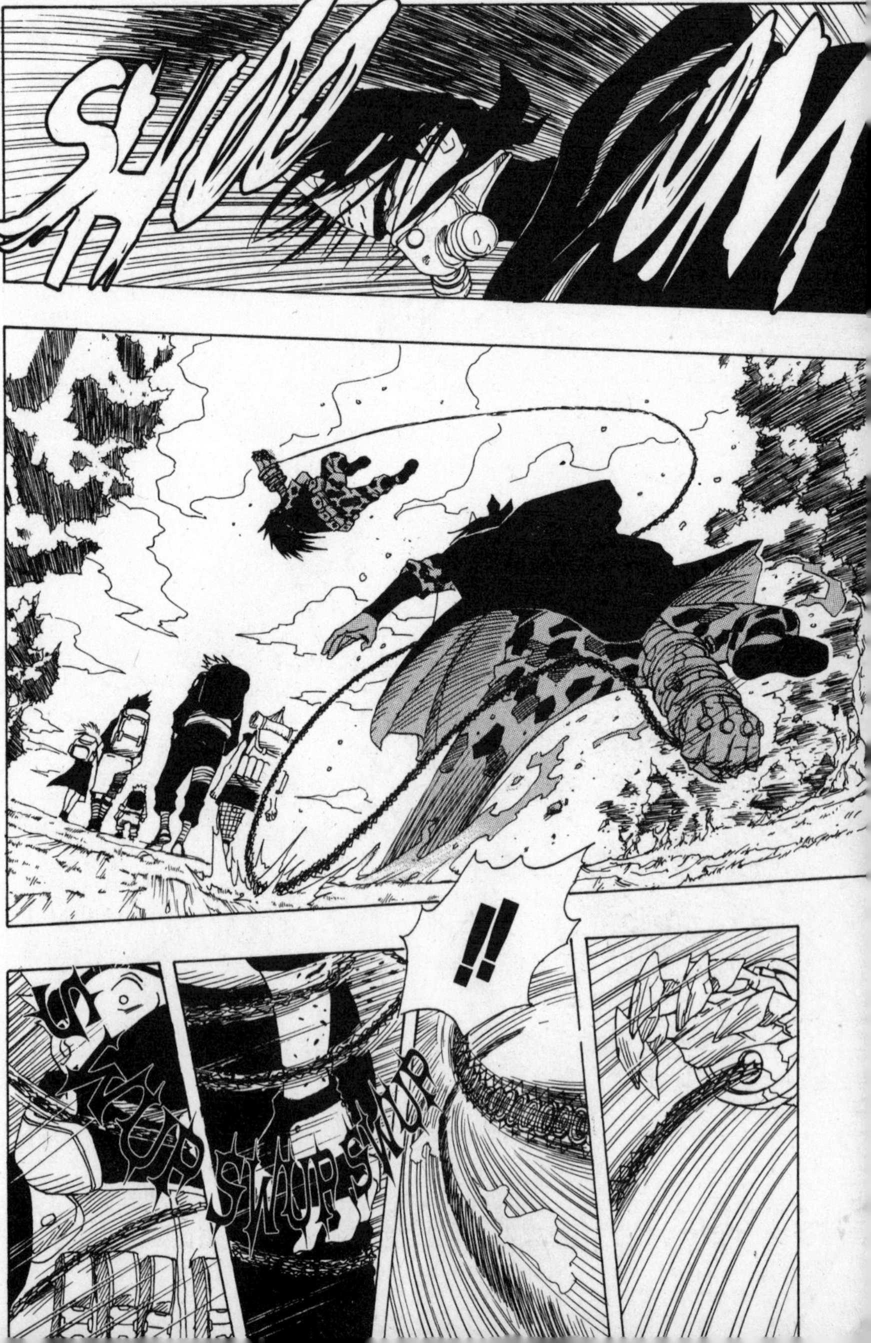
!!
SWOOP SWOOP SWOOP

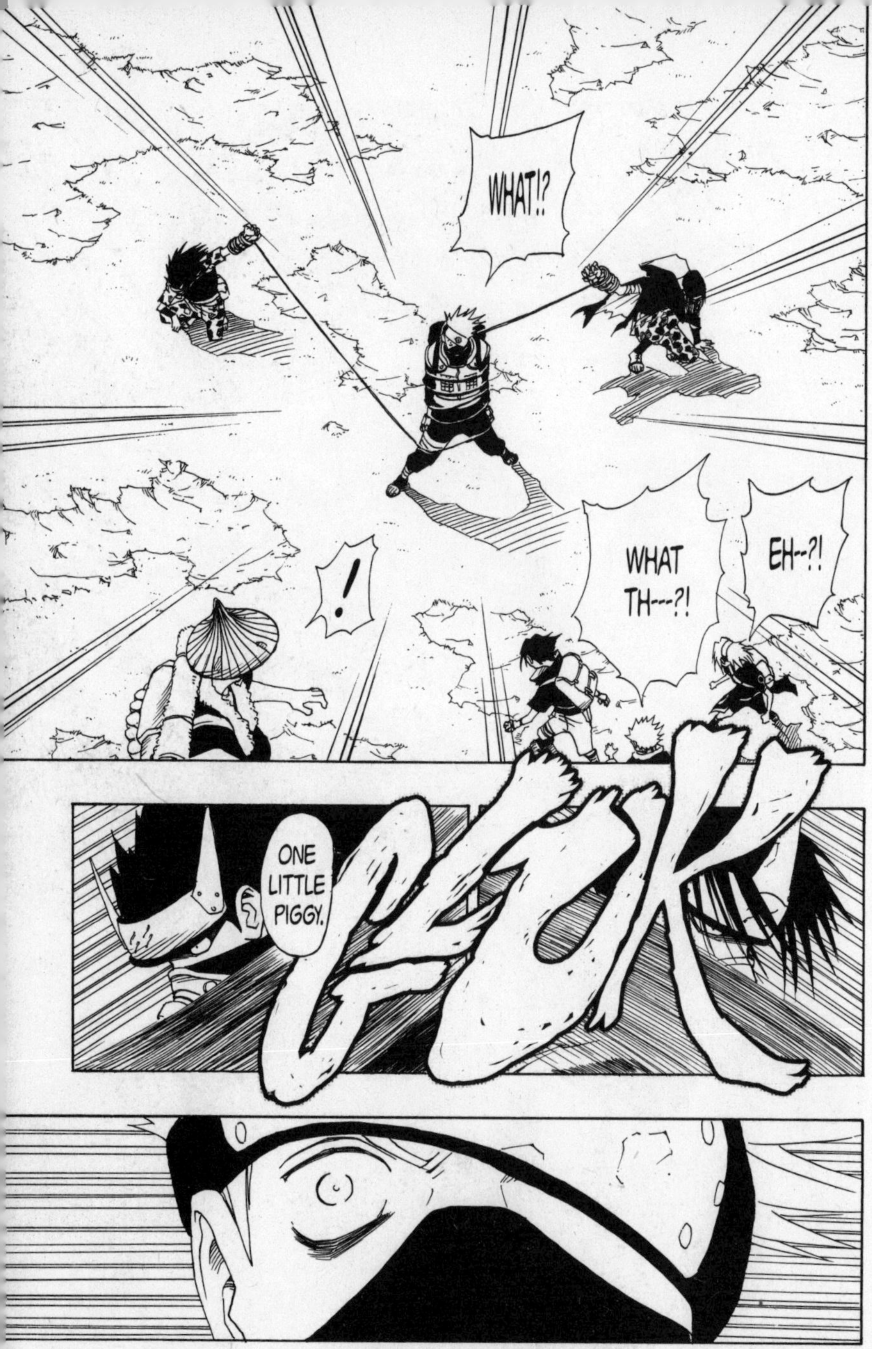
WHAT!?
EH--?!
WHAT TH---?!
!
ONE LITTLE PIGGY.

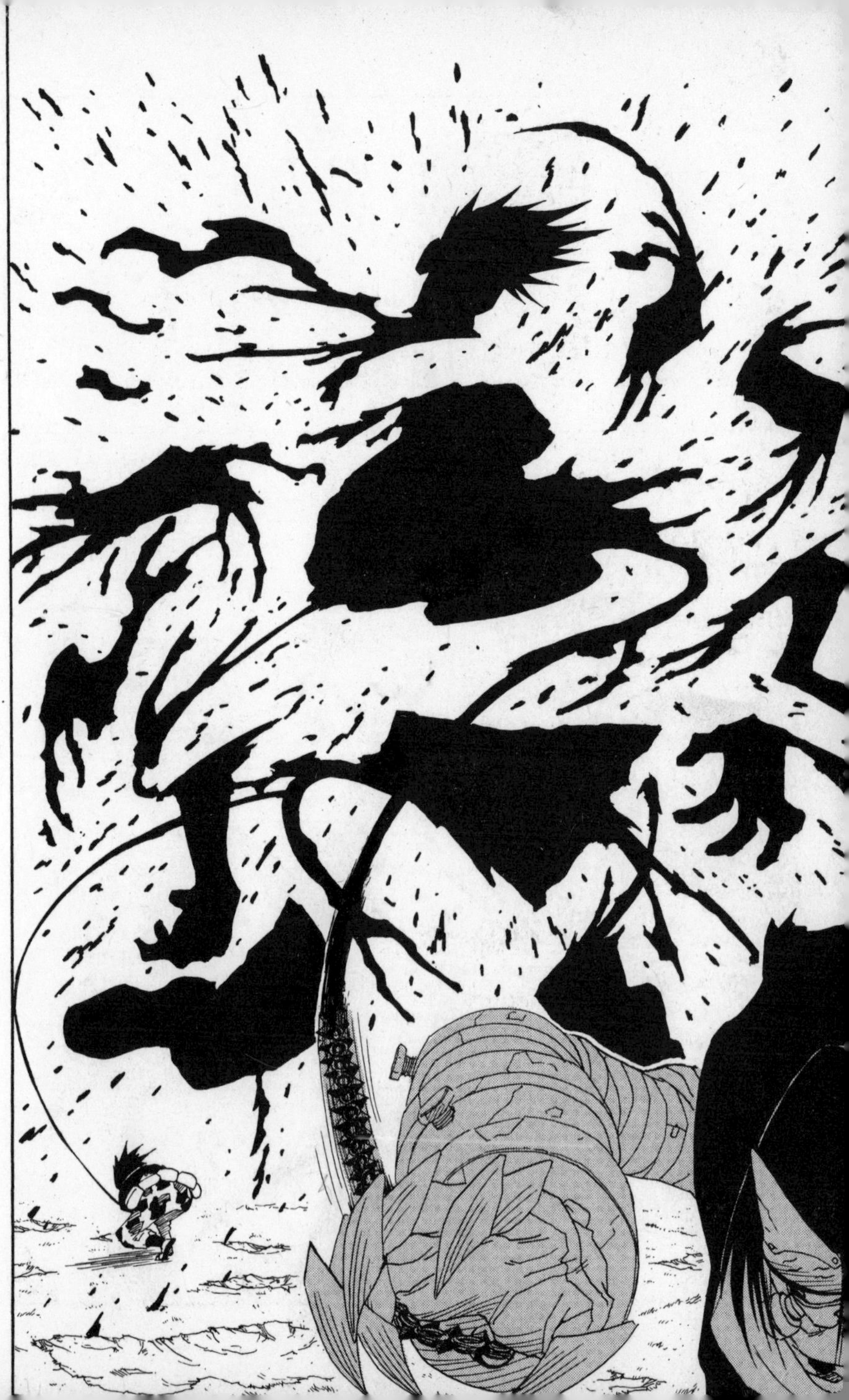

READ THIS WAY

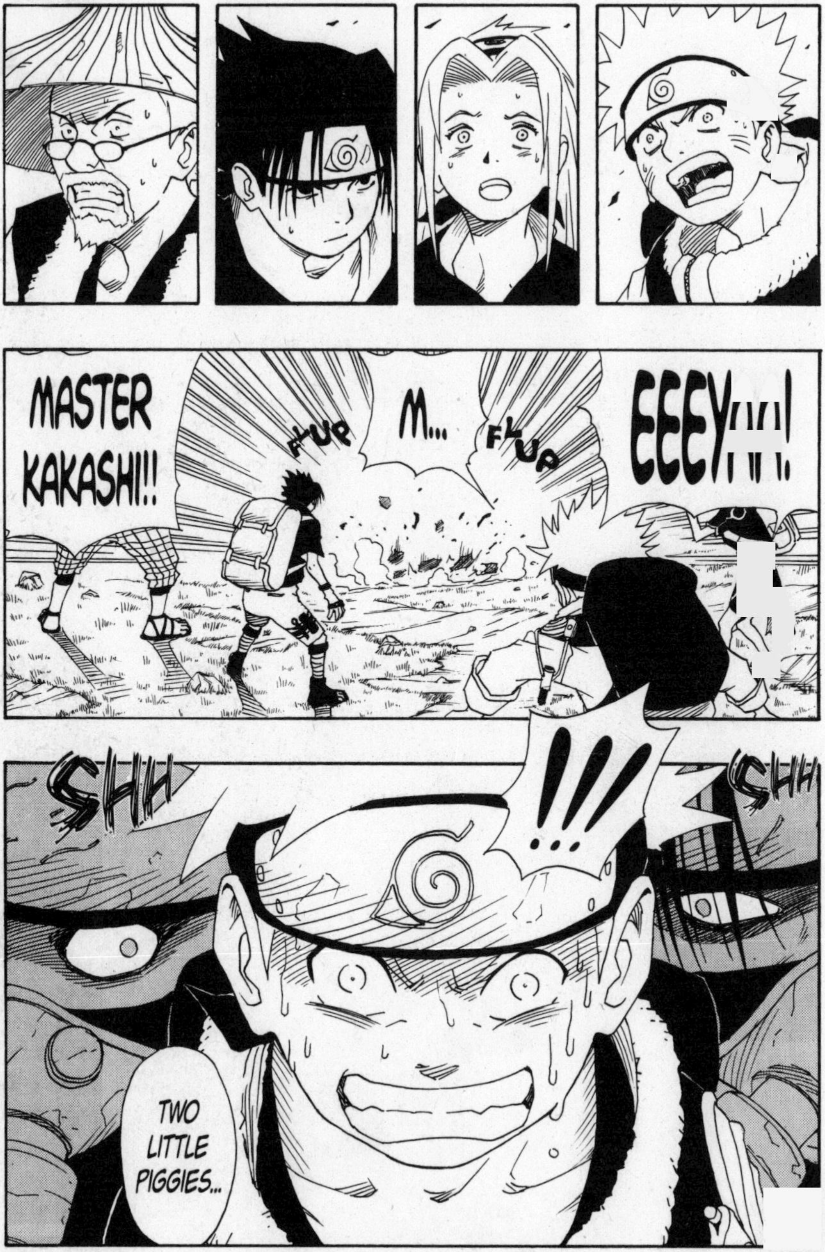

EEEY
FLUP
M...
FLUP
MASTER KAKASHI!!
SHH
!!!...
SHH
TWO LITTLE PIGGIES...

Number 10: Target #2

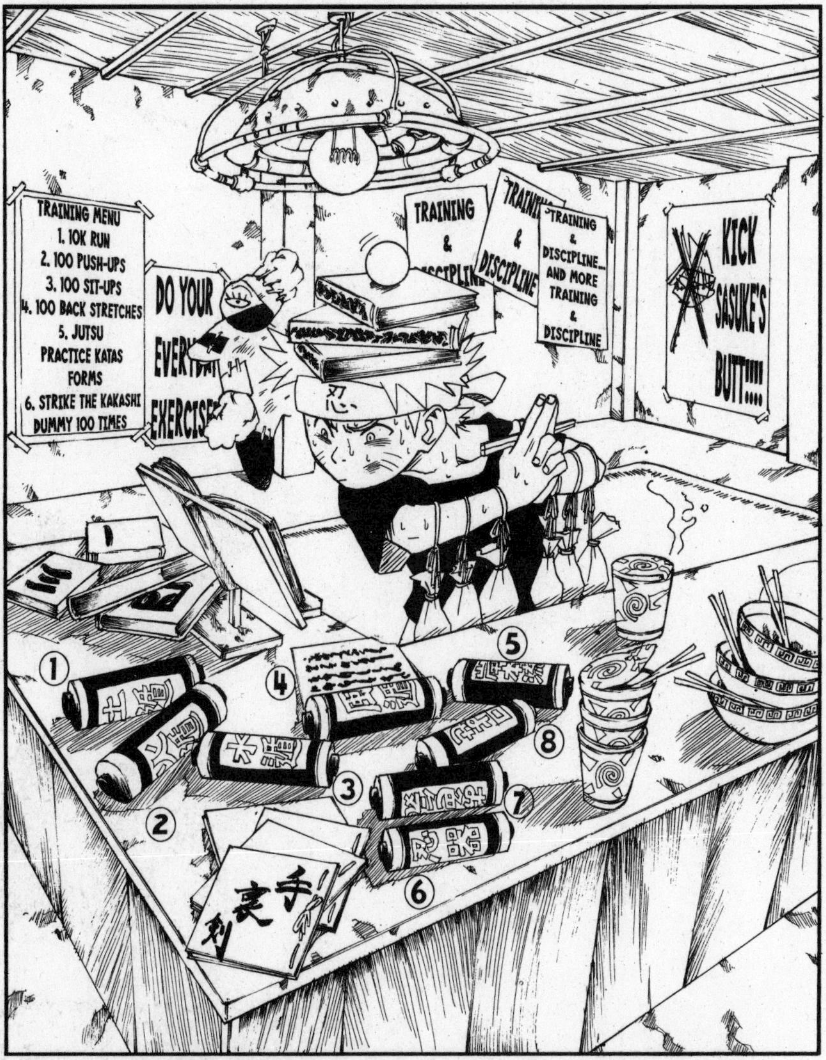
TRAINING MENU
1. 10K RUN
2. 100 PUSH-UPS
3. 100 SIT-UPS
4. 100 BACK STRETCHES
5. JUTSU PRACTICE KATAS FORMS
6. STRIKE THE KAKASHI DUMMY 100 TIMES
DO YOUR EVERYDA EXERCISE
TRAINING & DISCIPLINE
TRAINING & DISCIPLINE
TRAINING & DISCIPLINE... AND MORE TRAINING & DISCIPLINE
KICK SASUKE'S BUTT!!!!
1
2
3
4
5
6
7
8

SCROLLS: (1) EARTH STYLE (2) FIRE STYLE (3) WATER STYLE (4) WIND STYLE (5) KISHIMOTO TECHNIQUE (6) NINJA WEAPONRY (7) NINJA CENTERFOLD (8) SUMMONING

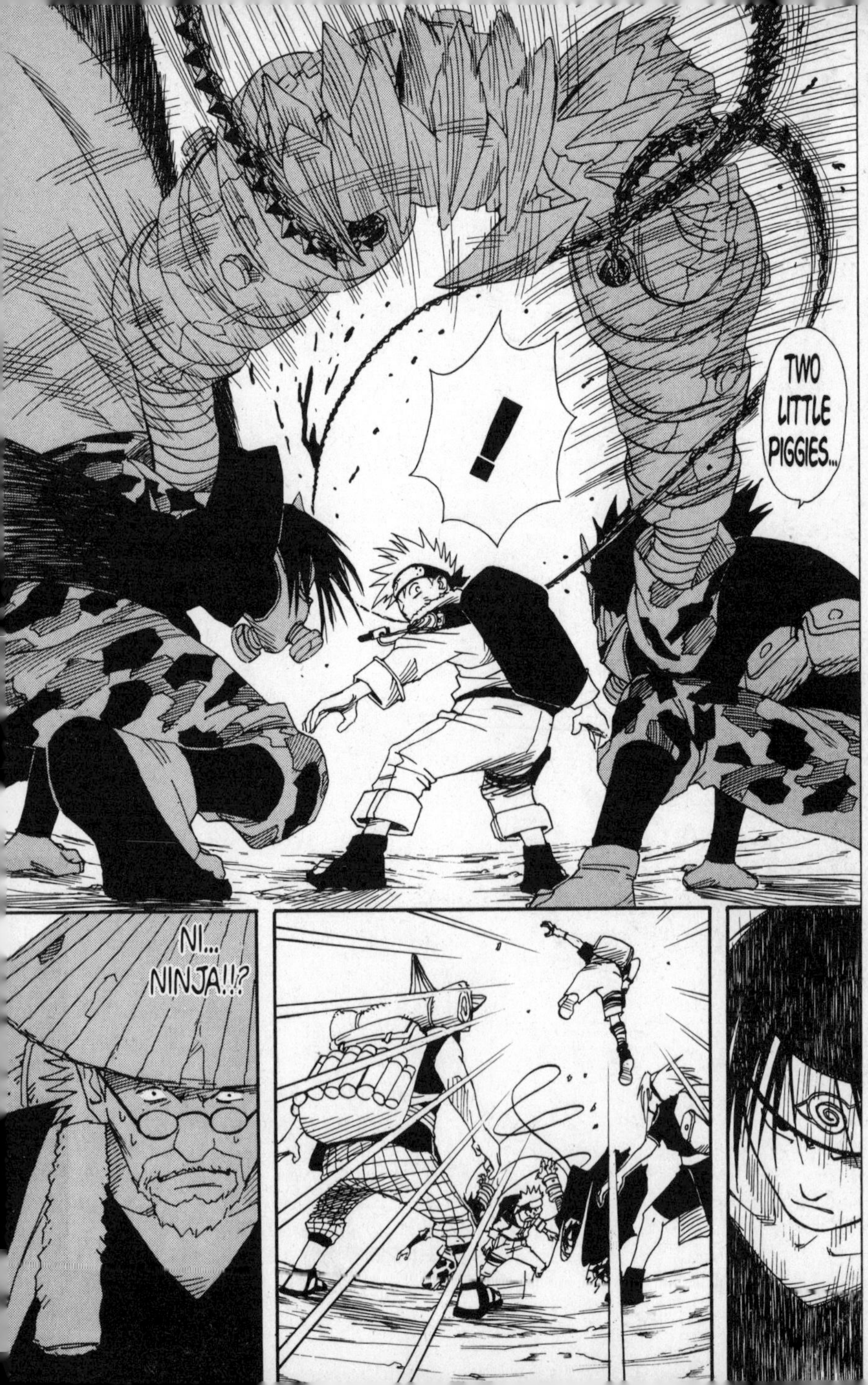
TWO LITTLE PIGGIES...
!
NI... NINJA!!?

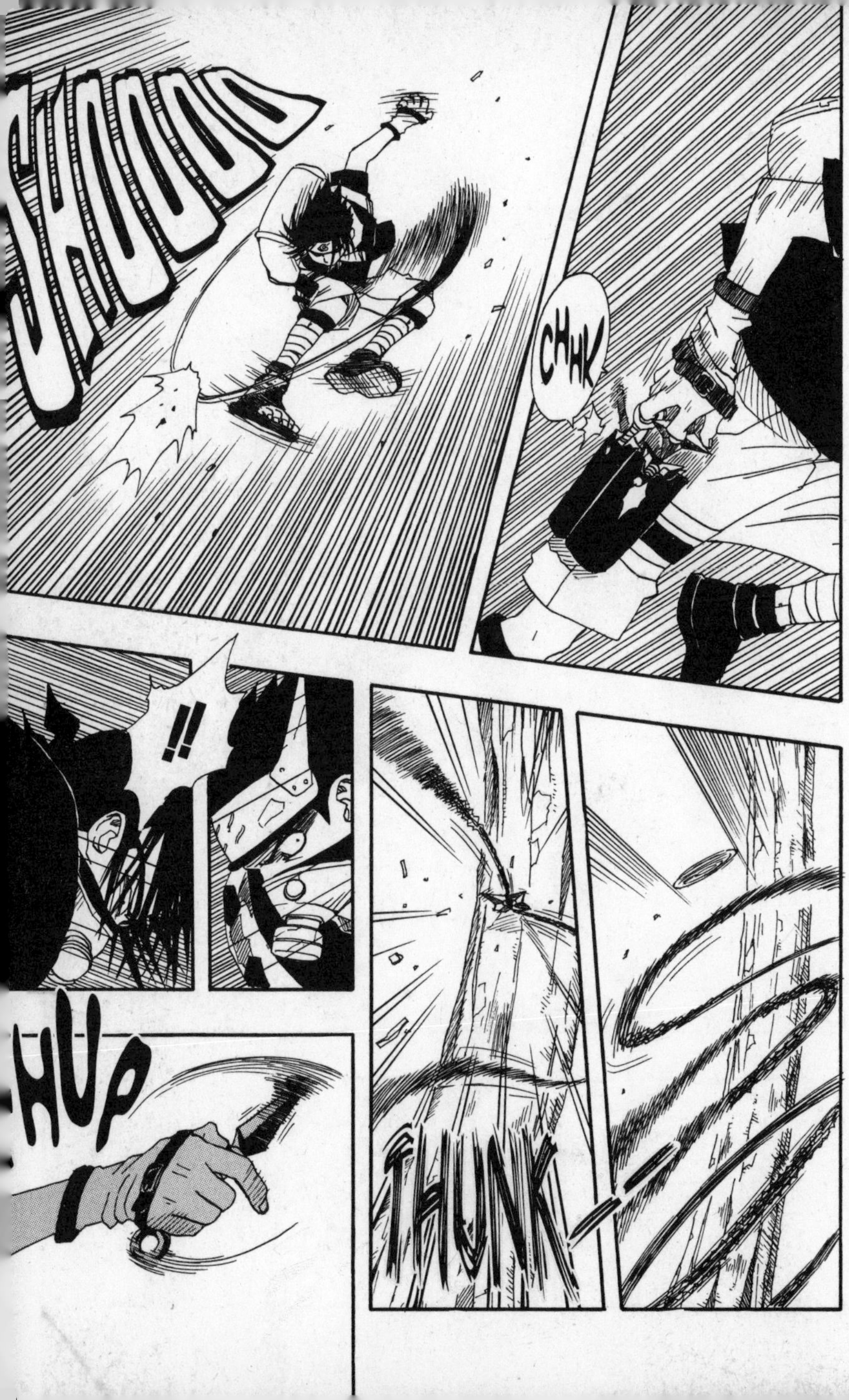
CHHK
SHOOOO
THUNK
!!
SHUP

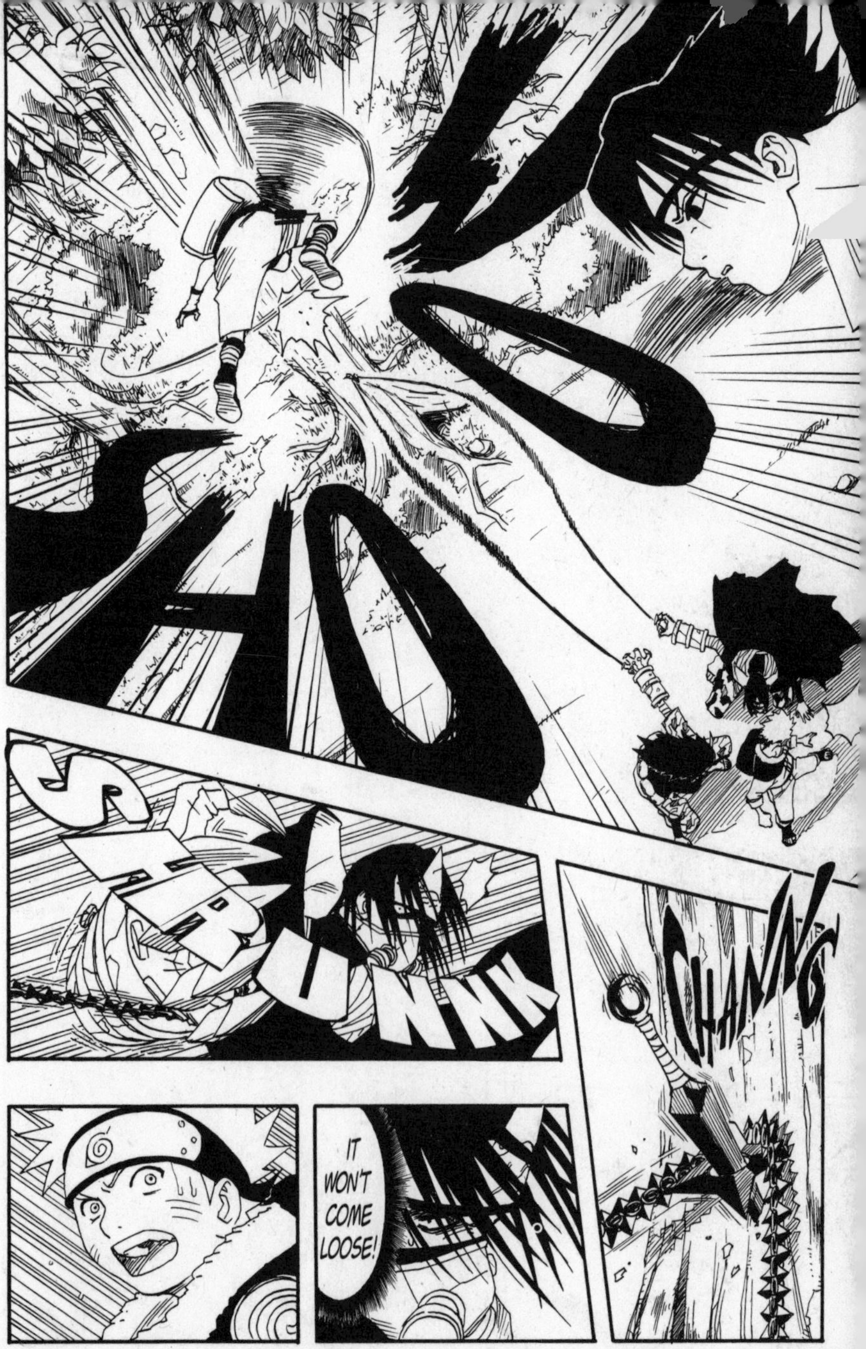
SHOO
CHANNG
SHUNKK
IT WON'T COME LOOSE!

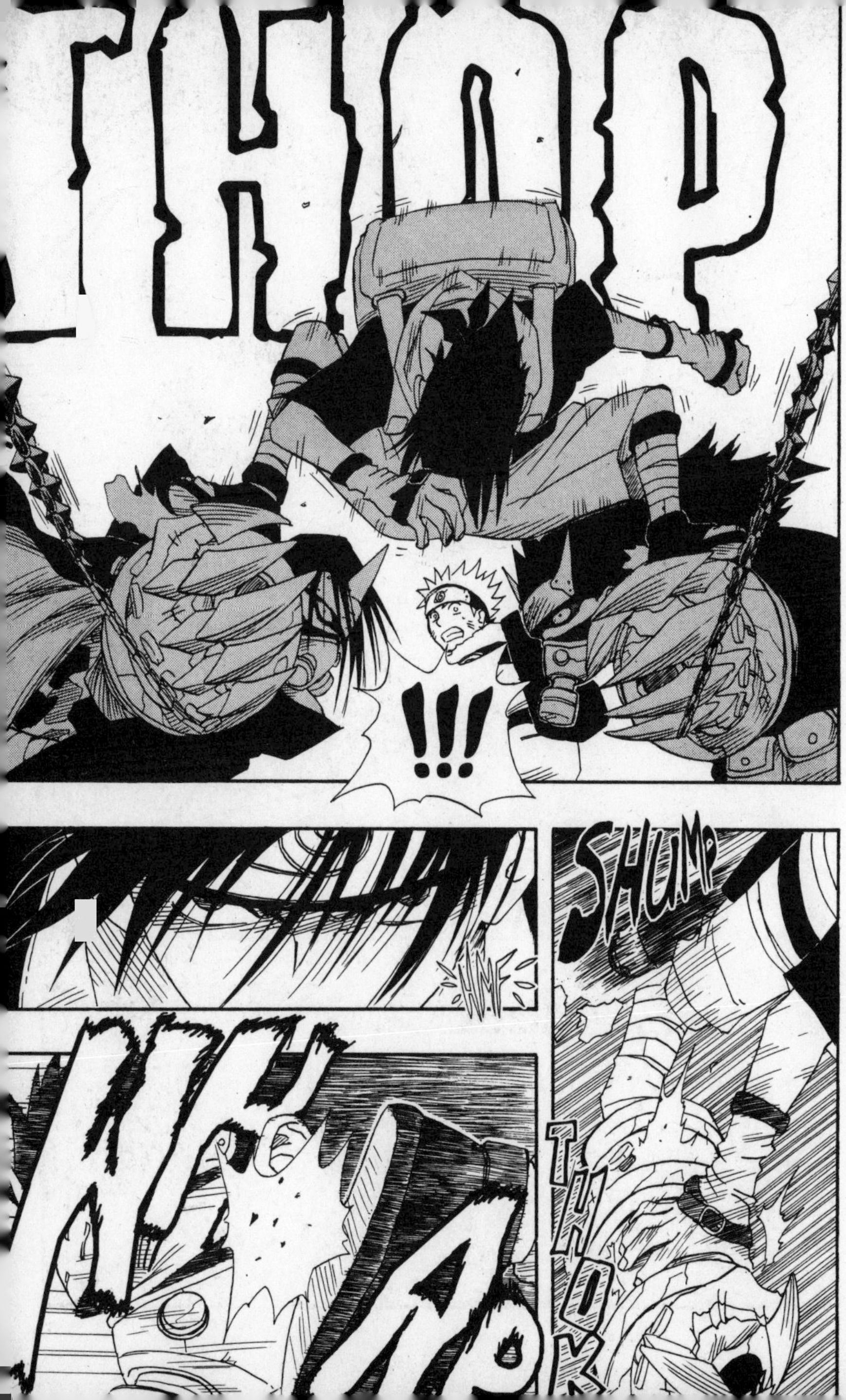
THOP
!!!
SHUMP
THOK
HMF
THWAP

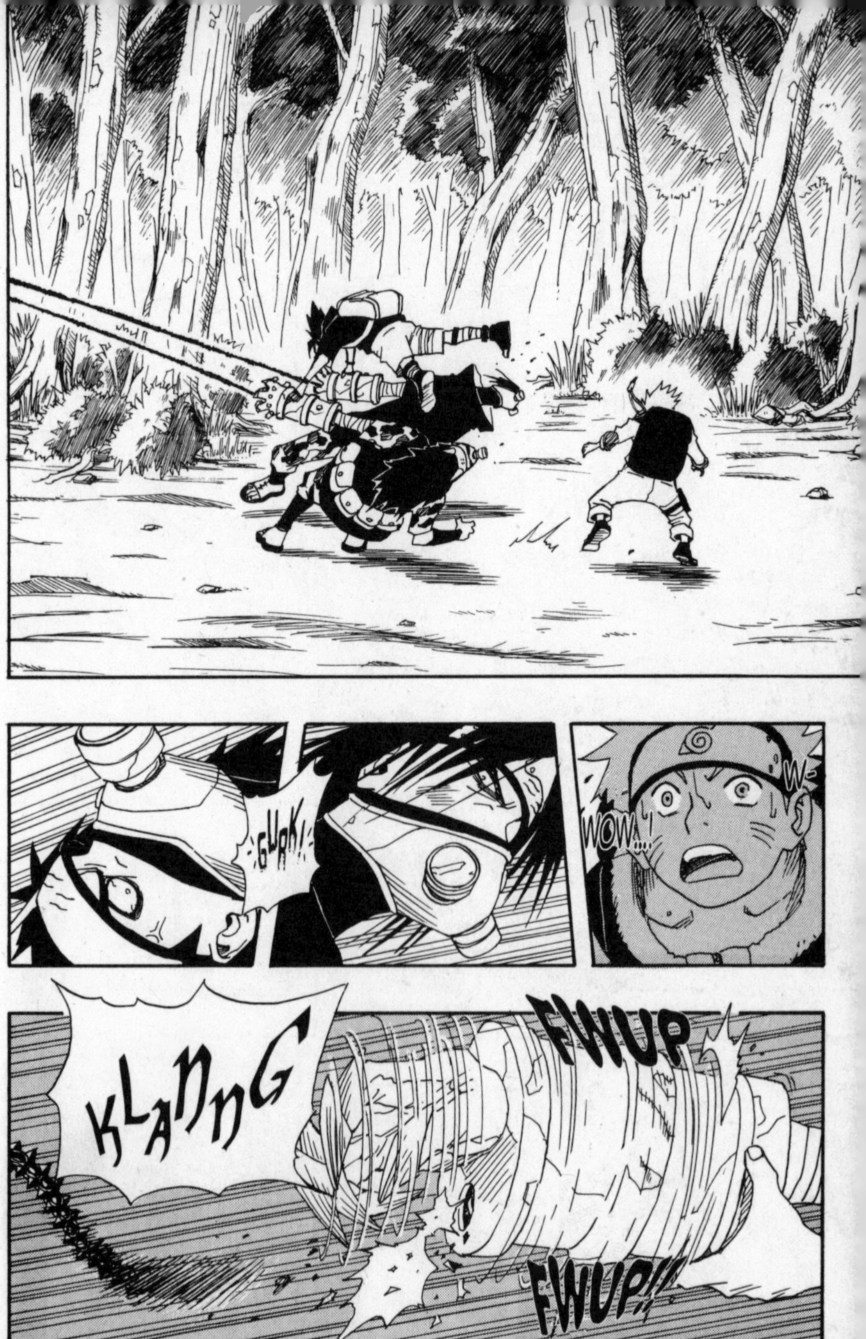
W-WOW...!
GURK!
FWUP
KLANNG
FWUP!!

READ THIS WAY

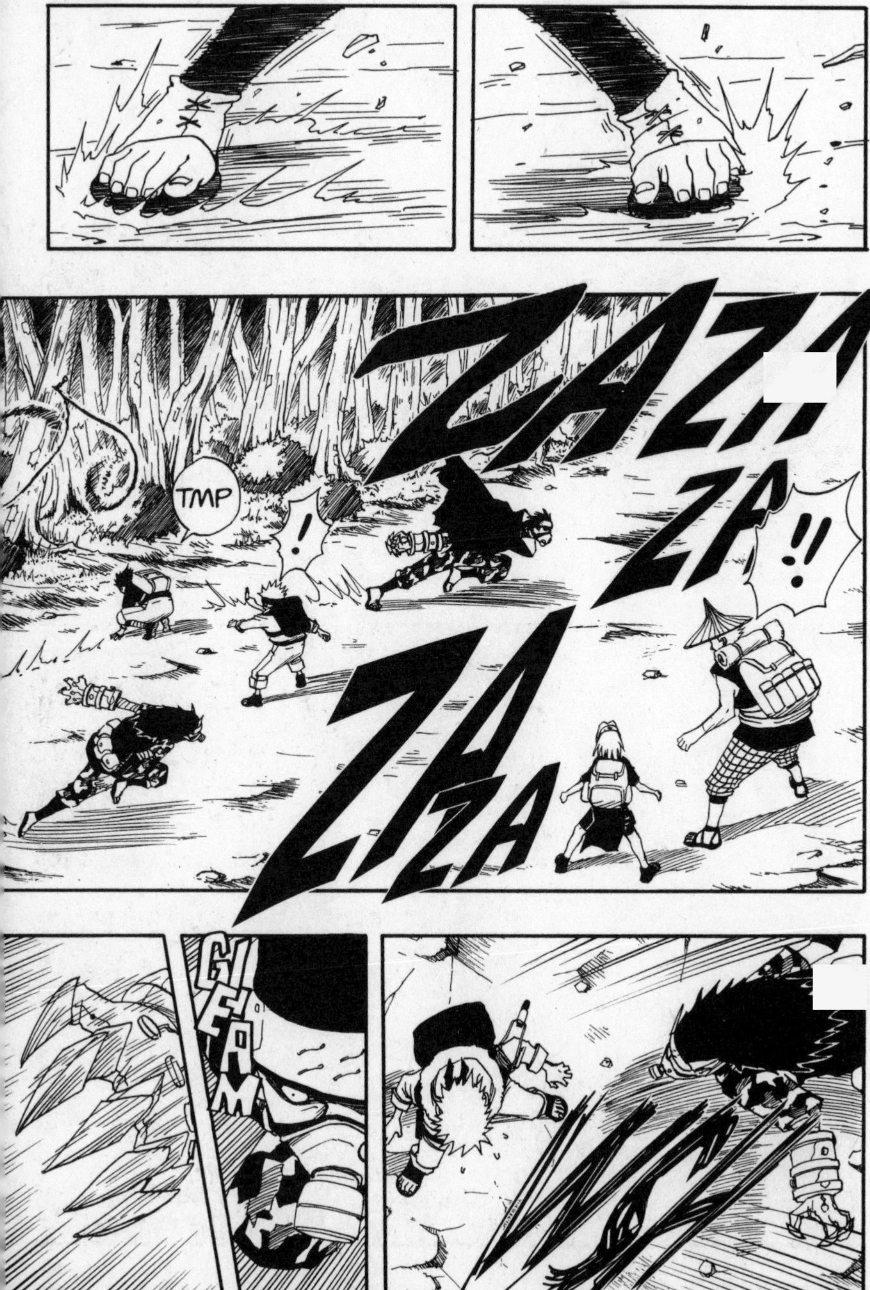
!!
!
TMP

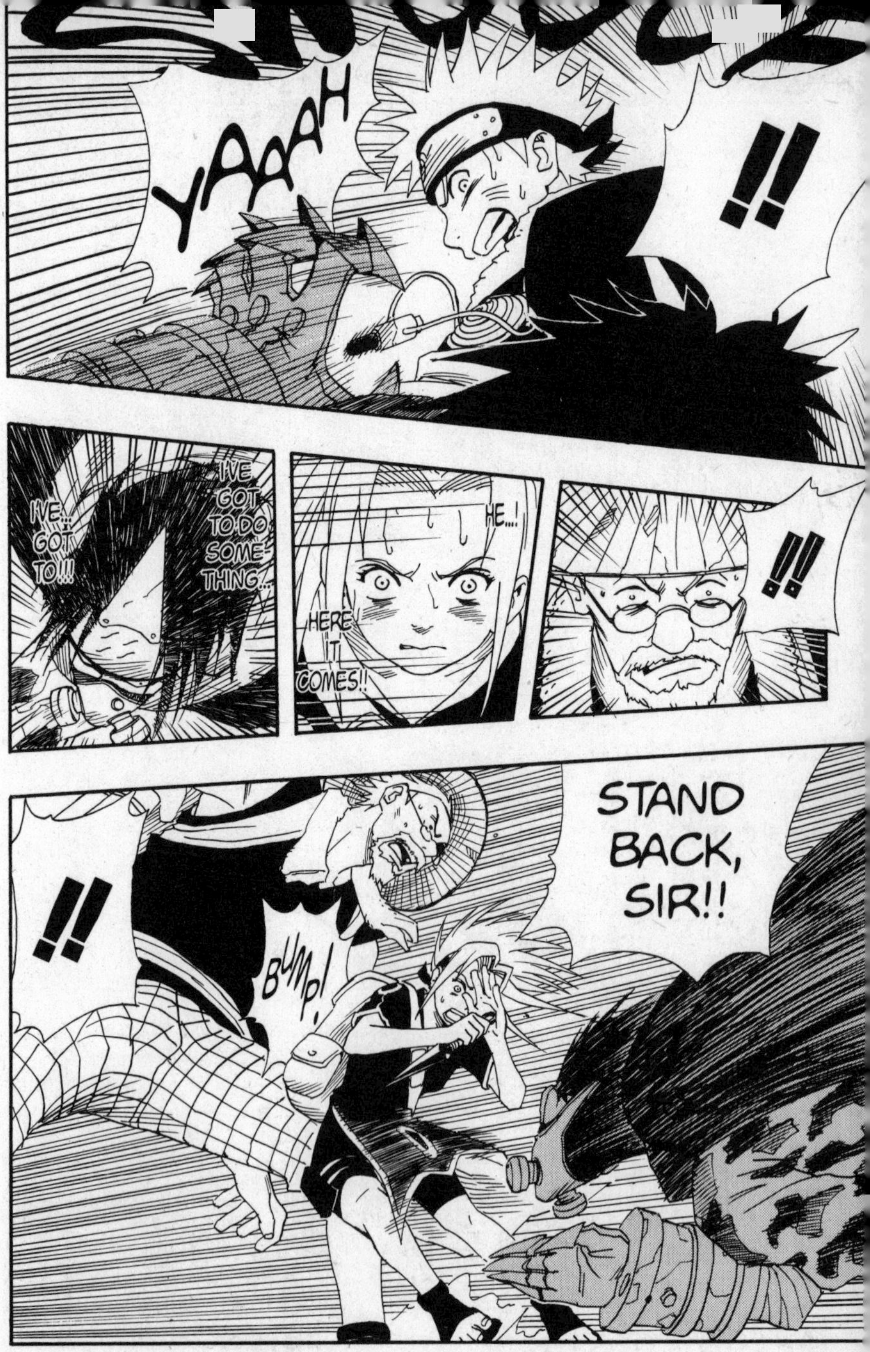
!!
YAAAH
!!
HE...!
HERE IT COMES!!
I'VE GOT TO DO SOME-THING...
I'VE... GOT TO!!!
STAND BACK, SIR!!
!!
BUMP!

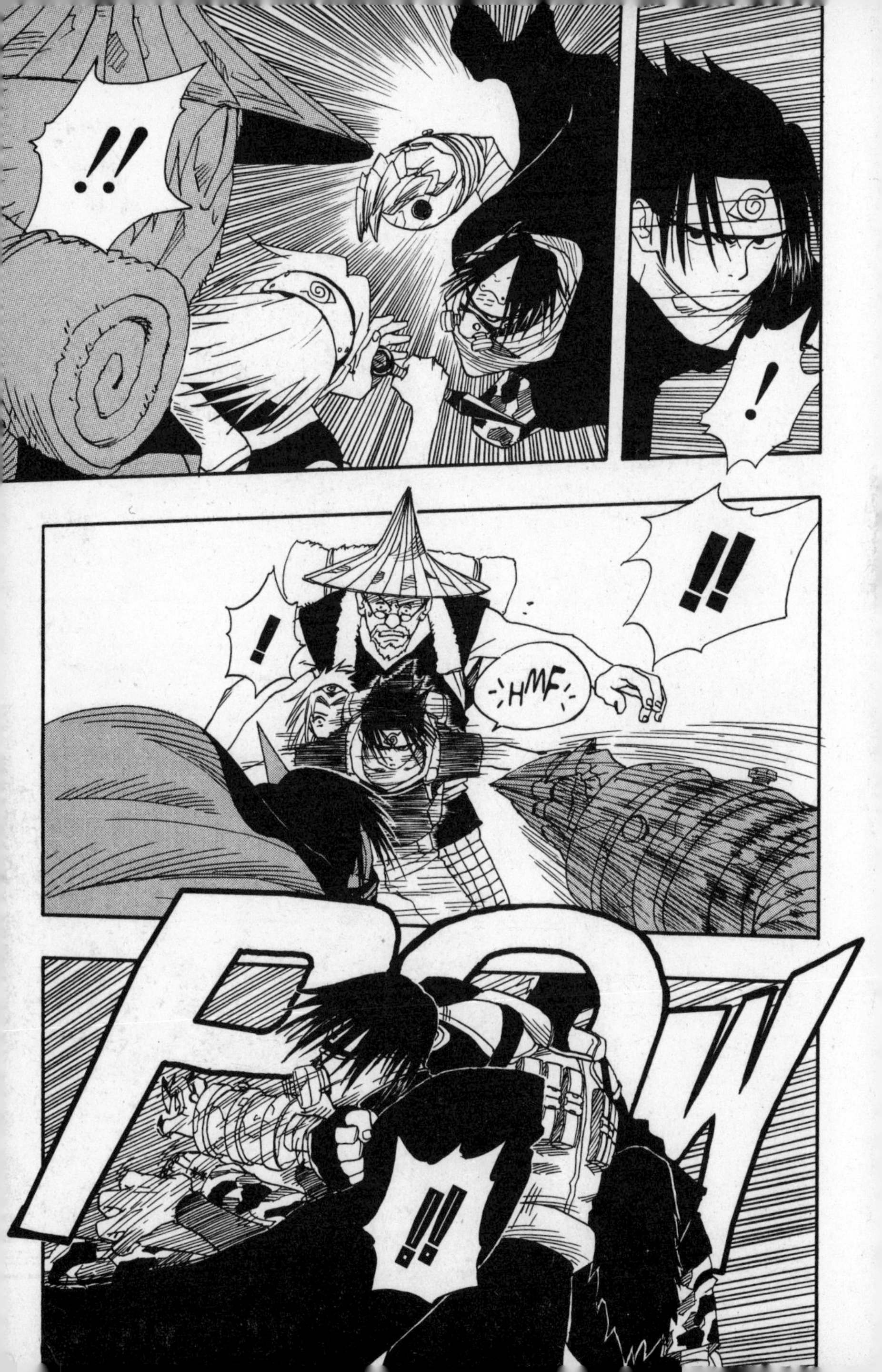
!
!!
!!
!
HMF
!!

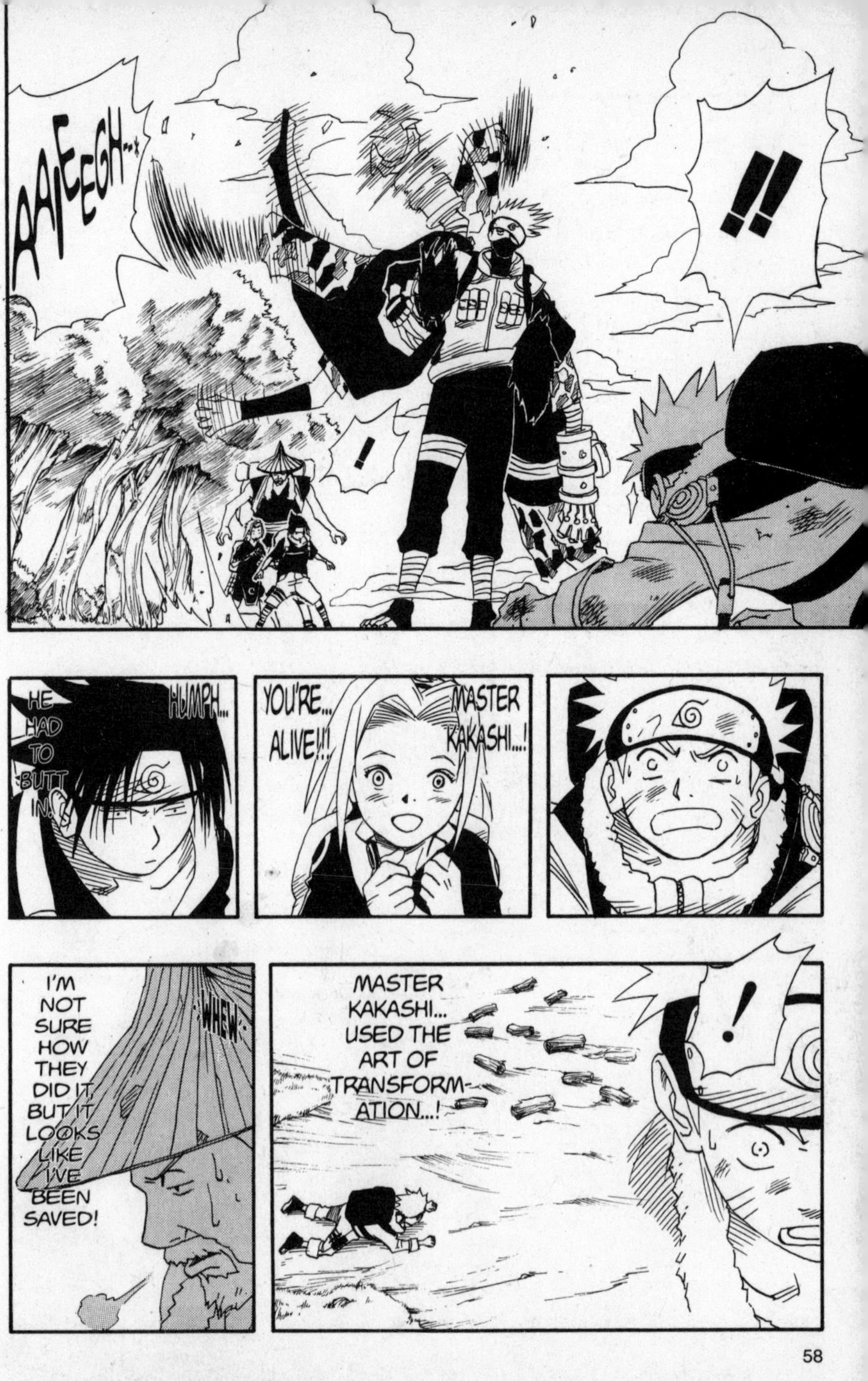
!!
AAIEEGH--
!
MASTER KAKASHI...!
YOU'RE... ALIVE!!!
HUMPH...
HE HAD TO BUTT IN.
!
MASTER KAKASHI... USED THE ART OF TRANSFORM-ATION...!
WHEW
I'M NOT SURE HOW THEY DID IT, BUT IT LOOKS LIKE I'VE BEEN SAVED!

READ THIS WAY

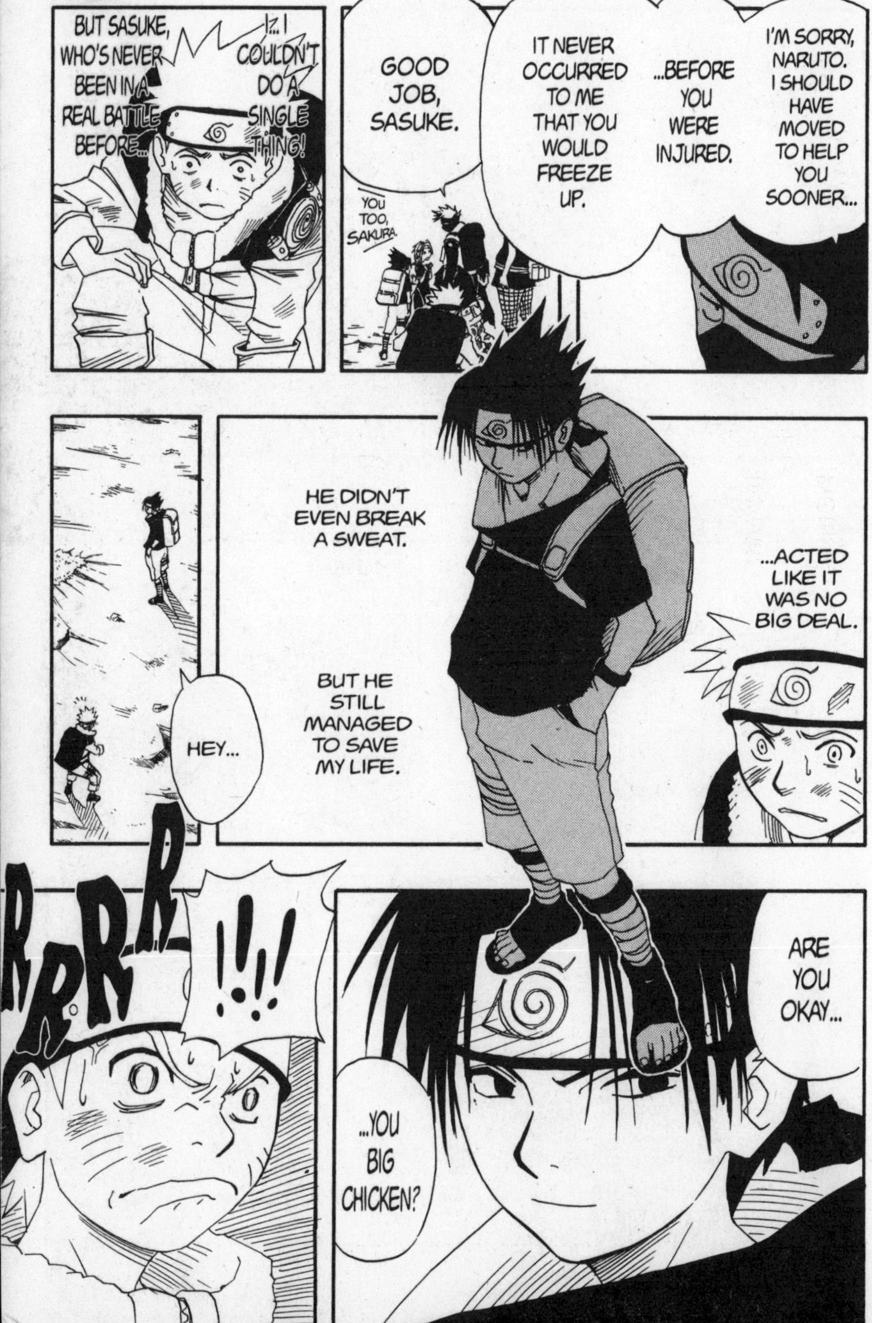
I'M SORRY, NARUTO. I SHOULD HAVE MOVED TO HELP YOU SOONER...
...BEFORE YOU WERE INJURED.
IT NEVER OCCURRED TO ME THAT YOU WOULD FREEZE UP.
GOOD JOB, SASUKE.
YOU TOO, SAKURA.
I...I COULDN'T DO A SINGLE THING!
BUT SASUKE, WHO'S NEVER BEEN IN A REAL BATTLE BEFORE...
...ACTED LIKE IT WAS NO BIG DEAL.
HE DIDN'T EVEN BREAK A SWEAT.
BUT HE STILL MANAGED TO SAVE MY LIFE.
HEY...
ARE YOU OKAY...
...YOU BIG CHICKEN?
!!
RRRR

READ THIS WAY

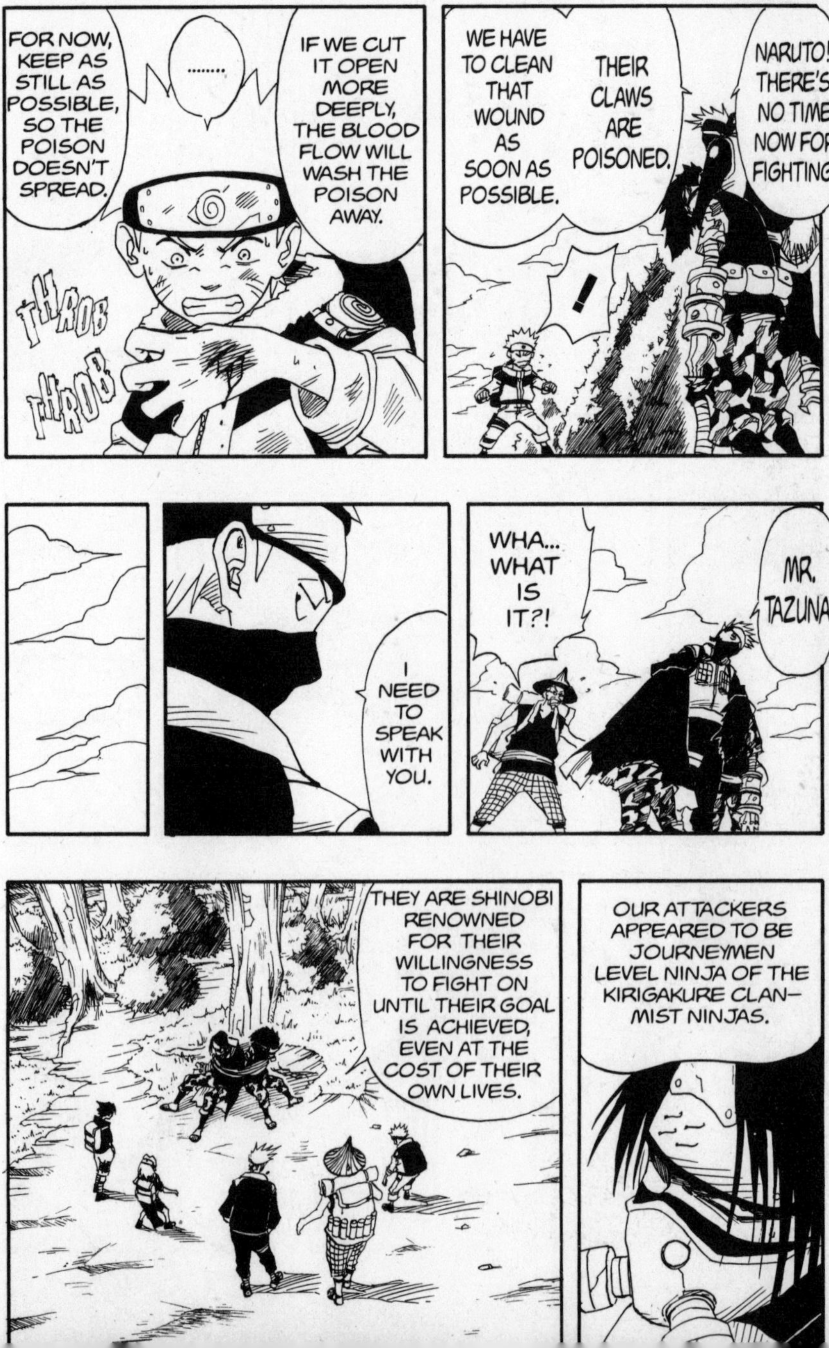
NARUTO! THERE'S NO TIME NOW FOR FIGHTING.
THEIR CLAWS ARE POISONED.
WE HAVE TO CLEAN THAT WOUND AS SOON AS POSSIBLE.
!
IF WE CUT IT OPEN MORE DEEPLY, THE BLOOD FLOW WILL WASH THE POISON AWAY.
....
FOR NOW, KEEP AS STILL AS POSSIBLE, SO THE POISON DOESN'T SPREAD.
THROB
THROB
MR. TAZUNA.
WHA... WHAT IS IT?!
I NEED TO SPEAK WITH YOU.
OUR ATTACKERS APPEARED TO BE JOURNEYMEN LEVEL NINJA OF THE KIRIGAKURE CLAN—MIST NINJAS.
THEY ARE SHINOBI RENOWNED FOR THEIR WILLINGNESS TO FIGHT ON UNTIL THEIR GOAL IS ACHIEVED, EVEN AT THE COST OF THEIR OWN LIVES.

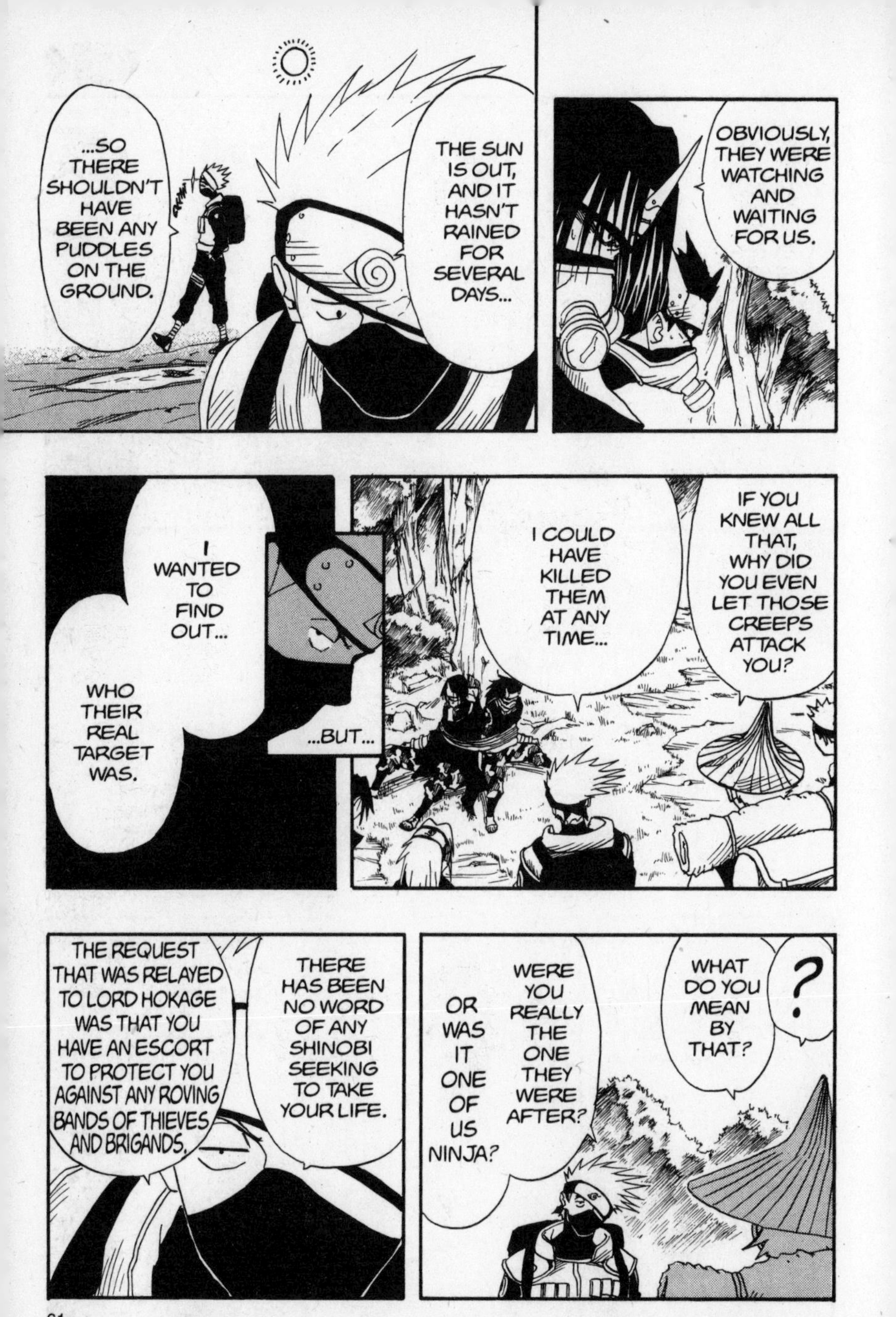
OBVIOUSLY, THEY WERE WATCHING AND WAITING FOR US.
THE SUN IS OUT, AND IT HASN'T RAINED FOR SEVERAL DAYS...
...SO THERE SHOULDN'T HAVE BEEN ANY PUDDLES ON THE GROUND.
IF YOU KNEW ALL THAT, WHY DID YOU EVEN LET THOSE CREEPS ATTACK YOU?
I COULD HAVE KILLED THEM AT ANY TIME...
...BUT...
I WANTED TO FIND OUT...
WHO THEIR REAL TARGET WAS.
?
WHAT DO YOU MEAN BY THAT?
WERE YOU REALLY THE ONE THEY WERE AFTER?
OR WAS IT ONE OF US NINJA?
THE REQUEST THAT WAS RELAYED TO LORD HOKAGE WAS THAT YOU HAVE AN ESCORT TO PROTECT YOU AGAINST ANY ROVING BANDS OF THIEVES AND BRIGANDS.
THERE HAS BEEN NO WORD OF ANY SHINOBI SEEKING TO TAKE YOUR LIFE.

READ THIS WAY

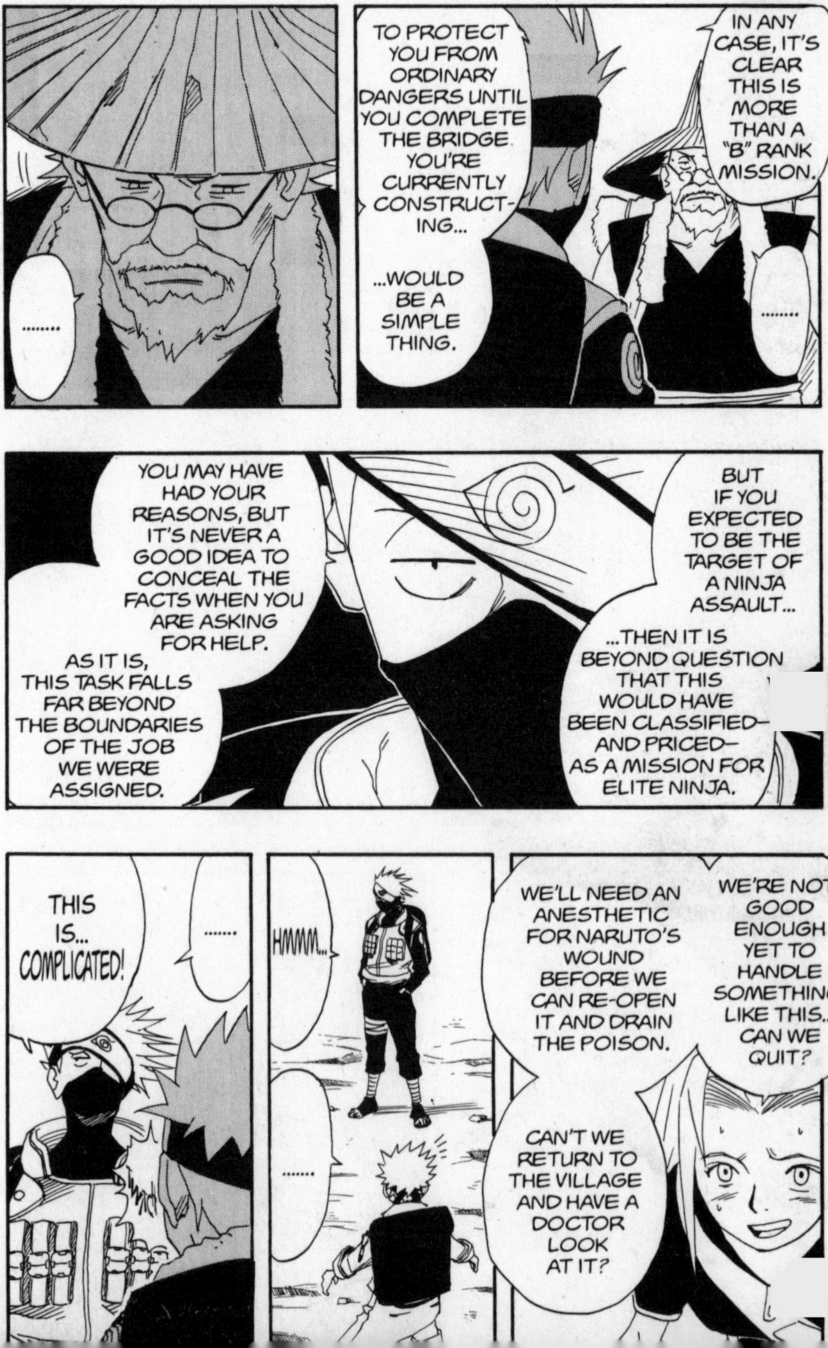

IN ANY CASE, IT'S CLEAR THIS IS MORE THAN A "B" RANK MISSION.
TO PROTECT YOU FROM ORDINARY DANGERS UNTIL YOU COMPLETE THE BRIDGE YOU'RE CURRENTLY CONSTRUCTING...
...WOULD BE A SIMPLE THING.
....
....
BUT IF YOU EXPECTED TO BE THE TARGET OF A NINJA ASSAULT...
...THEN IT IS BEYOND QUESTION THAT THIS WOULD HAVE BEEN CLASSIFIED— AND PRICED— AS A MISSION FOR ELITE NINJA.
YOU MAY HAVE HAD YOUR REASONS, BUT IT'S NEVER A GOOD IDEA TO CONCEAL THE FACTS WHEN YOU ARE ASKING FOR HELP.
AS IT IS, THIS TASK FALLS FAR BEYOND THE BOUNDARIES OF THE JOB WE WERE ASSIGNED.
WE'RE NOT GOOD ENOUGH YET TO HANDLE SOMETHING LIKE THIS... CAN WE QUIT?
WE'LL NEED AN ANESTHETIC FOR NARUTO'S WOUND BEFORE WE CAN RE-OPEN IT AND DRAIN THE POISON.
CAN'T WE RETURN TO THE VILLAGE AND HAVE A DOCTOR LOOK AT IT?
HMMM...
....
....
THIS IS... COMPLICATED!

READ THIS WAY

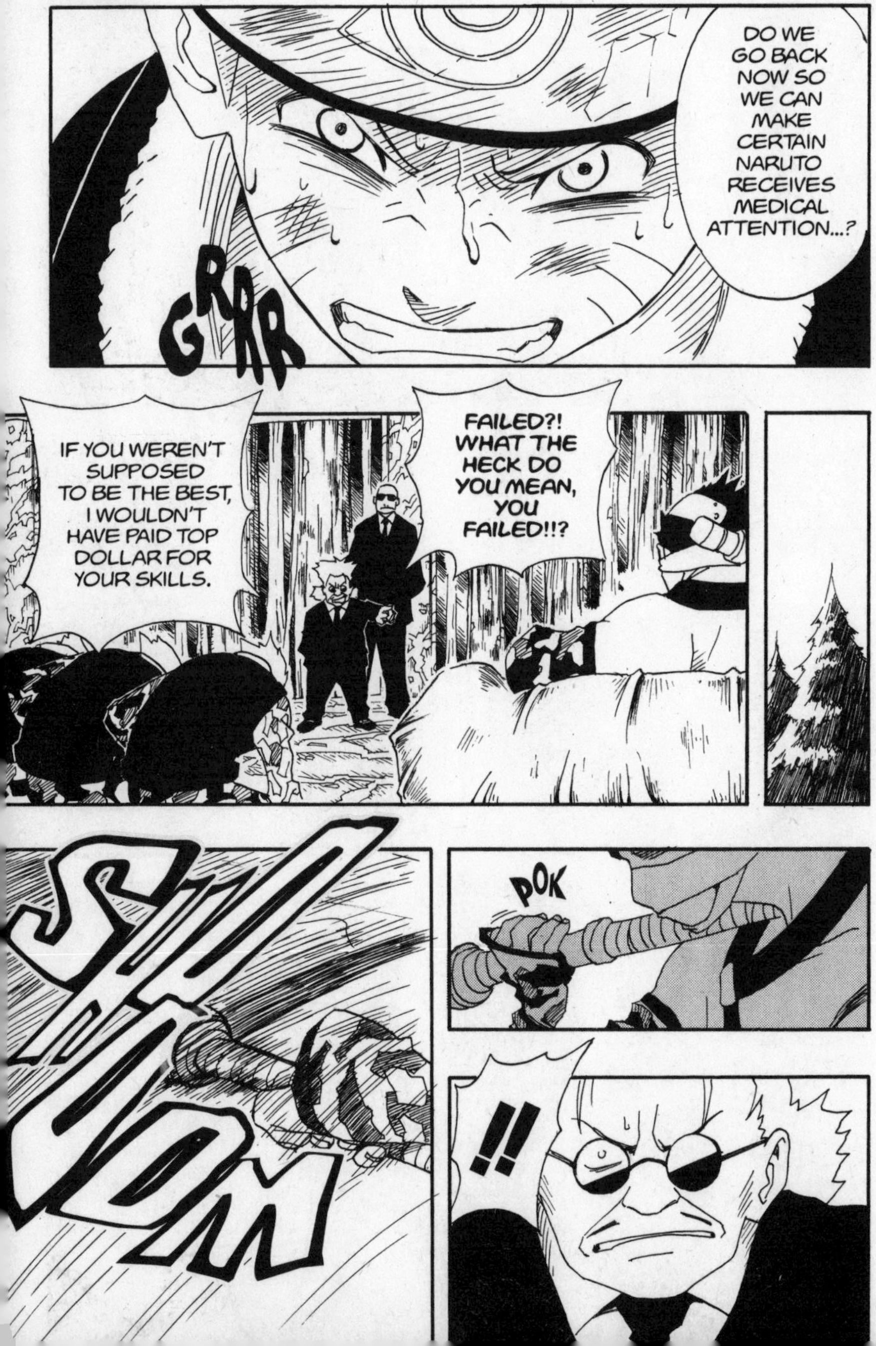

DO WE GO BACK NOW SO WE CAN MAKE CERTAIN NARUTO RECEIVES MEDICAL ATTENTION...?
GRRR
FAILED?! WHAT THE HECK DO YOU MEAN, YOU FAILED!!?
IF YOU WEREN'T SUPPOSED TO BE THE BEST, I WOULDN'T HAVE PAID TOP DOLLAR FOR YOUR SKILLS.
POK
!!
SHOOM

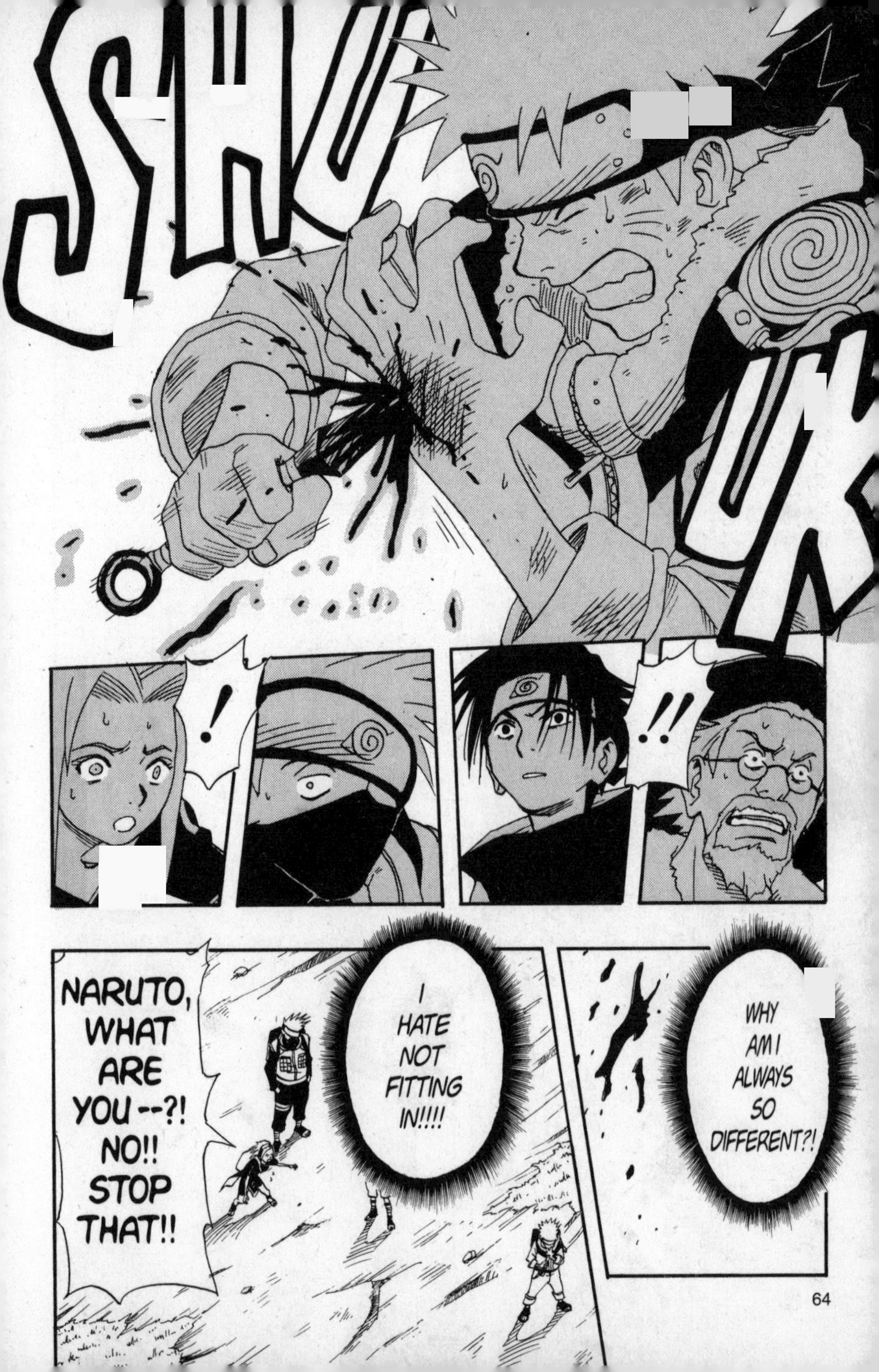
!!
!
WHY AM I ALWAYS SO DIFFERENT?!
I HATE NOT FITTING IN!!!!
NARUTO, WHAT ARE YOU --?! NO!! STOP THAT!!

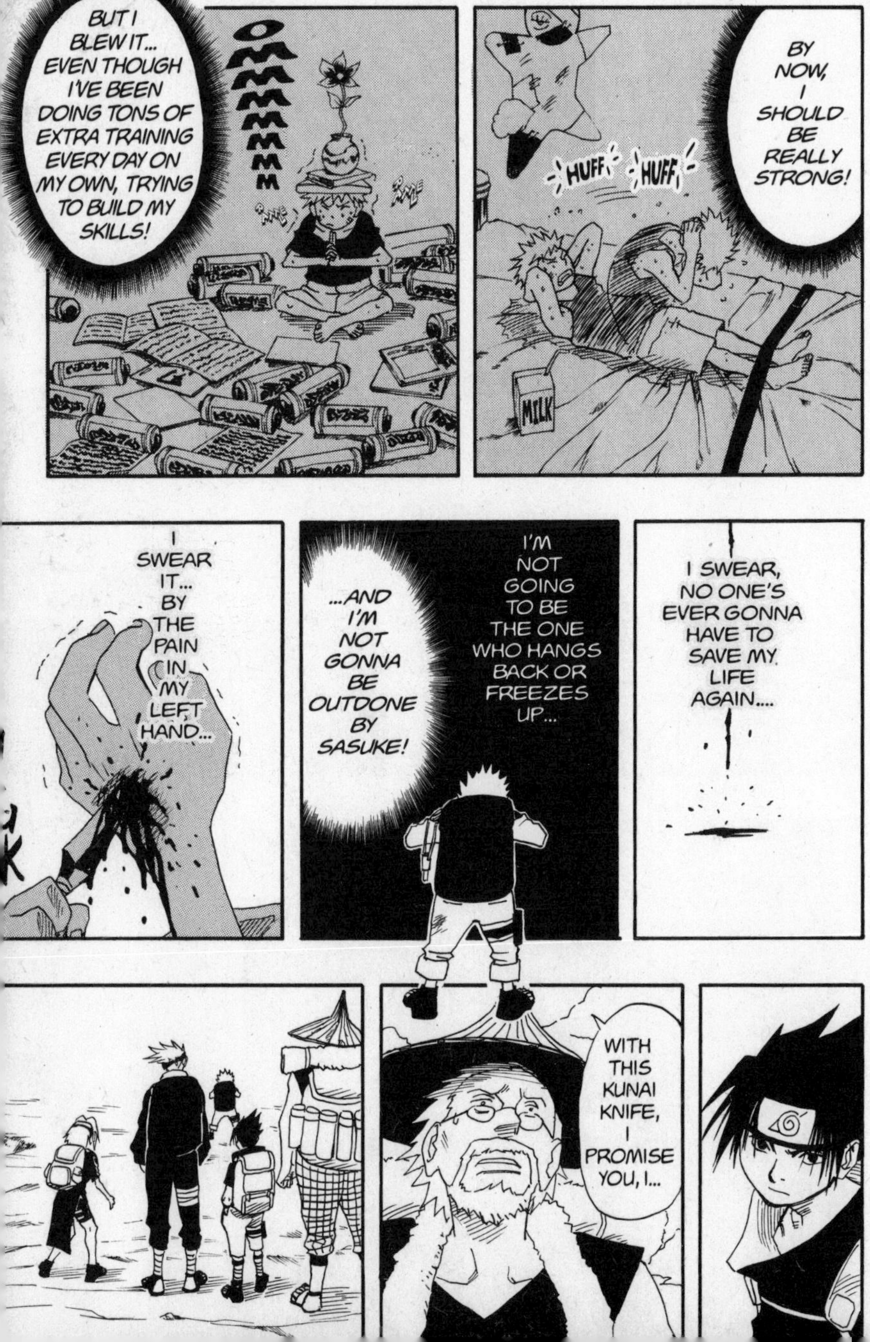
BY NOW, I SHOULD BE REALLY STRONG!
HUFF HUFF
MILK
BUT I BLEW IT... EVEN THOUGH I'VE BEEN DOING TONS OF EXTRA TRAINING EVERY DAY ON MY OWN, TRYING TO BUILD MY SKILLS!
OMMMMMMM
I SWEAR, NO ONE'S EVER GONNA HAVE TO SAVE MY LIFE AGAIN....
I'M NOT GOING TO BE THE ONE WHO HANGS BACK OR FREEZES UP...
...AND I'M NOT GONNA BE OUTDONE BY SASUKE!
I SWEAR IT... BY THE PAIN IN MY LEFT HAND...
WITH THIS KUNAI KNIFE, I PROMISE YOU, I...

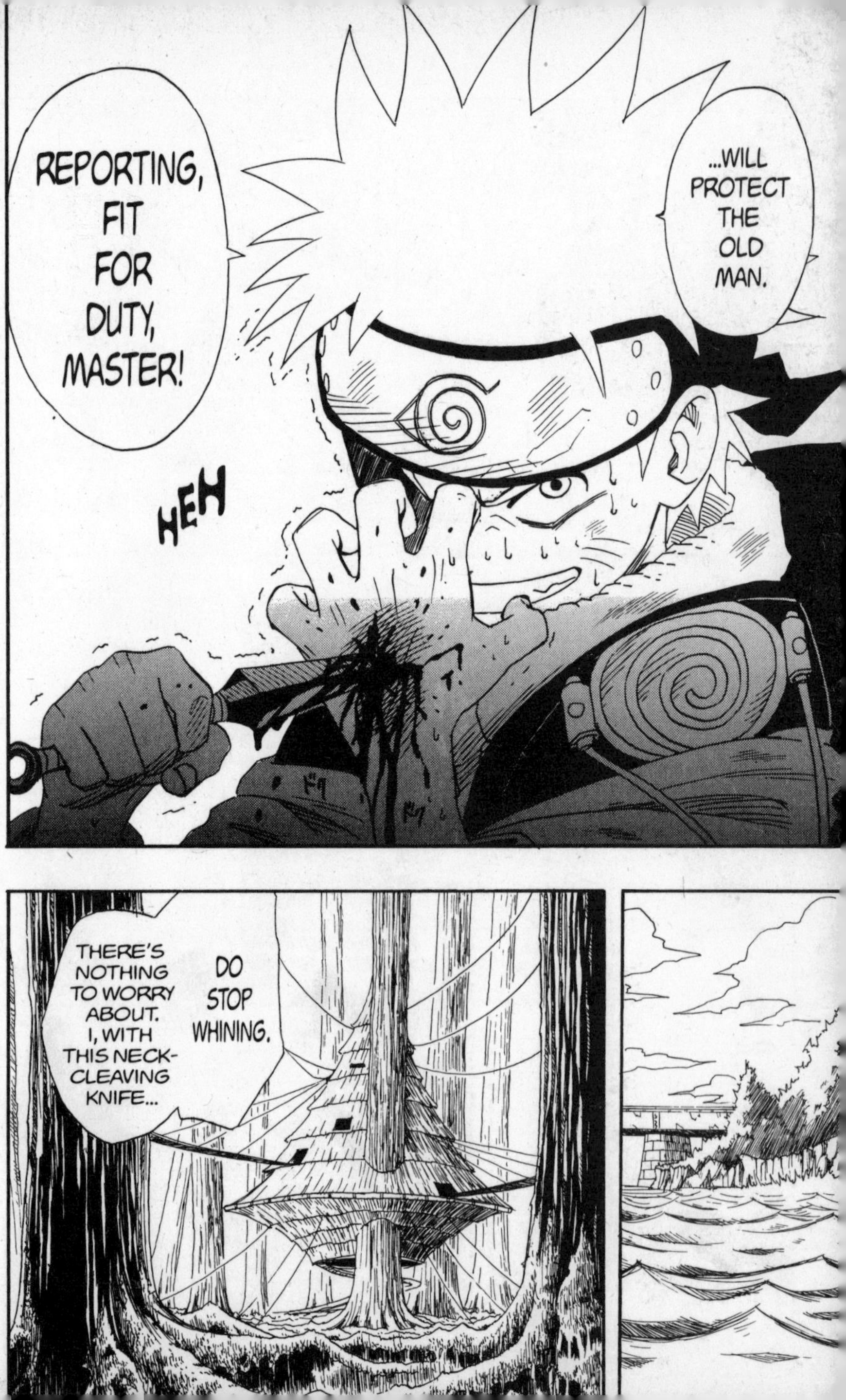
...WILL PROTECT THE OLD MAN.
REPORTING, FIT FOR DUTY, MASTER!
HEH
DO STOP WHINING.
THERE'S NOTHING TO WORRY ABOUT. I, WITH THIS NECK-CLEAVING KNIFE...

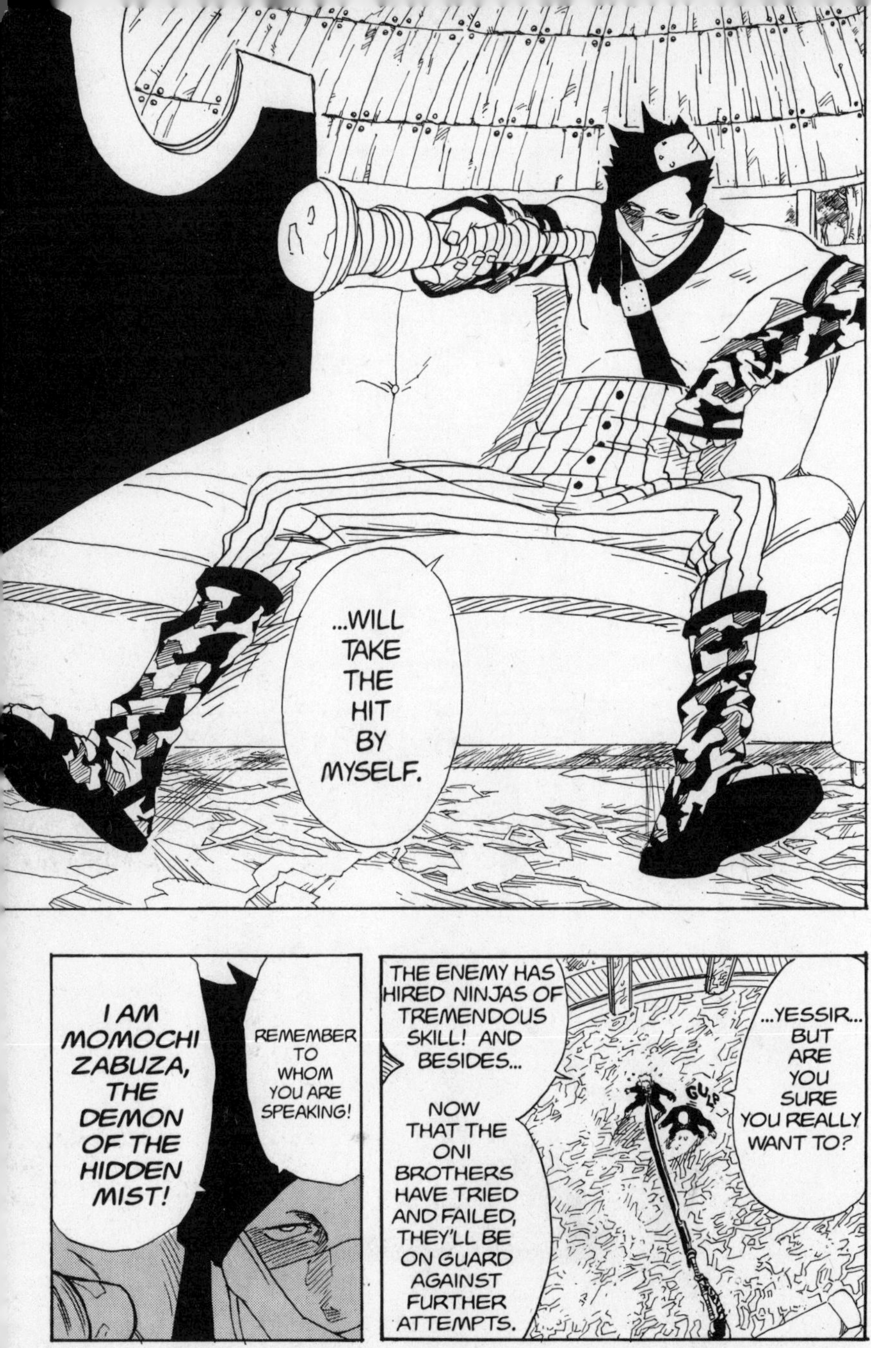
...WILL TAKE THE HIT BY MYSELF.
...YESSIR... BUT ARE YOU SURE YOU REALLY WANT TO?
GULP
THE ENEMY HAS HIRED NINJAS OF TREMENDOUS SKILL! AND BESIDES...
NOW THAT THE ONI BROTHERS HAVE TRIED AND FAILED, THEY'LL BE ON GUARD AGAINST FURTHER ATTEMPTS.
REMEMBER TO WHOM YOU ARE SPEAKING!
I AM MOMOCHI ZABUZA, THE DEMON OF THE HIDDEN MIST!

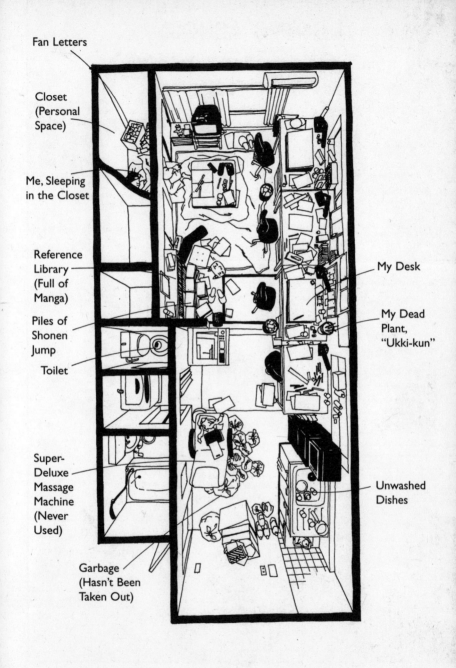

Fan Letters

Closet
(Personal
Space)

Me, Sleeping
in the Closet

Reference
Library
(Full of
Manga)

Piles of
Shonen
Jump

Toilet

Super-
Deluxe
Massage
Machine
(Never
Used)

Garbage
(Hasn't Been
Taken Out)

My Desk

My Dead
Plant,
"Ukki-kun"

Unwashed
Dishes

Number 11: GOING ASHORE

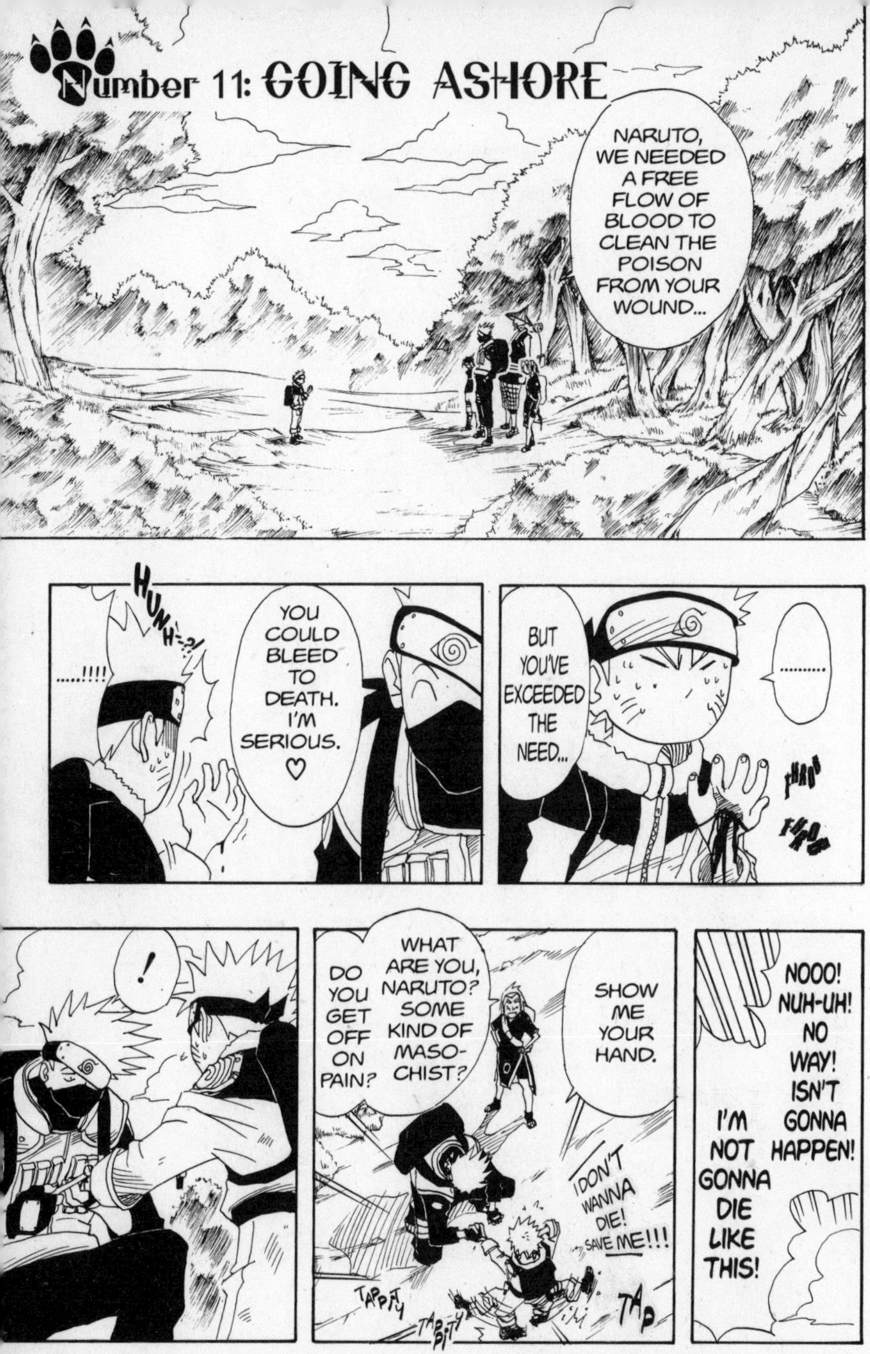

NARUTO, WE NEEDED A FREE FLOW OF BLOOD TO CLEAN THE POISON FROM YOUR WOUND...
BUT YOU'VE EXCEEDED THE NEED...
....
THROB
THROB
YOU COULD BLEED TO DEATH. I'M SERIOUS. ♡
HUNH-?!
.....!!!!
NOOO! NUH-UH! NO WAY! ISN'T GONNA HAPPEN!
I'M NOT GONNA DIE LIKE THIS!
SHOW ME YOUR HAND.
WHAT ARE YOU, NARUTO? SOME KIND OF MASOCHIST?
DO YOU GET OFF ON PAIN?
I DON'T WANNA DIE! SAVE ME!!!
TAP
TAPPITY
TAPPITY
!

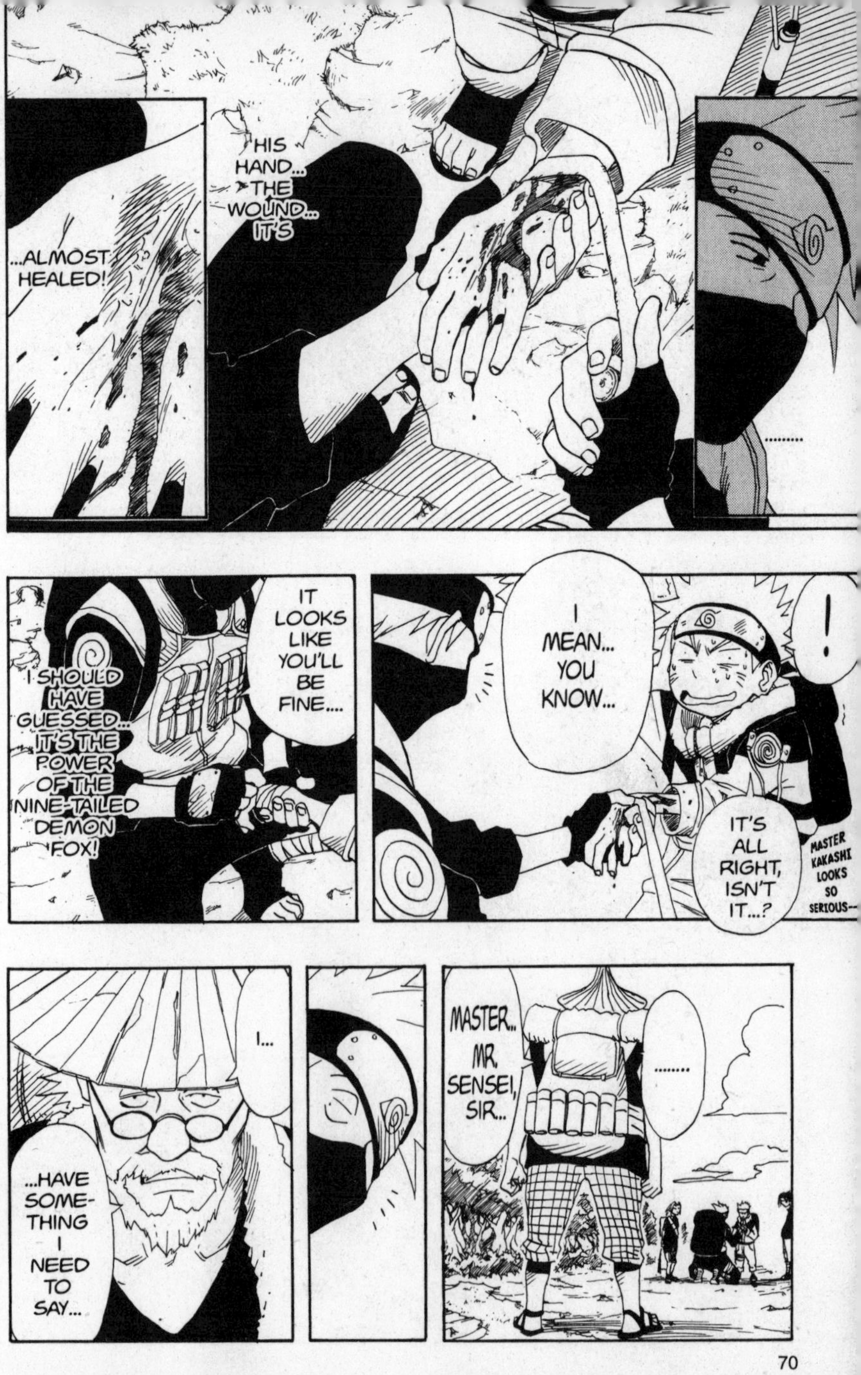
....
HIS HAND... THE WOUND... IT'S
...ALMOST HEALED!
!
MASTER KAKASHI LOOKS SO SERIOUS--
I MEAN... YOU KNOW...
IT'S ALL RIGHT, ISN'T IT...?
IT LOOKS LIKE YOU'LL BE FINE....
I SHOULD HAVE GUESSED... IT'S THE POWER OF THE NINE-TAILED DEMON FOX!
....
MASTER... MR. SENSEI, SIR...
I...
...HAVE SOMETHING I NEED TO SAY...

Chapter 11: Going Ashore

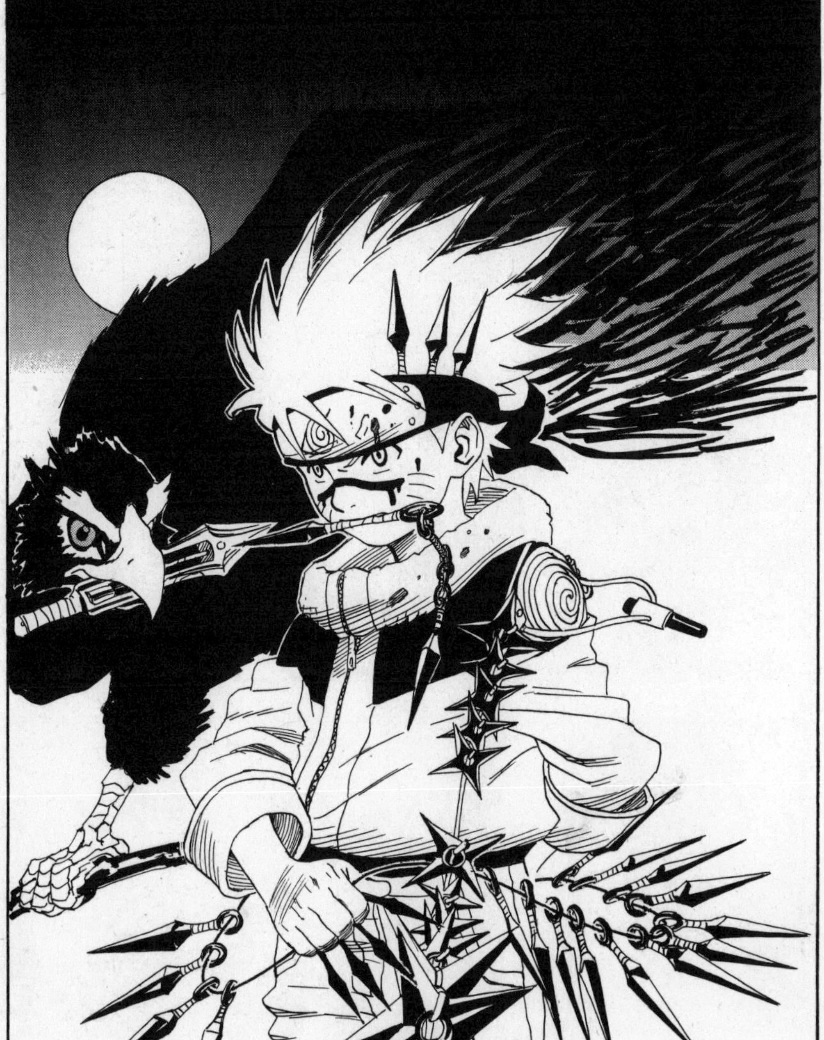

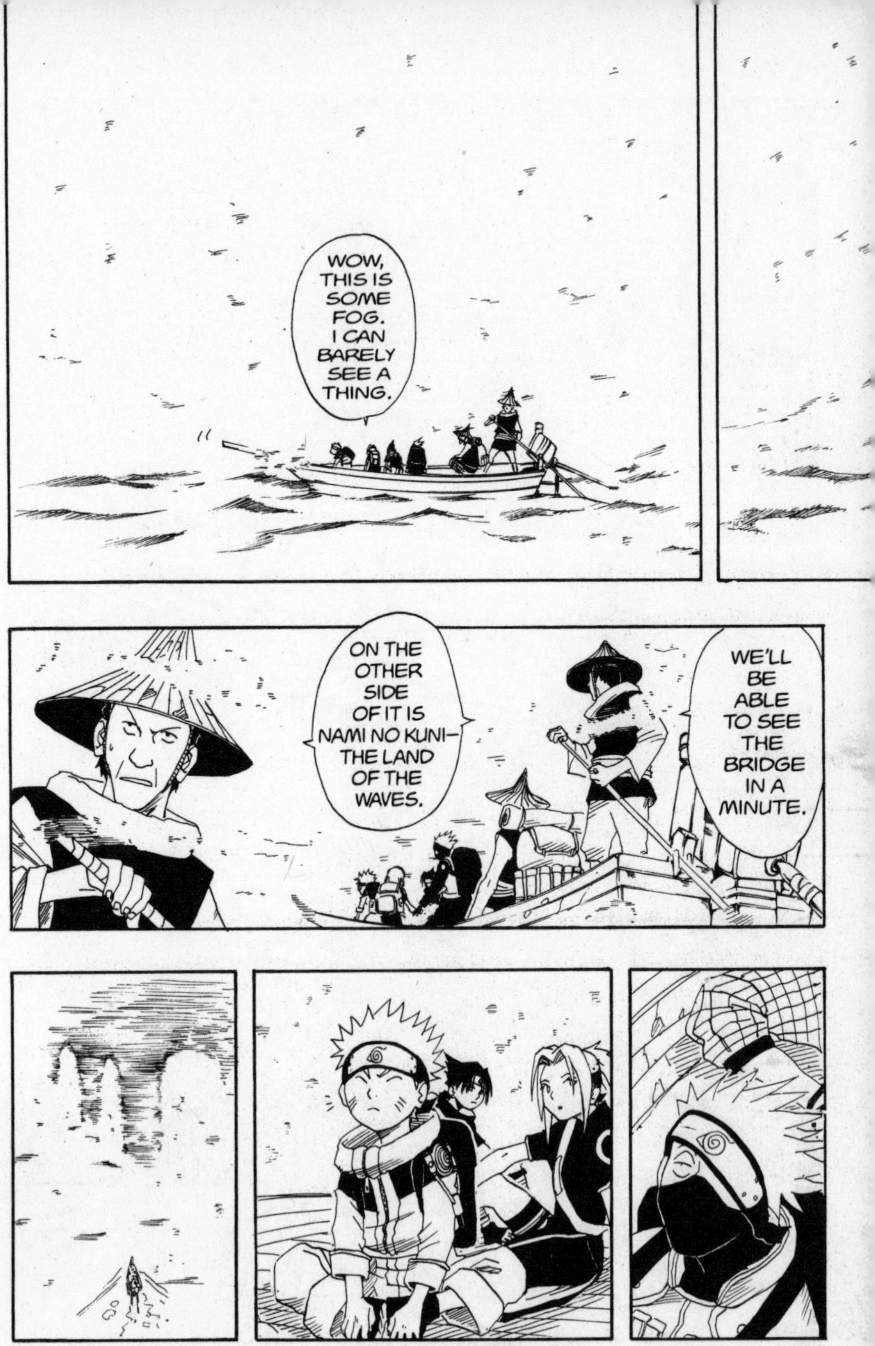
WOW, THIS IS SOME FOG. I CAN BARELY SEE A THING.
WE'LL BE ABLE TO SEE THE BRIDGE IN A MINUTE.
ON THE OTHER SIDE OF IT IS NAMI NO KUNI— THE LAND OF THE WAVES.

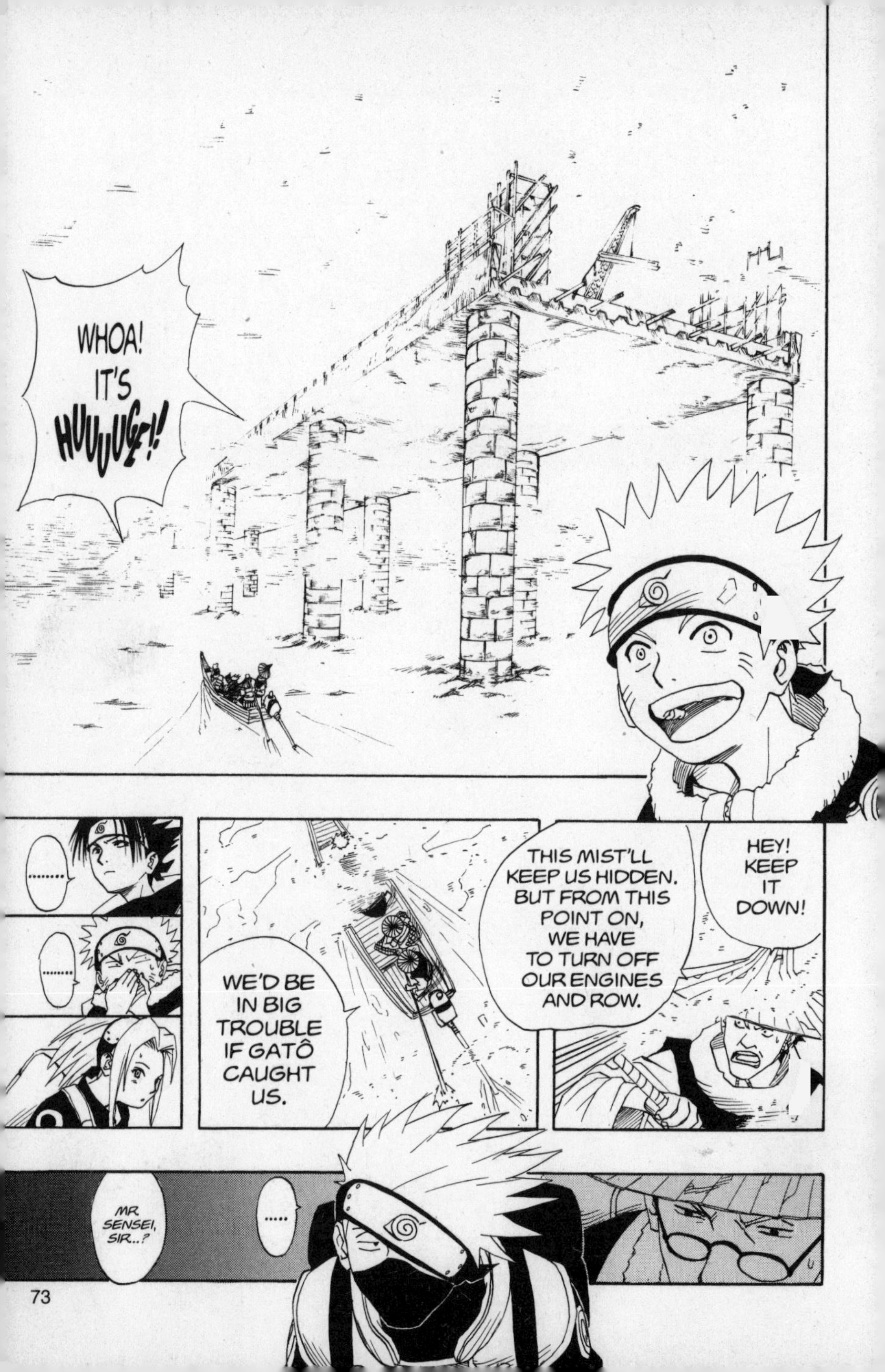

WHOA! IT'S HUUUUGE!!
HEY! KEEP IT DOWN!
THIS MIST'LL KEEP US HIDDEN. BUT FROM THIS POINT ON, WE HAVE TO TURN OFF OUR ENGINES AND ROW.
WE'D BE IN BIG TROUBLE IF GATÔ CAUGHT US.
....
....
.....
MR. SENSEI, SIR...?

READ THIS WAY

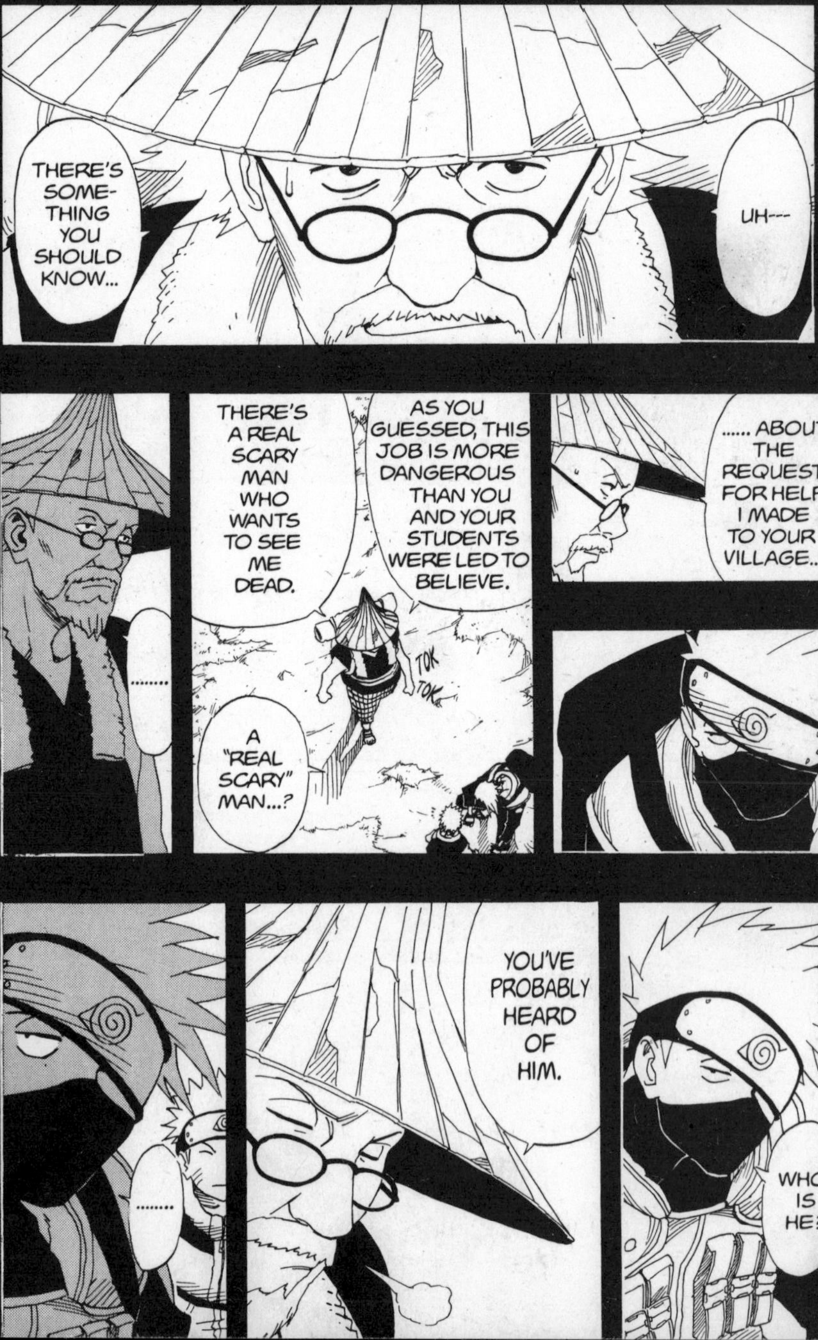

UH---
THERE'S SOMETHING YOU SHOULD KNOW...
...... ABOUT THE REQUEST FOR HELP I MADE TO YOUR VILLAGE...
AS YOU GUESSED, THIS JOB IS MORE DANGEROUS THAN YOU AND YOUR STUDENTS WERE LED TO BELIEVE.
THERE'S A REAL SCARY MAN WHO WANTS TO SEE ME DEAD.
TOK TOK
A "REAL SCARY" MAN...?
....
WHO IS HE?
YOU'VE PROBABLY HEARD OF HIM.
....

READ THIS WAY

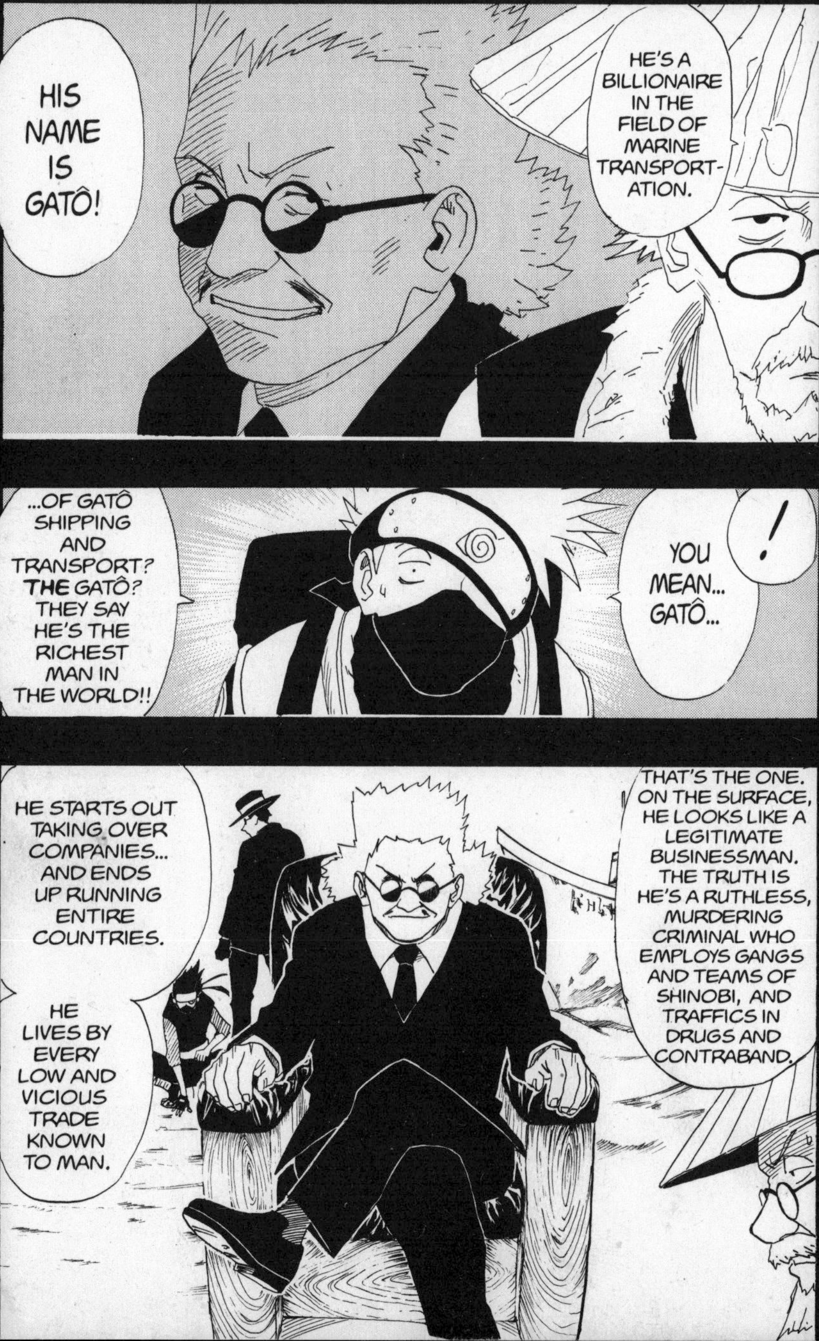
HE'S A BILLIONAIRE IN THE FIELD OF MARINE TRANSPORT-ATION.
HIS NAME IS GATÔ!
!
YOU MEAN... GATÔ...
...OF GATÔ SHIPPING AND TRANSPORT? THE GATÔ? THEY SAY HE'S THE RICHEST MAN IN THE WORLD!!
THAT'S THE ONE. ON THE SURFACE, HE LOOKS LIKE A LEGITIMATE BUSINESSMAN. THE TRUTH IS HE'S A RUTHLESS, MURDERING CRIMINAL WHO EMPLOYS GANGS AND TEAMS OF SHINOBI, AND TRAFFICS IN DRUGS AND CONTRABAND.
HE STARTS OUT TAKING OVER COMPANIES... AND ENDS UP RUNNING ENTIRE COUNTRIES.
HE LIVES BY EVERY LOW AND VICIOUS TRADE KNOWN TO MAN.

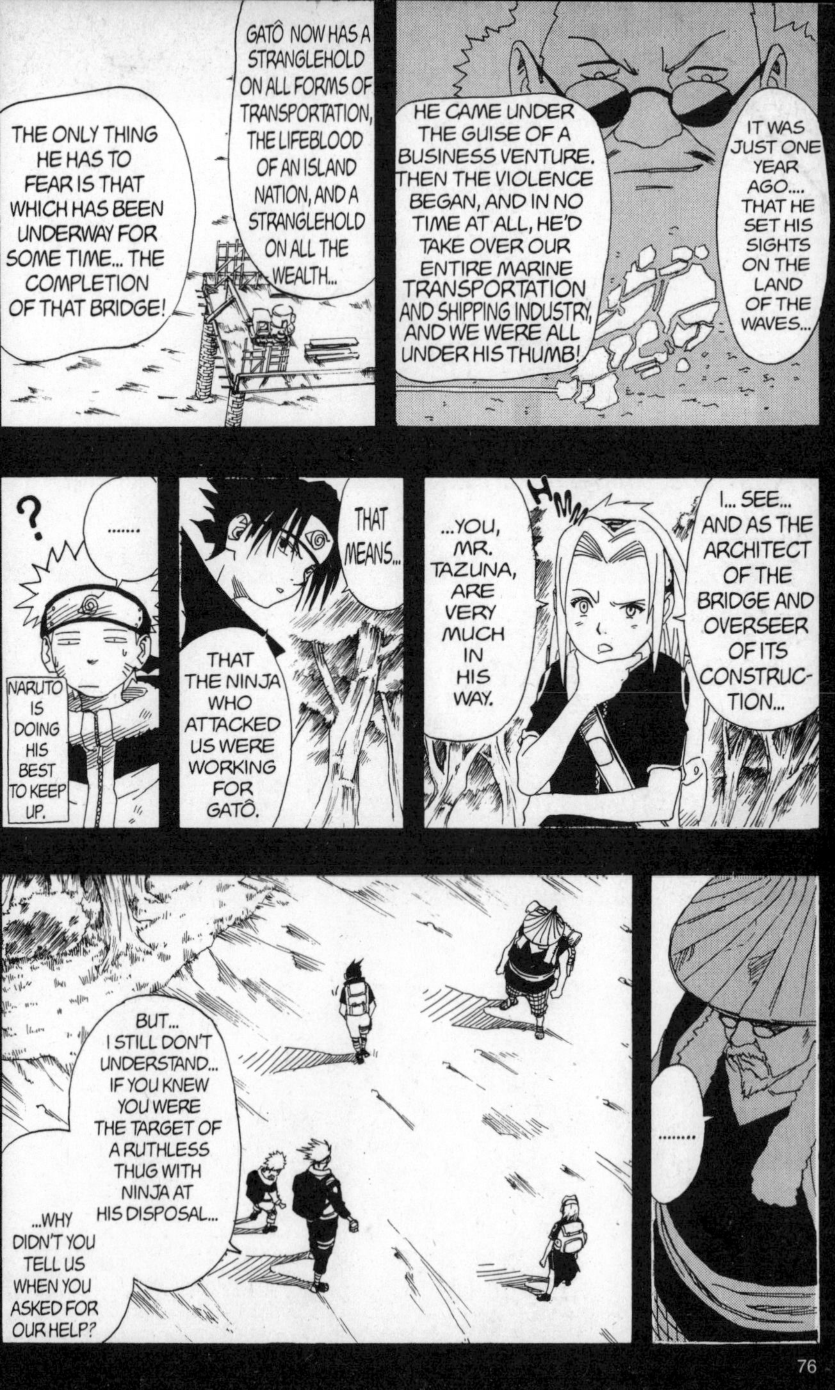
IT WAS JUST ONE YEAR AGO.... THAT HE SET HIS SIGHTS ON THE LAND OF THE WAVES...
HE CAME UNDER THE GUISE OF A BUSINESS VENTURE. THEN THE VIOLENCE BEGAN, AND IN NO TIME AT ALL, HE'D TAKE OVER OUR ENTIRE MARINE TRANSPORTATION AND SHIPPING INDUSTRY, AND WE WERE ALL UNDER HIS THUMB!
GATÔ NOW HAS A STRANGLEHOLD ON ALL FORMS OF TRANSPORTATION, THE LIFEBLOOD OF AN ISLAND NATION, AND A STRANGLEHOLD ON ALL THE WEALTH...
THE ONLY THING HE HAS TO FEAR IS THAT WHICH HAS BEEN UNDERWAY FOR SOME TIME... THE COMPLETION OF THAT BRIDGE!
I... SEE... AND AS THE ARCHITECT OF THE BRIDGE AND OVERSEER OF ITS CONSTRUCTION...
HMM
...YOU, MR. TAZUNA, ARE VERY MUCH IN HIS WAY.
THAT MEANS...
THAT THE NINJA WHO ATTACKED US WERE WORKING FOR GATÔ.
....
?
NARUTO IS DOING HIS BEST TO KEEP UP.
....
BUT... I STILL DON'T UNDERSTAND... IF YOU KNEW YOU WERE THE TARGET OF A RUTHLESS THUG WITH NINJA AT HIS DISPOSAL...
...WHY DIDN'T YOU TELL US WHEN YOU ASKED FOR OUR HELP?

READ THIS WAY

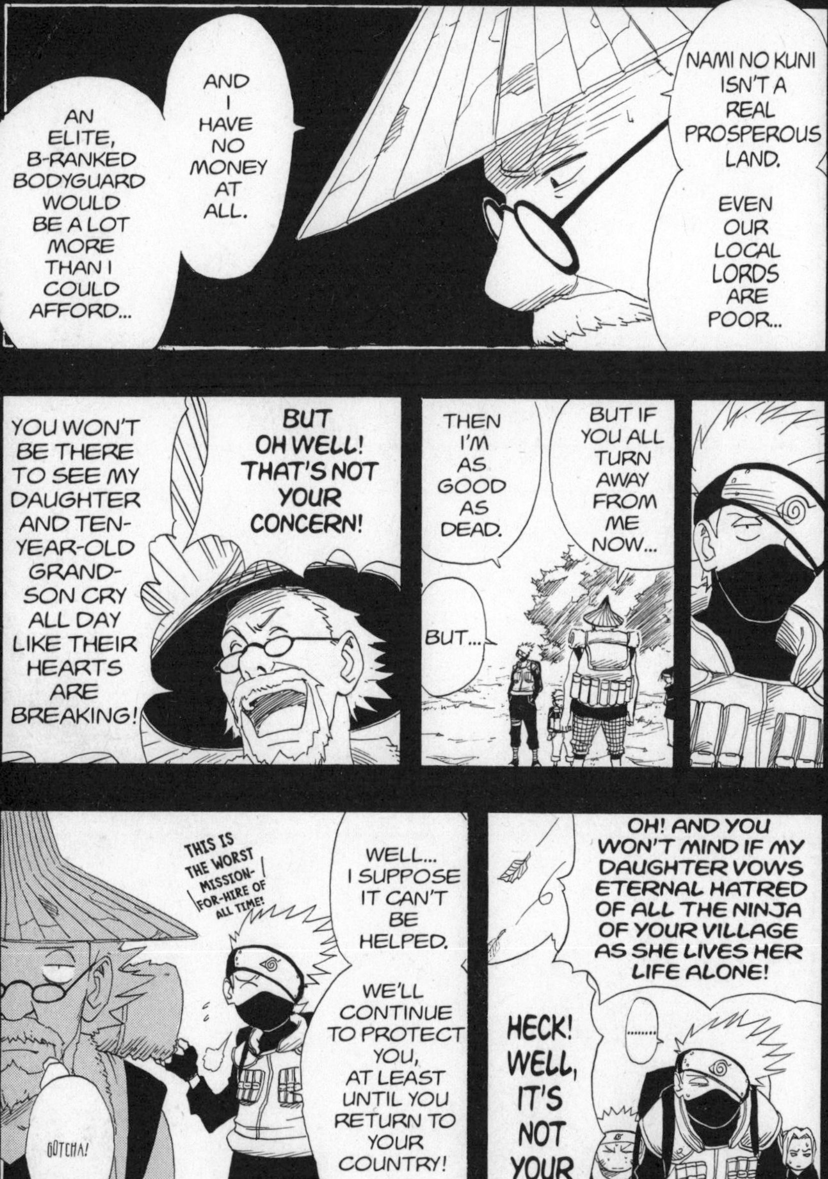

NAMI NO KUNI ISN'T A REAL PROSPEROUS LAND.
EVEN OUR LOCAL LORDS ARE POOR...
AND I HAVE NO MONEY AT ALL.
AN ELITE, B-RANKED BODYGUARD WOULD BE A LOT MORE THAN I COULD AFFORD...
BUT IF YOU ALL TURN AWAY FROM ME NOW...
THEN I'M AS GOOD AS DEAD.
BUT...
BUT OH WELL! THAT'S NOT YOUR CONCERN!
YOU WON'T BE THERE TO SEE MY DAUGHTER AND TEN-YEAR-OLD GRANDSON CRY ALL DAY LIKE THEIR HEARTS ARE BREAKING!
OH! AND YOU WON'T MIND IF MY DAUGHTER VOWS ETERNAL HATRED OF ALL THE NINJA OF YOUR VILLAGE AS SHE LIVES HER LIFE ALONE!
....
HECK! WELL, IT'S NOT YOUR FAULT!
WELL... I SUPPOSE IT CAN'T BE HELPED.
WE'LL CONTINUE TO PROTECT YOU, AT LEAST UNTIL YOU RETURN TO YOUR COUNTRY!
THIS IS THE WORST MISSION-FOR-HIRE OF ALL TIME!
GOTCHA!

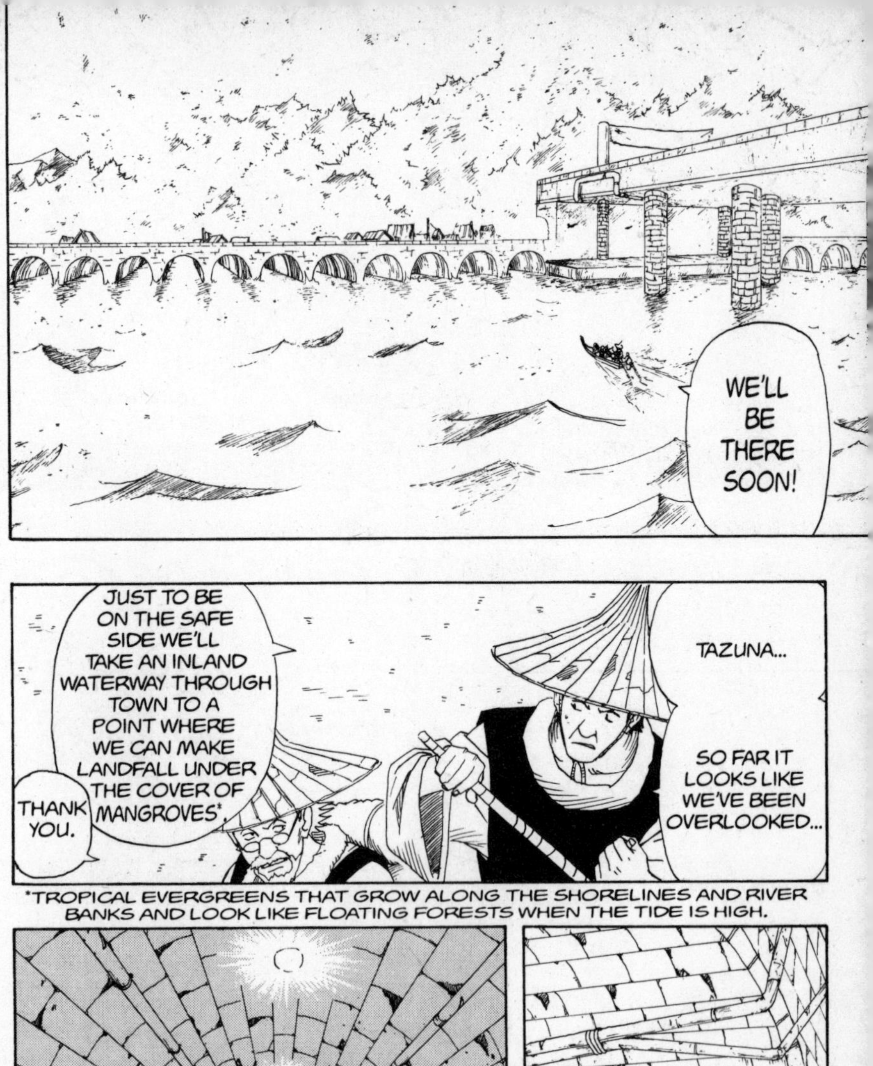
WE'LL BE THERE SOON!
TAZUNA...
SO FAR IT LOOKS LIKE WE'VE BEEN OVERLOOKED...
JUST TO BE ON THE SAFE SIDE WE'LL TAKE AN INLAND WATERWAY THROUGH TOWN TO A POINT WHERE WE CAN MAKE LANDFALL UNDER THE COVER OF MANGROVES*.
THANK YOU.

*TROPICAL EVERGREENS THAT GROW ALONG THE SHORELINES AND RIVER BANKS AND LOOK LIKE FLOATING FORESTS WHEN THE TIDE IS HIGH.

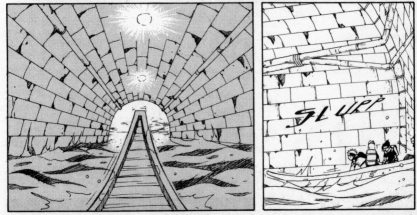

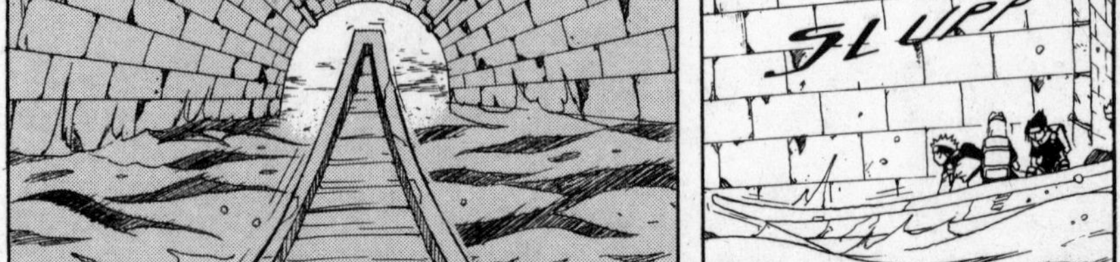
SLURP

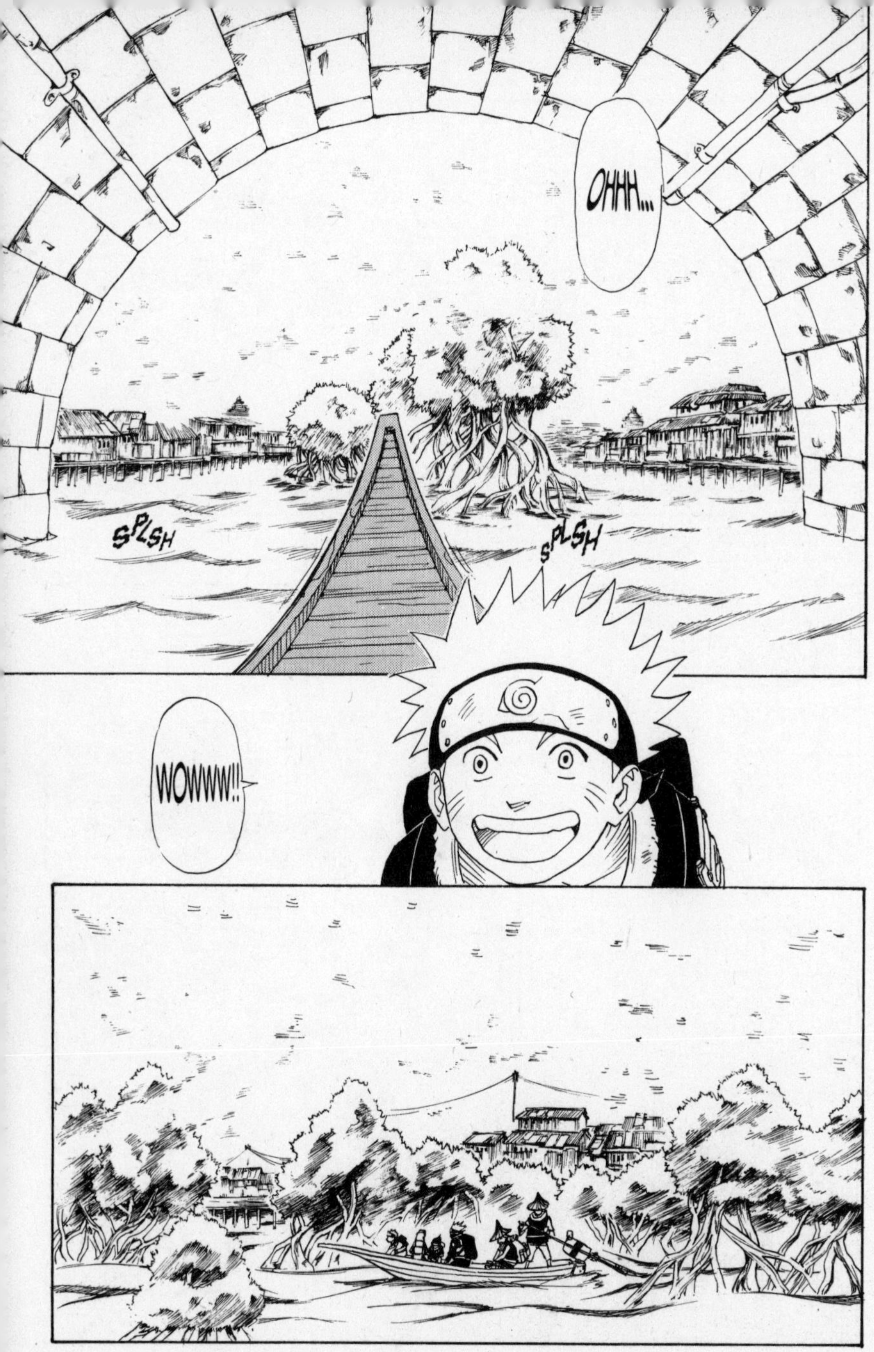
OHHH...
SPLSH
SPLSH
WOWWW!!

READ THIS WAY

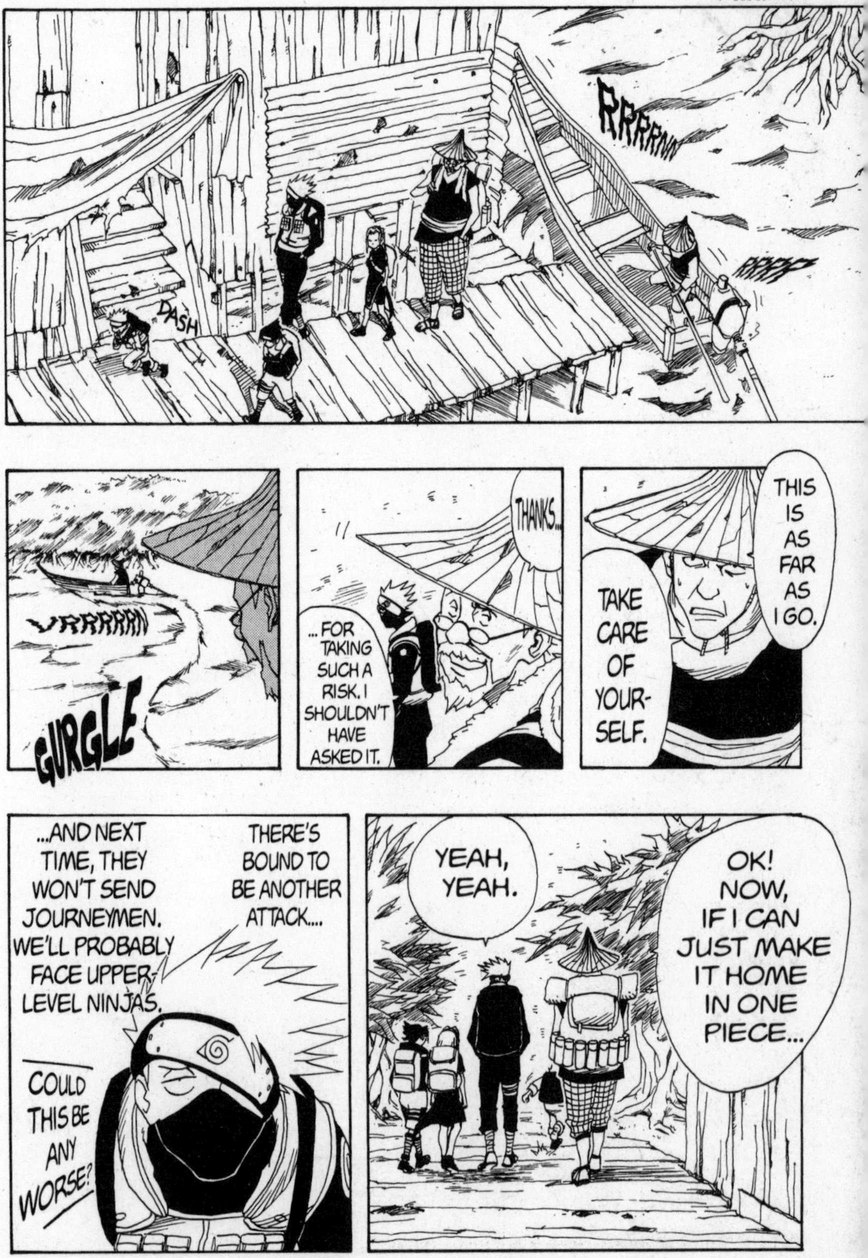
RRRRNN
DASH
THIS IS AS FAR AS I GO.
TAKE CARE OF YOURSELF.
THANKS...
...FOR TAKING SUCH A RISK. I SHOULDN'T HAVE ASKED IT.
VRRRRRN
GURGLE
OK! NOW, IF I CAN JUST MAKE IT HOME IN ONE PIECE...
YEAH, YEAH.
THERE'S BOUND TO BE ANOTHER ATTACK....
...AND NEXT TIME, THEY WON'T SEND JOURNEYMEN. WE'LL PROBABLY FACE UPPER-LEVEL NINJAS.
COULD THIS BE ANY WORSE?

READ THIS WAY

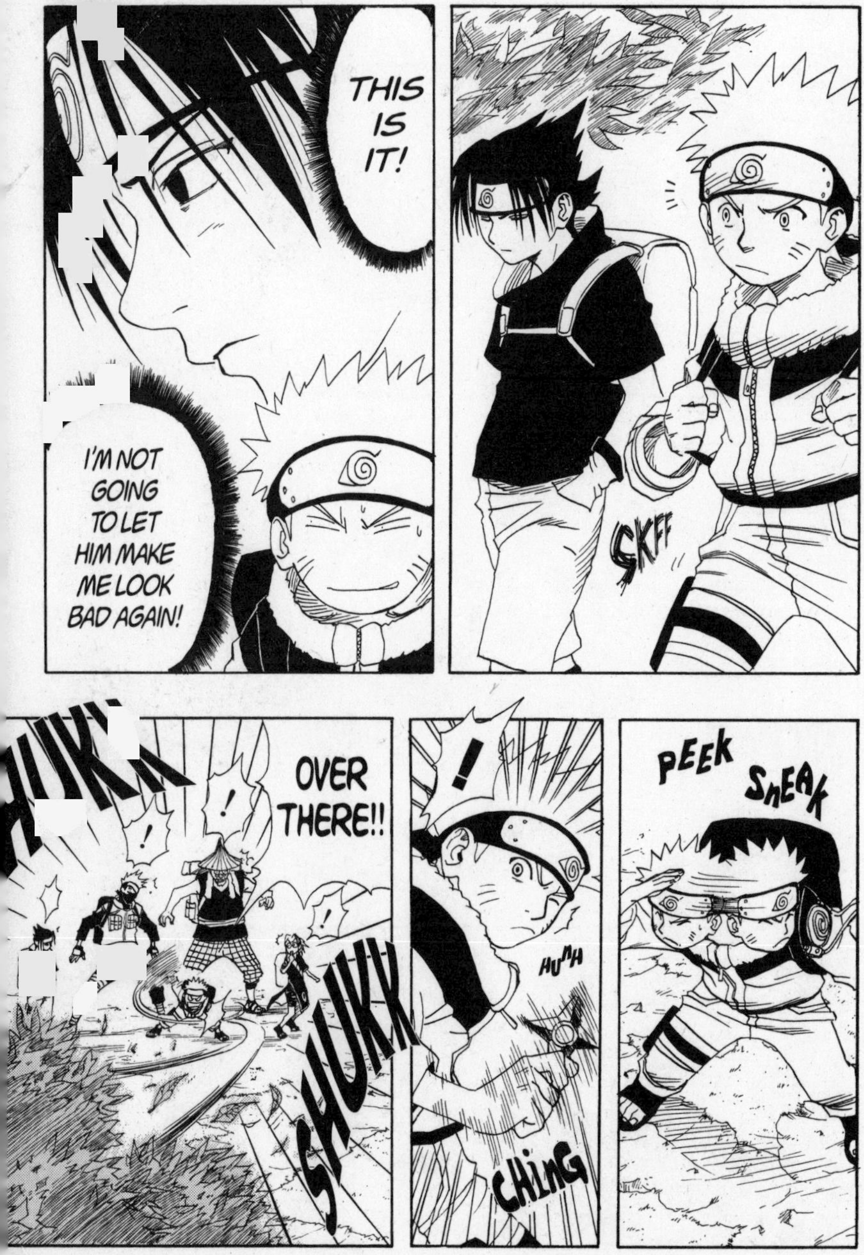
SKFF
THIS IS IT!
I'M NOT GOING TO LET HIM MAKE ME LOOK BAD AGAIN!
PEEK
SNEAK
!
HUNH
CHING
SHUKK
OVER THERE!!
!
!
!
!
SHUKK

READ THIS WAY

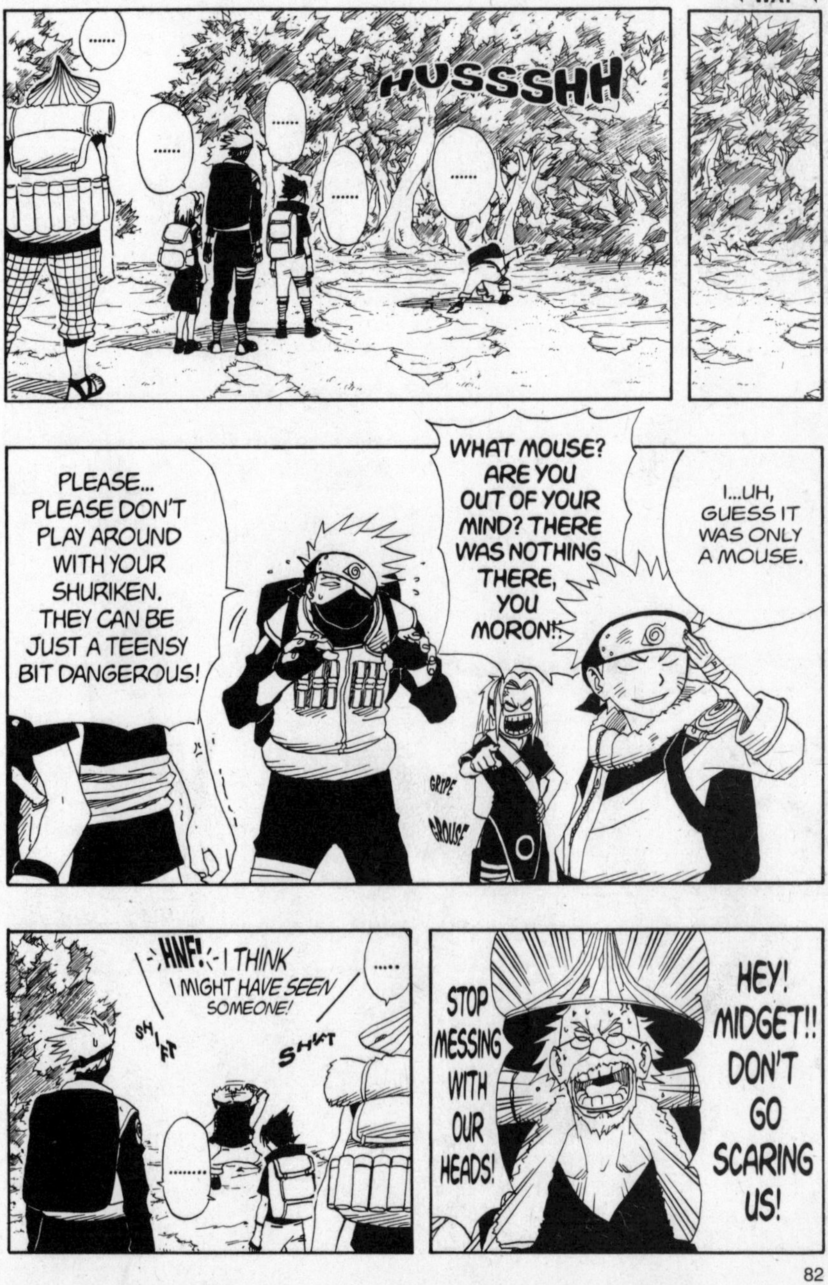

......
HUSSSHH
......
......
......
......
I...UH, GUESS IT WAS ONLY A MOUSE.
WHAT MOUSE? ARE YOU OUT OF YOUR MIND? THERE WAS NOTHING THERE, YOU MORON!!
PLEASE... PLEASE DON'T PLAY AROUND WITH YOUR SHURIKEN. THEY CAN BE JUST A TEENSY BIT DANGEROUS!
GRIPE
GROUSE
HEY! MIDGET!! DON'T GO SCARING US!
STOP MESSING WITH OUR HEADS!
.....
HNF! I THINK I MIGHT HAVE SEEN SOMEONE!
SHIFT
....

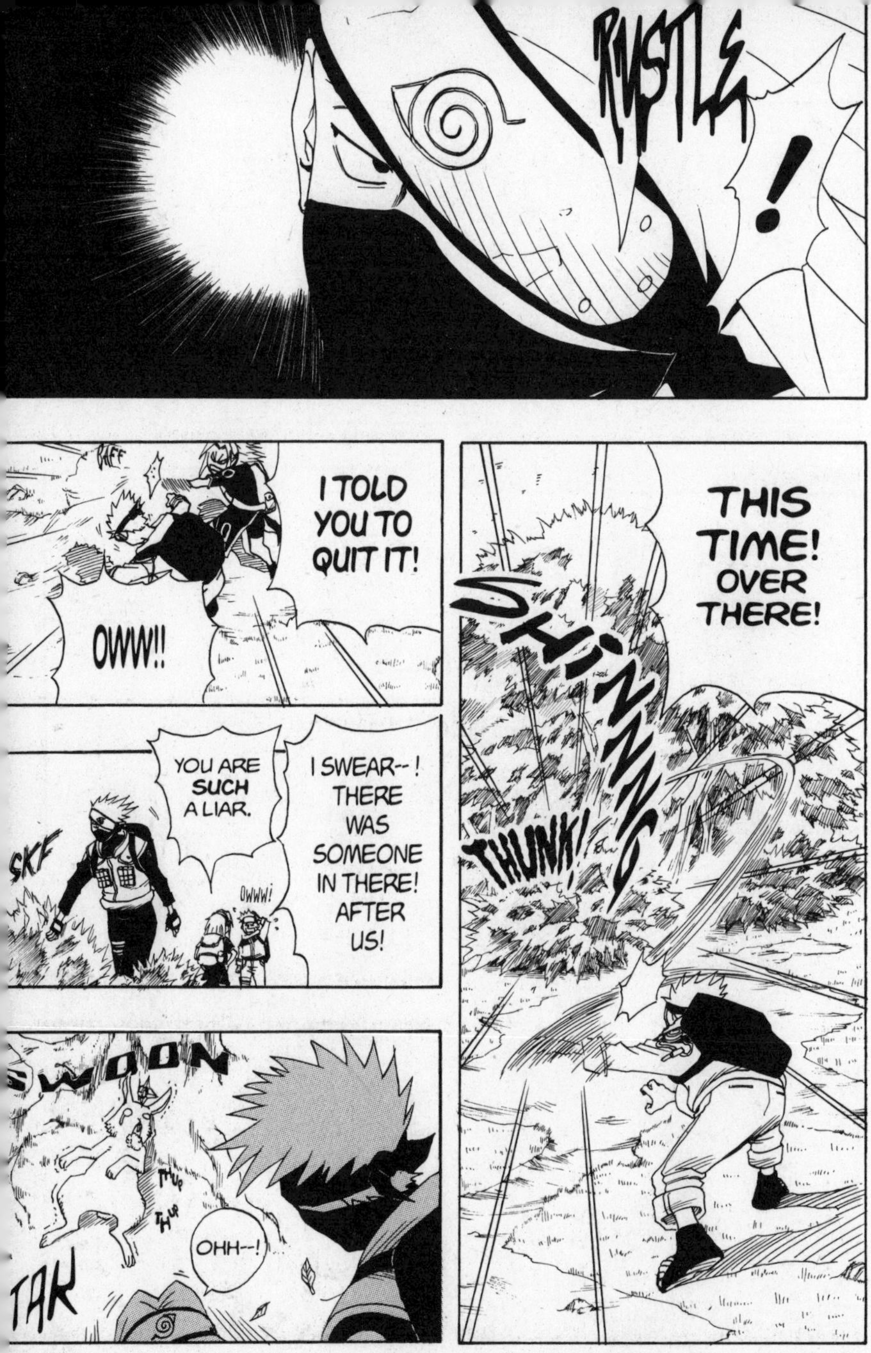
RUSTLE
!
THIS TIME! OVER THERE!
SHINNNG
THUNK!
I TOLD YOU TO QUIT IT!
OWW!!
I SWEAR--! THERE WAS SOMEONE IN THERE! AFTER US!
YOU ARE SUCH A LIAR.
OWWW!
SKF
SWOON
THUP
THUP
OHH--!
TAK

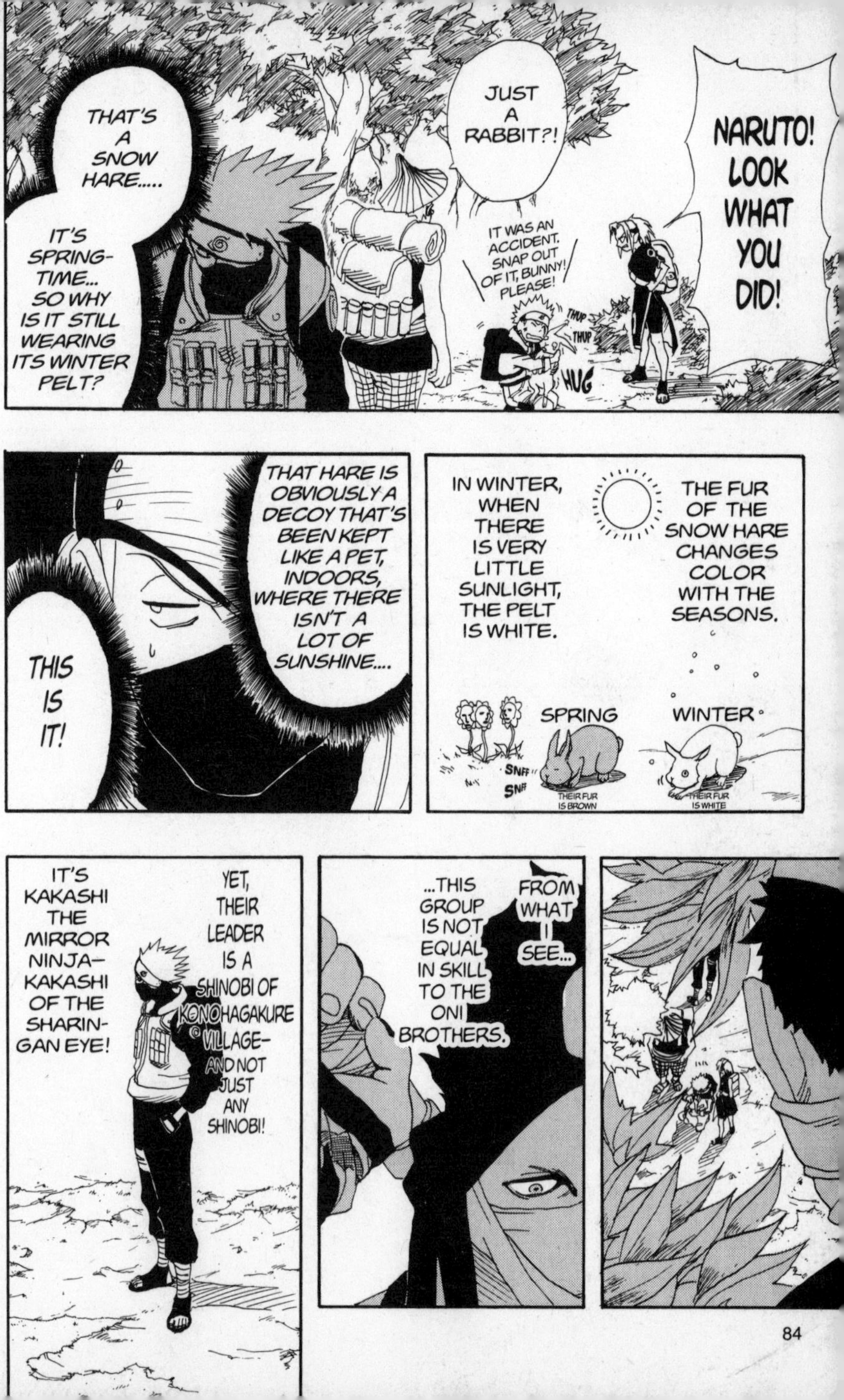
NARUTO! LOOK WHAT YOU DID!
JUST A RABBIT?!
THAT'S A SNOW HARE.....
IT WAS AN ACCIDENT. SNAP OUT OF IT, BUNNY! PLEASE!
THUP
THUP
HUG
IT'S SPRING-TIME... SO WHY IS IT STILL WEARING ITS WINTER PELT?
THE FUR OF THE SNOW HARE CHANGES COLOR WITH THE SEASONS.
IN WINTER, WHEN THERE IS VERY LITTLE SUNLIGHT, THE PELT IS WHITE.
WINTER
THEIR FUR IS WHITE
SPRING
SNFF
SNFF
THEIR FUR IS BROWN
THAT HARE IS OBVIOUSLY A DECOY THAT'S BEEN KEPT LIKE A PET, INDOORS, WHERE THERE ISN'T A LOT OF SUNSHINE....
THIS IS IT!
FROM WHAT I SEE...
...THIS GROUP IS NOT EQUAL IN SKILL TO THE ONI BROTHERS.
YET, THEIR LEADER IS A SHINOBI OF KONOHAGAKURE VILLAGE— AND NOT JUST ANY SHINOBI!
IT'S KAKASHI THE MIRROR NINJA— KAKASHI OF THE SHARIN-GAN EYE!

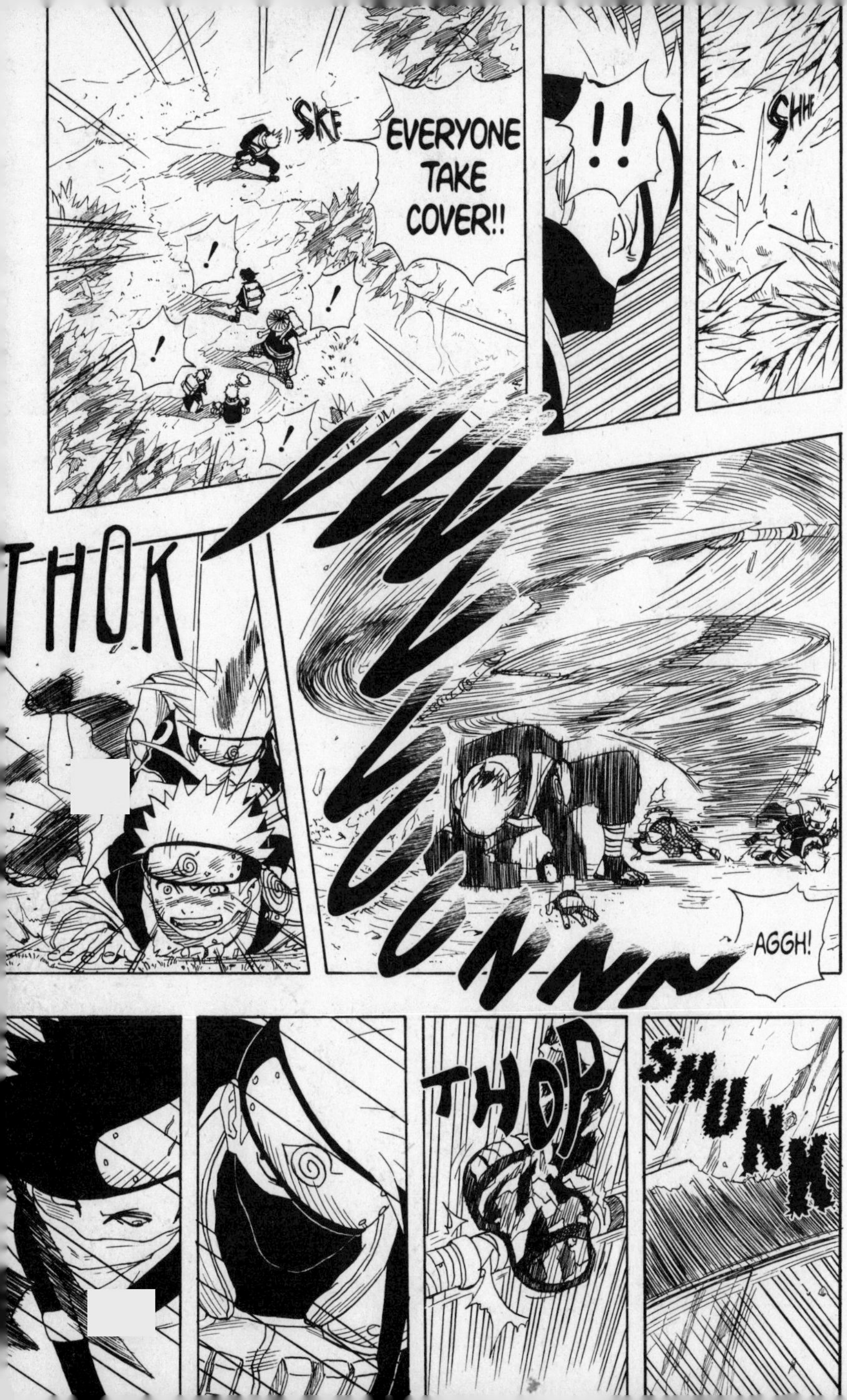
SHH
!!
SKF
EVERYONE TAKE COVER!!
!
!
!
!
AGGH!
THOK
SHUNK
THOP

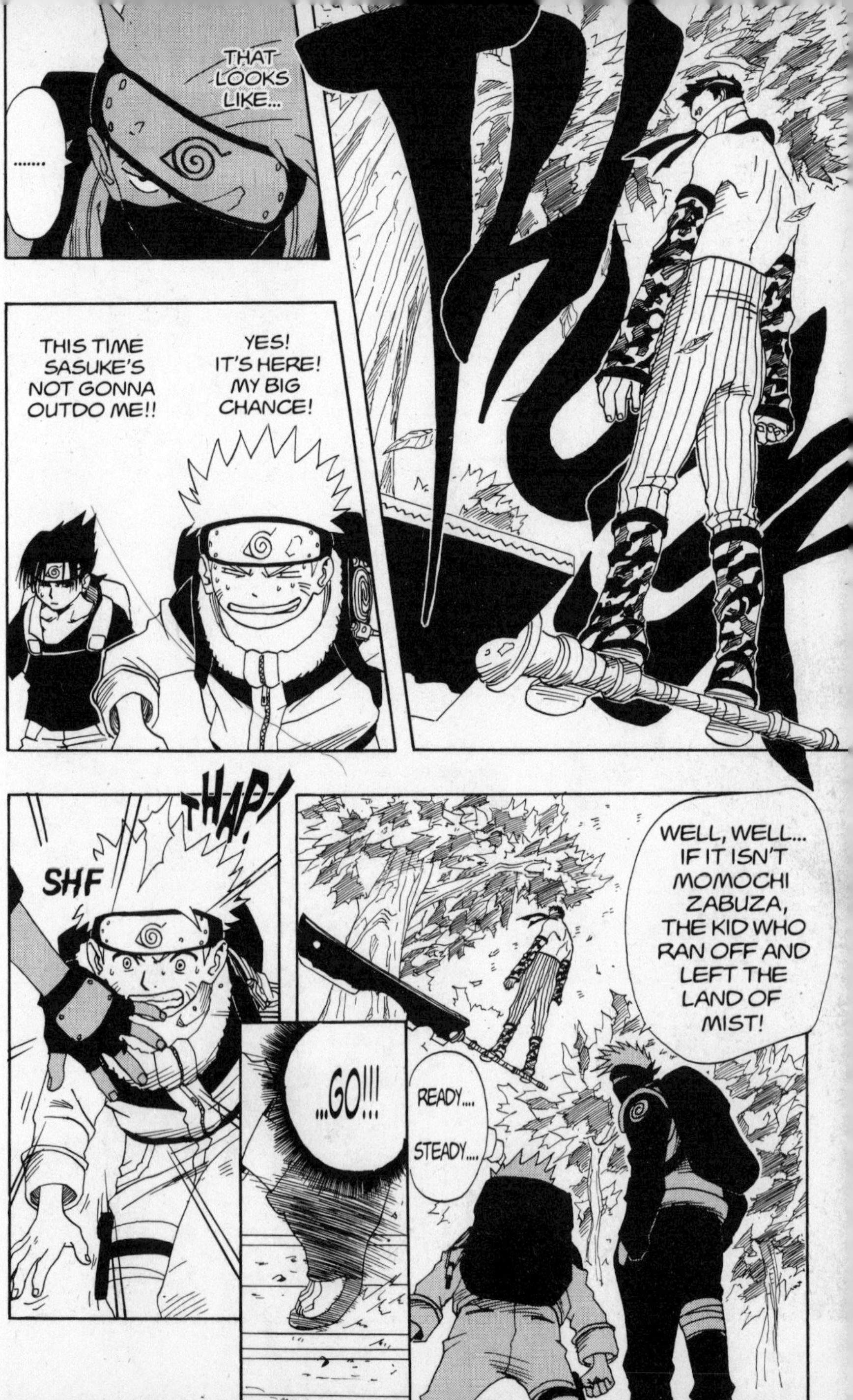
THAT LOOKS LIKE...
......
YES! IT'S HERE! MY BIG CHANCE!
THIS TIME SASUKE'S NOT GONNA OUTDO ME!!
WELL, WELL... IF IT ISN'T MOMOCHI ZABUZA, THE KID WHO RAN OFF AND LEFT THE LAND OF MIST!
READY....
STEADY....
...GO!!!
THAP!
SHF

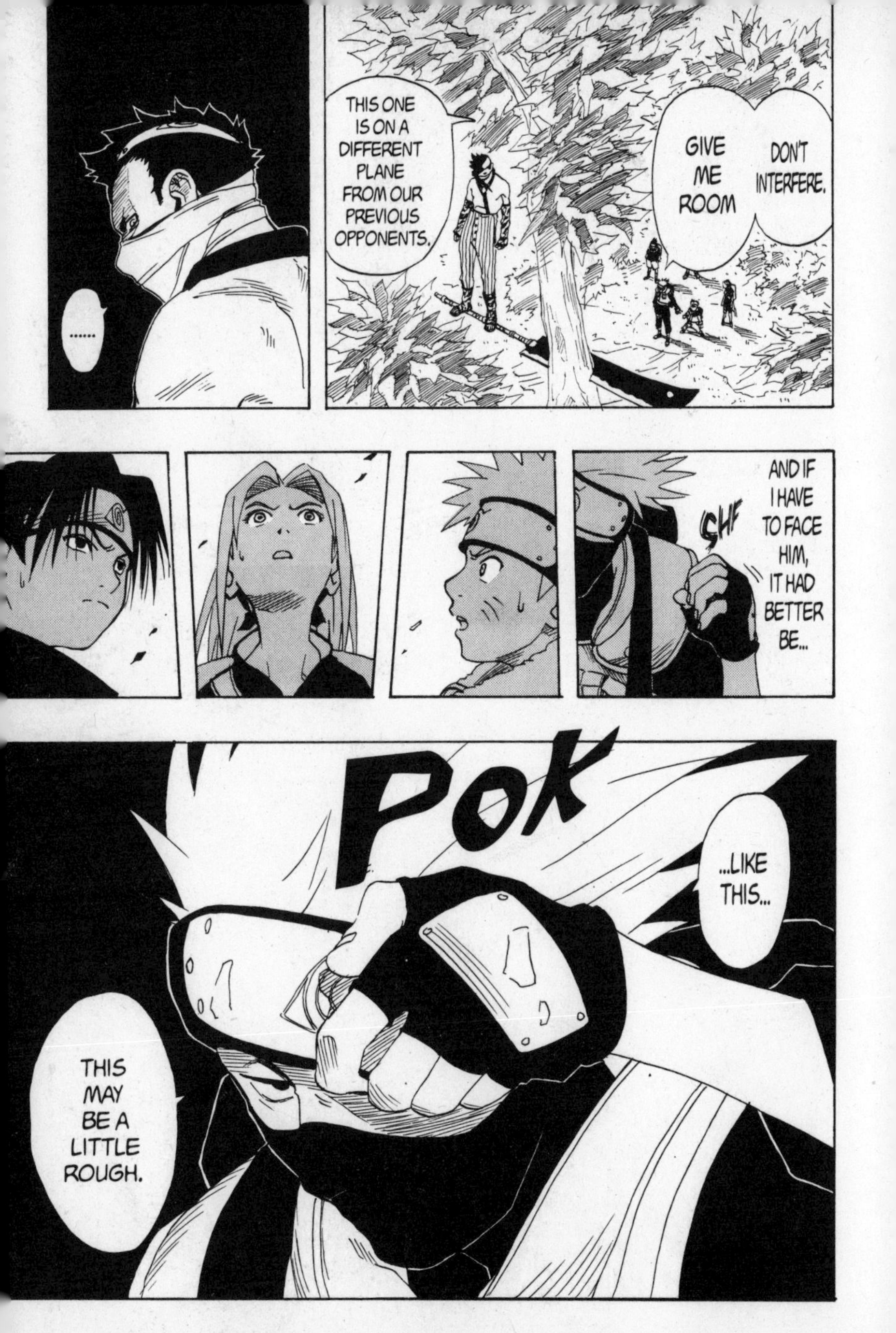
DON'T INTERFERE.
GIVE ME ROOM
THIS ONE IS ON A DIFFERENT PLANE FROM OUR PREVIOUS OPPONENTS.
......
CHF
AND IF I HAVE TO FACE HIM, IT HAD BETTER BE...
POK
...LIKE THIS...
THIS MAY BE A LITTLE ROUGH.

Number 12: Game Over!!!

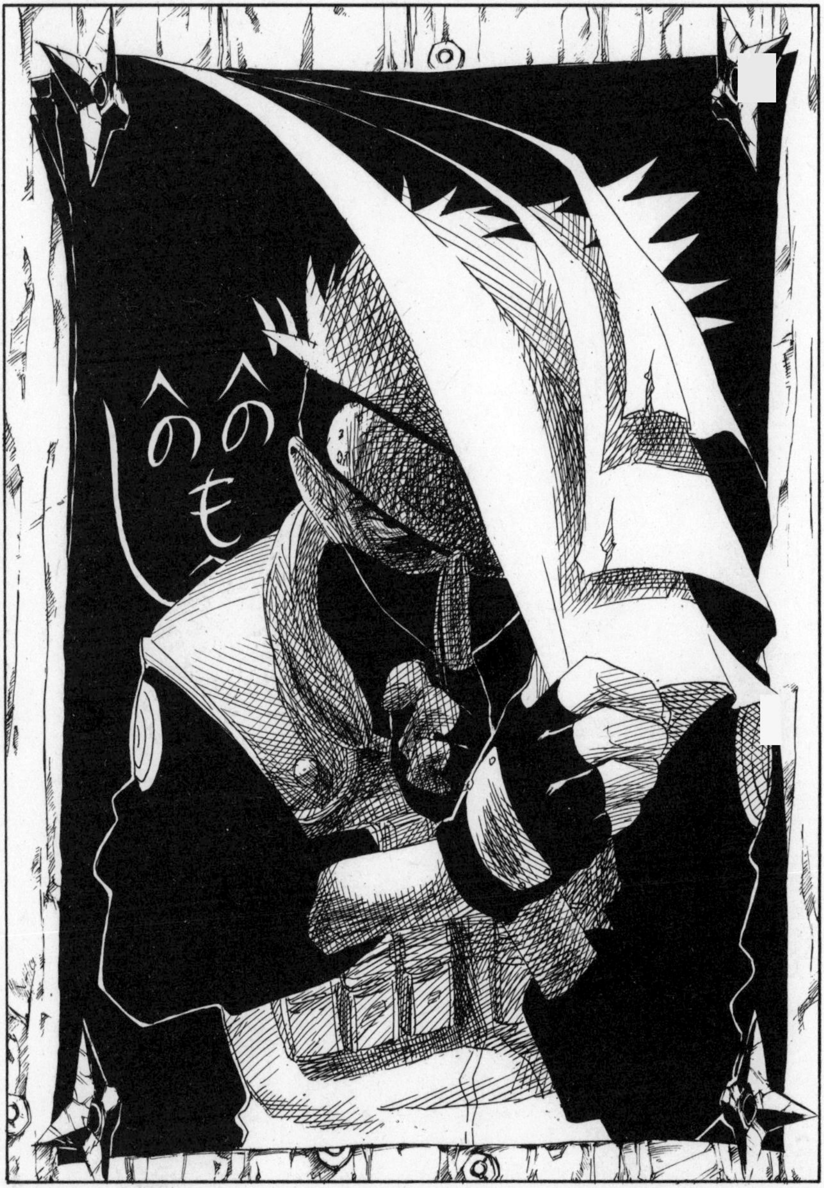

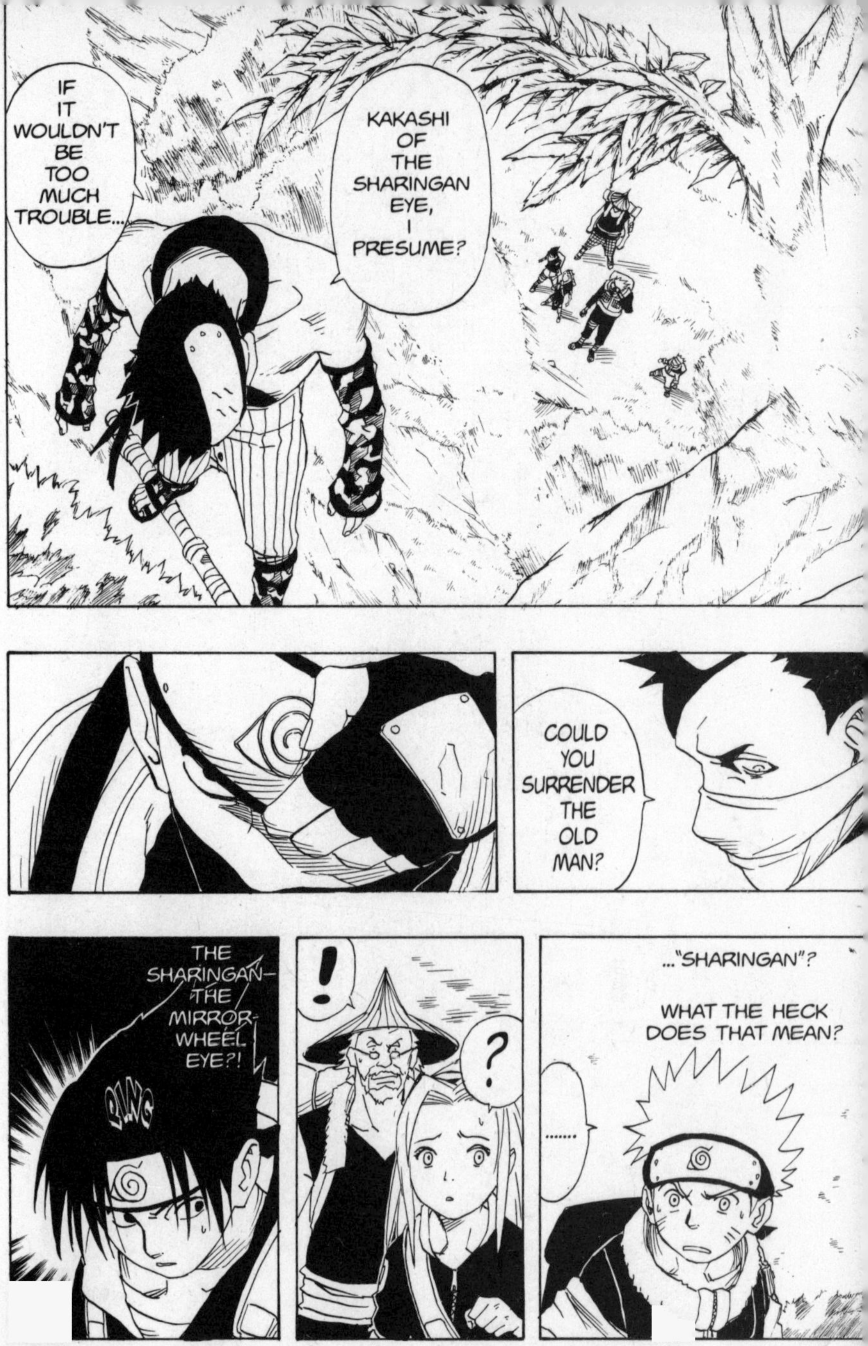
KAKASHI OF THE SHARINGAN EYE, I PRESUME?
IF IT WOULDN'T BE TOO MUCH TROUBLE...
COULD YOU SURRENDER THE OLD MAN?
..."SHARINGAN"?
WHAT THE HECK DOES THAT MEAN?
....
!
?
THE SHARINGAN—THE MIRROR-WHEEL EYE?!

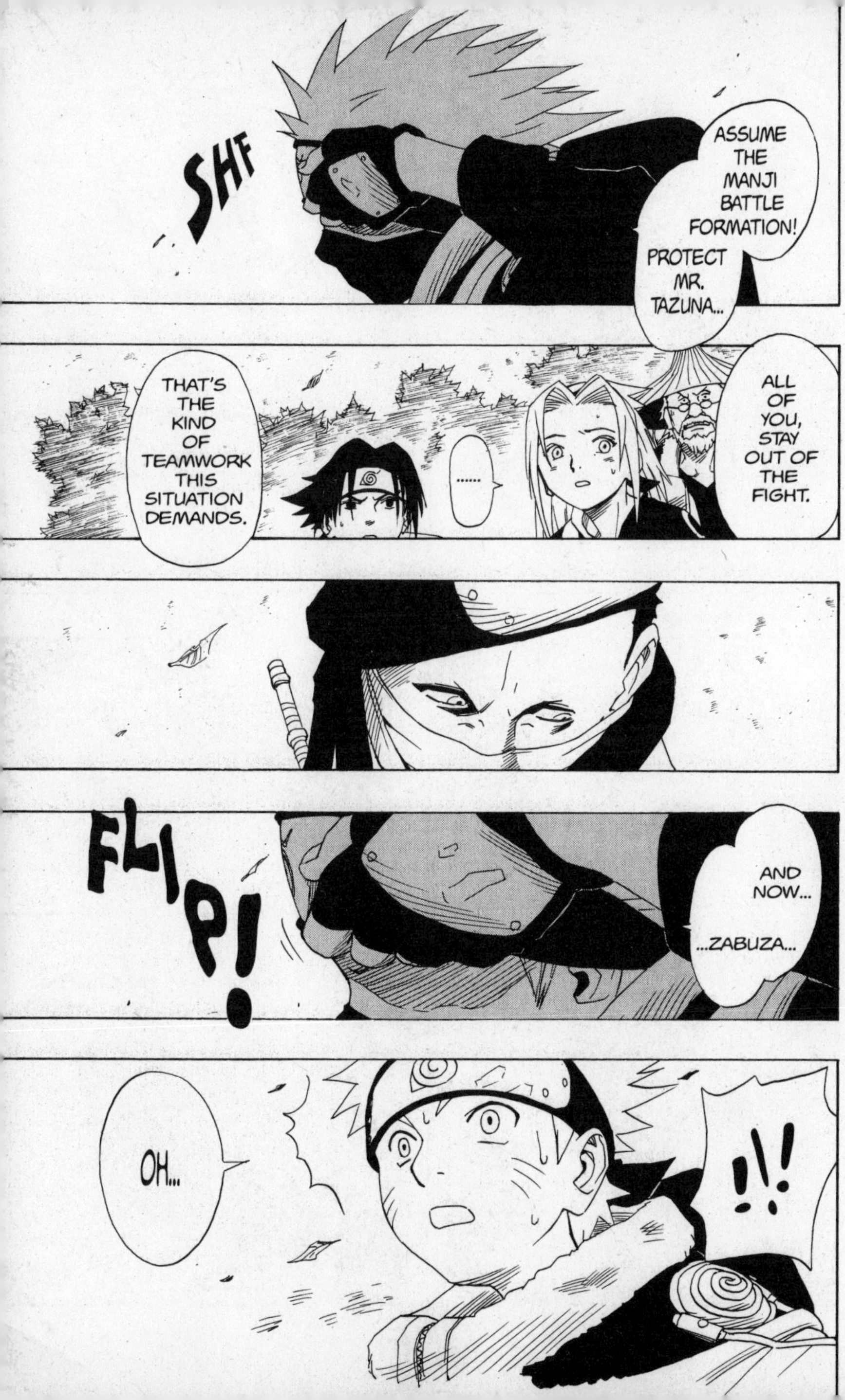
ASSUME THE MANJI BATTLE FORMATION!
PROTECT MR. TAZUNA...
SHF
ALL OF YOU, STAY OUT OF THE FIGHT.
......
THAT'S THE KIND OF TEAMWORK THIS SITUATION DEMANDS.
AND NOW...
...ZABUZA...
FLIP!
!!
OH...

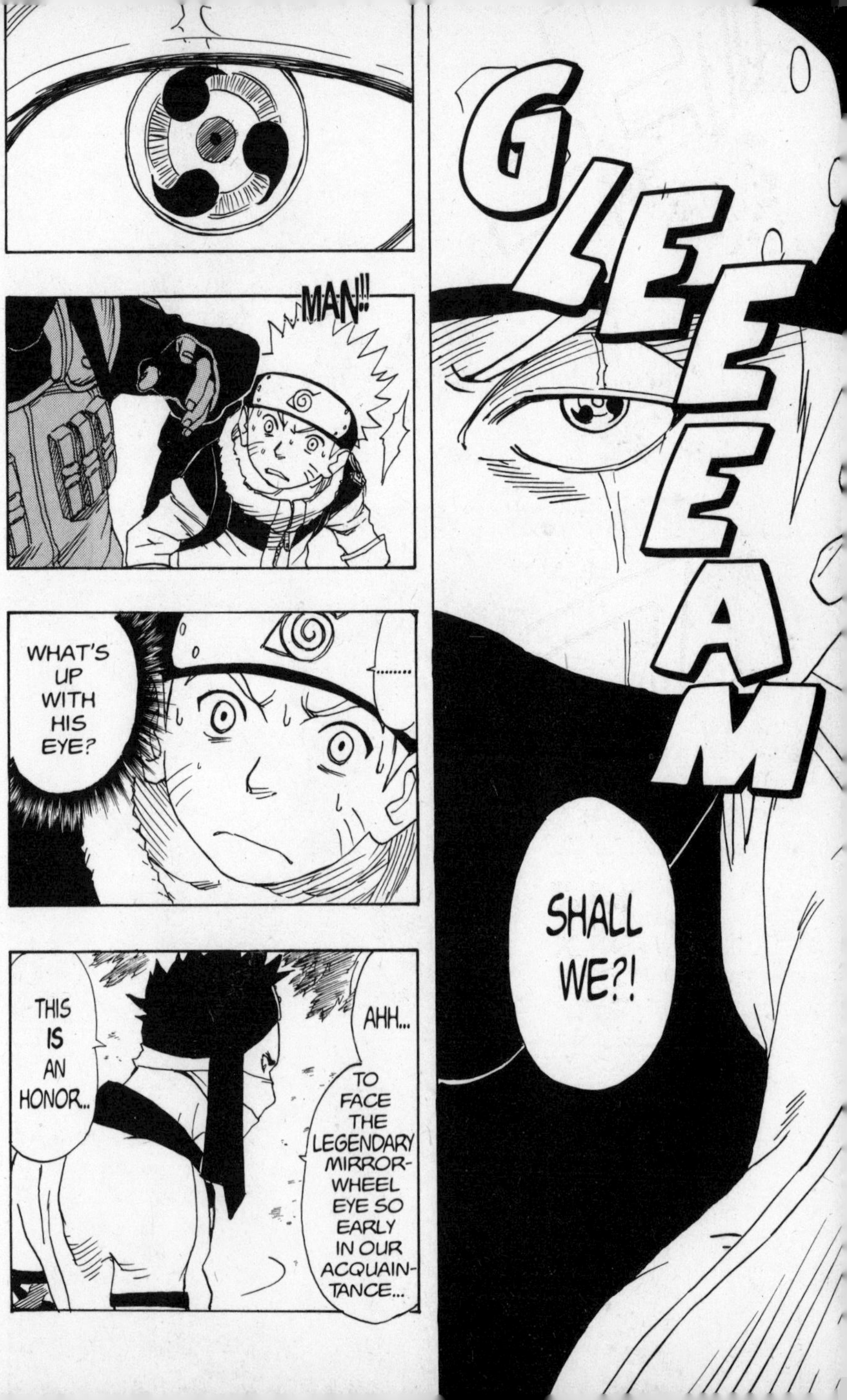
GLEEEAM
SHALL WE?!
MAN!!
......
WHAT'S UP WITH HIS EYE?
AHH...
TO FACE THE LEGENDARY MIRROR-WHEEL EYE SO EARLY IN OUR ACQUAINTANCE...
THIS IS AN HONOR..

READ THIS WAY

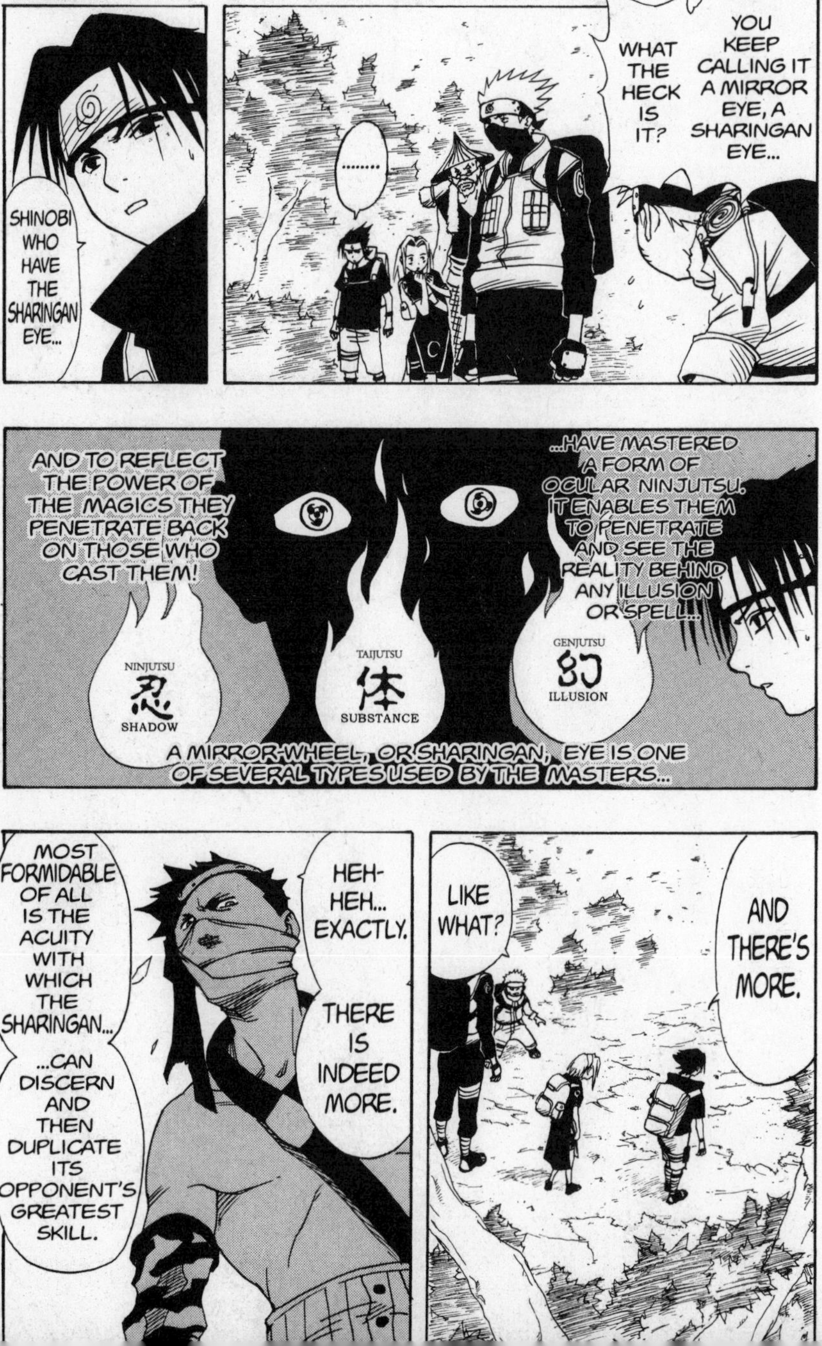
YOU KEEP CALLING IT A MIRROR EYE, A SHARINGAN EYE...
WHAT THE HECK IS IT?
....
SHINOBI WHO HAVE THE SHARINGAN EYE...
...HAVE MASTERED A FORM OF OCULAR NINJUTSU. IT ENABLES THEM TO PENETRATE AND SEE THE REALITY BEHIND ANY ILLUSION OR SPELL...
AND TO REFLECT THE POWER OF THE MAGICS THEY PENETRATE BACK ON THOSE WHO CAST THEM!
GENJUTSU 幻 ILLUSION
TAIJUTSU 体 SUBSTANCE
NINJUTSU 忍 SHADOW
A MIRROR-WHEEL, OR SHARINGAN, EYE IS ONE OF SEVERAL TYPES USED BY THE MASTERS...
AND THERE'S MORE.
LIKE WHAT?
HEH-HEH... EXACTLY.
THERE IS INDEED MORE.
MOST FORMIDABLE OF ALL IS THE ACUITY WITH WHICH THE SHARINGAN...
...CAN DISCERN AND THEN DUPLICATE ITS OPPONENT'S GREATEST SKILL.

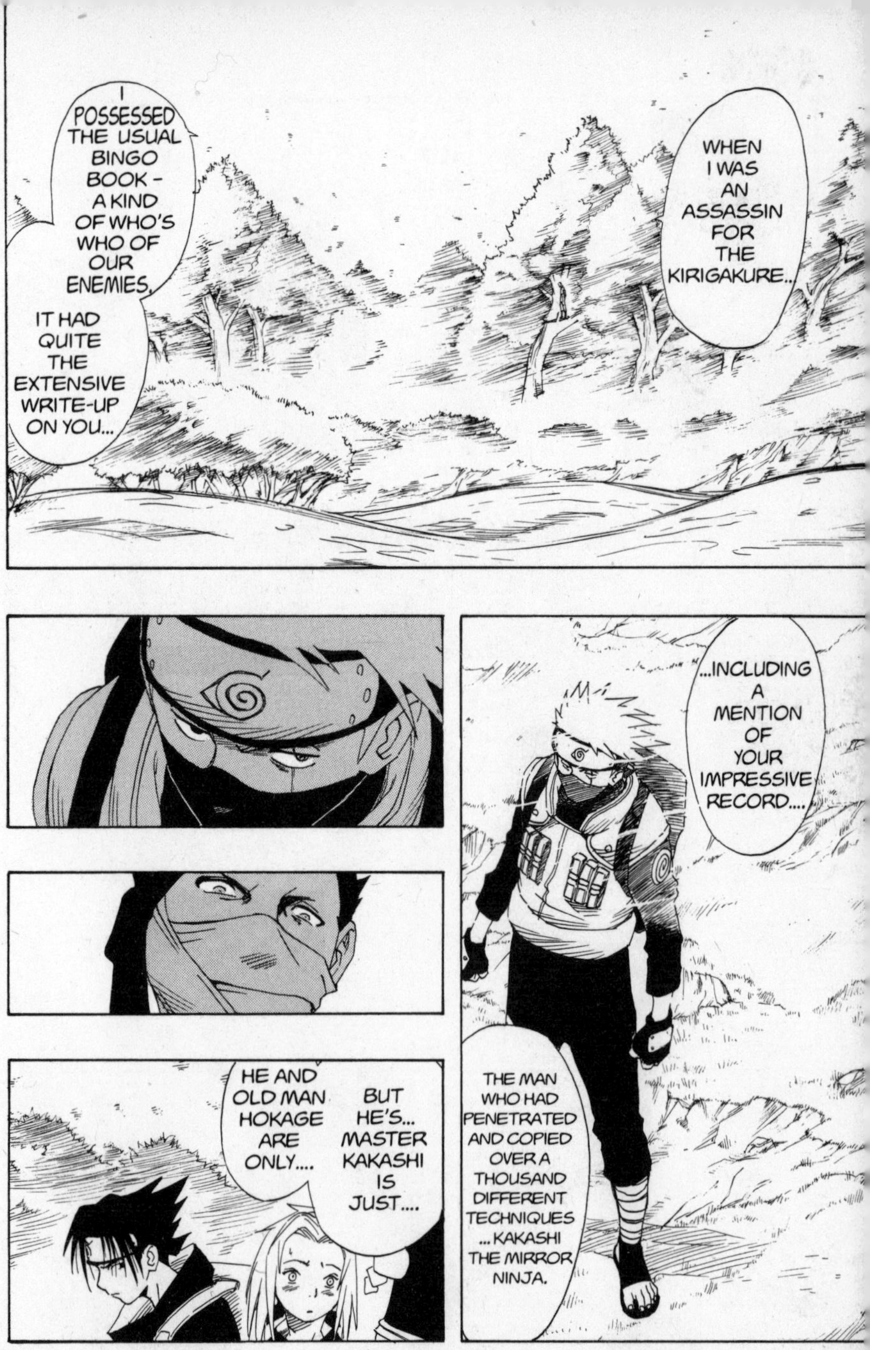
WHEN I WAS AN ASSASSIN FOR THE KIRIGAKURE..
I POSSESSED THE USUAL BINGO BOOK - A KIND OF WHO'S WHO OF OUR ENEMIES.
IT HAD QUITE THE EXTENSIVE WRITE-UP ON YOU...
...INCLUDING A MENTION OF YOUR IMPRESSIVE RECORD....
THE MAN WHO HAD PENETRATED AND COPIED OVER A THOUSAND DIFFERENT TECHNIQUES ...KAKASHI THE MIRROR NINJA.
BUT HE'S... MASTER KAKASHI IS JUST....
HE AND OLD MAN HOKAGE ARE ONLY....

READ THIS WAY

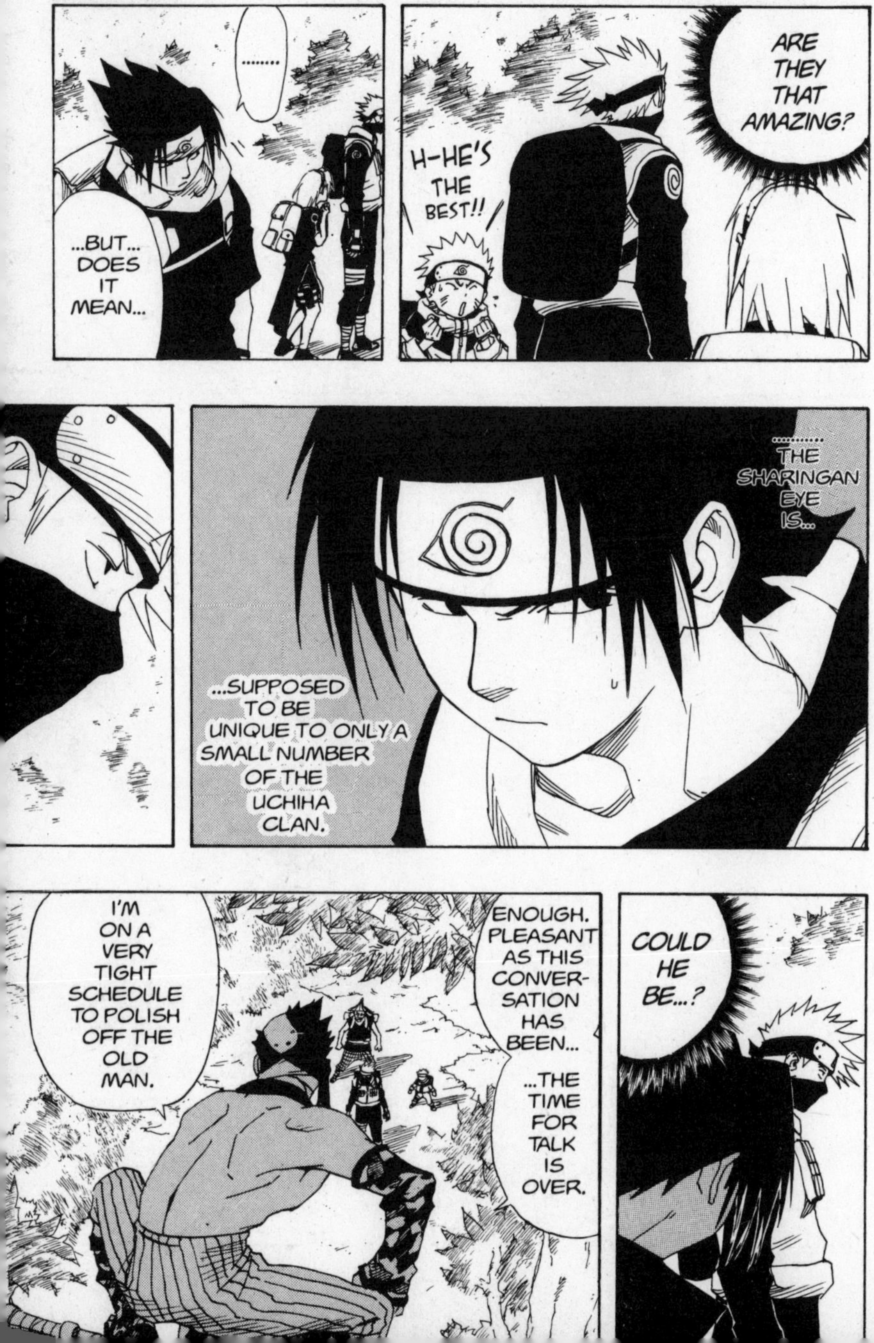

ARE THEY THAT AMAZING?
H-HE'S THE BEST!!
....
...BUT... DOES IT MEAN...
..........THE SHARINGAN EYE IS...
...SUPPOSED TO BE UNIQUE TO ONLY A SMALL NUMBER OF THE UCHIHA CLAN.
COULD HE BE...?
ENOUGH. PLEASANT AS THIS CONVER-SATION HAS BEEN...
...THE TIME FOR TALK IS OVER.
I'M ON A VERY TIGHT SCHEDULE TO POLISH OFF THE OLD MAN.

READ THIS WAY

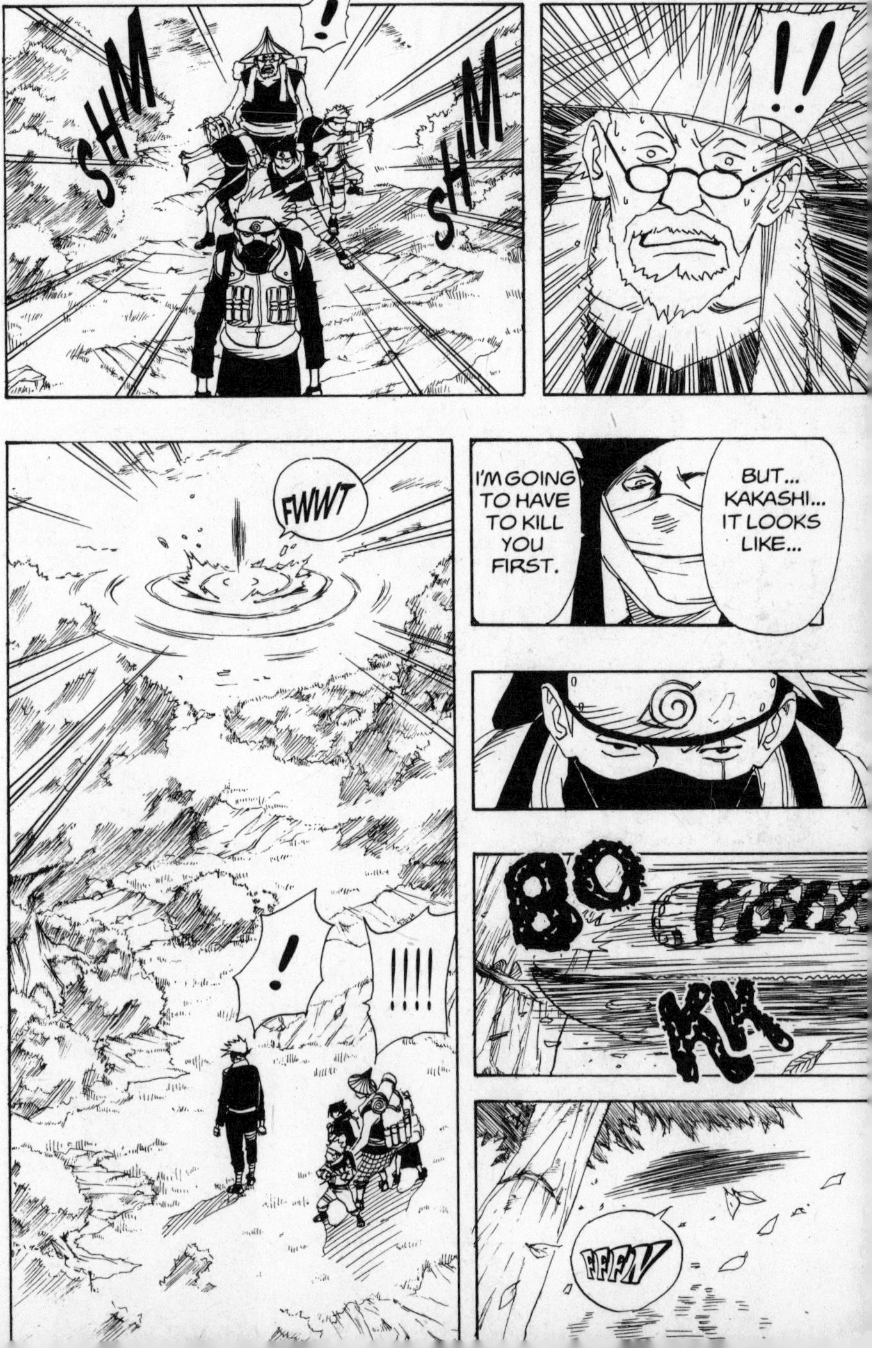
!!
SHM
!
SHM
BUT... KAKASHI... IT LOOKS LIKE...
I'M GOING TO HAVE TO KILL YOU FIRST.
KK
FFFN
FWWT
!
!!!!

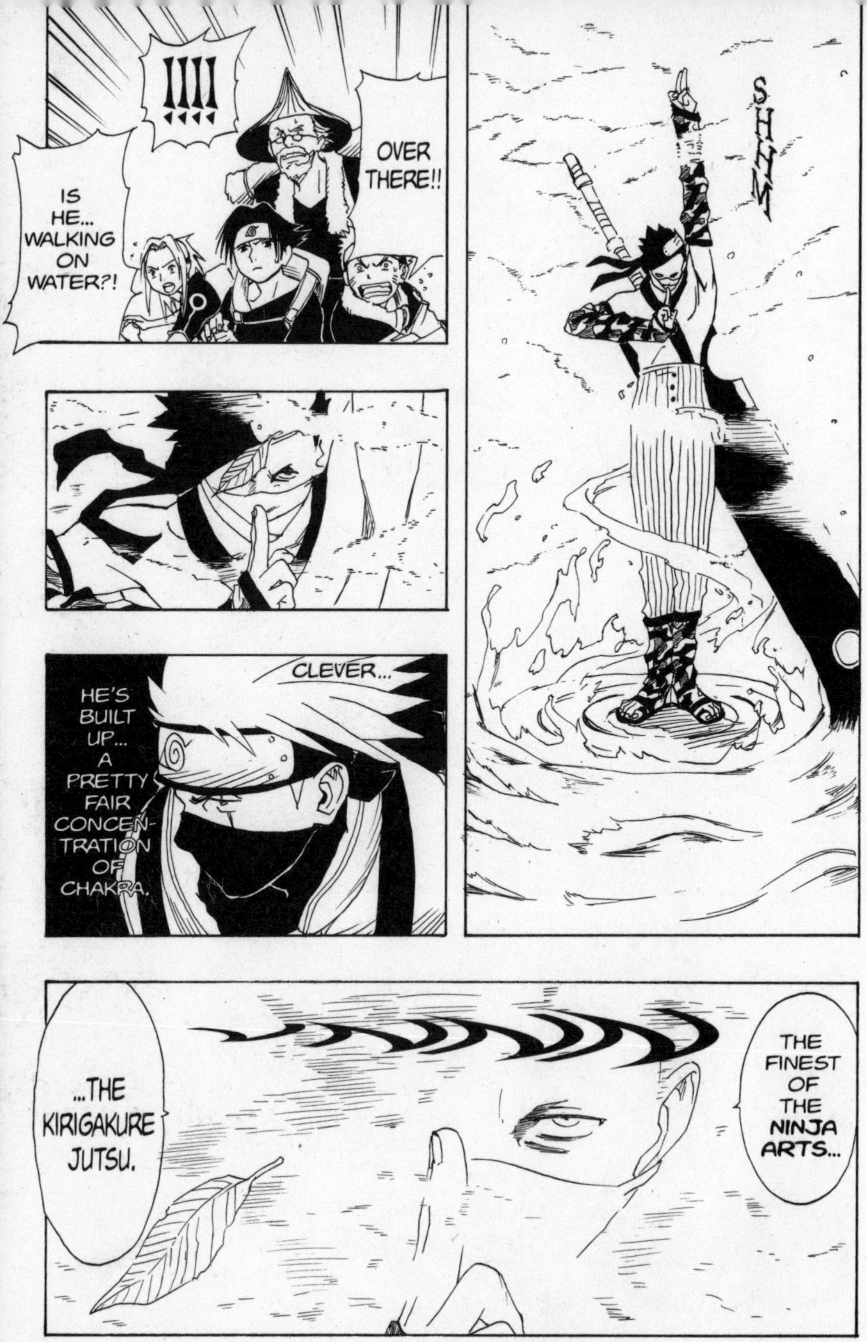
SHHH
!!!!
OVER THERE!!
IS HE... WALKING ON WATER?!
CLEVER...
HE'S BUILT UP... A PRETTY FAIR CONCEN-TRATION OF CHAKRA.
THE FINEST OF THE NINJA ARTS...
...THE KIRIGAKURE JUTSU.

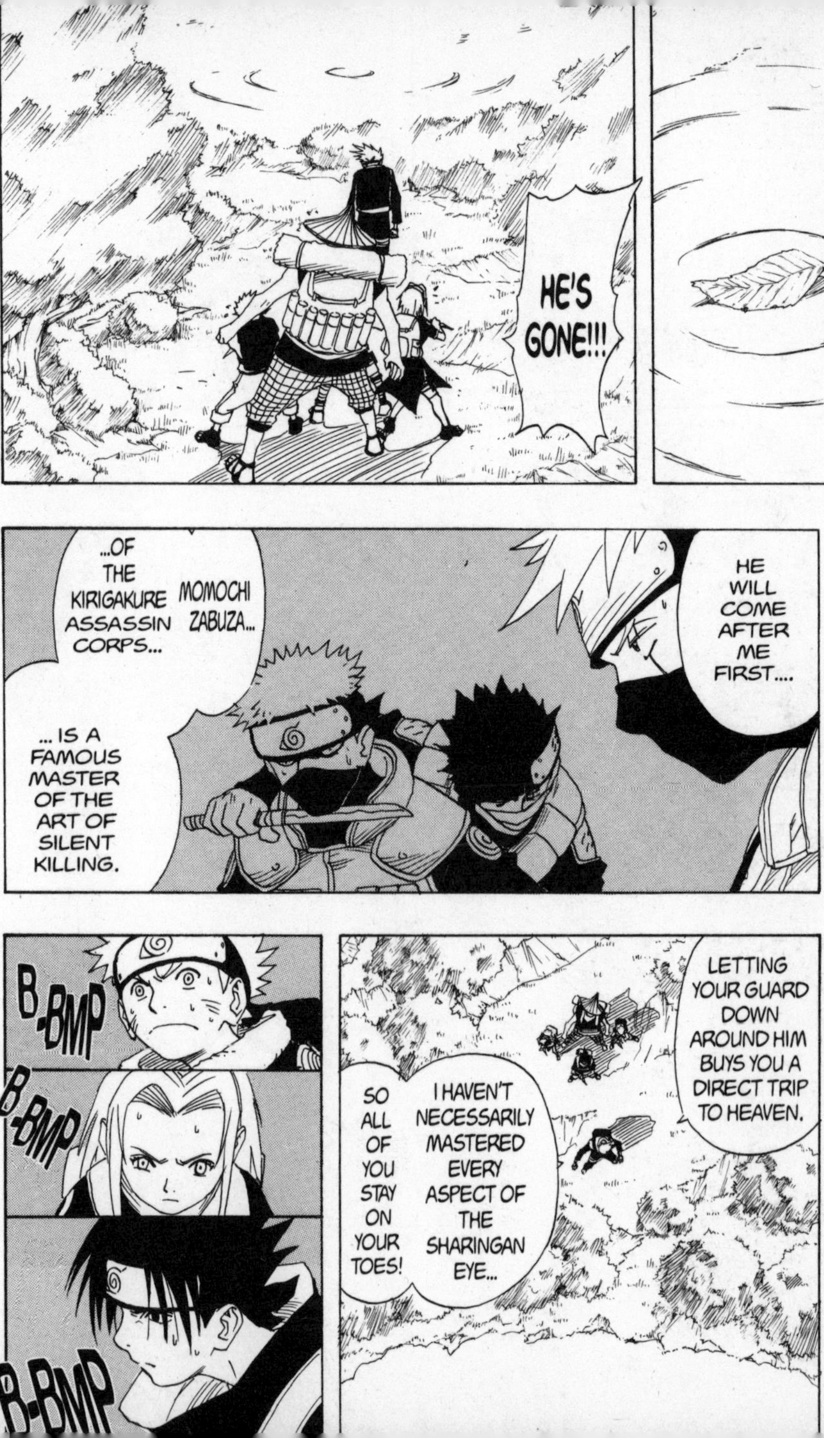

HE'S GONE!!!
HE WILL COME AFTER ME FIRST....
MOMOCHI ZABUZA...
...OF THE KIRIGAKURE ASSASSIN CORPS...
... IS A FAMOUS MASTER OF THE ART OF SILENT KILLING.
LETTING YOUR GUARD DOWN AROUND HIM BUYS YOU A DIRECT TRIP TO HEAVEN.
I HAVEN'T NECESSARILY MASTERED EVERY ASPECT OF THE SHARINGAN EYE...
SO ALL OF YOU STAY ON YOUR TOES!
B-BMP
B-BMP
B-BMP

READ THIS WAY

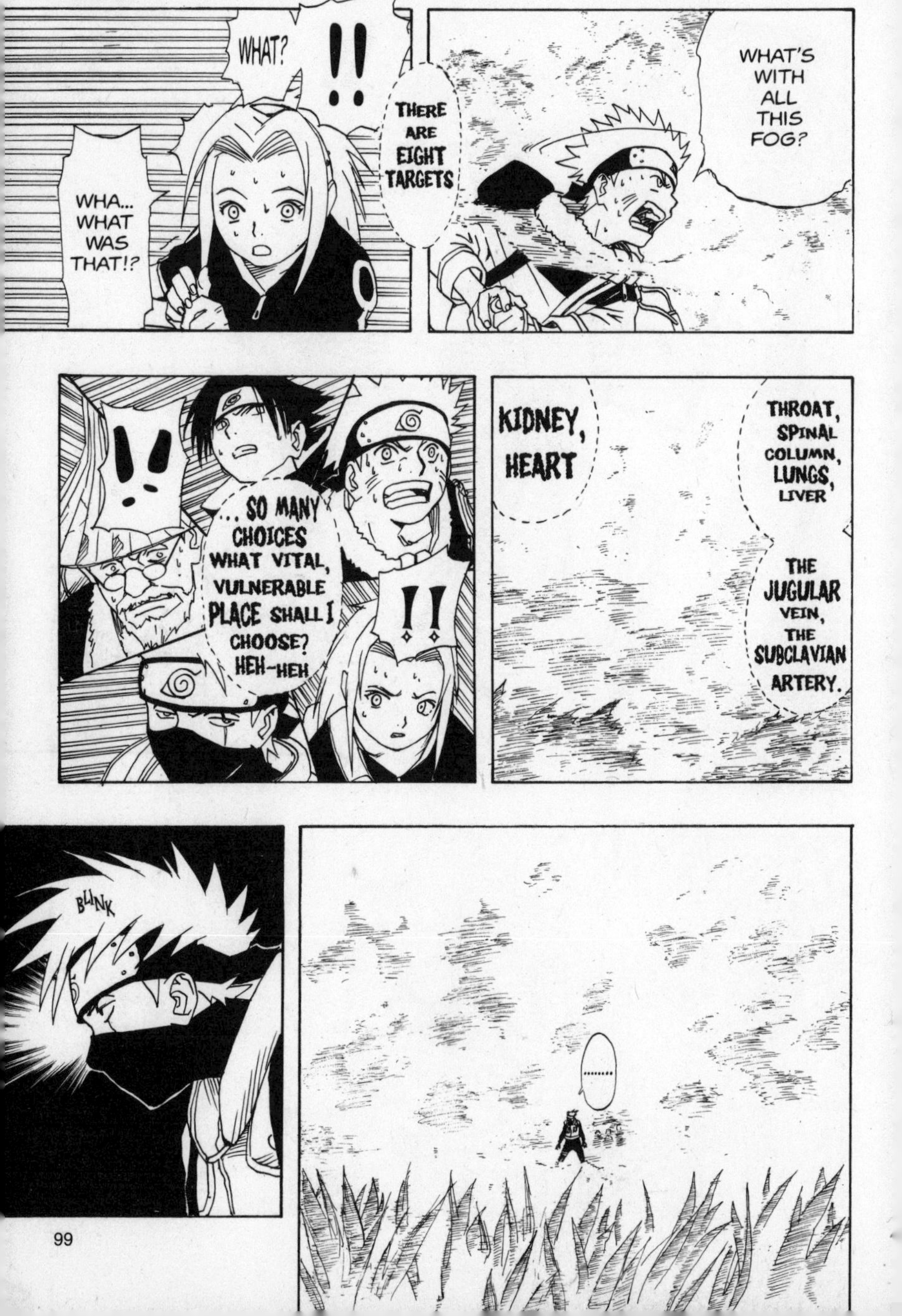
WHAT'S WITH ALL THIS FOG?
THERE ARE EIGHT TARGETS
!!
WHAT?
WHA... WHAT WAS THAT!?
THROAT, SPINAL COLUMN, LUNGS, LIVER
THE JUGULAR VEIN, THE SUBCLAVIAN ARTERY.
KIDNEY, HEART
!!
...SO MANY CHOICES WHAT VITAL, VULNERABLE PLACE SHALL I CHOOSE? HEH-HEH
!!
....
BLINK

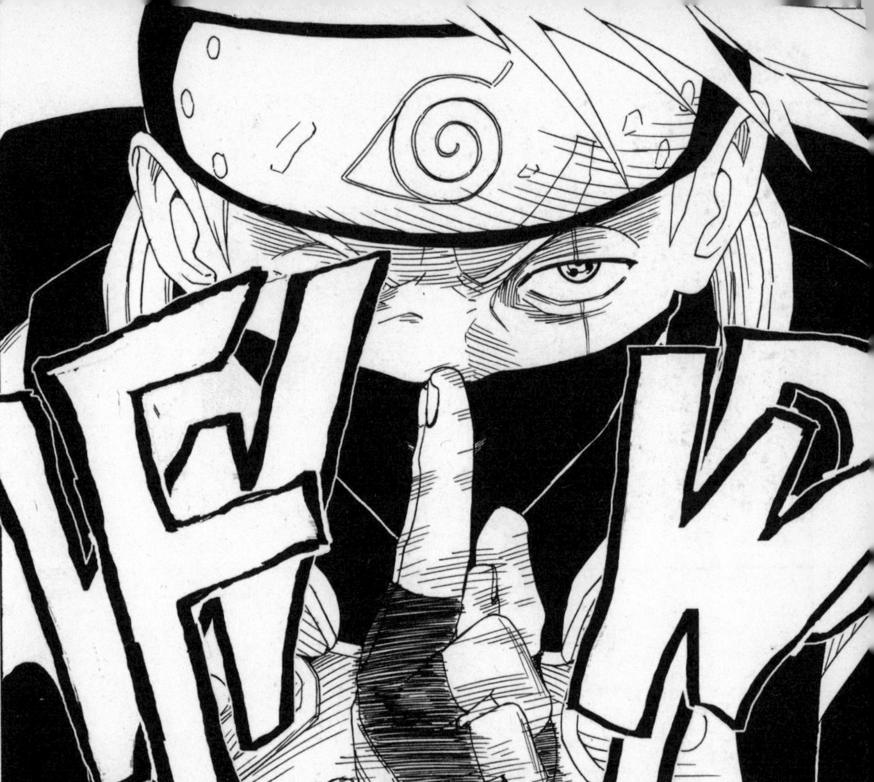

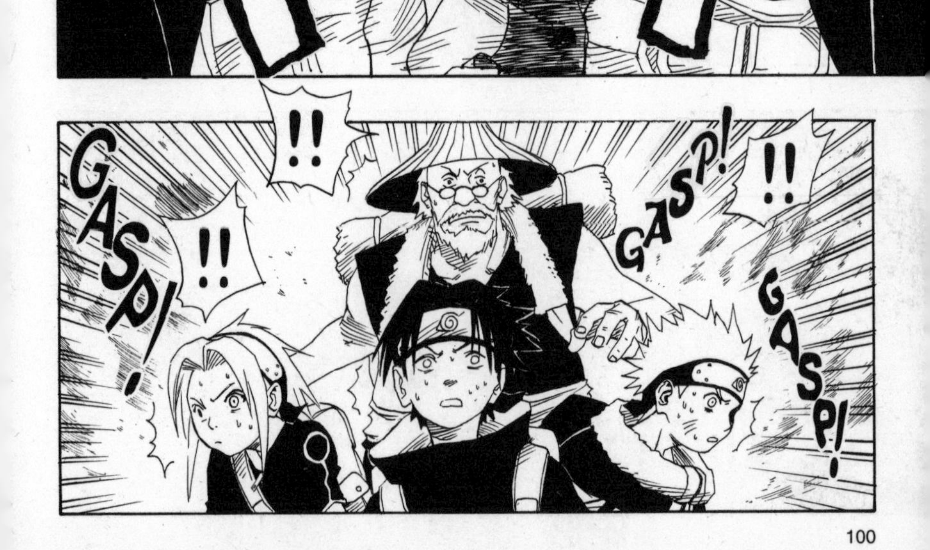
!!
GASP!
GASP!
!!
!!
GASP!

READ THIS WAY

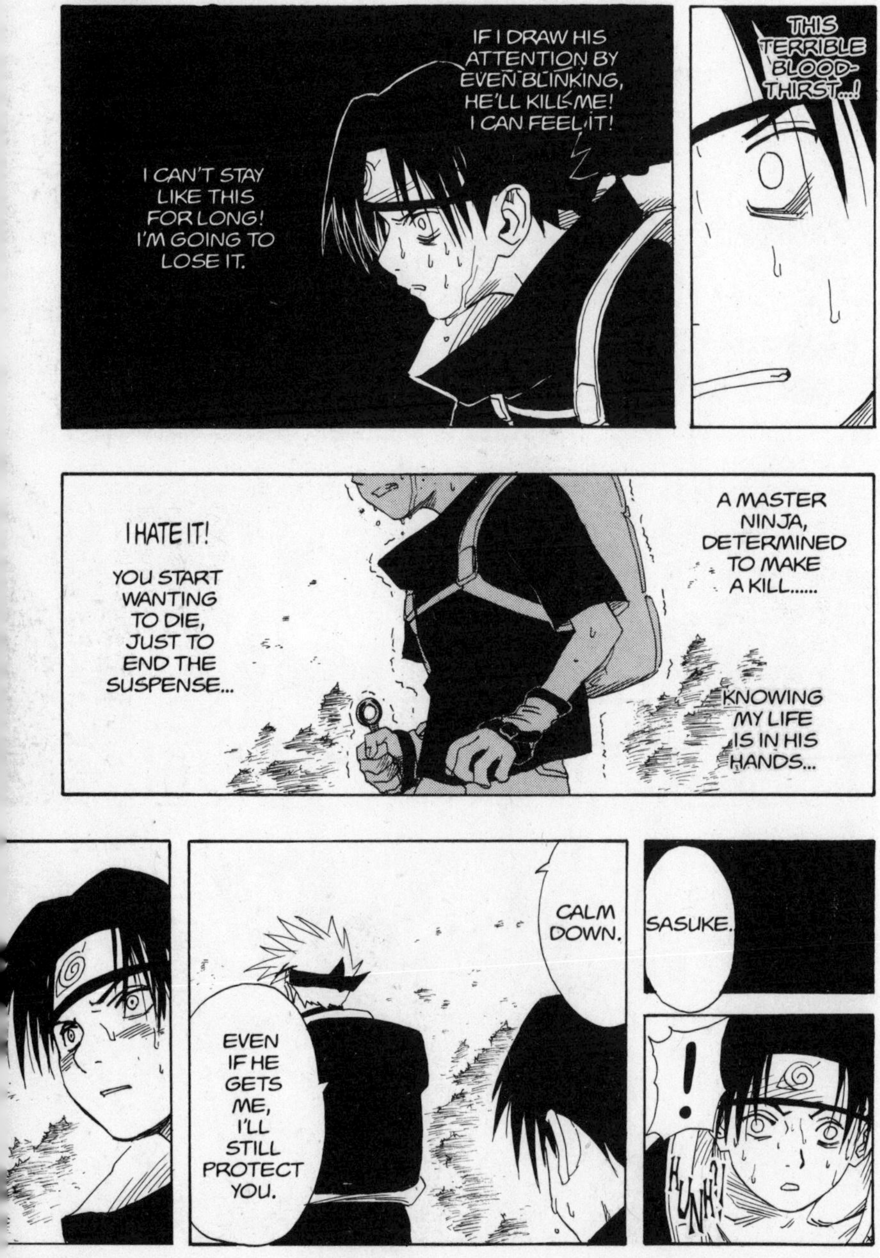

THIS TERRIBLE BLOOD-THIRST...!
IF I DRAW HIS ATTENTION BY EVEN BLINKING, HE'LL KILL ME! I CAN FEEL IT!
I CAN'T STAY LIKE THIS FOR LONG! I'M GOING TO LOSE IT.
A MASTER NINJA, DETERMINED TO MAKE A KILL......
KNOWING MY LIFE IS IN HIS HANDS...
I HATE IT!
YOU START WANTING TO DIE, JUST TO END THE SUSPENSE...
SASUKE.
!
HUNH!?
CALM DOWN.
EVEN IF HE GETS ME, I'LL STILL PROTECT YOU.

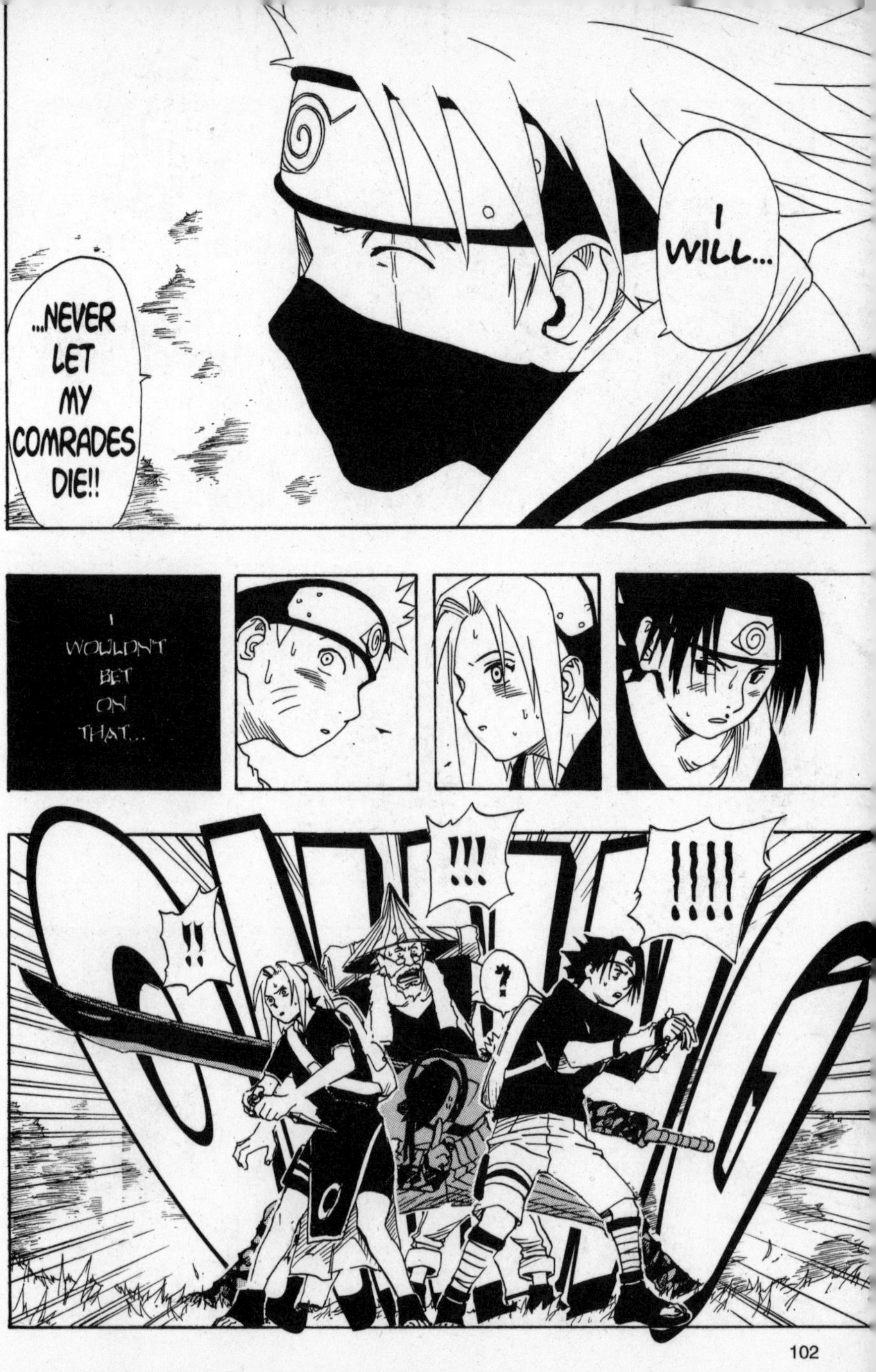
I WILL...
...NEVER LET MY COMRADES DIE!!
I WOULDN'T BET ON THAT...
!!!!
!!!
?
!!

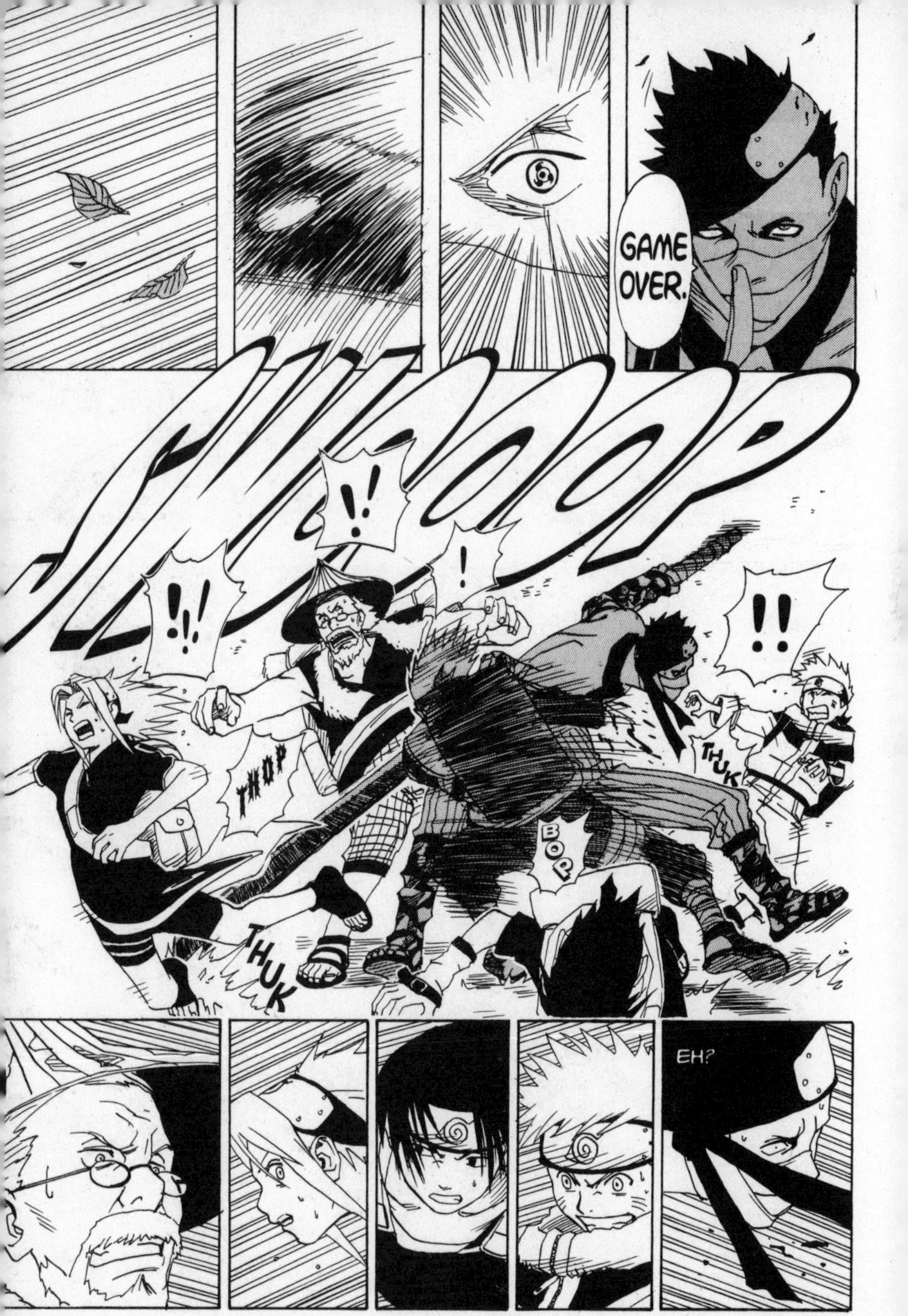
GAME OVER.
SHWOOP
!!
!
!!
!!!
THUK
BOP
THOP
THUK
EH?

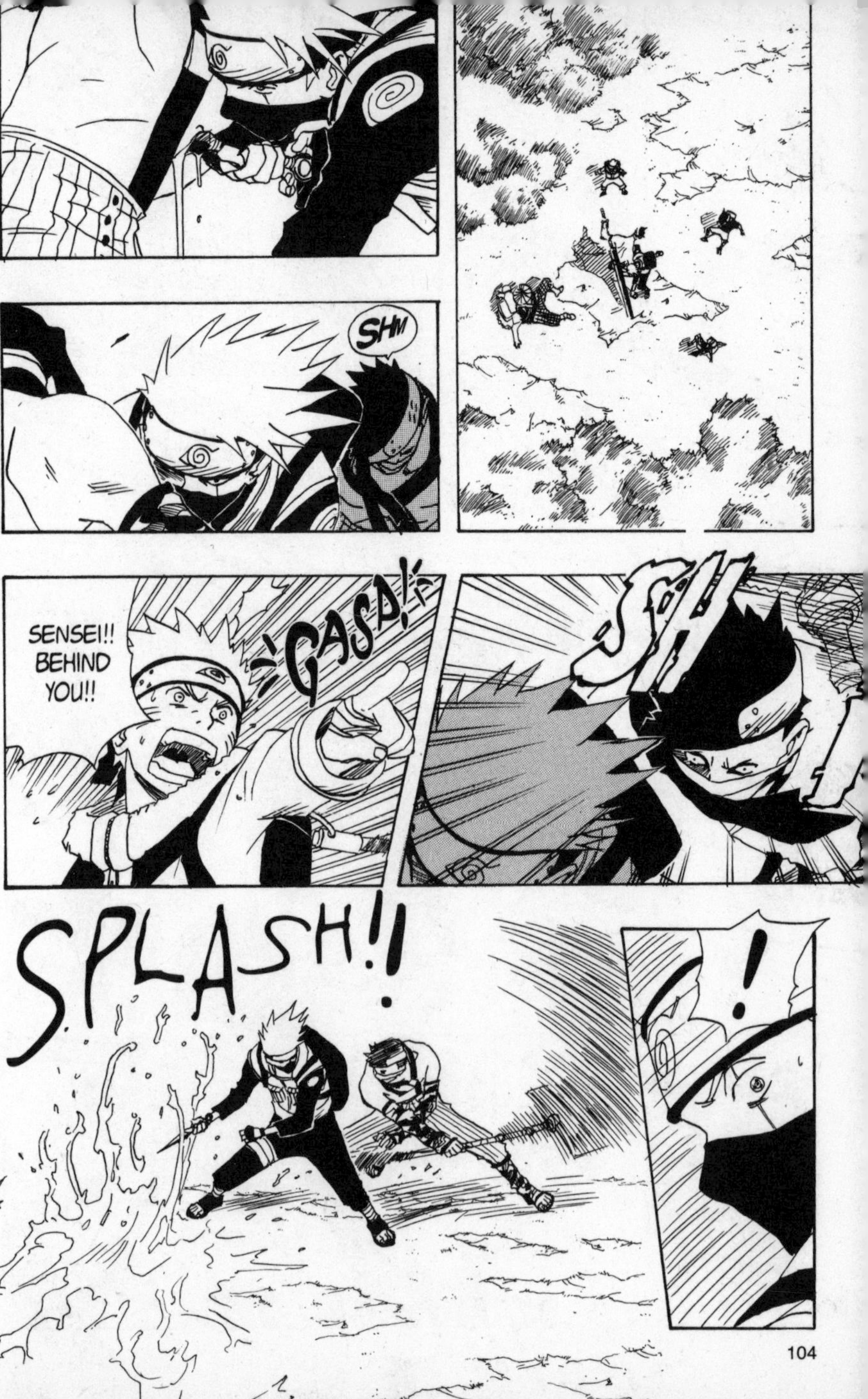
SHM
GASA!
SENSEI!!! BEHIND YOU!!
!
SPLASH!!

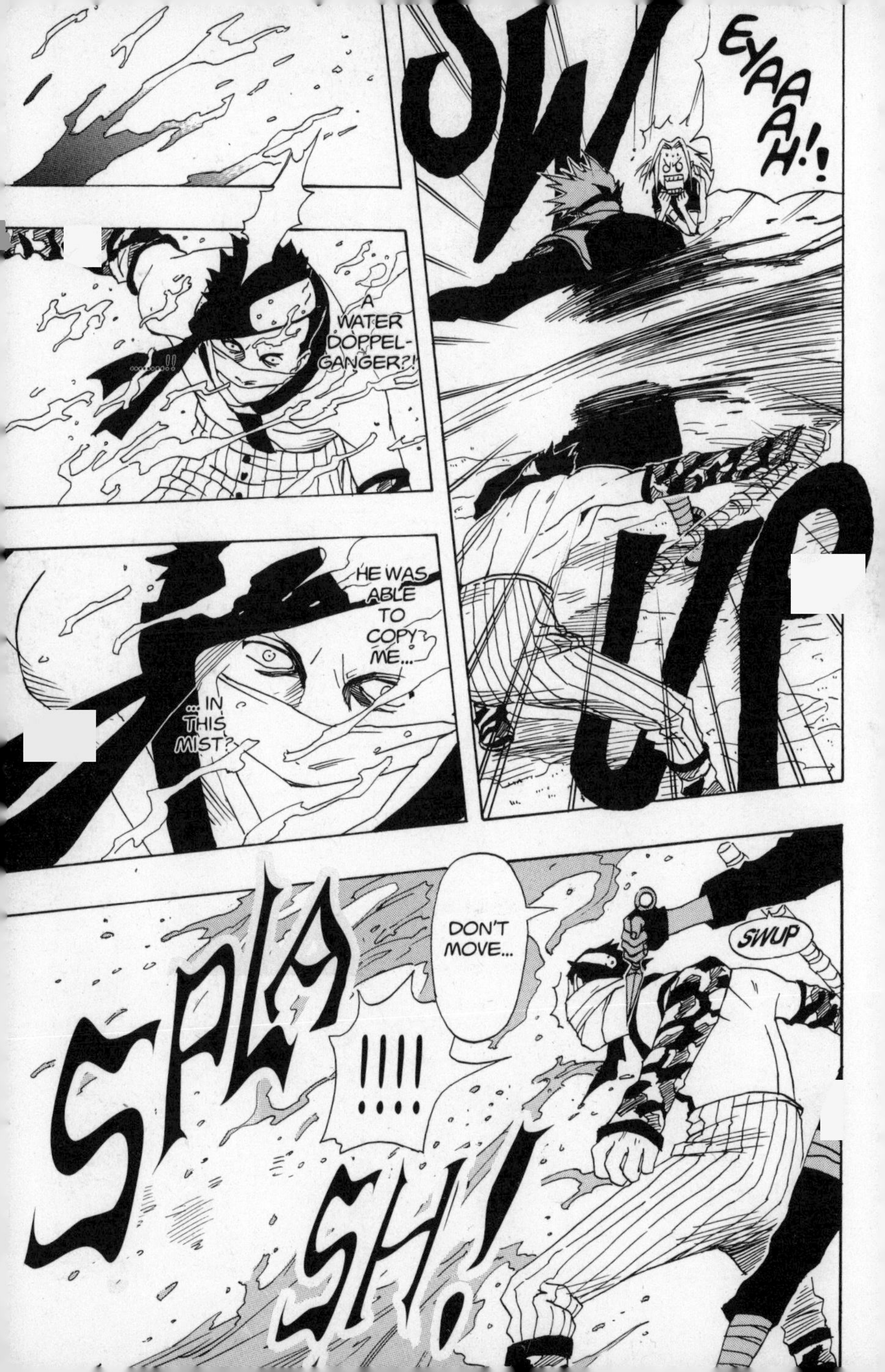

EYAAAH!!
SWUP
A WATER DOPPEL-GANGER?!
......!!
HE WAS ABLE TO COPY ME...
...IN THIS MIST?
SWUP
DON'T MOVE...
!!!!
SPLASH

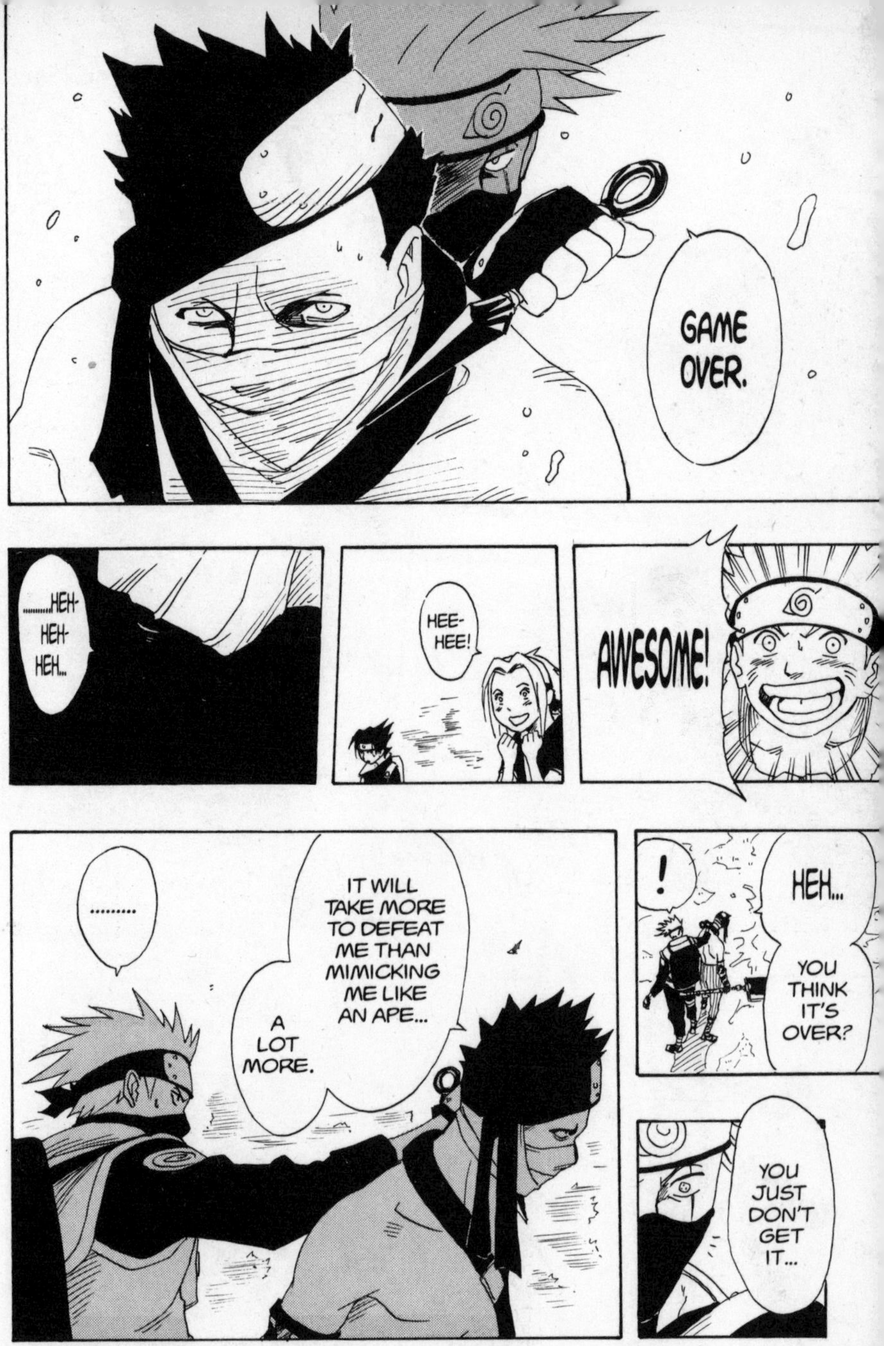
GAME OVER.
AWESOME!
HEE-HEE!
..........HEH-HEH-HEH...
HEH...
YOU THINK IT'S OVER?
!
YOU JUST DON'T GET IT...
IT WILL TAKE MORE TO DEFEAT ME THAN MIMICKING ME LIKE AN APE...
A LOT MORE.
....

NUMBER 13: NINJA!!

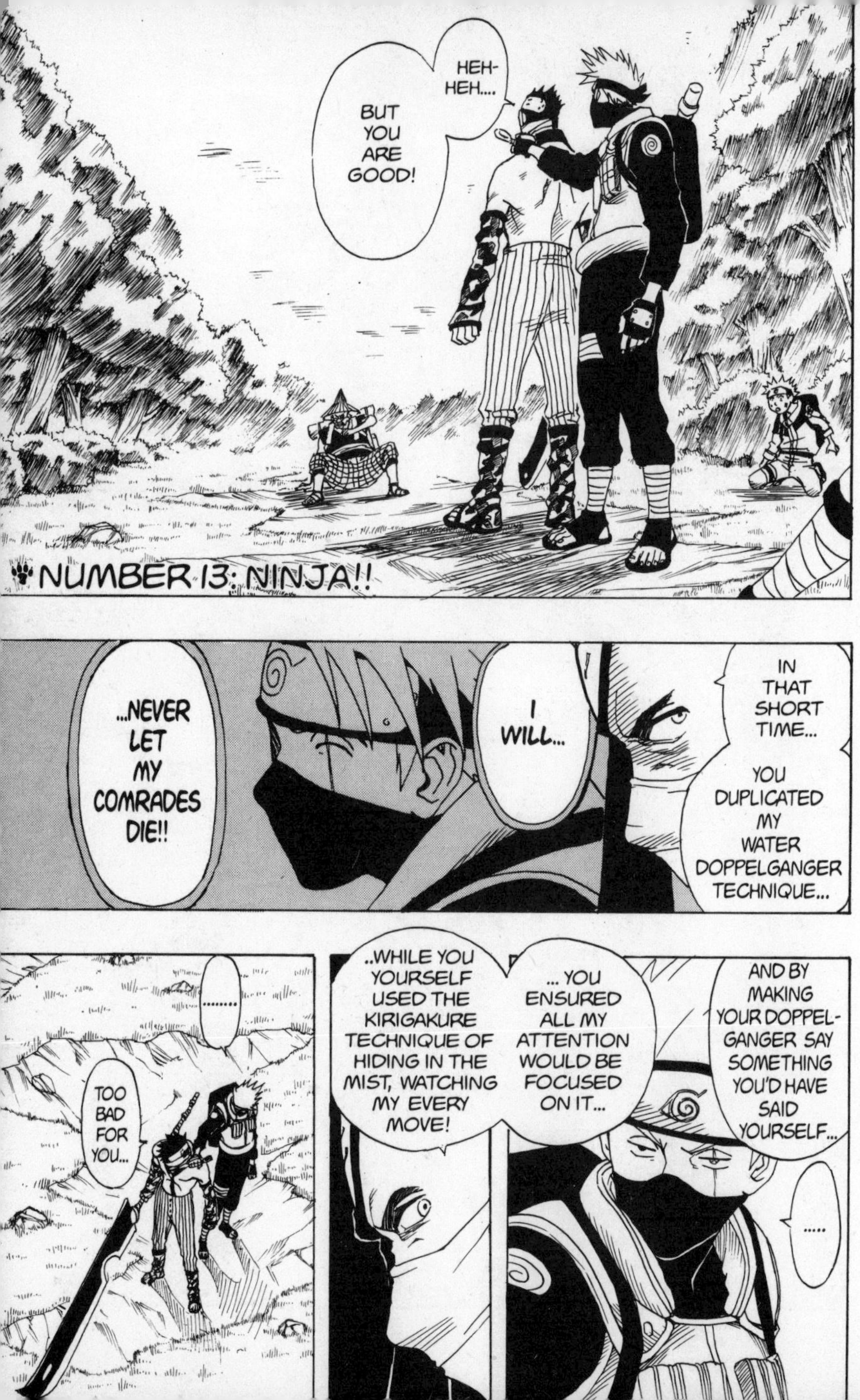
HEH-HEH....
BUT YOU ARE GOOD!
IN THAT SHORT TIME...
YOU DUPLICATED MY WATER DOPPELGANGER TECHNIQUE...
I WILL...
...NEVER LET MY COMRADES DIE!!
AND BY MAKING YOUR DOPPEL-GANGER SAY SOMETHING YOU'D HAVE SAID YOURSELF...
... YOU ENSURED ALL MY ATTENTION WOULD BE FOCUSED ON IT...
..WHILE YOU YOURSELF USED THE KIRIGAKURE TECHNIQUE OF HIDING IN THE MIST, WATCHING MY EVERY MOVE!
.....
....
TOO BAD FOR YOU...

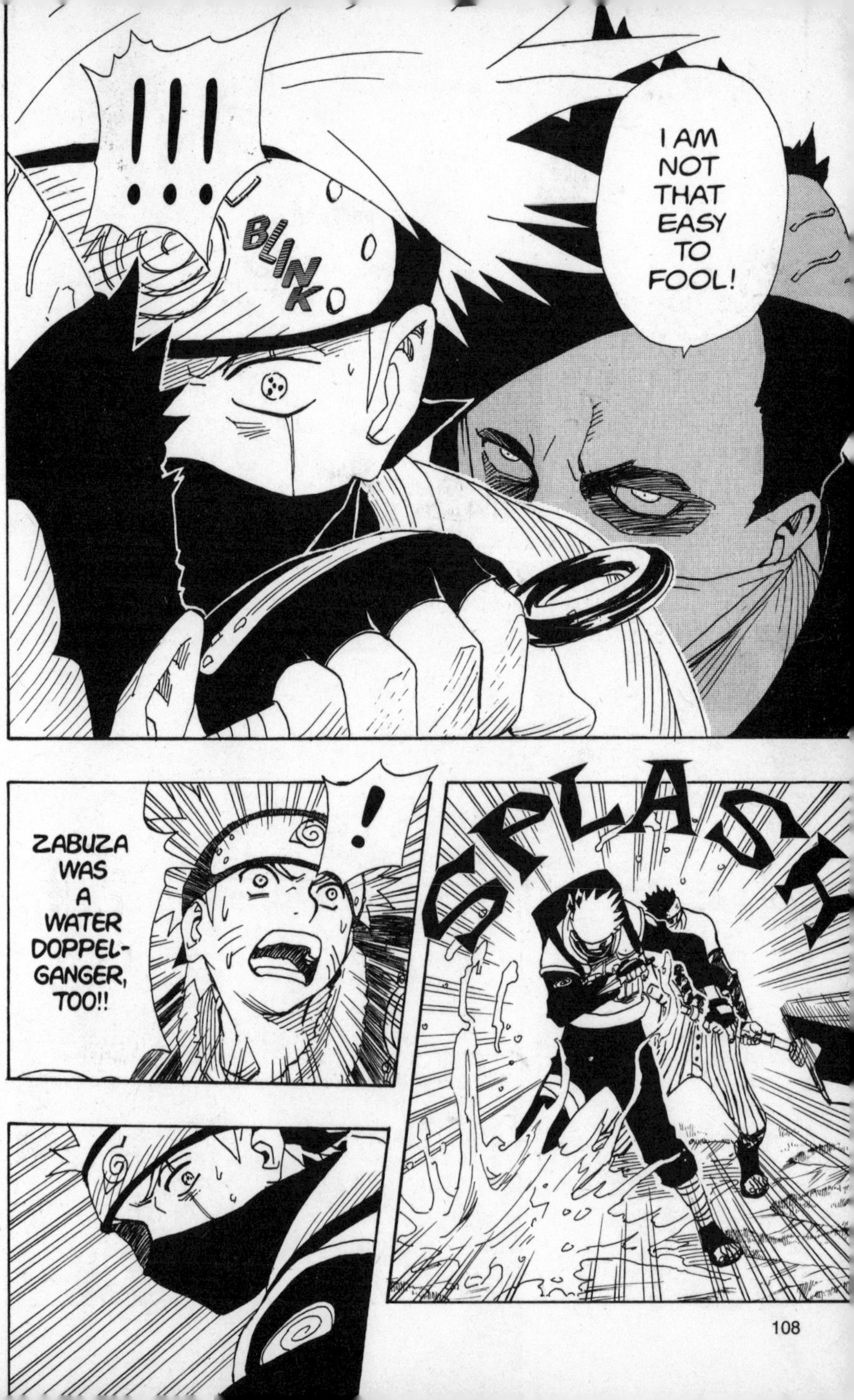
I AM NOT THAT EASY TO FOOL!
!!!...
BLINK
SPLASH
!
ZABUZA WAS A WATER DOPPEL-GANGER, TOO!!

Number 13: Ninja!!!

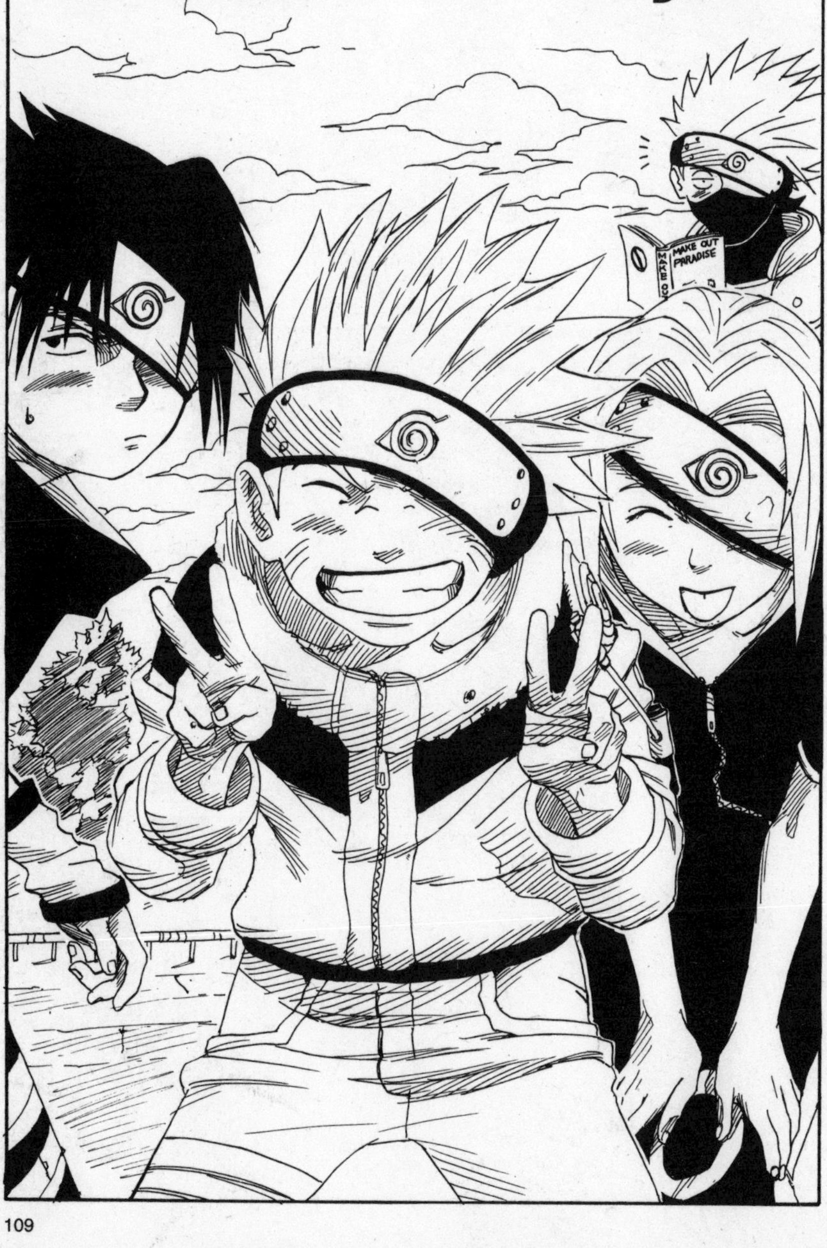
MAKE OUT PARADISE
MAKE OUT

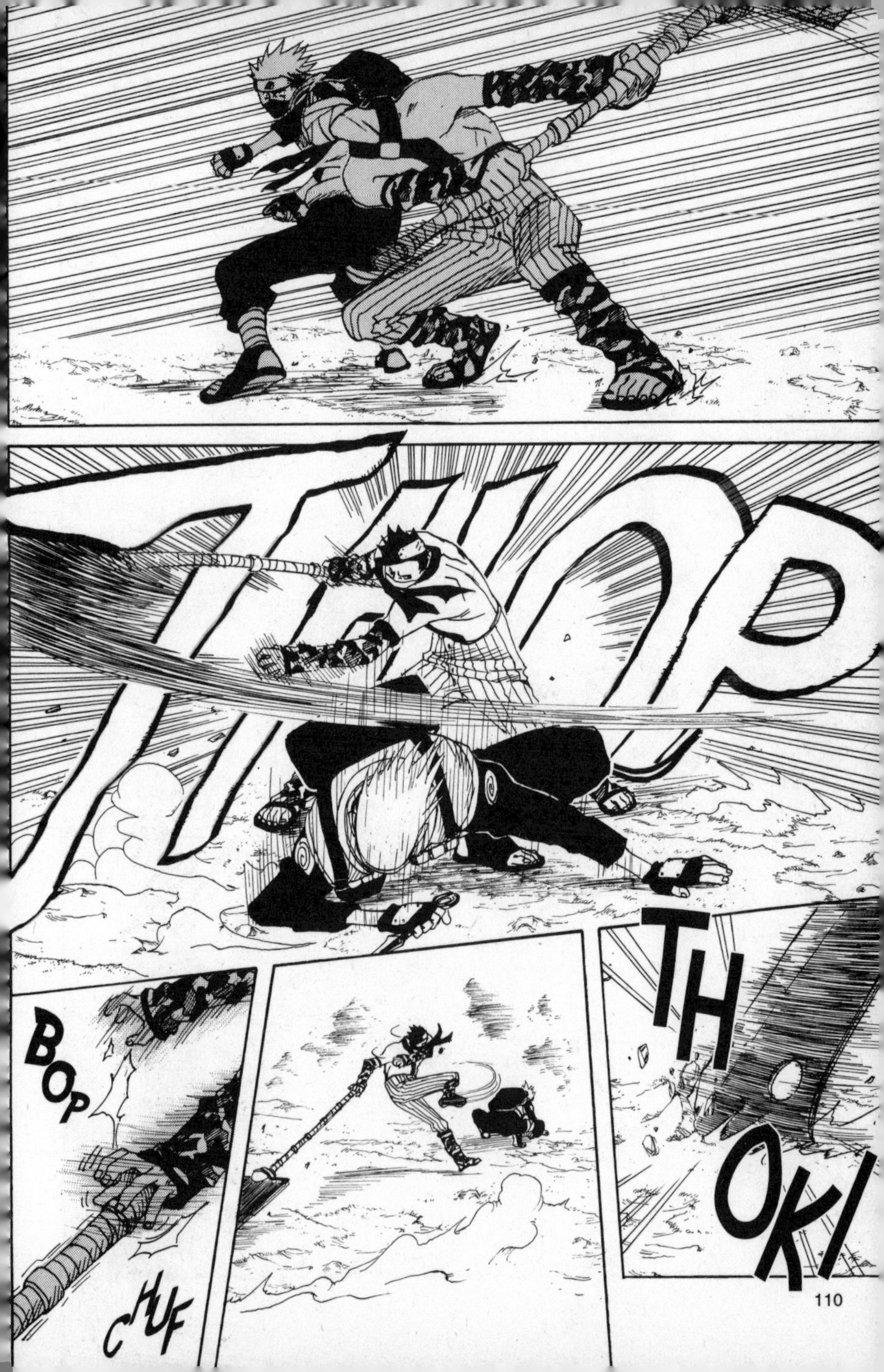
THOP
THOK!
BOP
CHUF

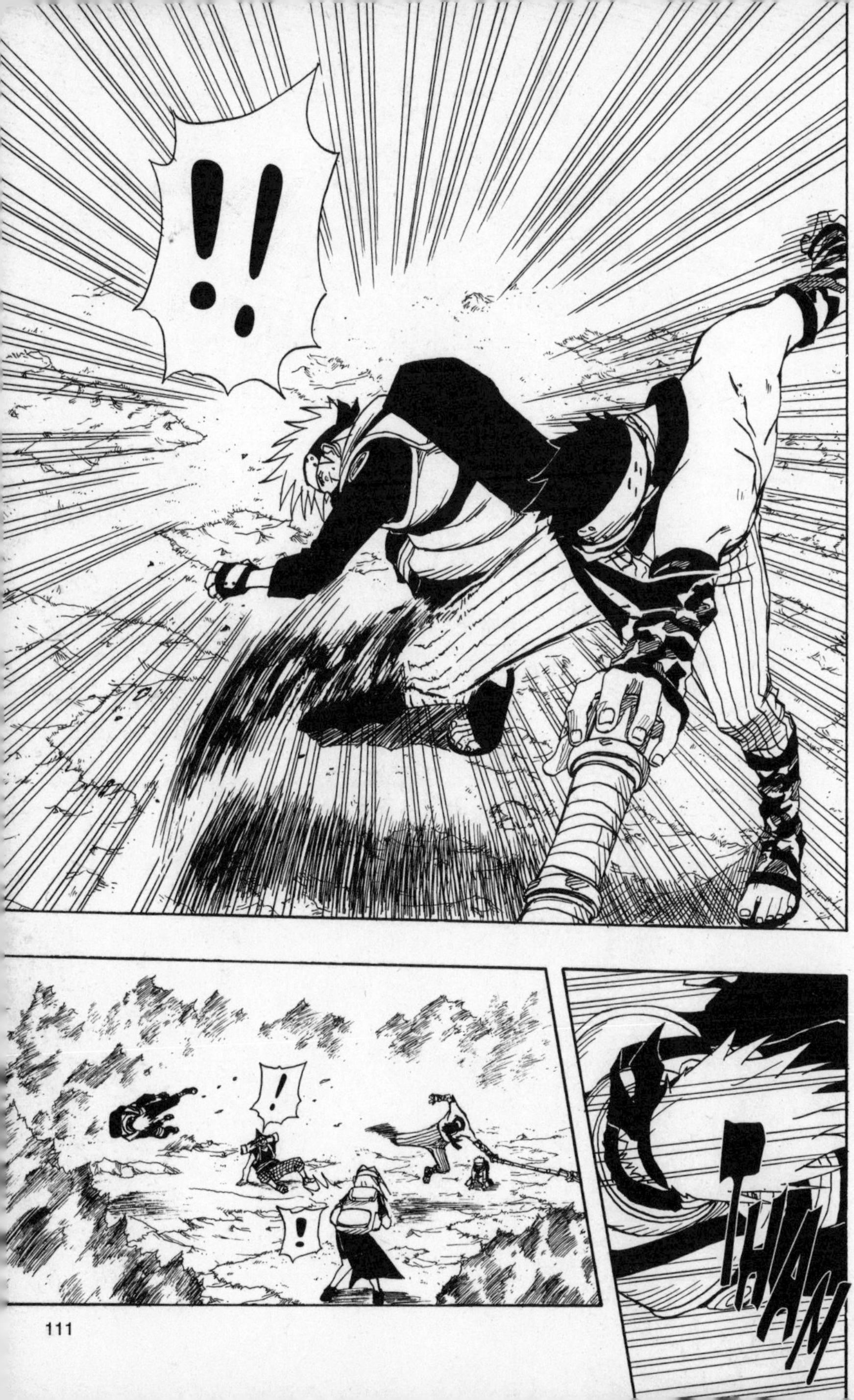
!!
CHAM
!
!

READ THIS WAY

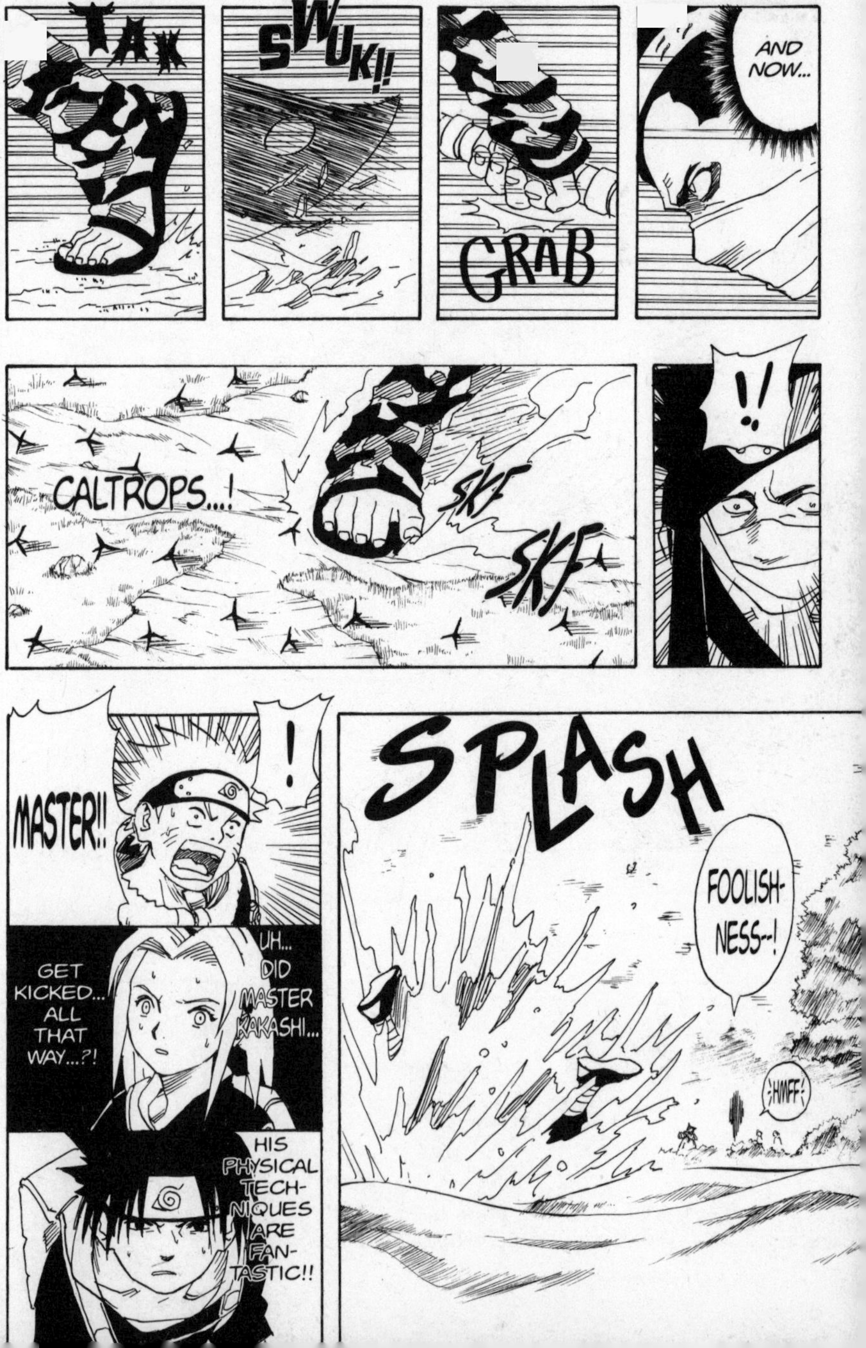
AND NOW...
GRAB
SWUK!!
TAK
!!
CALTROPS...!
SKF
SKF
SPLASH
FOOLISH-NESS--!
HMFF
!
MASTER!!
UH... DID MASTER KAKASHI...
GET KICKED... ALL THAT WAY...?!
HIS PHYSICAL TECH-NIQUES ARE FAN-TASTIC!!

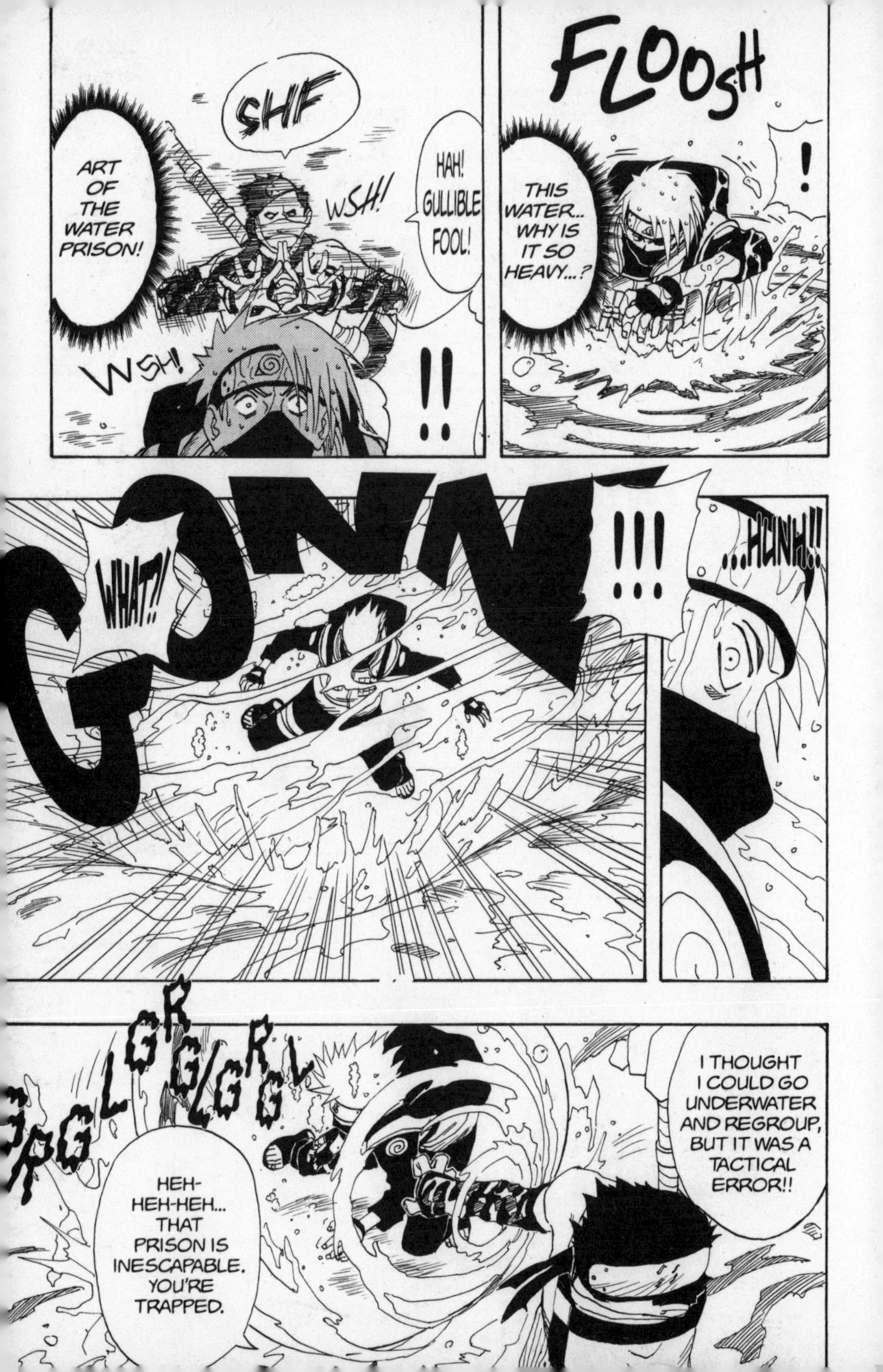
FLOOSH
!
THIS WATER... WHY IS IT SO HEAVY...?
SHF
HAH! GULLIBLE FOOL!
WSH!
ART OF THE WATER PRISON!
WSH!
!!
...HUNH!!
!!!
GONN
WHAT?!
I THOUGHT I COULD GO UNDERWATER AND REGROUP, BUT IT WAS A TACTICAL ERROR!!
HEH-HEH-HEH... THAT PRISON IS INESCAPABLE. YOU'RE TRAPPED.

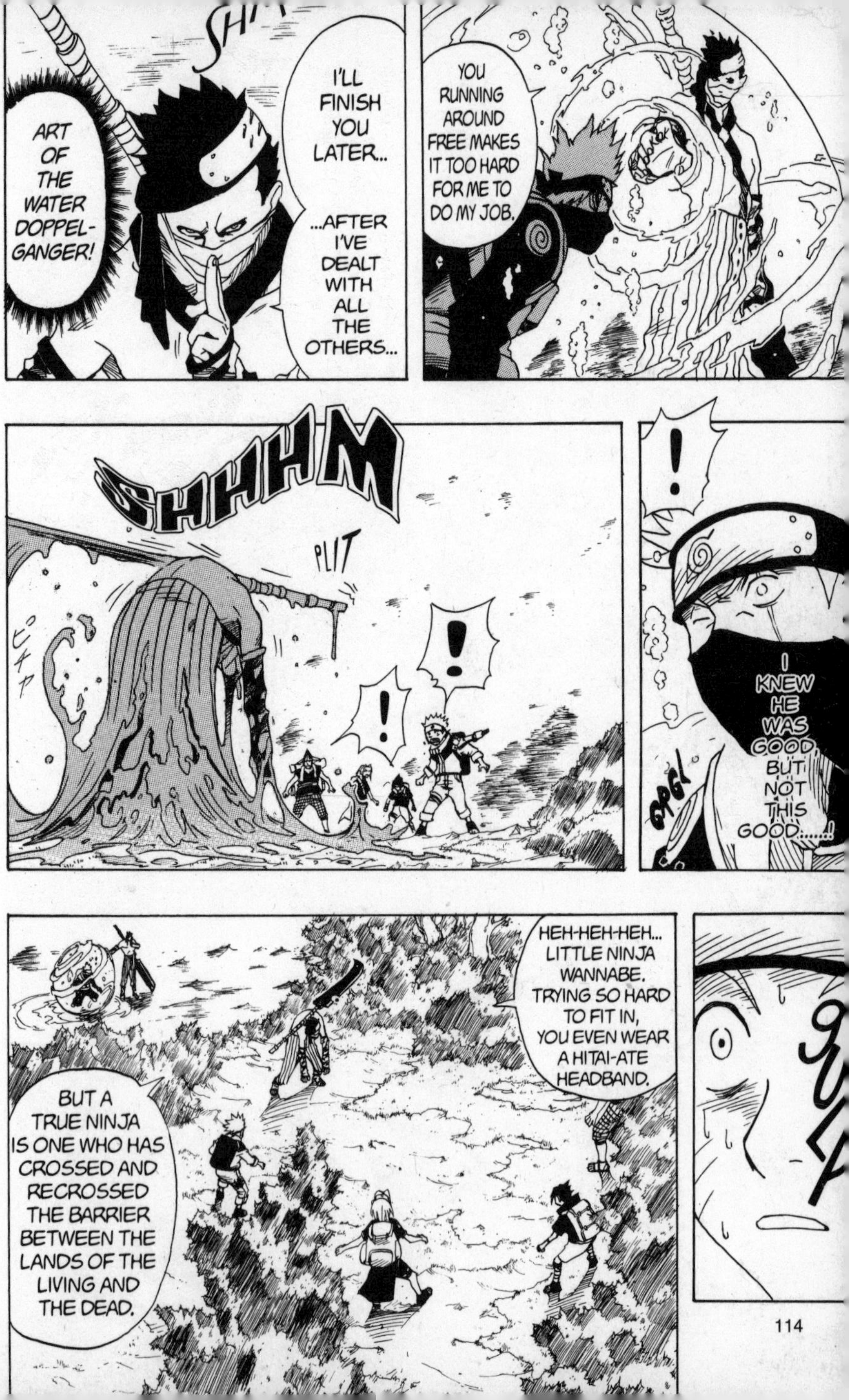
YOU RUNNING AROUND FREE MAKES IT TOO HARD FOR ME TO DO MY JOB.
I'LL FINISH YOU LATER...
...AFTER I'VE DEALT WITH ALL THE OTHERS...
ART OF THE WATER DOPPEL-GANGER!
!
I KNEW HE WAS GOOD BUT NOT THIS GOOD......!
SHHHM
PLIT
!
!
GULP
HEH-HEH-HEH... LITTLE NINJA WANNABE. TRYING SO HARD TO FIT IN, YOU EVEN WEAR A HITAI-ATE HEADBAND.
BUT A TRUE NINJA IS ONE WHO HAS CROSSED AND RECROSSED THE BARRIER BETWEEN THE LANDS OF THE LIVING AND THE DEAD.

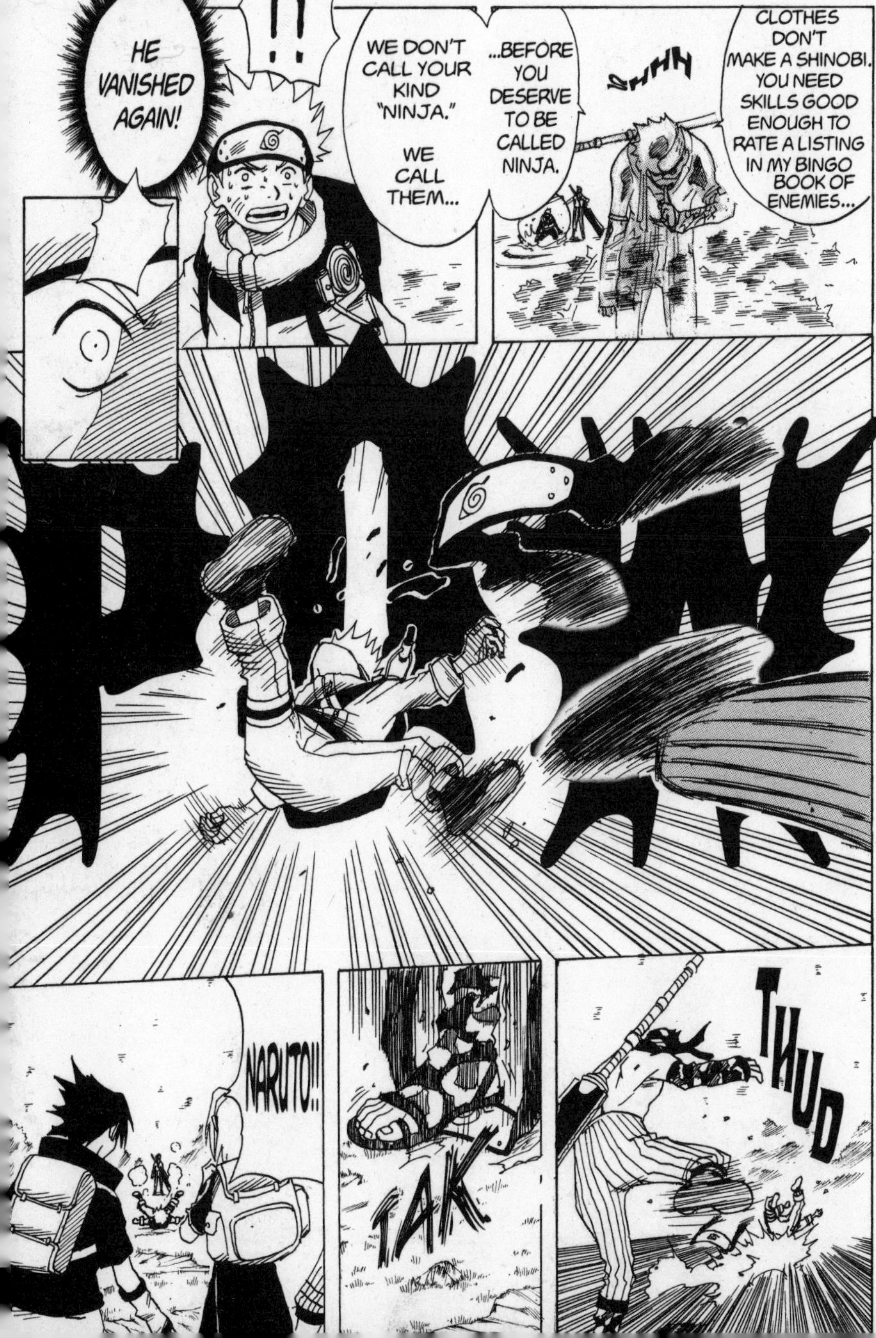
CLOTHES DON'T MAKE A SHINOBI. YOU NEED SKILLS GOOD ENOUGH TO RATE A LISTING IN MY BINGO BOOK OF ENEMIES...
...BEFORE YOU DESERVE TO BE CALLED NINJA.
WE DON'T CALL YOUR KIND "NINJA." WE CALL THEM...
!!
HE VANISHED AGAIN!
THUD
TAK
NARUTO!!

READ THIS WAY

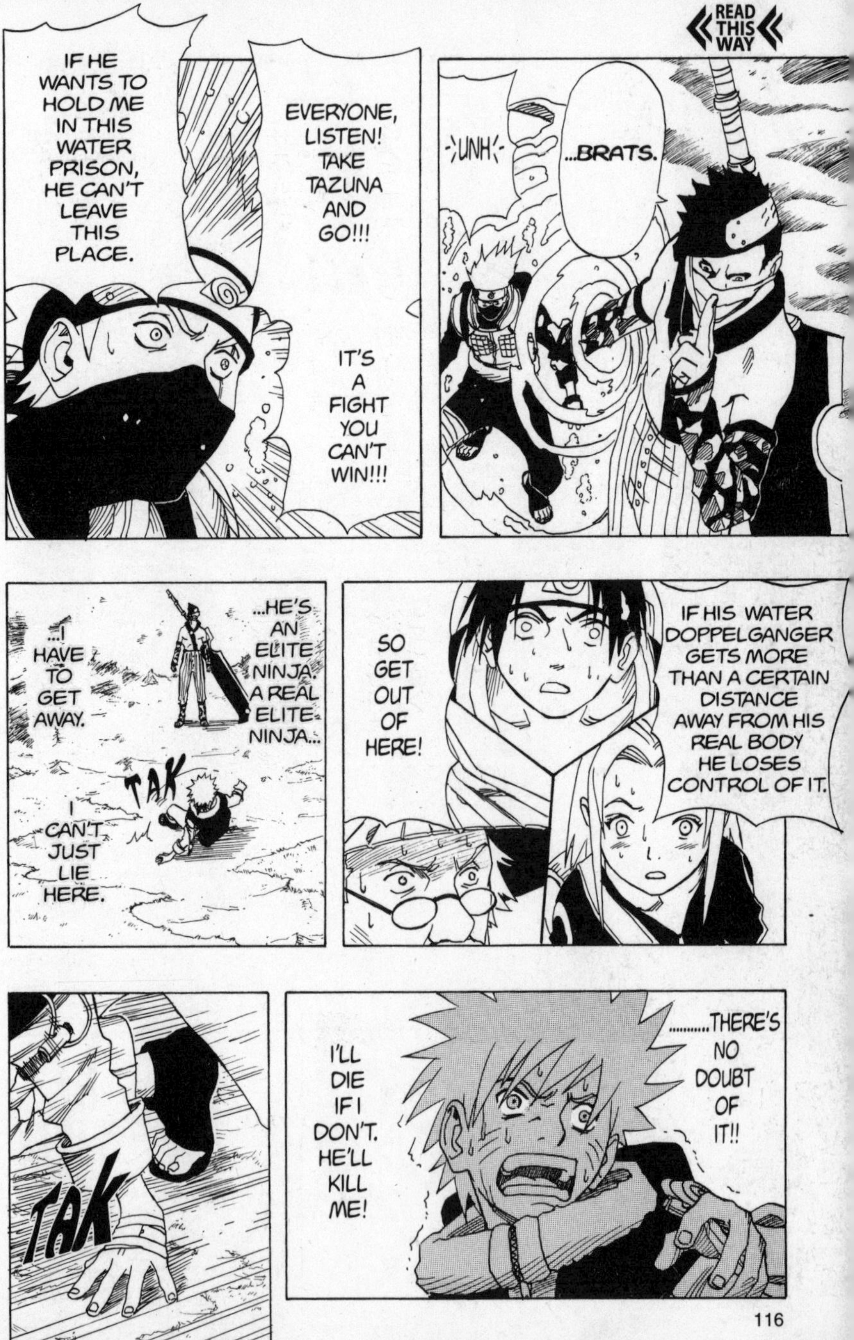

UNH
...BRATS.
IF HE WANTS TO HOLD ME IN THIS WATER PRISON, HE CAN'T LEAVE THIS PLACE.
EVERYONE, LISTEN! TAKE TAZUNA AND GO!!!
IT'S A FIGHT YOU CAN'T WIN!!!
IF HIS WATER DOPPELGANGER GETS MORE THAN A CERTAIN DISTANCE AWAY FROM HIS REAL BODY HE LOSES CONTROL OF IT.
SO GET OUT OF HERE!
...HE'S AN ELITE NINJA. A REAL ELITE NINJA...
...I HAVE TO GET AWAY.
TAK
I CAN'T JUST LIE HERE.
..........THERE'S NO DOUBT OF IT!!
I'LL DIE IF I DON'T. HE'LL KILL ME!
TAK

READ THIS WAY

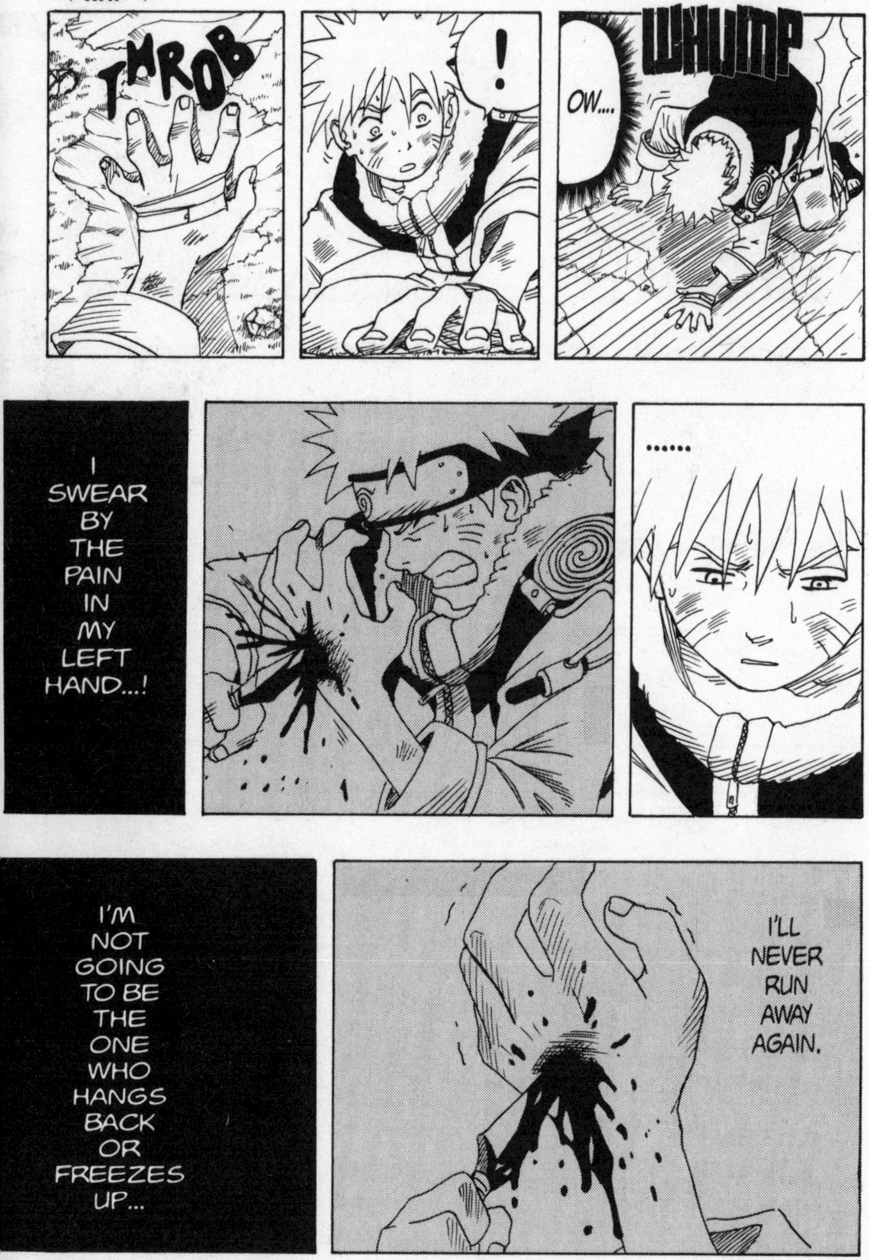
WHUMP
OW....
!
THROB
......
I SWEAR BY THE PAIN IN MY LEFT HAND...!
I'LL NEVER RUN AWAY AGAIN.
I'M NOT GOING TO BE THE ONE WHO HANGS BACK OR FREEZES UP...

READ THIS WAY

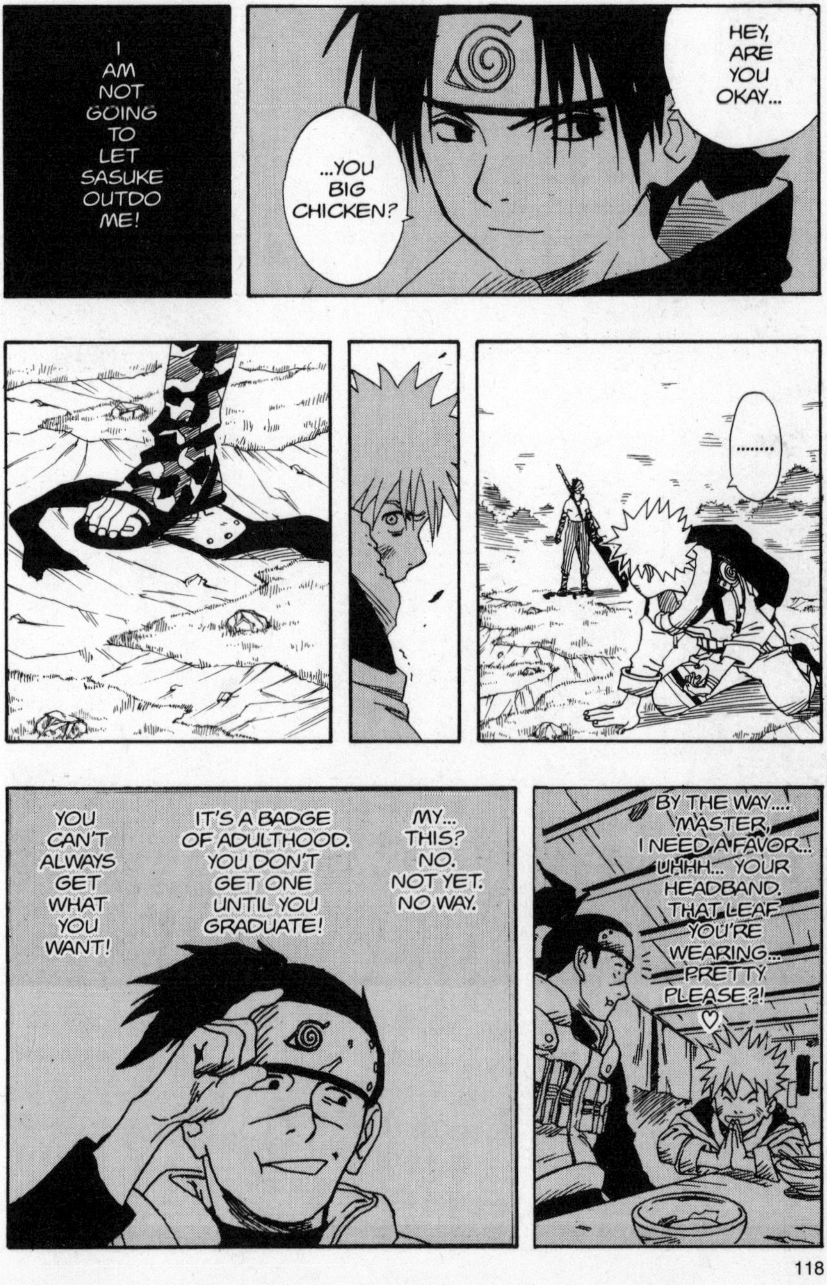
HEY, ARE YOU OKAY...
...YOU BIG CHICKEN?
I AM NOT GOING TO LET SASUKE OUTDO ME!
....
BY THE WAY.... MASTER, I NEED A FAVOR... UHHH... YOUR HEADBAND. THAT LEAF YOU'RE WEARING... PRETTY PLEASE?!
MY... THIS? NO. NOT YET. NO WAY.
IT'S A BADGE OF ADULTHOOD. YOU DON'T GET ONE UNTIL YOU GRADUATE!
YOU CAN'T ALWAYS GET WHAT YOU WANT!

READ THIS WAY

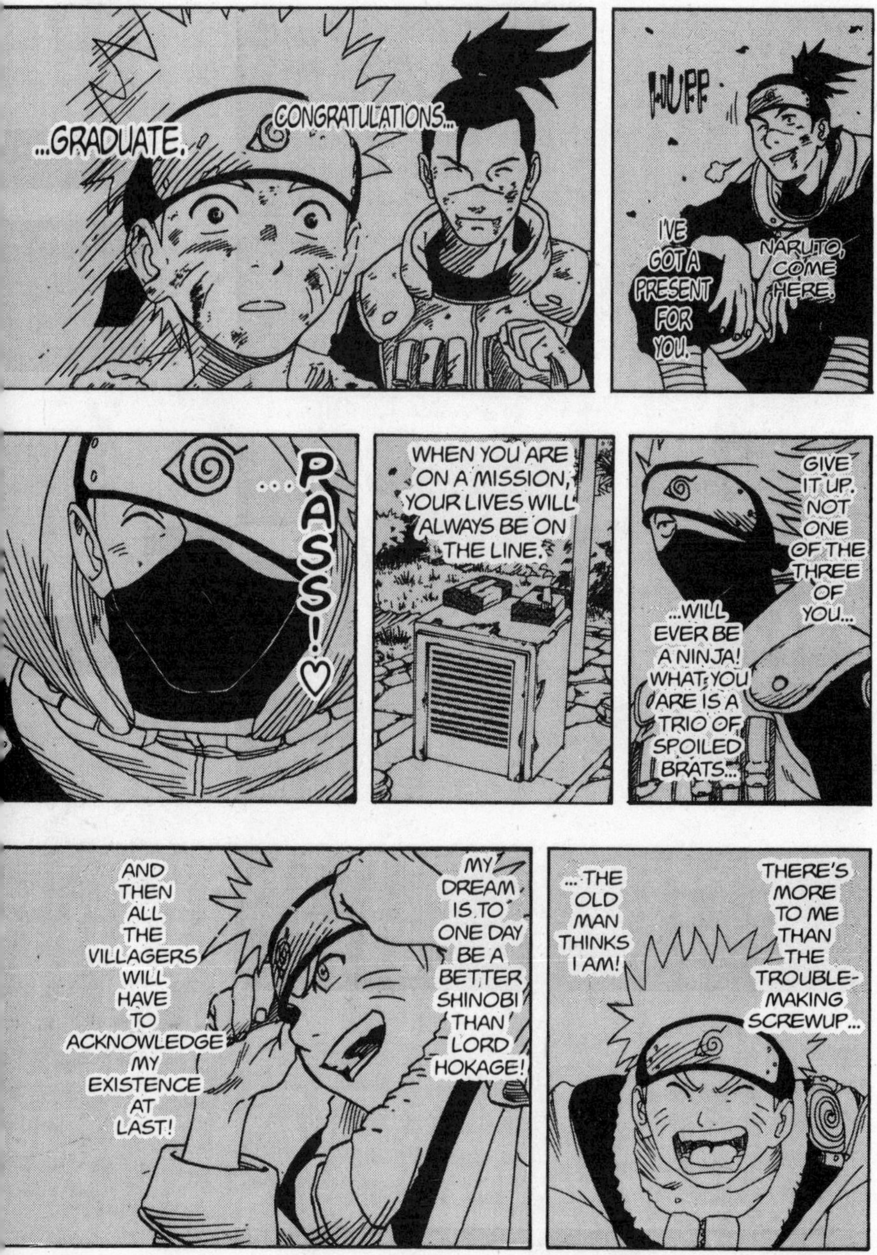
WUFF
NARUTO, COME HERE.
I'VE GOT A PRESENT FOR YOU.
CONGRATULATIONS...
...GRADUATE.
GIVE IT UP. NOT ONE OF THE THREE OF YOU...
...WILL EVER BE A NINJA! WHAT YOU ARE IS A TRIO OF SPOILED BRATS...
WHEN YOU ARE ON A MISSION, YOUR LIVES WILL ALWAYS BE ON THE LINE.
...PASS!♥
THERE'S MORE TO ME THAN THE TROUBLE-MAKING SCREWUP...
...THE OLD MAN THINKS I AM!
MY DREAM IS TO ONE DAY BE A BETTER SHINOBI THAN LORD HOKAGE!
AND THEN ALL THE VILLAGERS WILL HAVE TO ACKNOWLEDGE MY EXISTENCE AT LAST!

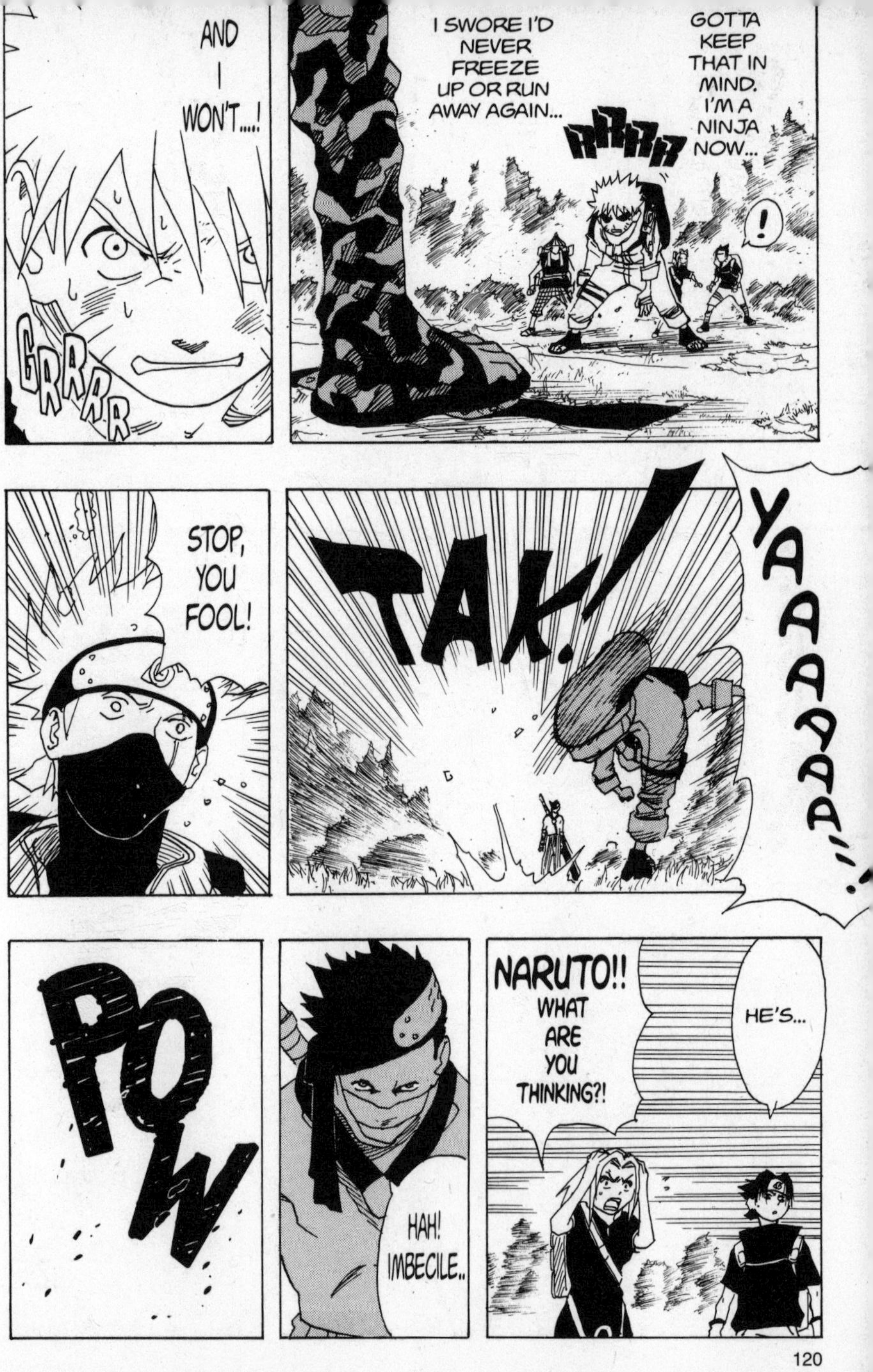
GOTTA KEEP THAT IN MIND. I'M A NINJA NOW...
I SWORE I'D NEVER FREEZE UP OR RUN AWAY AGAIN...
RRRR
!
AND I WON'T....!
GRRRR
YAAAAAA!!
TAK!!
STOP, YOU FOOL!
HE'S...
NARUTO!! WHAT ARE YOU THINKING?!
HAH! IMBECILE..
POW

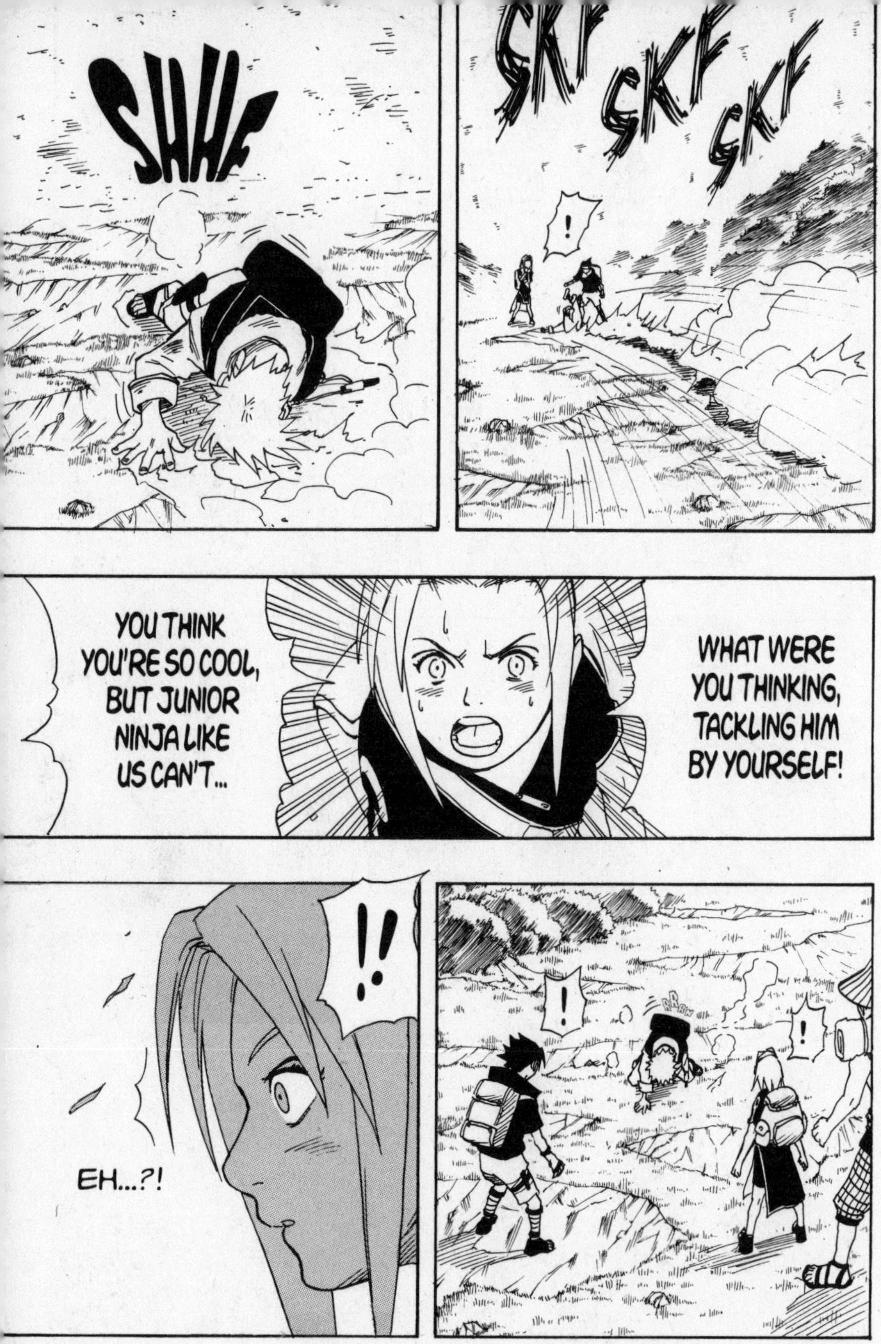
SKF SKF SKF
!
SWHF
WHAT WERE YOU THINKING, TACKLING HIM BY YOURSELF!
YOU THINK YOU'RE SO COOL, BUT JUNIOR NINJA LIKE US CAN'T...
!
!
!!
EH...?!

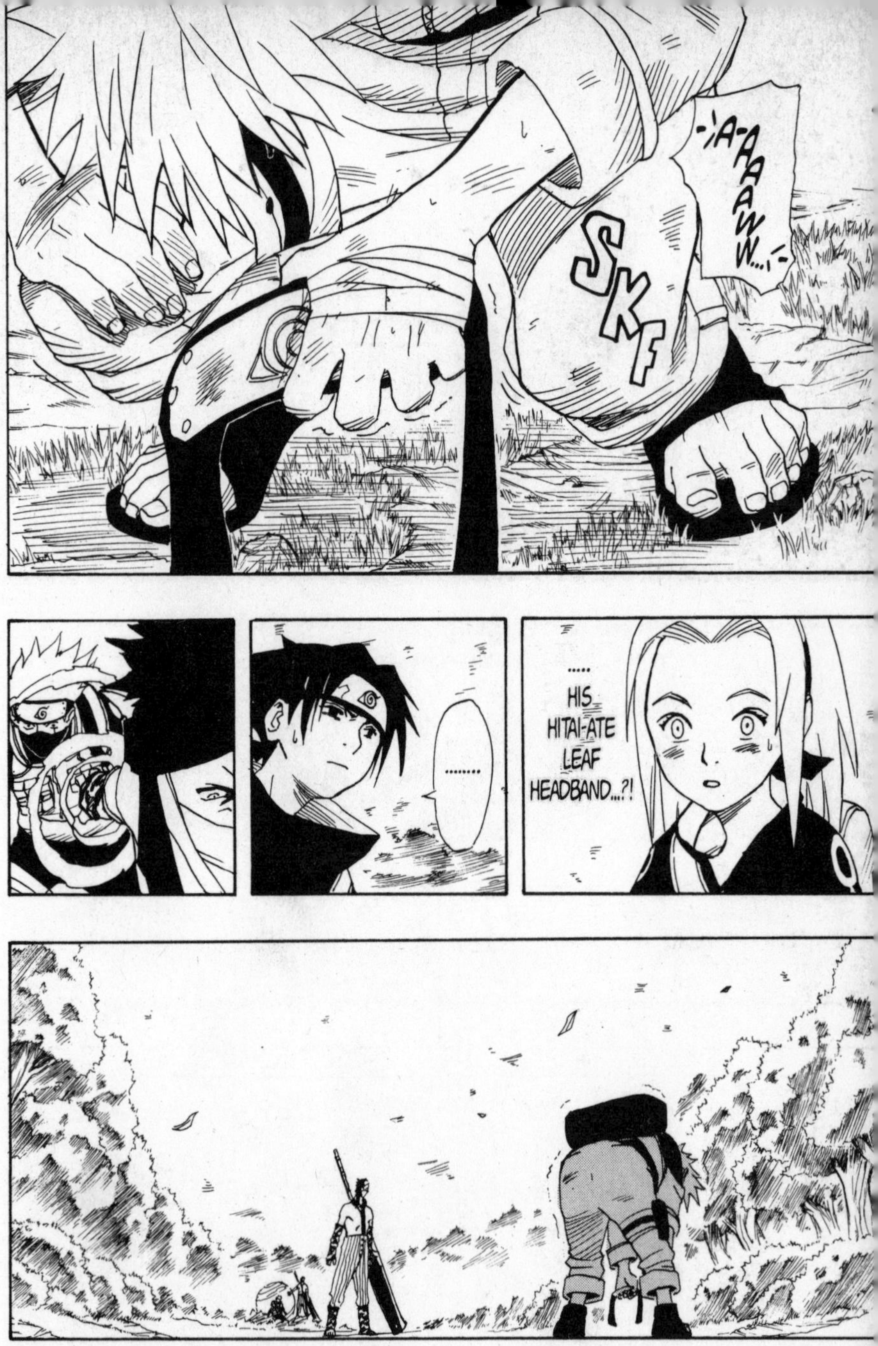
¡A-AAAWW...!
SKF
..... HIS HITAI-ATE LEAF HEADBAND...?!
....

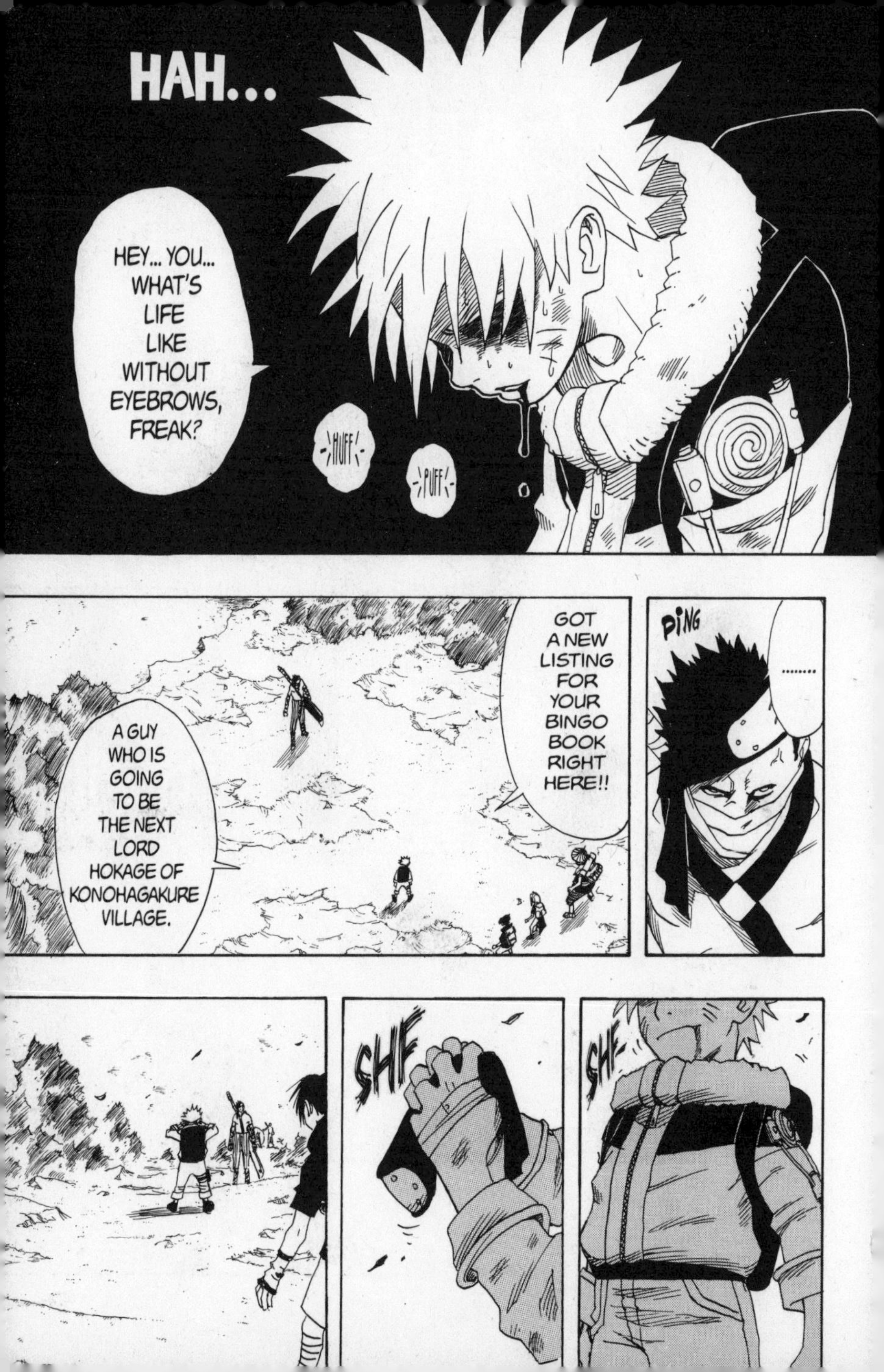
HAH...
HEY... YOU... WHAT'S LIFE LIKE WITHOUT EYEBROWS, FREAK?
HUFF
PUFF
PING
....
GOT A NEW LISTING FOR YOUR BINGO BOOK RIGHT HERE!!
A GUY WHO IS GOING TO BE THE NEXT LORD HOKAGE OF KONOHAGAKURE VILLAGE.
SHF
SHF

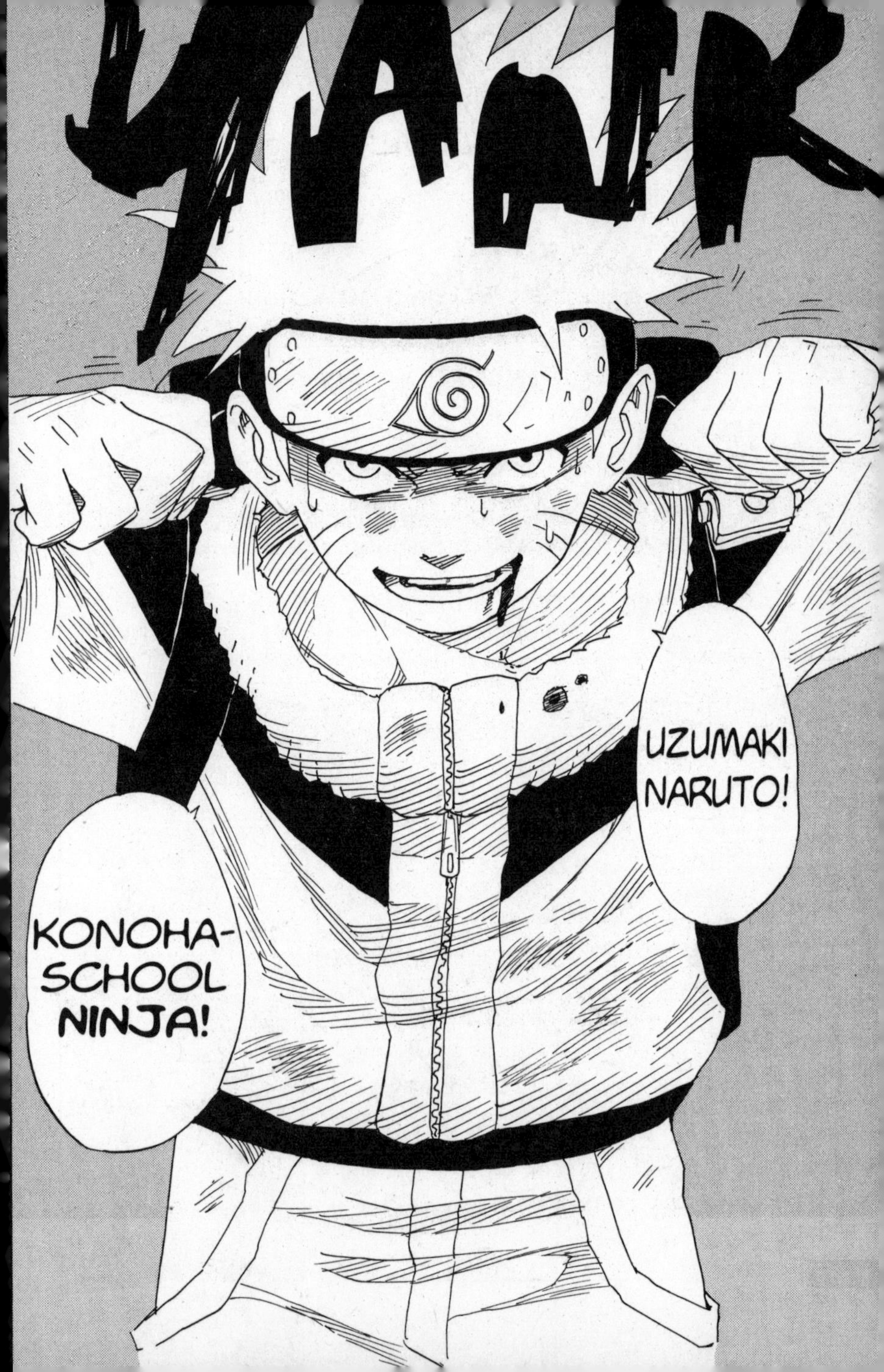
UZUMAKI NARUTO!
KONOHA-SCHOOL NINJA!

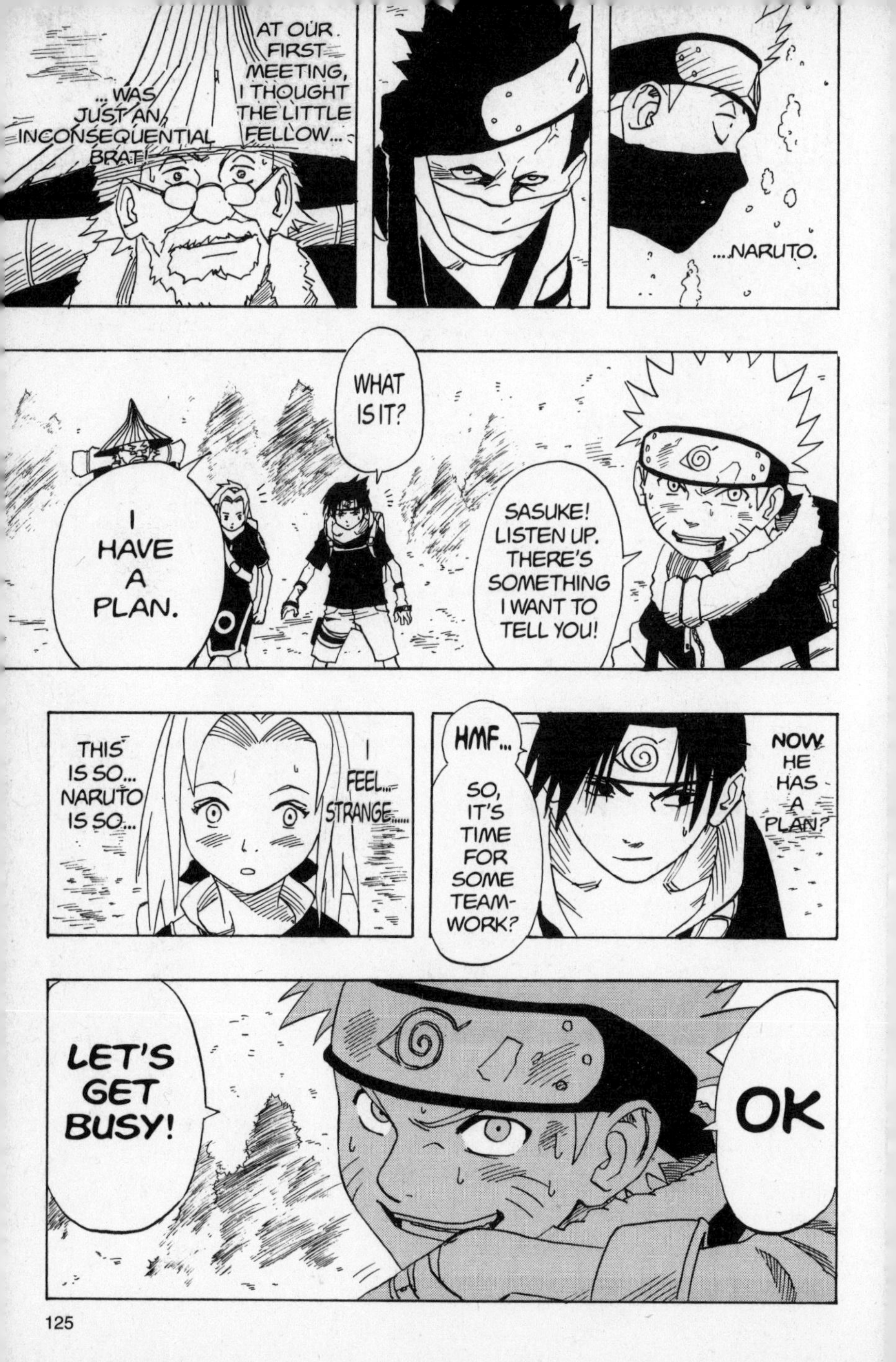
....NARUTO.
AT OUR FIRST MEETING, I THOUGHT THE LITTLE FELLOW...
... WAS JUST AN INCONSEQUENTIAL BRAT
SASUKE! LISTEN UP. THERE'S SOMETHING I WANT TO TELL YOU!
WHAT IS IT?
I HAVE A PLAN.
NOW HE HAS A PLAN?
HMF...
SO, IT'S TIME FOR SOME TEAM-WORK?
I FEEL... STRANGE.....
THIS IS SO... NARUTO IS SO...
OK
LET'S GET BUSY!

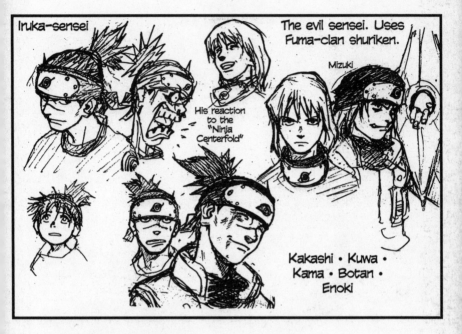

Iruka-sensei

The evil sensei. Uses Fuma-clan shuriken.

Mizuki

His reaction to the "Ninja Centerfold"

Kakashi • Kuwa • Kama • Botan • Enoki

IRUKA & MIZUKI

These were my first sketches of Iruka and Mizuki (see **Naruto** Vol. 1). In the final version, Mizuki's bangs are parted in the center, but otherwise he's pretty much the same. Iruka used to have a more evil look around his eyes, and sharper cheekbones, but I made him more relaxed and younger-looking.

One more thing. When I was originally planning who Iruka and Mizuki's teacher was going to be, I decided on the next teacher's name at the same time. If you look in the bottom right corner, you can see some of the names I considered: *Kakashi* ("scarecrow"), *Kuwa* ("hoe"), *Kama* ("scythe"), *Botan* ("peony" or "button") and *Enoki* (a Chinese nettle tree). Looking back at it, though, I'm really glad I used "Kakashi."

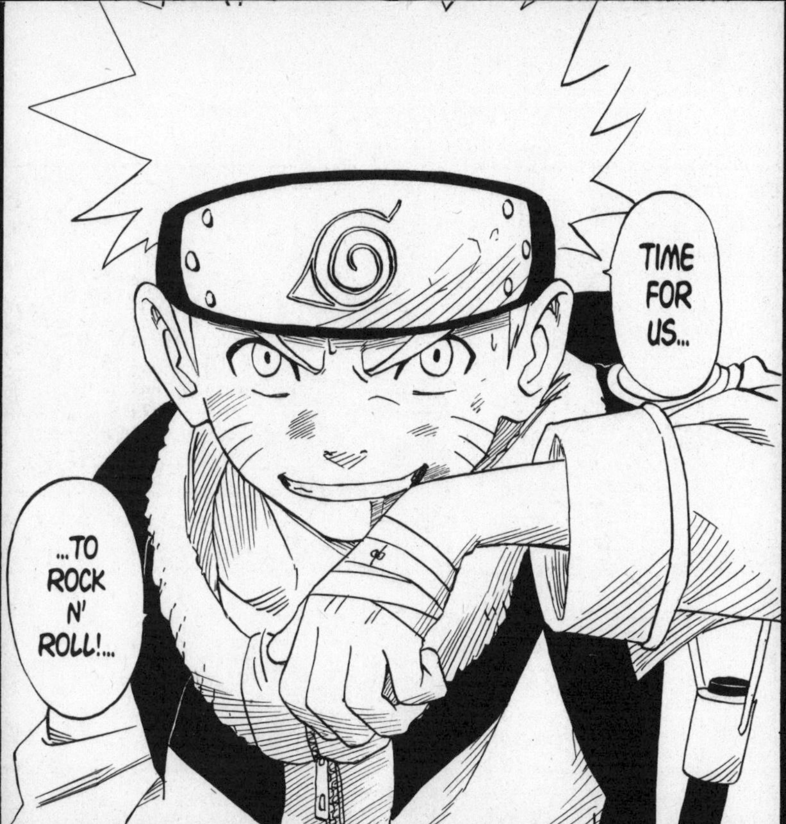
TIME FOR US...
...TO ROCK N' ROLL!...

Number 14: The Secret Plan !!!

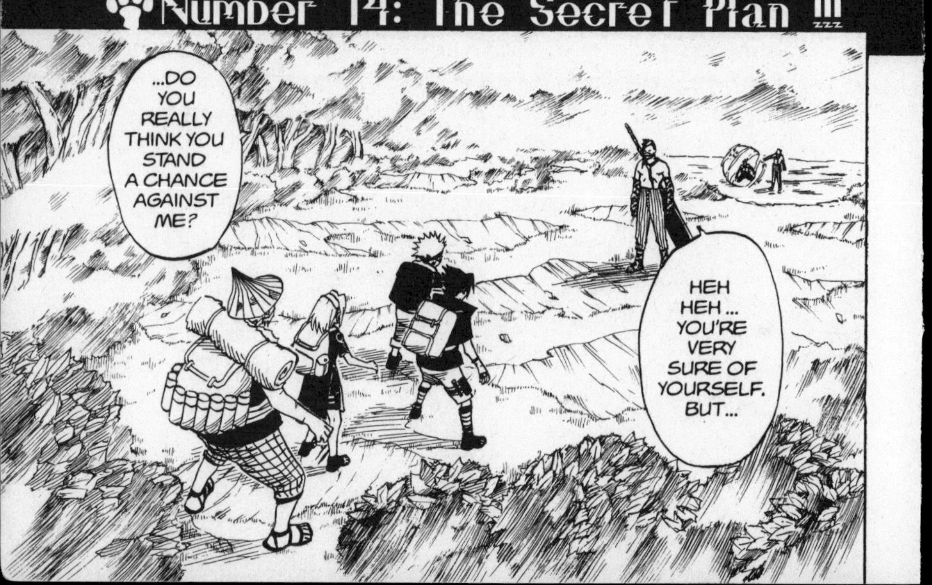
HEH HEH ... YOU'RE VERY SURE OF YOURSELF. BUT...
...DO YOU REALLY THINK YOU STAND A CHANCE AGAINST ME?

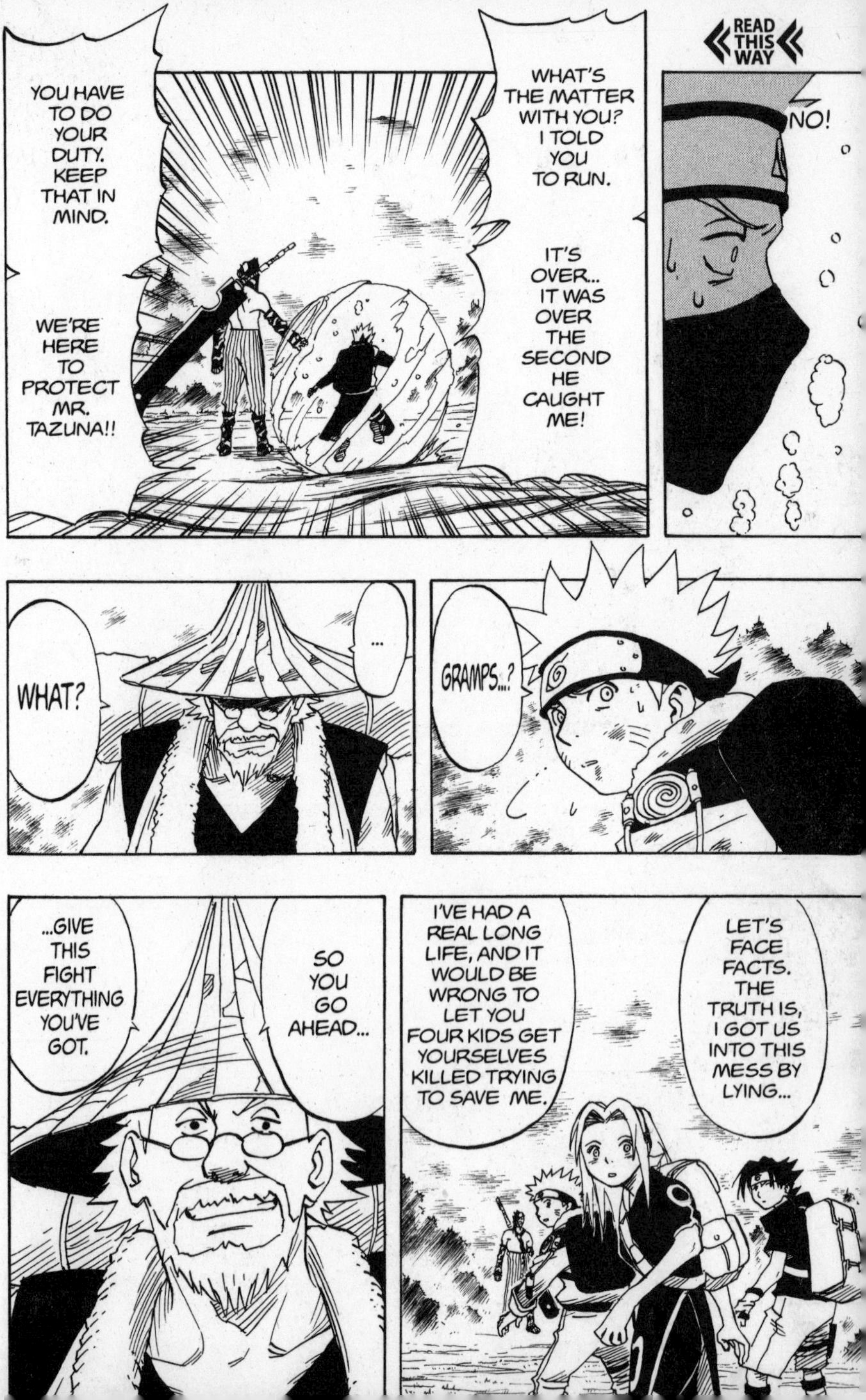
READ THIS WAY
NO!
WHAT'S THE MATTER WITH YOU? I TOLD YOU TO RUN.
IT'S OVER... IT WAS OVER THE SECOND HE CAUGHT ME!
YOU HAVE TO DO YOUR DUTY. KEEP THAT IN MIND.
WE'RE HERE TO PROTECT MR. TAZUNA!!
GRAMPS...?
...
WHAT?
LET'S FACE FACTS. THE TRUTH IS, I GOT US INTO THIS MESS BY LYING...
I'VE HAD A REAL LONG LIFE, AND IT WOULD BE WRONG TO LET YOU FOUR KIDS GET YOURSELVES KILLED TRYING TO SAVE ME.
SO YOU GO AHEAD...
...GIVE THIS FIGHT EVERYTHING YOU'VE GOT.

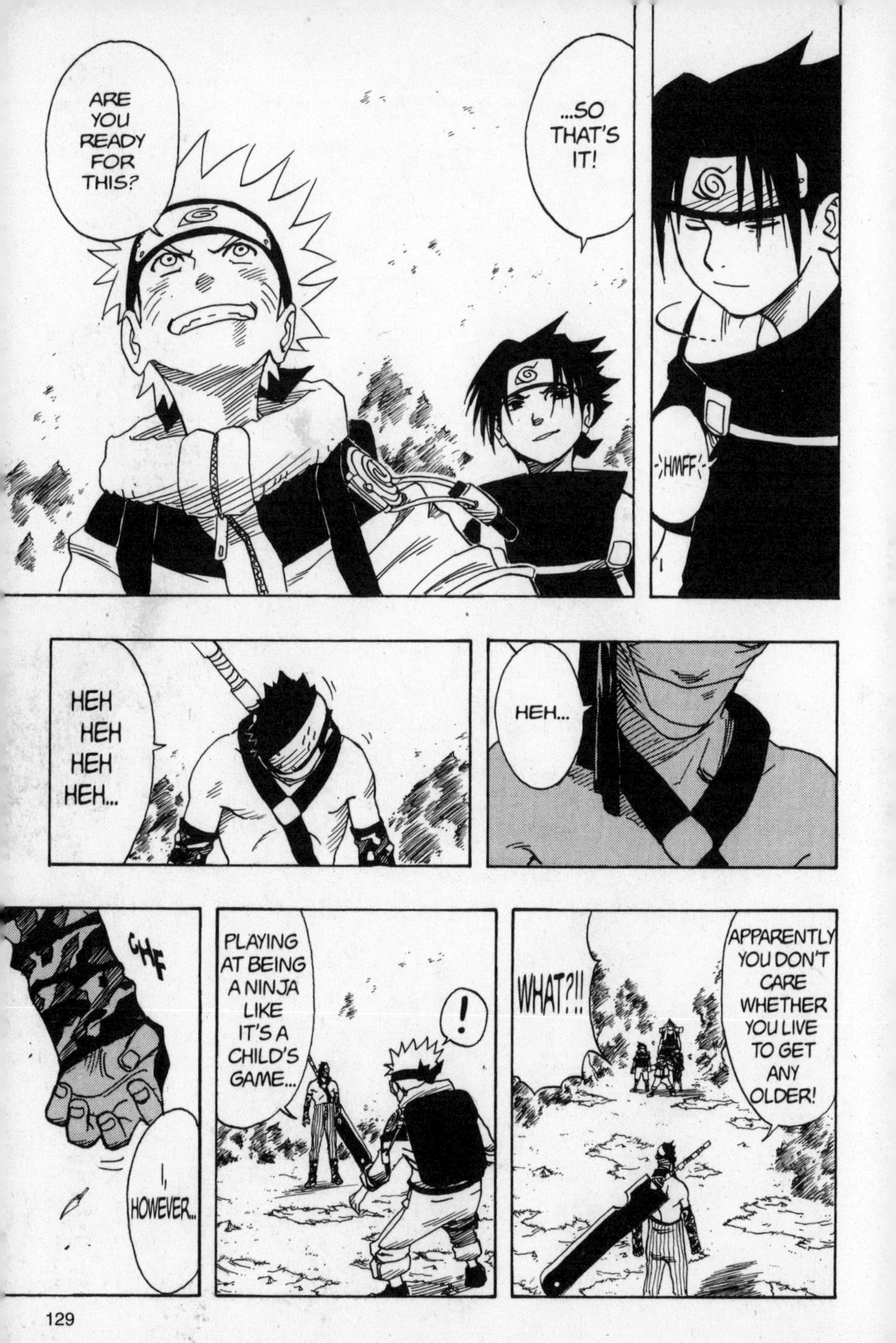
HMFF
...SO THAT'S IT!
ARE YOU READY FOR THIS?
HEH...
HEH HEH HEH HEH...
APPARENTLY YOU DON'T CARE WHETHER YOU LIVE TO GET ANY OLDER!
WHAT?!!
PLAYING AT BEING A NINJA LIKE IT'S A CHILD'S GAME...
!
CHF
I, HOWEVER...

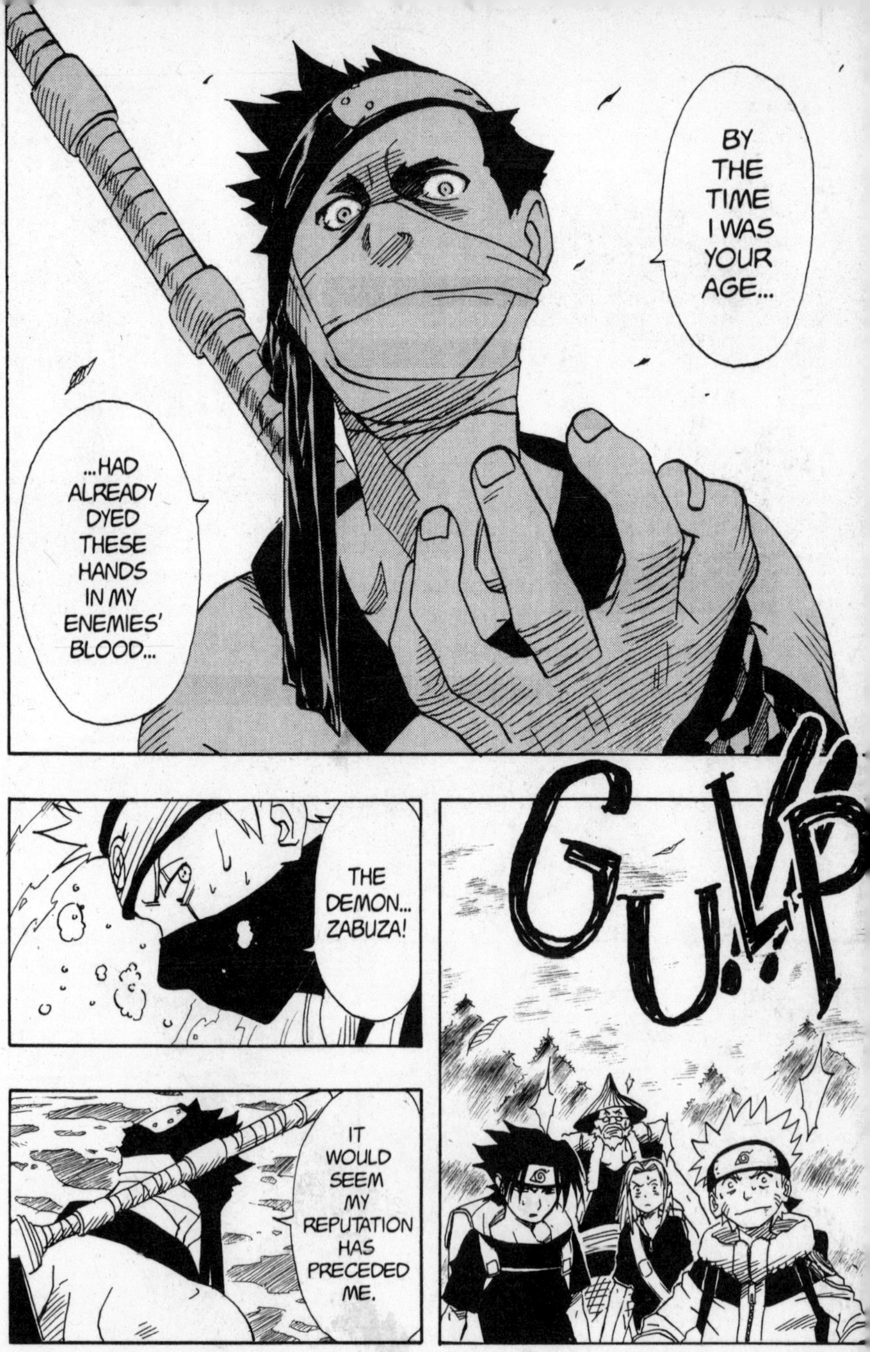
BY THE TIME I WAS YOUR AGE...
...HAD ALREADY DYED THESE HANDS IN MY ENEMIES' BLOOD...
GULP
THE DEMON... ZABUZA!
IT WOULD SEEM MY REPUTATION HAS PRECEDED ME.

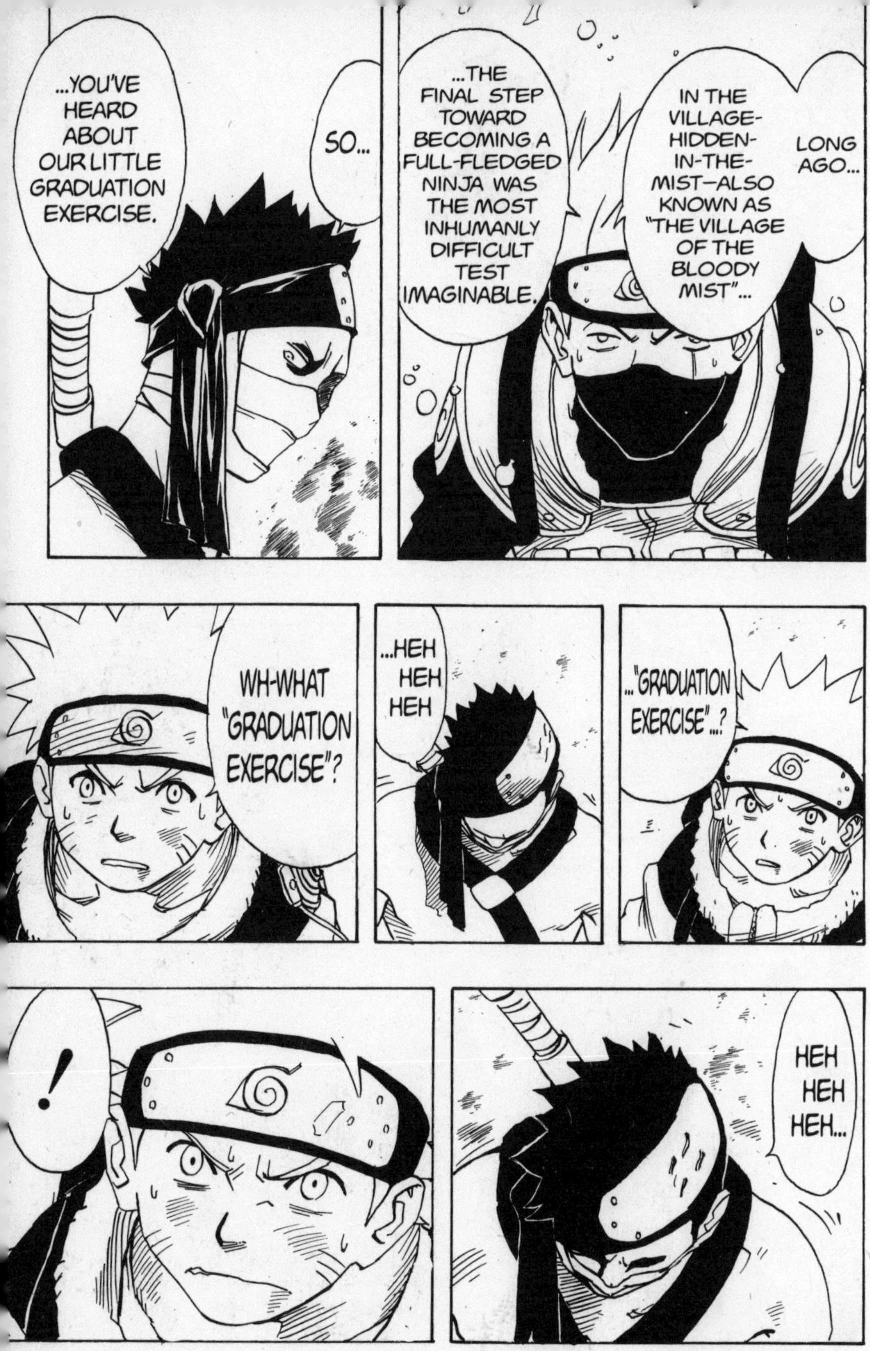
LONG AGO...
IN THE VILLAGE-HIDDEN-IN-THE-MIST—ALSO KNOWN AS "THE VILLAGE OF THE BLOODY MIST"...
...THE FINAL STEP TOWARD BECOMING A FULL-FLEDGED NINJA WAS THE MOST INHUMANLY DIFFICULT TEST IMAGINABLE.
SO...
...YOU'VE HEARD ABOUT OUR LITTLE GRADUATION EXERCISE.
..."GRADUATION EXERCISE"...?
...HEH HEH HEH
WH-WHAT "GRADUATION EXERCISE"?
HEH HEH HEH...
!

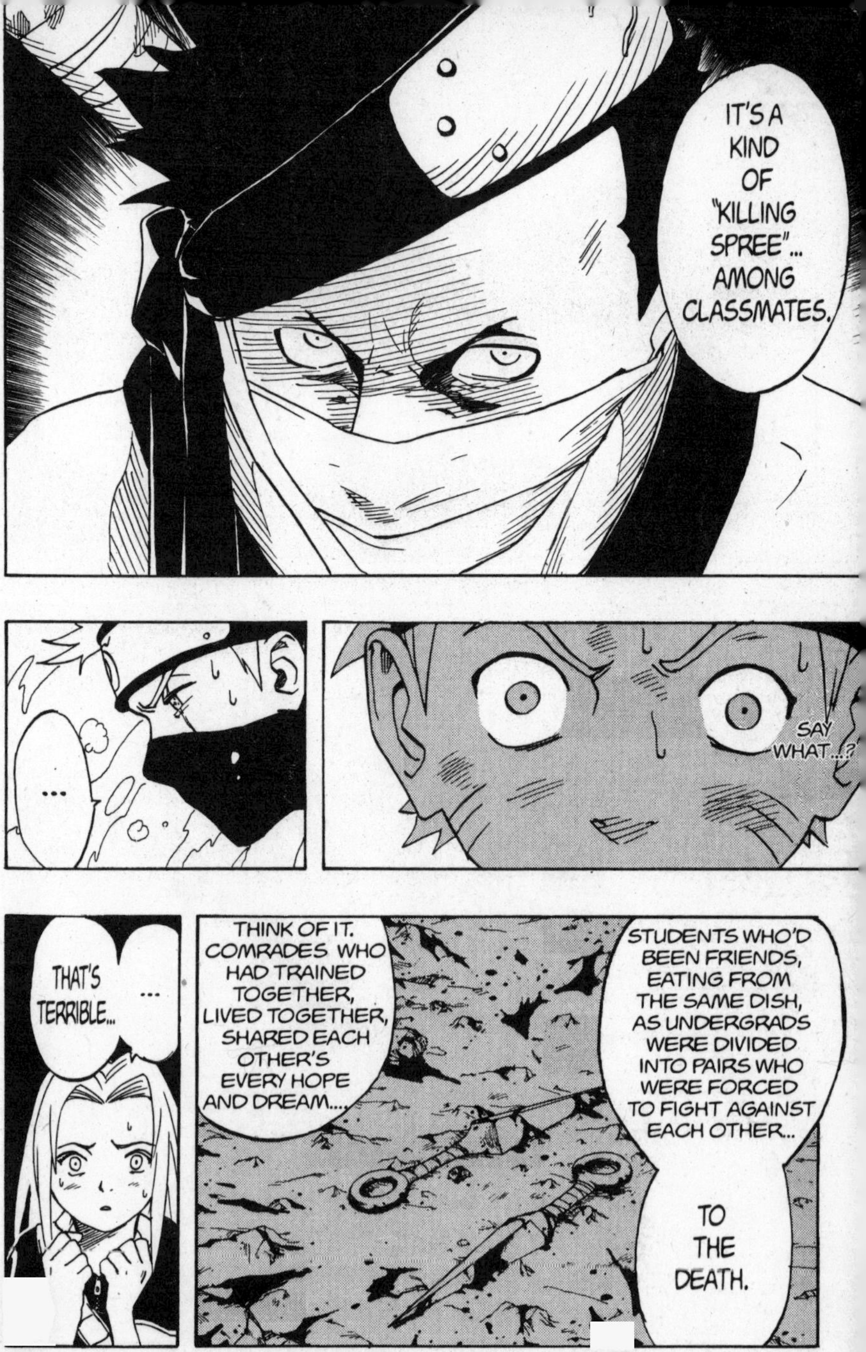

IT'S A KIND OF "KILLING SPREE"... AMONG CLASSMATES.
SAY WHAT...?
...
STUDENTS WHO'D BEEN FRIENDS, EATING FROM THE SAME DISH, AS UNDERGRADS WERE DIVIDED INTO PAIRS WHO WERE FORCED TO FIGHT AGAINST EACH OTHER...
TO THE DEATH.
THINK OF IT. COMRADES WHO HAD TRAINED TOGETHER, LIVED TOGETHER, SHARED EACH OTHER'S EVERY HOPE AND DREAM....
THAT'S TERRIBLE...
...

READ THIS WAY

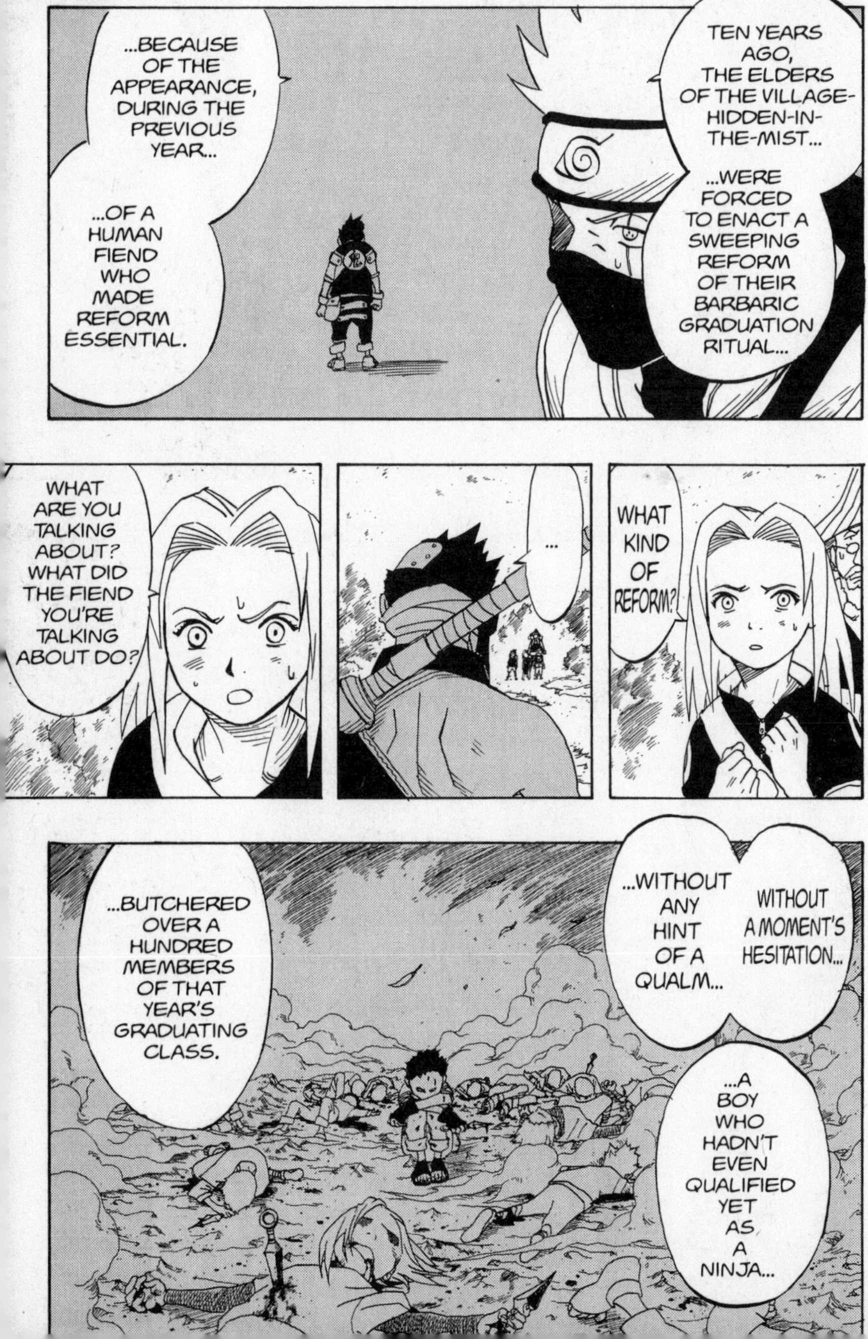
TEN YEARS AGO, THE ELDERS OF THE VILLAGE-HIDDEN-IN-THE-MIST...
...WERE FORCED TO ENACT A SWEEPING REFORM OF THEIR BARBARIC GRADUATION RITUAL...
...BECAUSE OF THE APPEARANCE, DURING THE PREVIOUS YEAR...
...OF A HUMAN FIEND WHO MADE REFORM ESSENTIAL.
WHAT KIND OF REFORM?
...
WHAT ARE YOU TALKING ABOUT? WHAT DID THE FIEND YOU'RE TALKING ABOUT DO?
WITHOUT A MOMENT'S HESITATION...
...WITHOUT ANY HINT OF A QUALM...
...A BOY WHO HADN'T EVEN QUALIFIED YET AS A NINJA...
...BUTCHERED OVER A HUNDRED MEMBERS OF THAT YEAR'S GRADUATING CLASS.

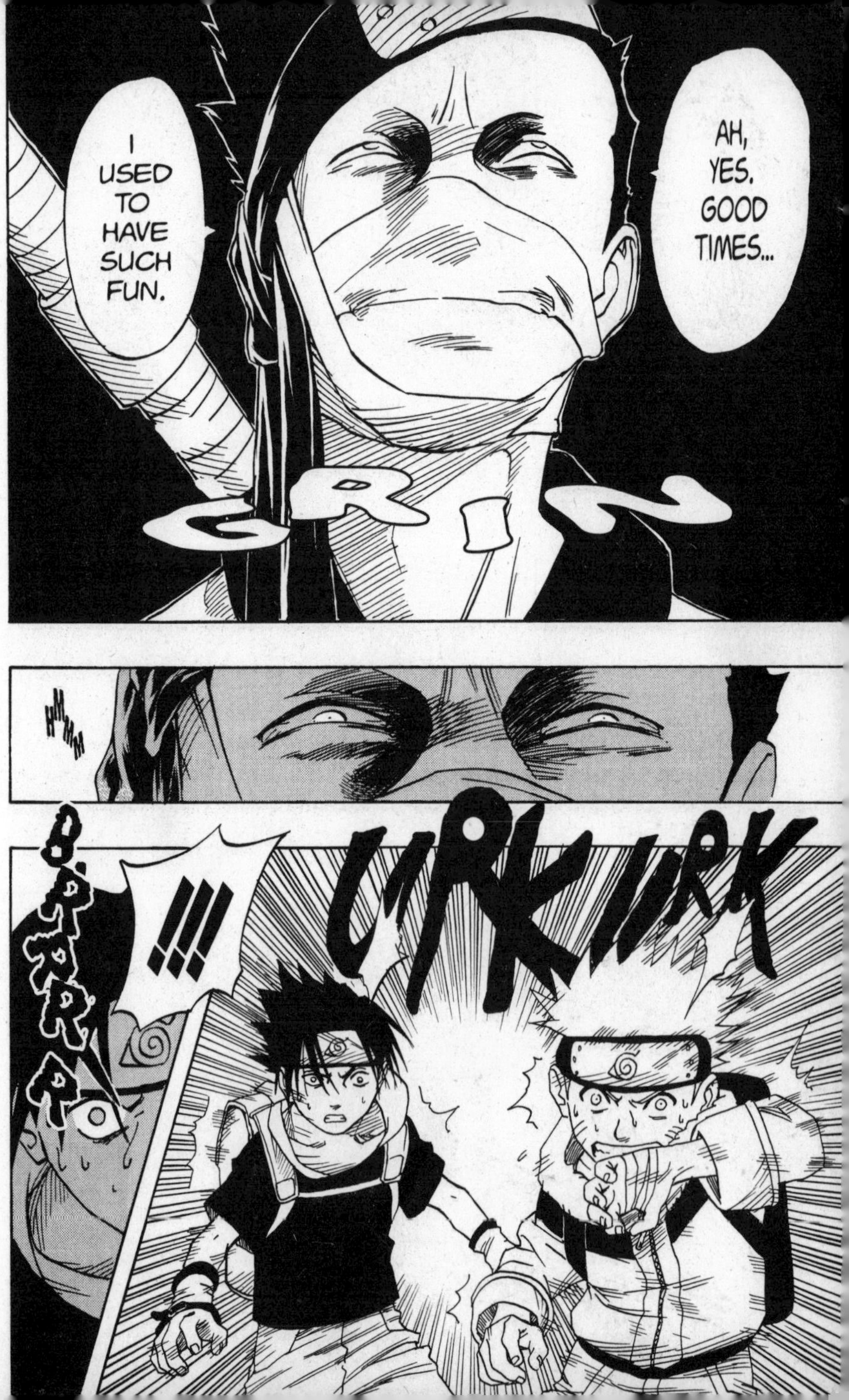
AH, YES. GOOD TIMES...
I USED TO HAVE SUCH FUN.
GRIN
HMMMM
URK
URK
!!!
BRRRR

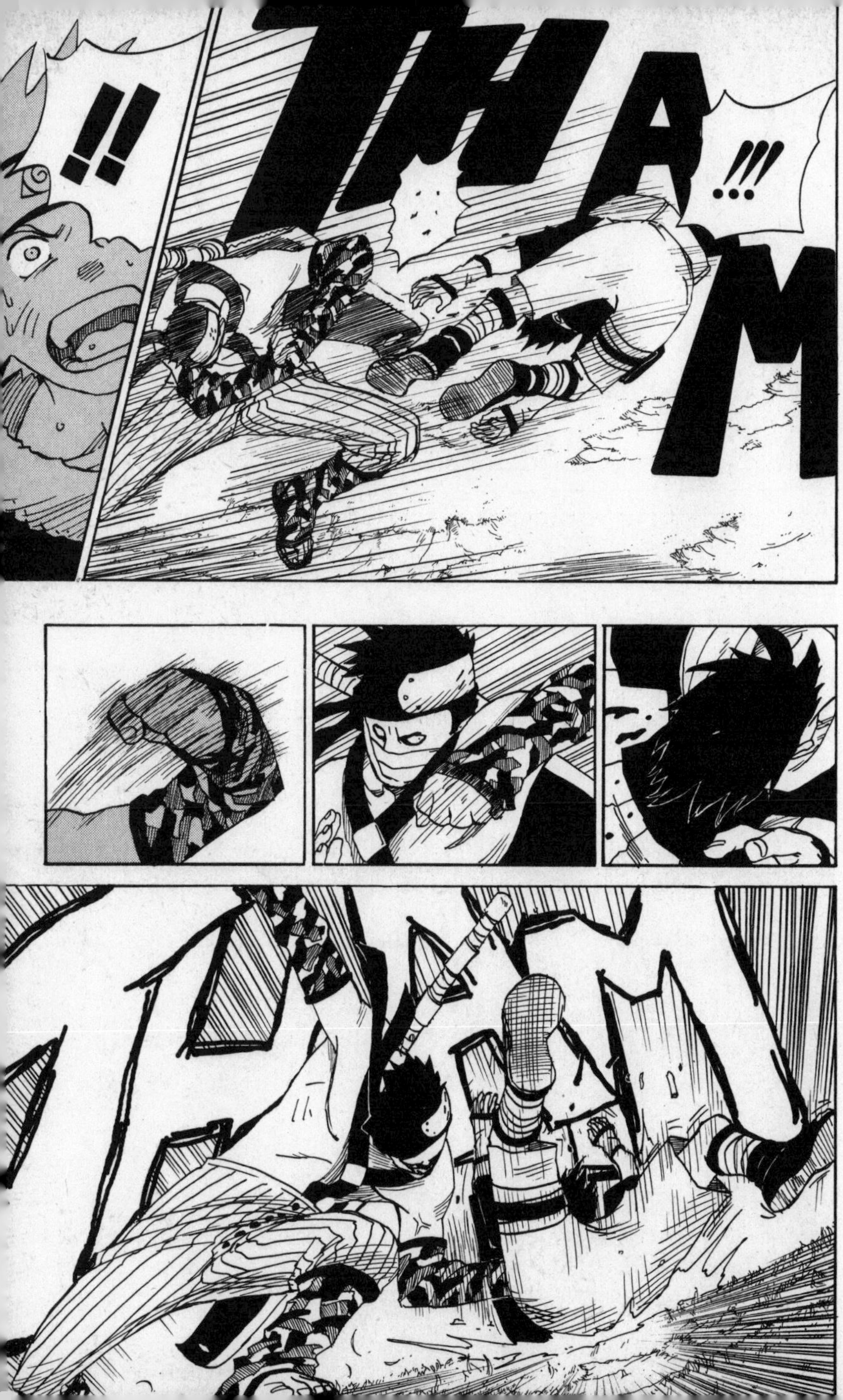
THAM
!!!
!!

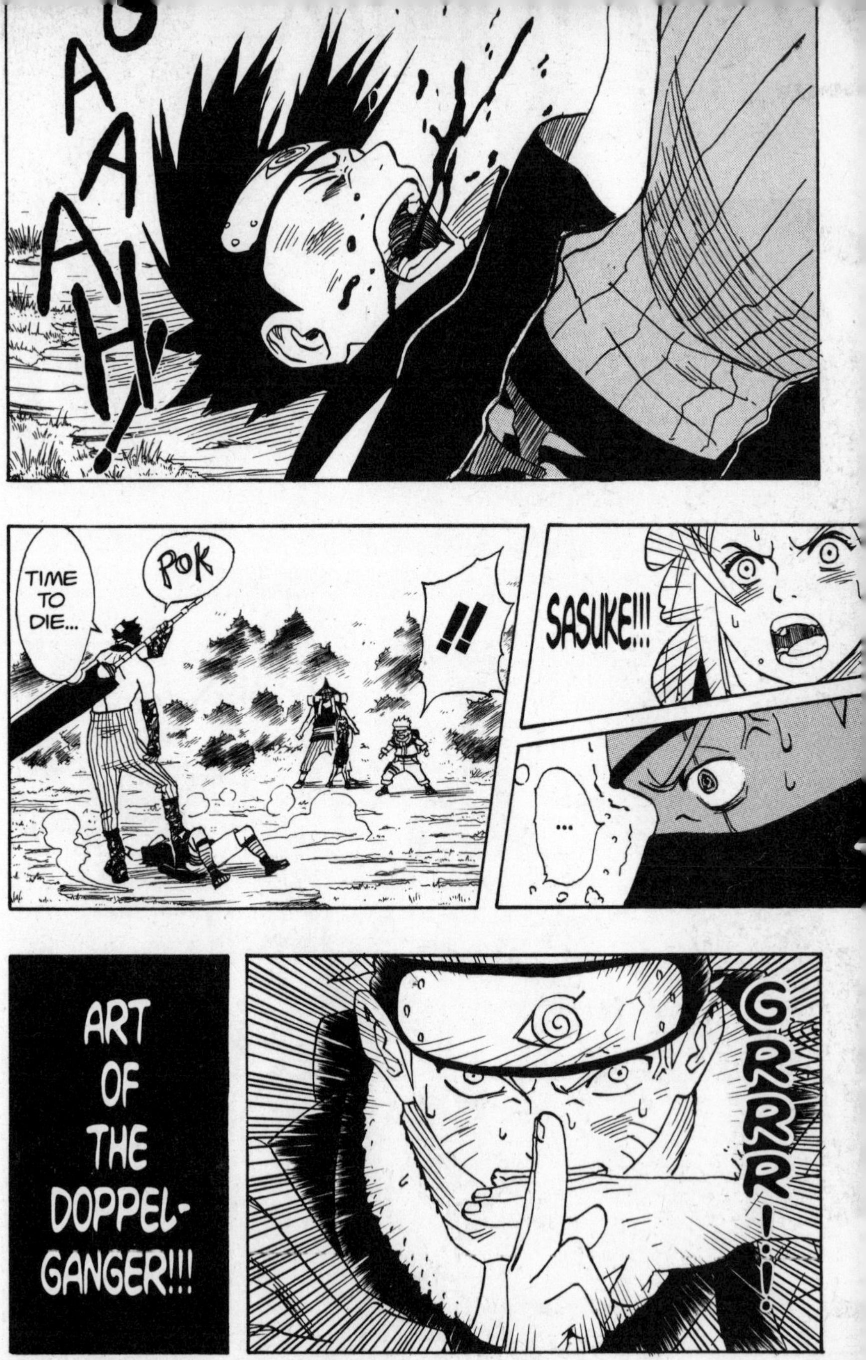
AAAH!
SASUKE!!!
...
!!
POK
TIME TO DIE...
GRRR!!!
ART OF THE DOPPEL-GANGER!!!

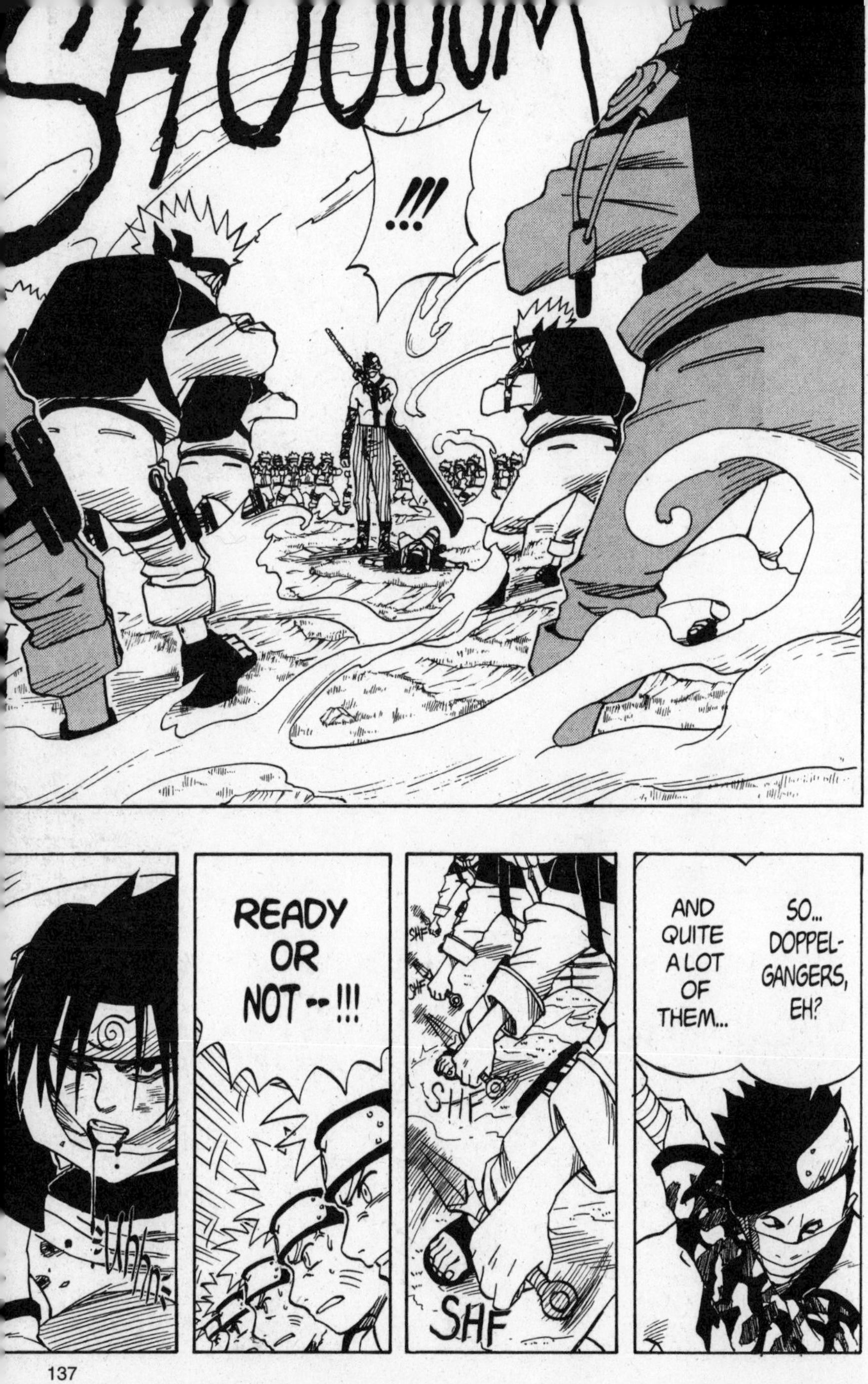
SHOOOOM
!!!
SO... DOPPEL-GANGERS, EH?
AND QUITE A LOT OF THEM...
SHF
SHF
SHF
SHF
READY OR NOT--!!!
Uhh

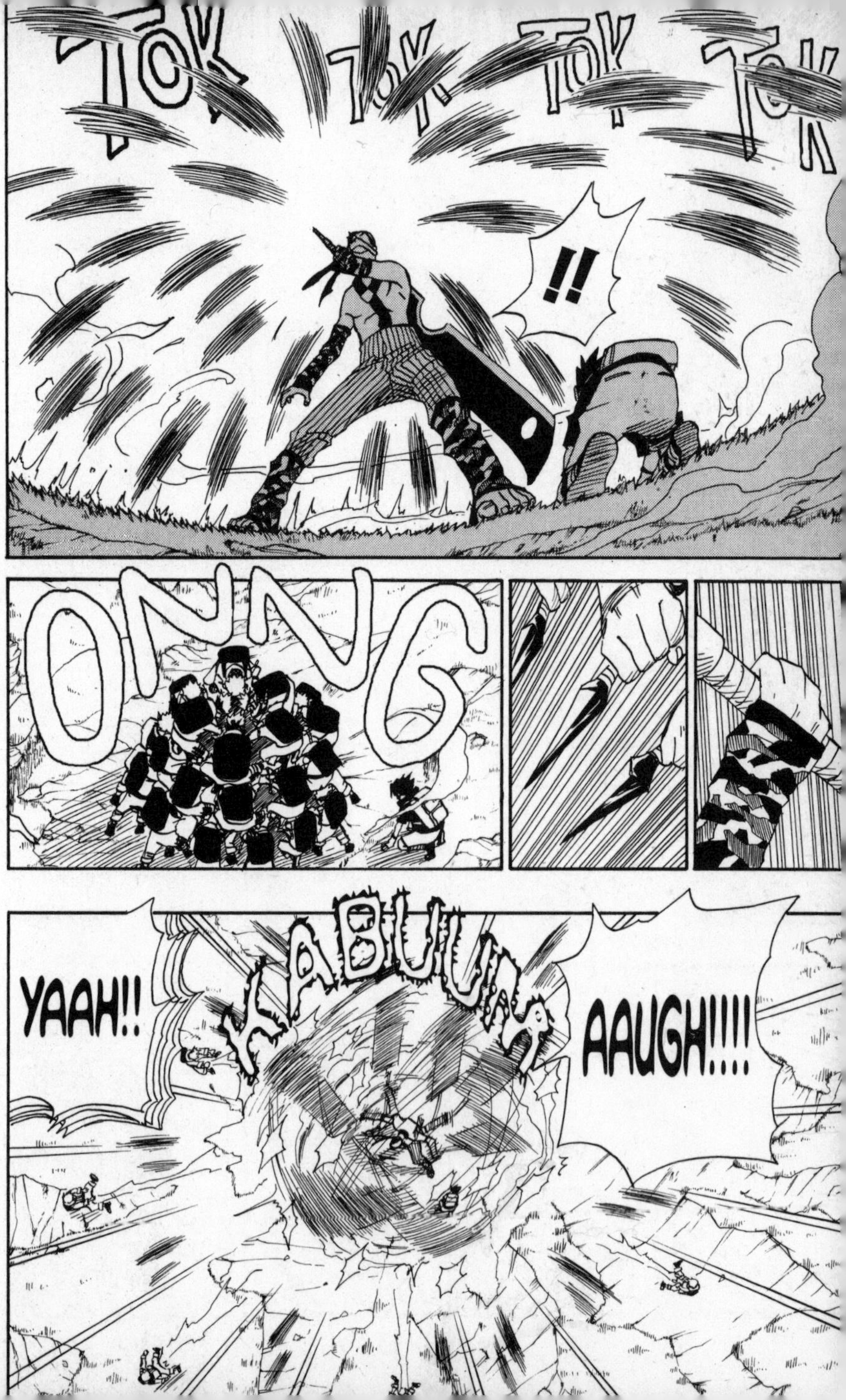
TOK TOK TOK TOK
!!
ONNG
AAUGH!!!!
KABUUM
YAAH!!

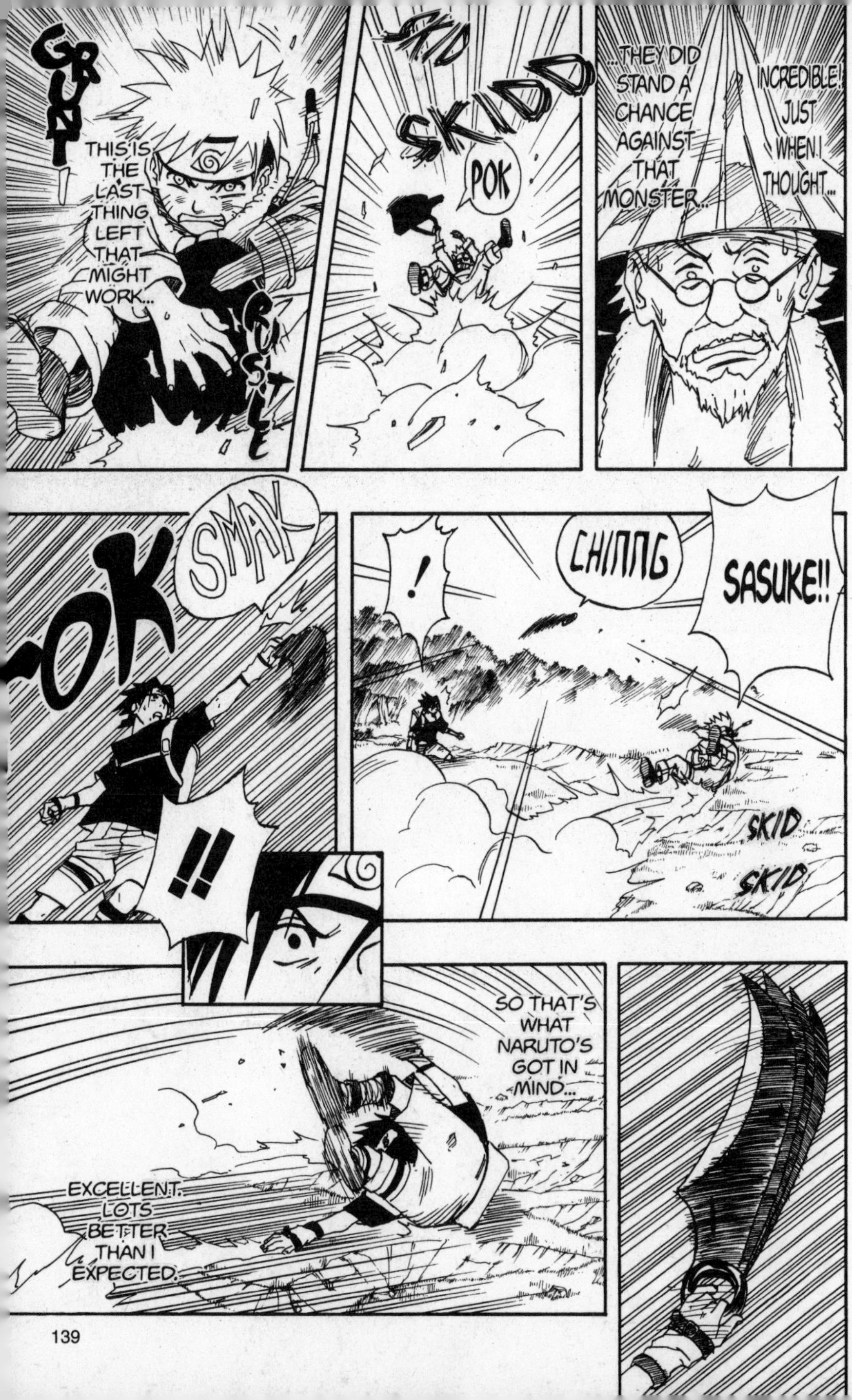
INCREDIBLE! JUST WHEN I THOUGHT...
...THEY DID STAND A CHANCE AGAINST THAT MONSTER...
SKID
SKIDD
POK
GRUNT!
THIS IS THE LAST THING LEFT THAT MIGHT WORK...
RUSTLE
SASUKE!!
CHINNG
!
SKID
SKID
POK
SMAK
!!
SO THAT'S WHAT NARUTO'S GOT IN MIND...
EXCELLENT. LOTS BETTER THAN I EXPECTED.

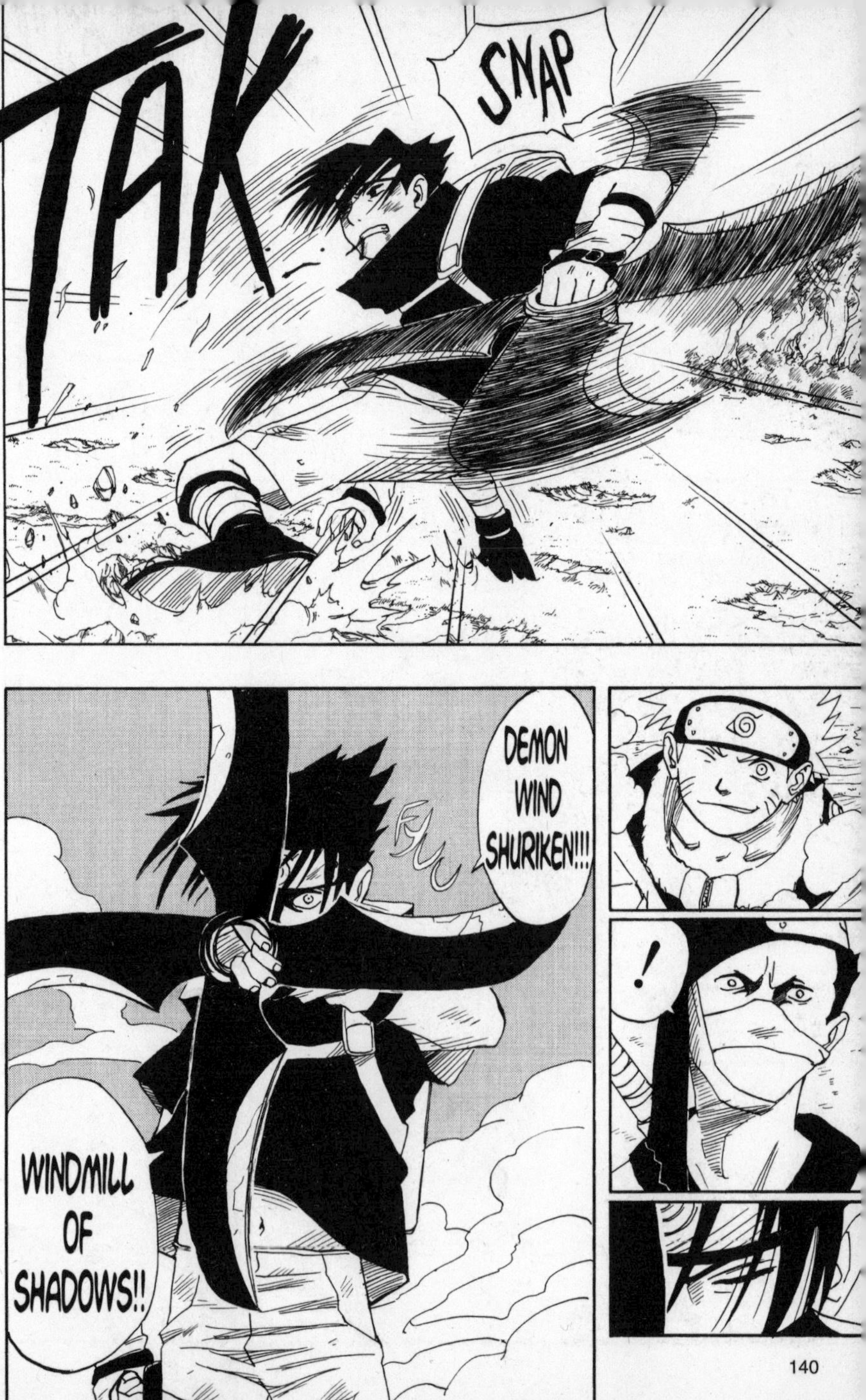
SNAP
TAK
!
DEMON WIND SHURIKEN!!!
WINDMILL OF SHADOWS!!

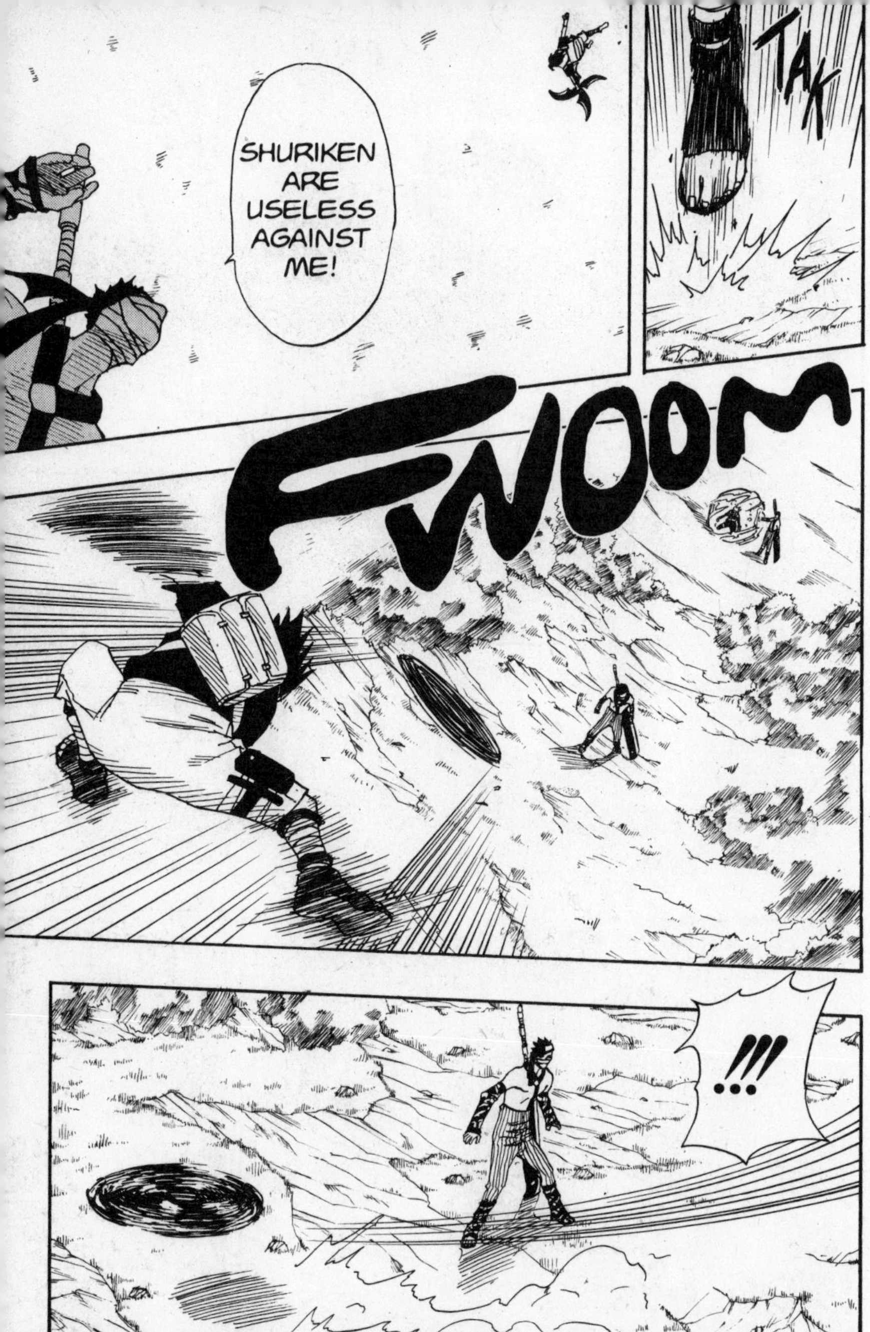
TAK
SHURIKEN ARE USELESS AGAINST ME!
FWOOM
!!!

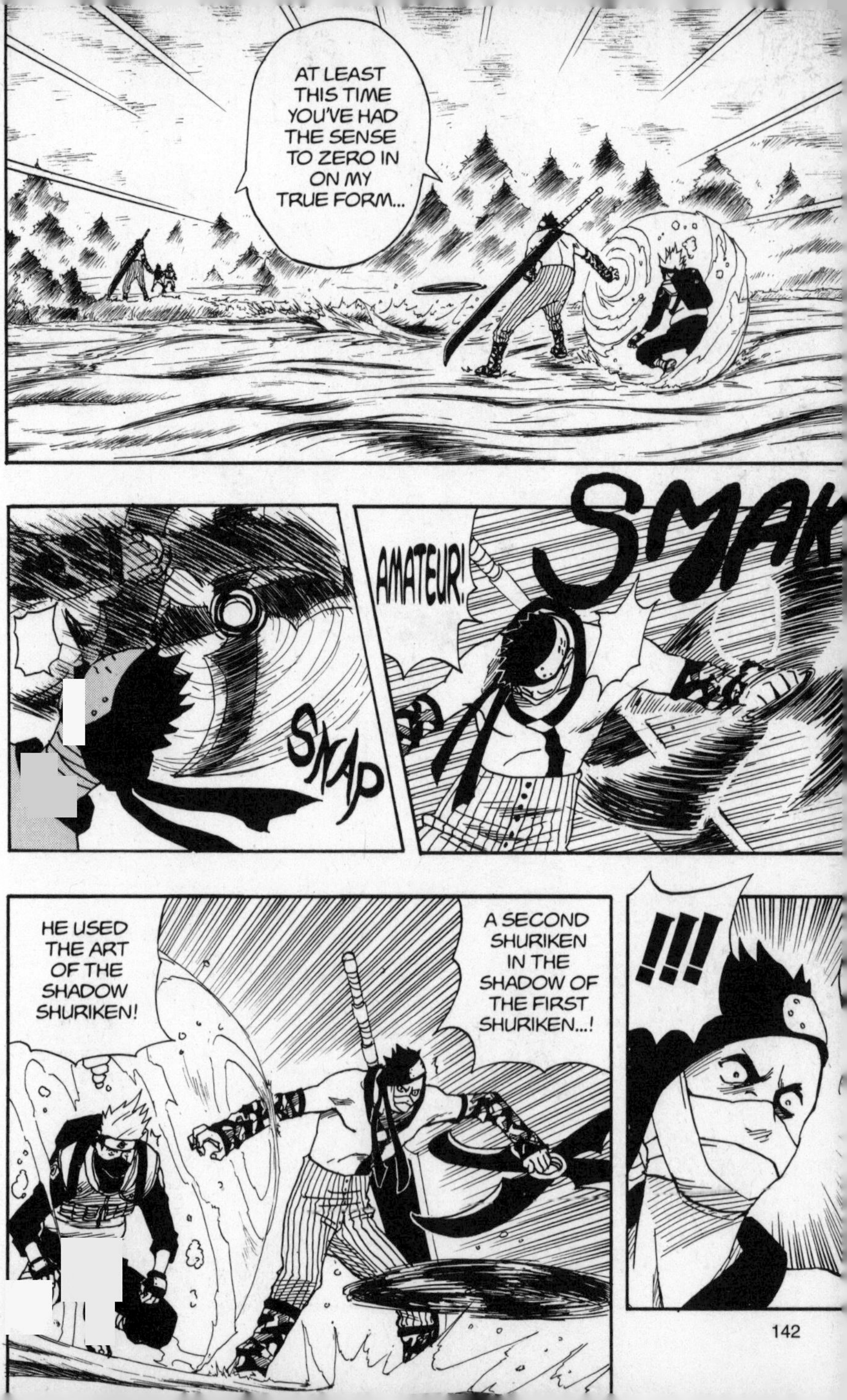
AT LEAST THIS TIME YOU'VE HAD THE SENSE TO ZERO IN ON MY TRUE FORM...
SMAK
AMATEUR!
SMAP
!!!
A SECOND SHURIKEN IN THE SHADOW OF THE FIRST SHURIKEN...!
HE USED THE ART OF THE SHADOW SHURIKEN!

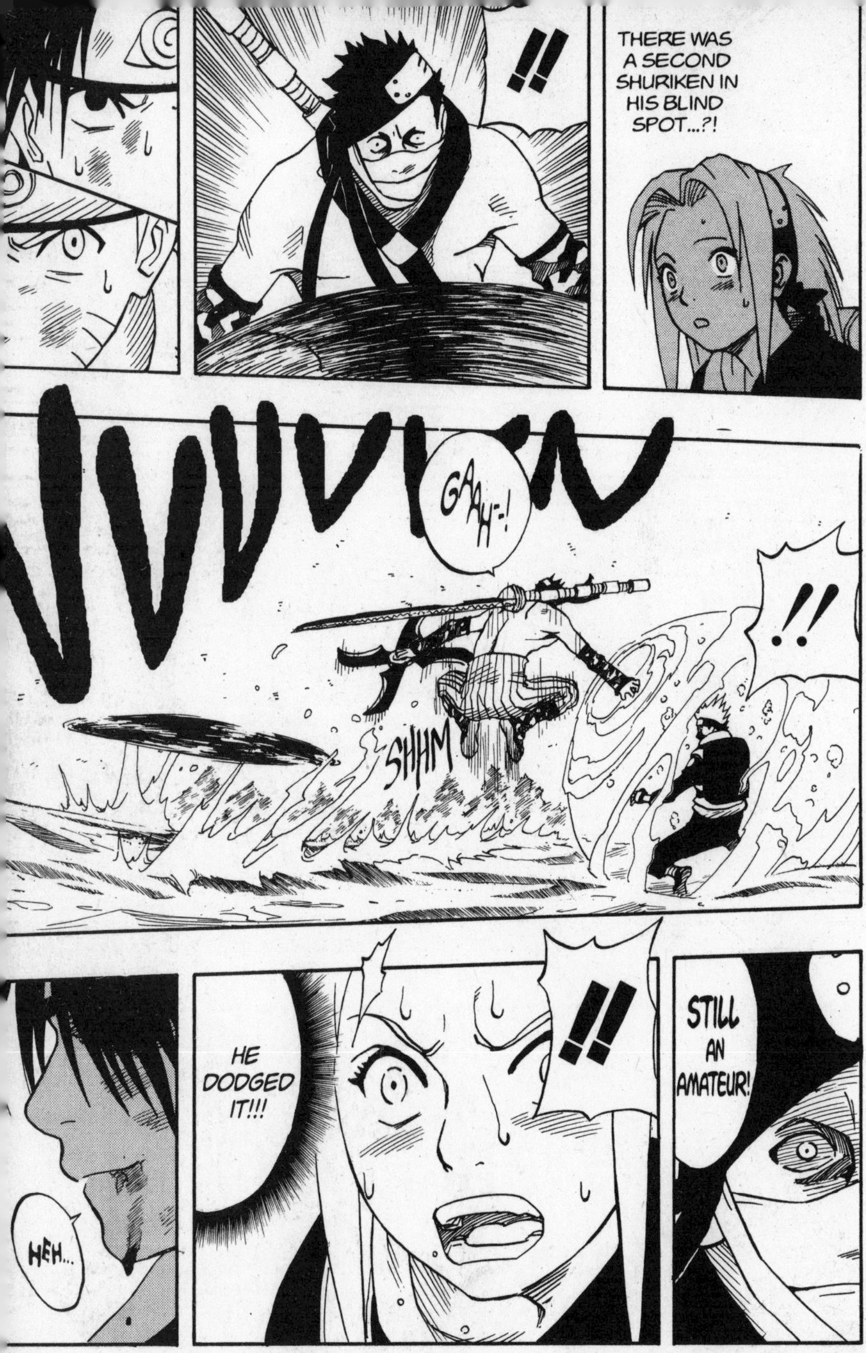
THERE WAS A SECOND SHURIKEN IN HIS BLIND SPOT...?!
!!
GAAH--!
!!
SHHM
STILL AN AMATEUR!
!!
HE DODGED IT!!!
HEH...

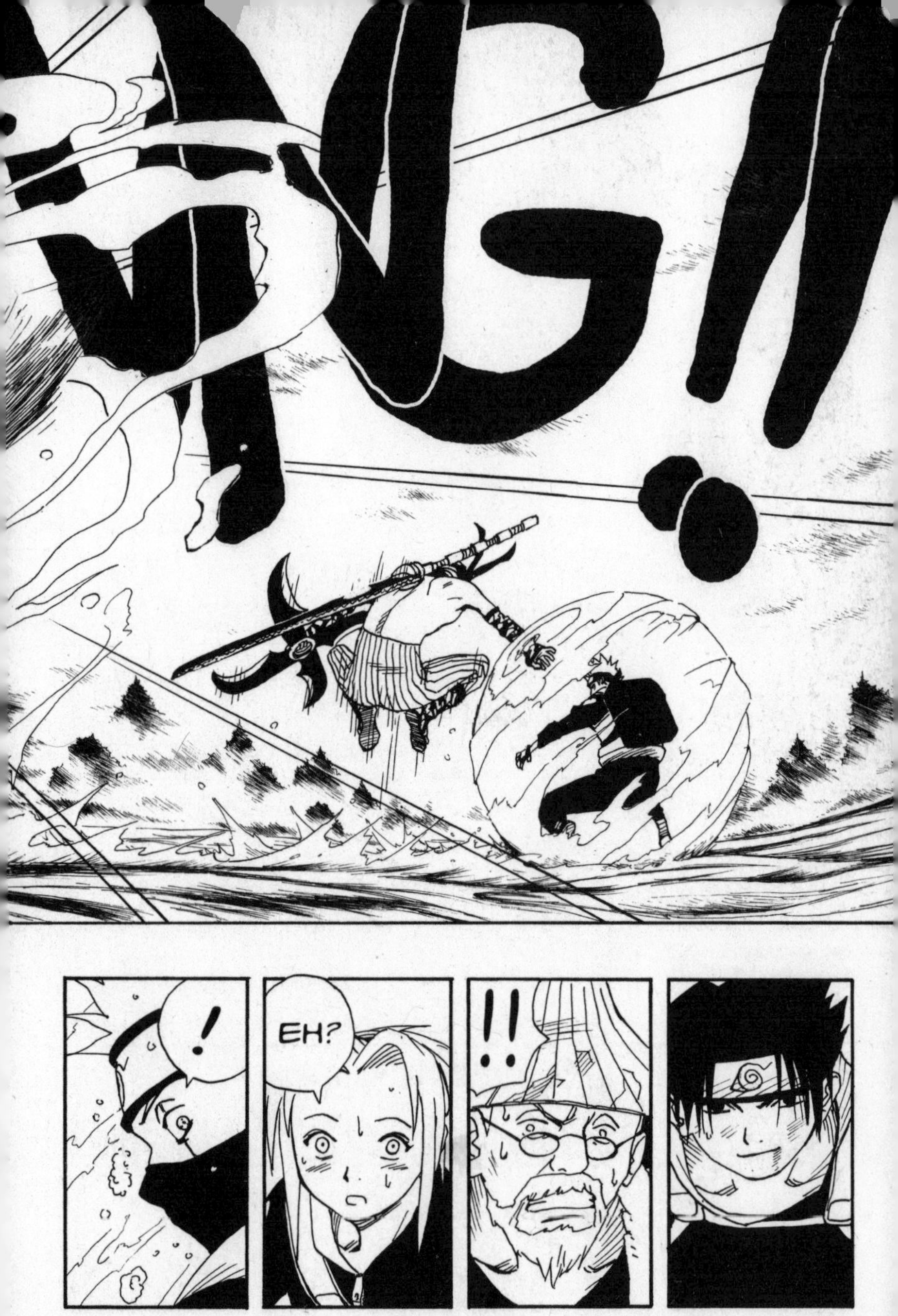
NG!!
!!
EH?
!

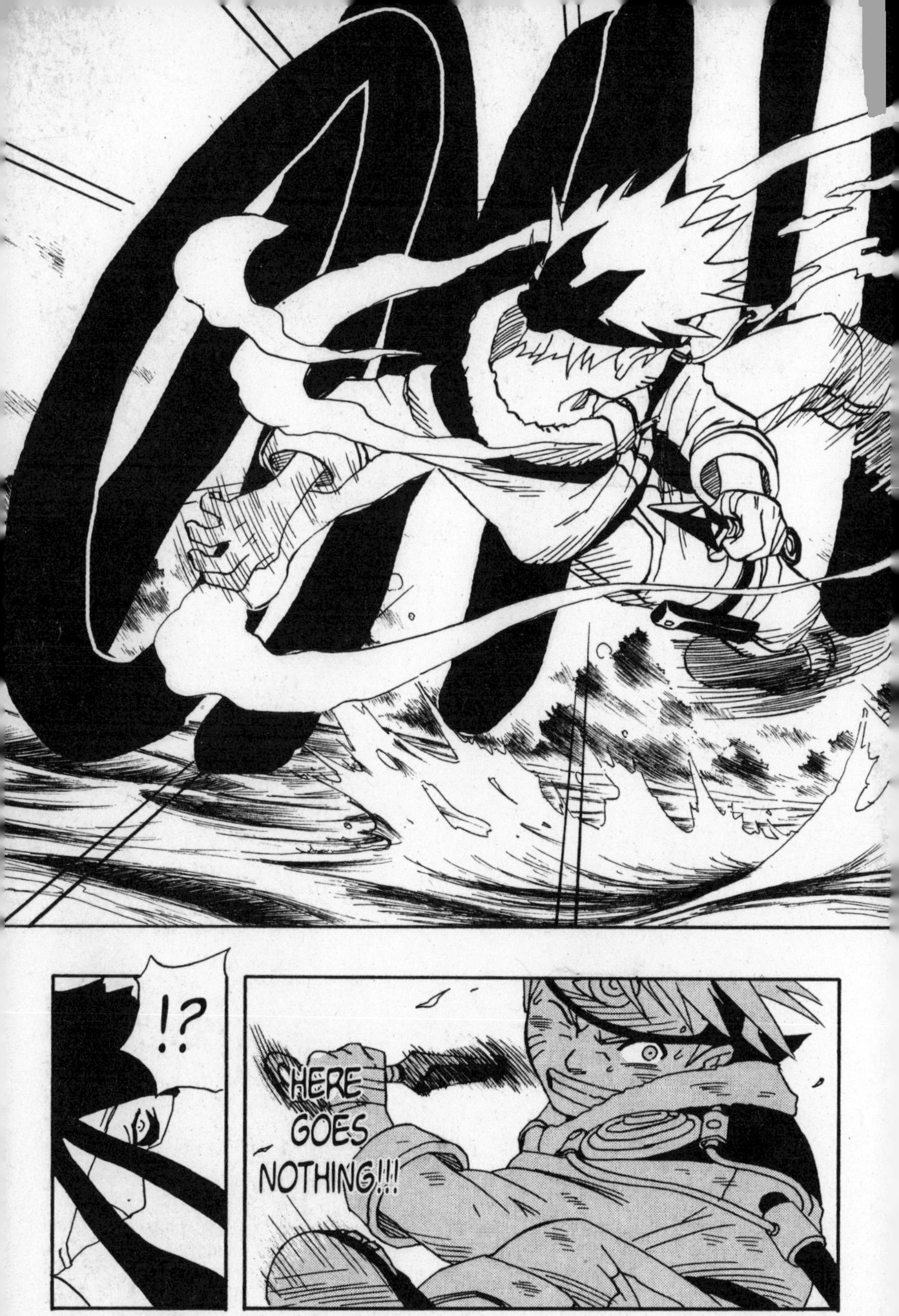
HERE GOES NOTHING!!!
!?

Number 15: Return of the Sharingan

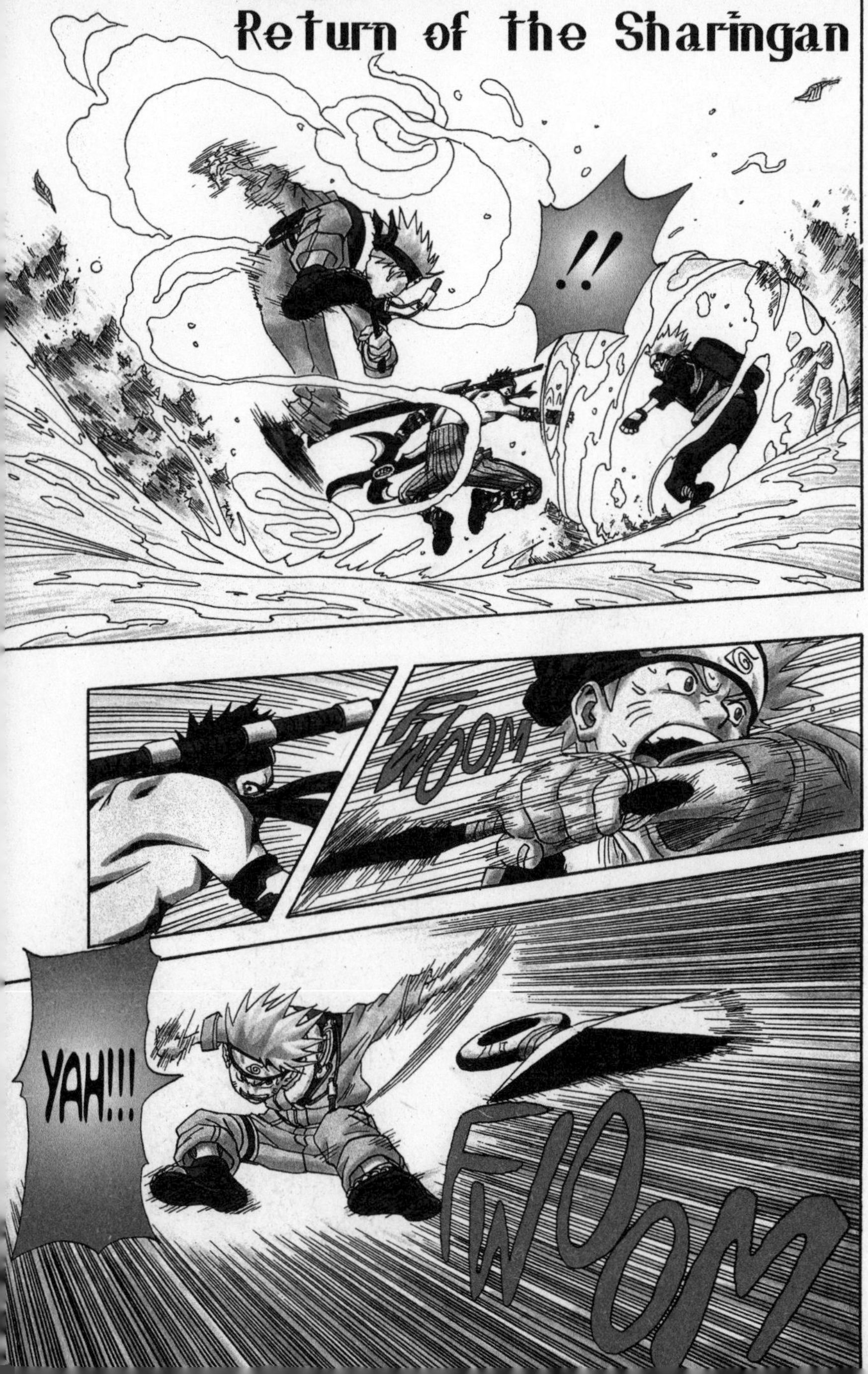
!!
FWOOM
YAH!!!
FWOOM

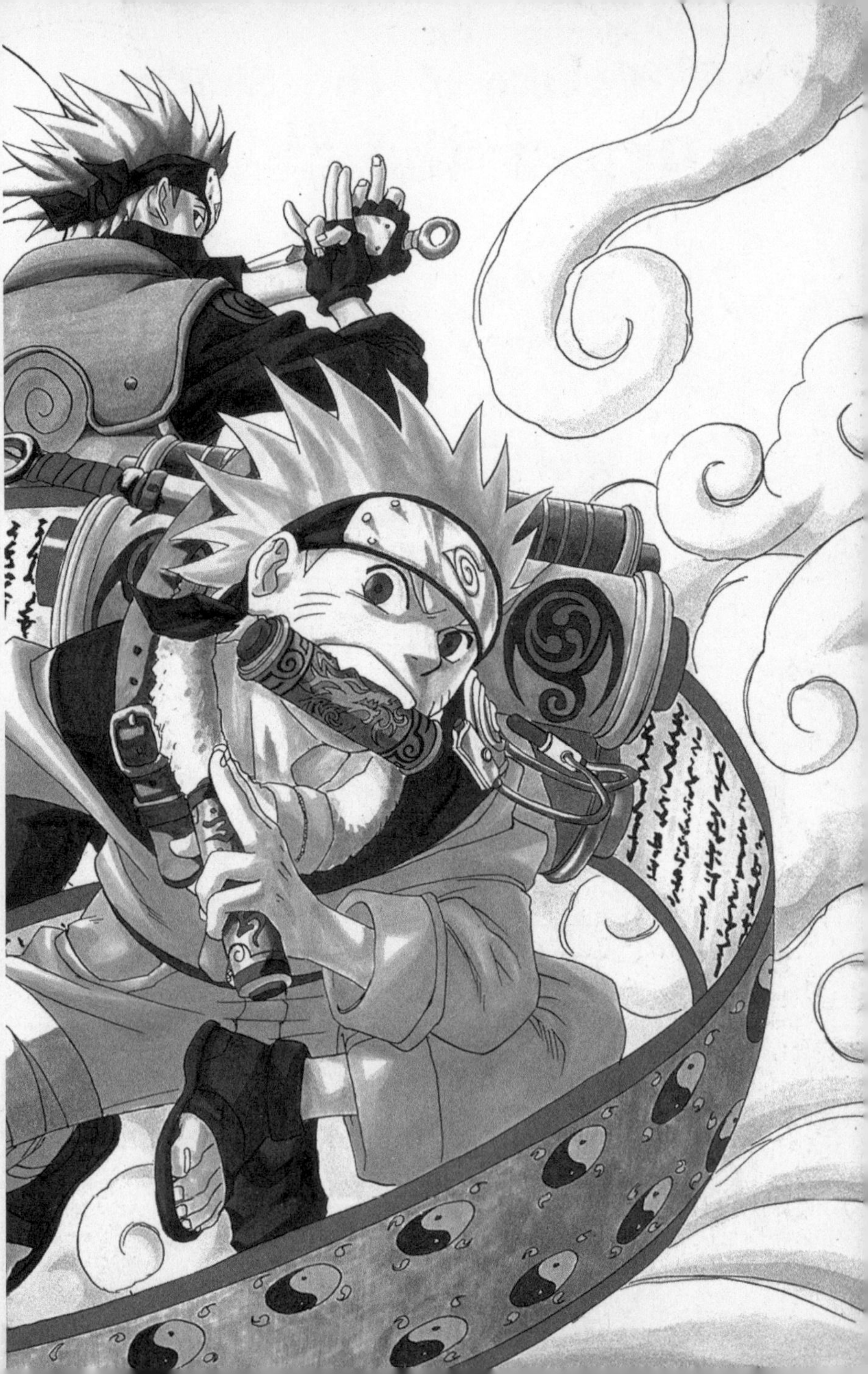

Number 15: Return of the Sharingan

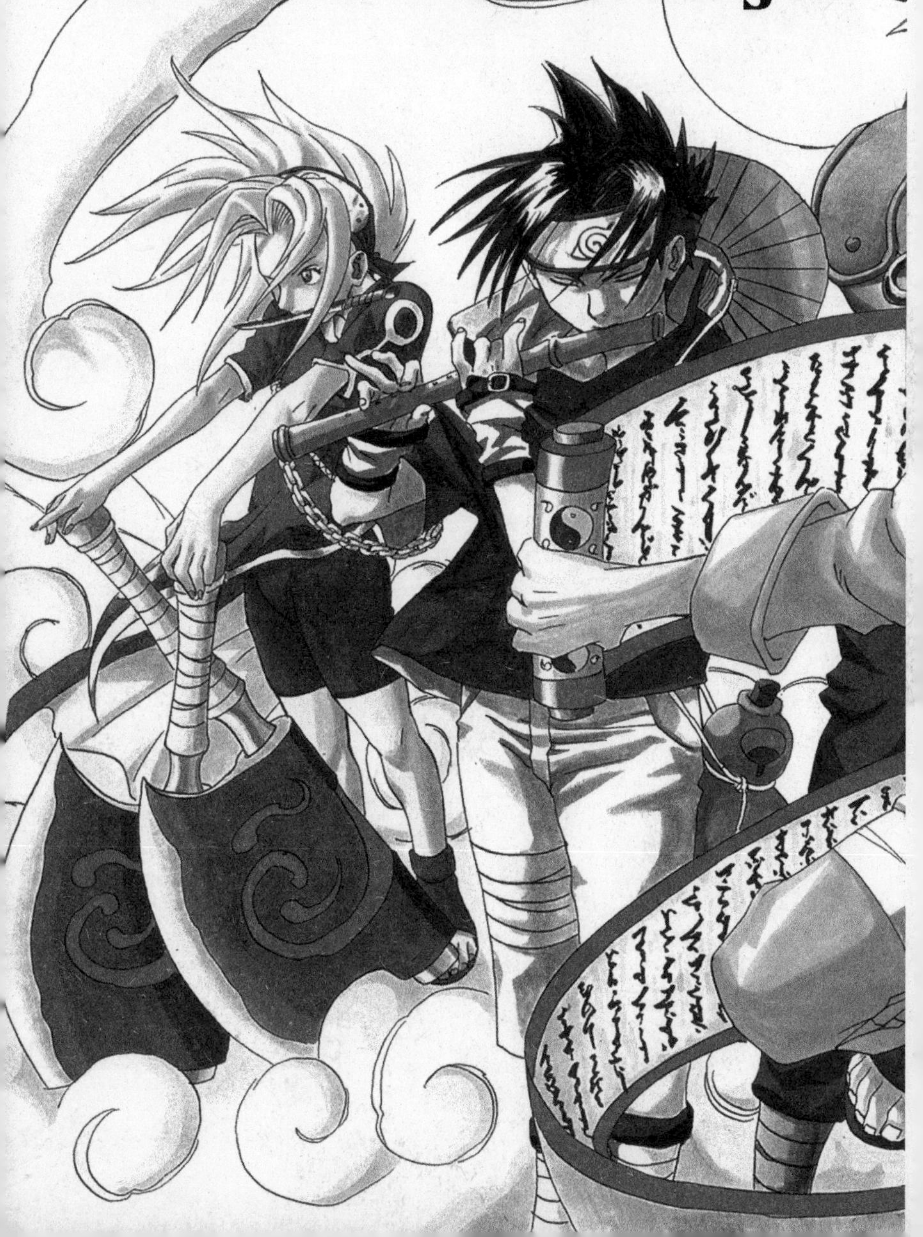

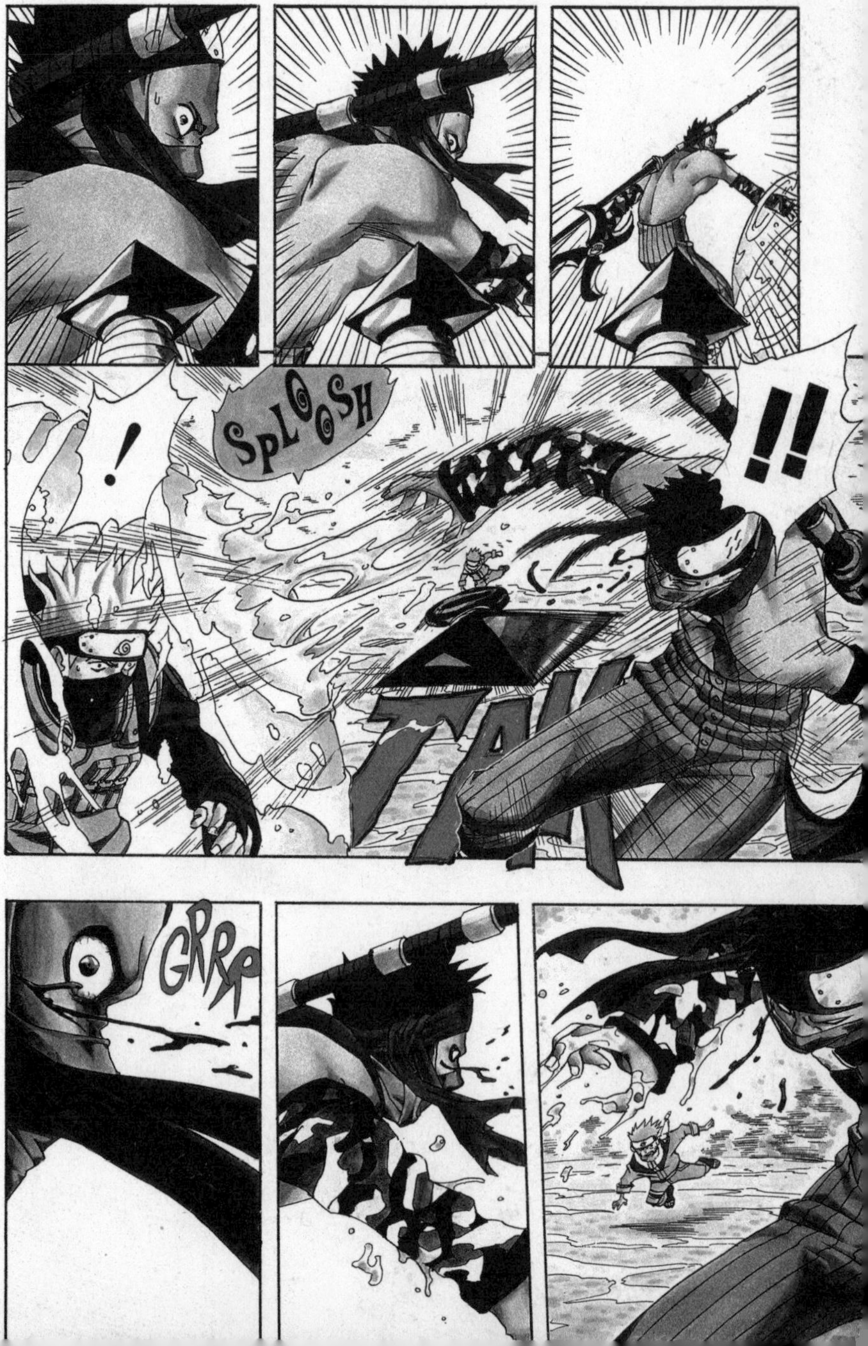
!!
SPLOOSH
!
TAK
GRRR

READ THIS WAY

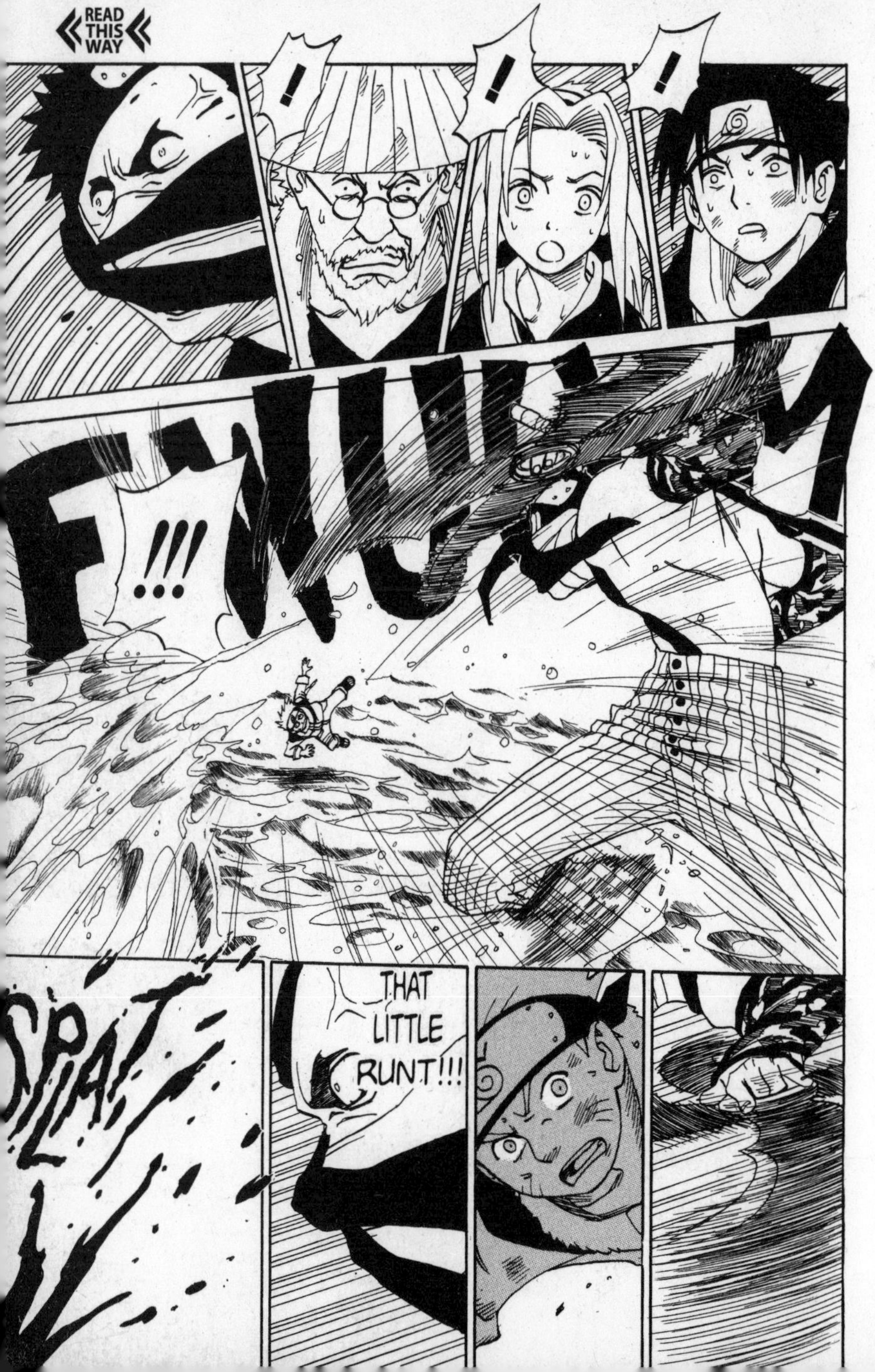
!
!
!
FWUMM!!!
THAT LITTLE RUNT!!!
SPLAT

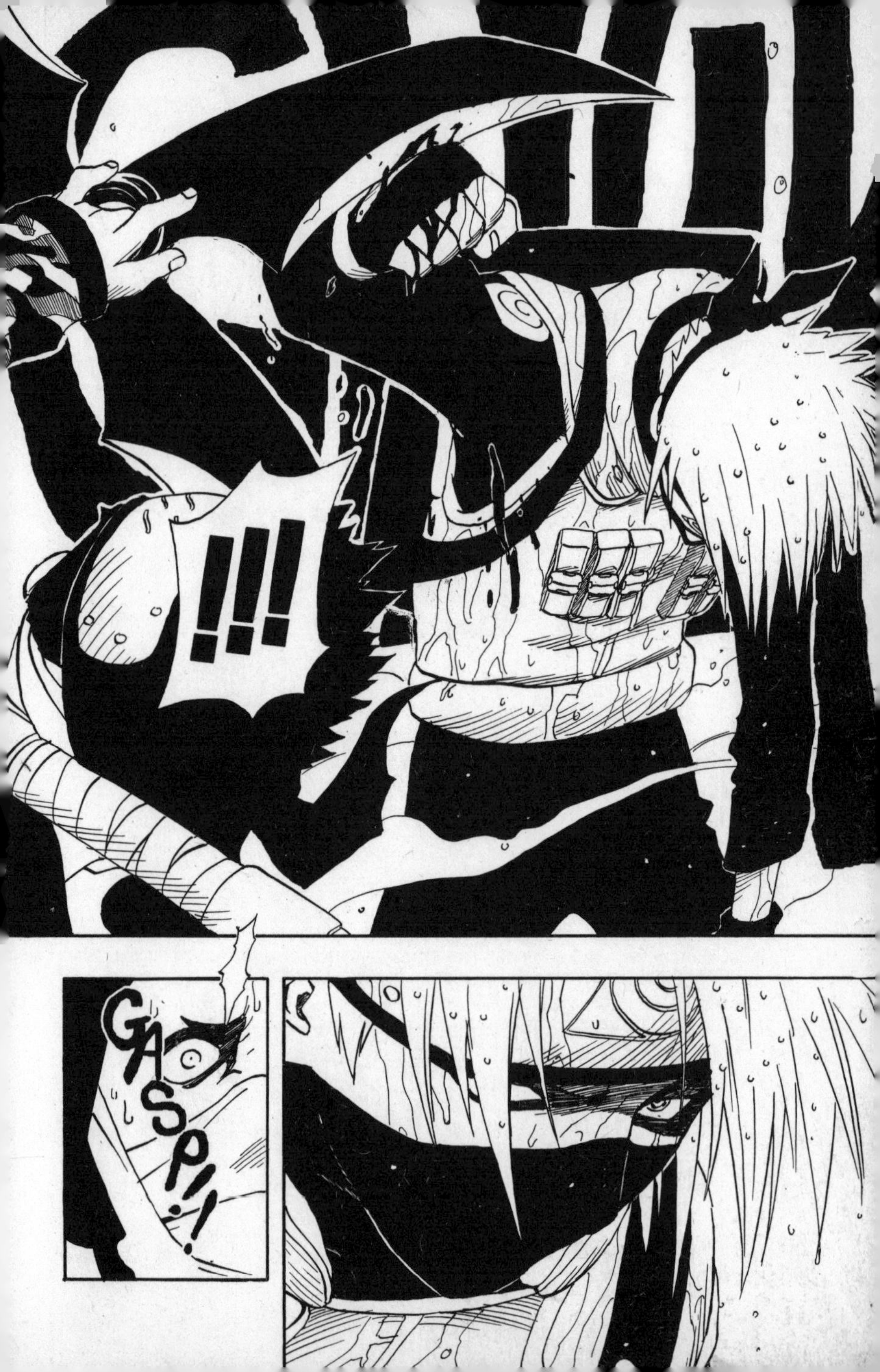
!!!
GASP!!

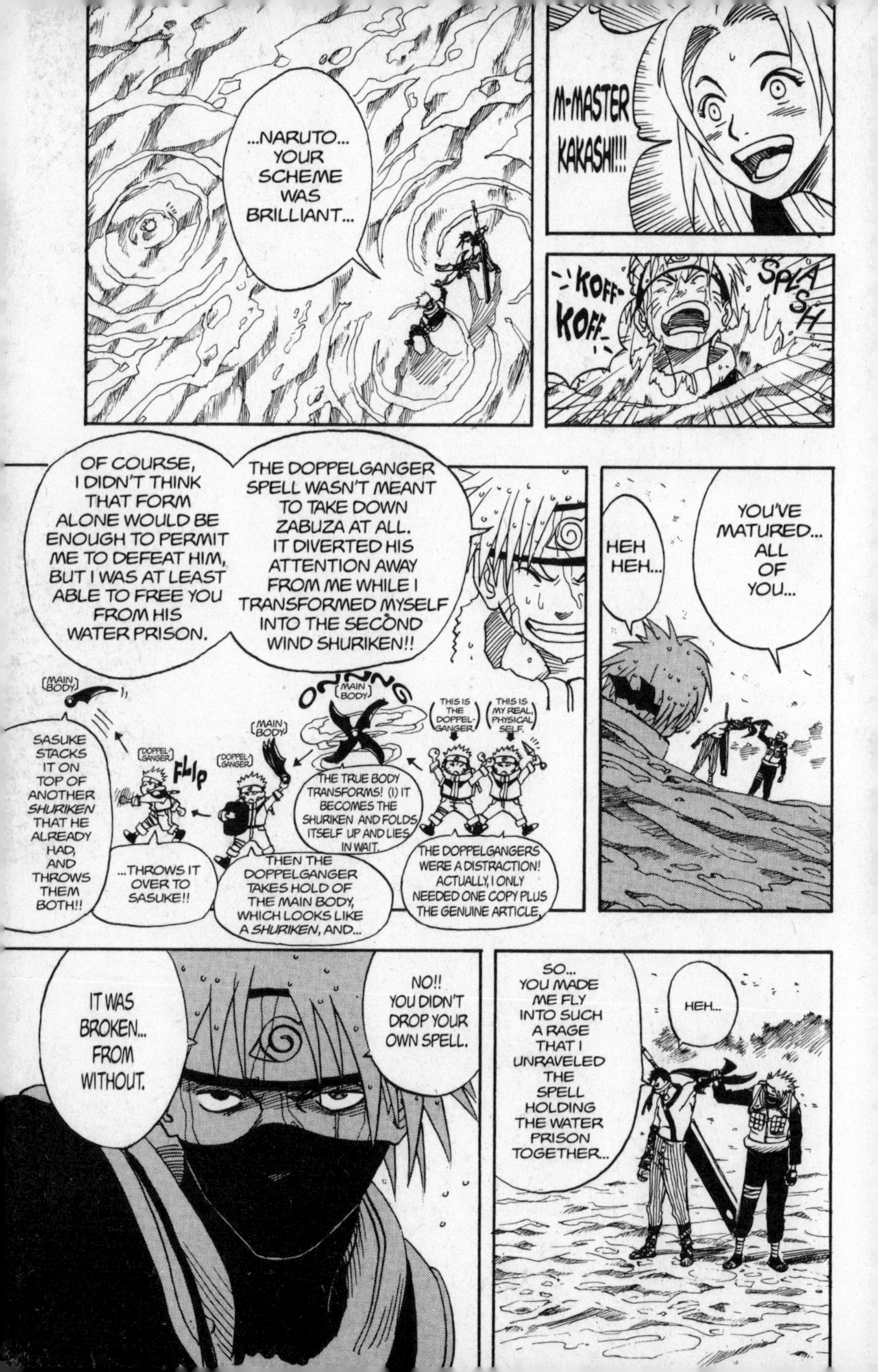
M-MASTER KAKASHI!!!
KOFF KOFF
SPLASH
...NARUTO... YOUR SCHEME WAS BRILLIANT...
YOU'VE MATURED... ALL OF YOU...
HEH HEH...
THE DOPPELGANGER SPELL WASN'T MEANT TO TAKE DOWN ZABUZA AT ALL. IT DIVERTED HIS ATTENTION AWAY FROM ME WHILE I TRANSFORMED MYSELF INTO THE SECOND WIND SHURIKEN!!
OF COURSE, I DIDN'T THINK THAT FORM ALONE WOULD BE ENOUGH TO PERMIT ME TO DEFEAT HIM, BUT I WAS AT LEAST ABLE TO FREE YOU FROM HIS WATER PRISON.
THIS IS MY REAL, PHYSICAL SELF.
THIS IS THE DOPPEL-GANGER.
THE DOPPELGANGERS WERE A DISTRACTION! ACTUALLY, I ONLY NEEDED ONE COPY PLUS THE GENUINE ARTICLE.
ONNNG
MAIN BODY
THE TRUE BODY TRANSFORMS! (I) IT BECOMES THE SHURIKEN AND FOLDS ITSELF UP AND LIES IN WAIT.
MAIN BODY
DOPPEL-GANGER
THEN THE DOPPELGANGER TAKES HOLD OF THE MAIN BODY, WHICH LOOKS LIKE A SHURIKEN, AND...
DOPPEL-GANGER
FLIP
...THROWS IT OVER TO SASUKE!!
MAIN BODY
SASUKE STACKS IT ON TOP OF ANOTHER SHURIKEN THAT HE ALREADY HAD, AND THROWS THEM BOTH!!
HEH...
SO... YOU MADE ME FLY INTO SUCH A RAGE THAT I UNRAVELED THE SPELL HOLDING THE WATER PRISON TOGETHER...
NO!! YOU DIDN'T DROP YOUR OWN SPELL.
IT WAS BROKEN... FROM WITHOUT.

JUST SO YOU KNOW, THE SAME SPELL WON'T WORK ON ME TWICE.

-HMMF-

YOUR MOVE.

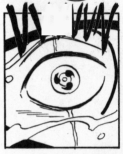

SPLASH SPLASH

壬子亥酉

子丑亥申酉

卯亥辰子未

寅巳子申酉

酉丑午未

壬申酉未

巳亥寅巳丑未

戌寅未子

午酉丑寅

子亥酉丑

丑申卯

壬子亥酉

子丑亥申酉

卯亥辰子未

寅巳子申酉

酉丑午未

壬申酉未

巳亥寅巳丑未

戌寅未子

午酉丑寅

子亥酉丑

丑申卯

FWUP FWUP FWUP FWUP FWUP FWUP FWUP FWUP FWUP

酉 TORI! SIGN OF THE BIRD!

READ THIS WAY

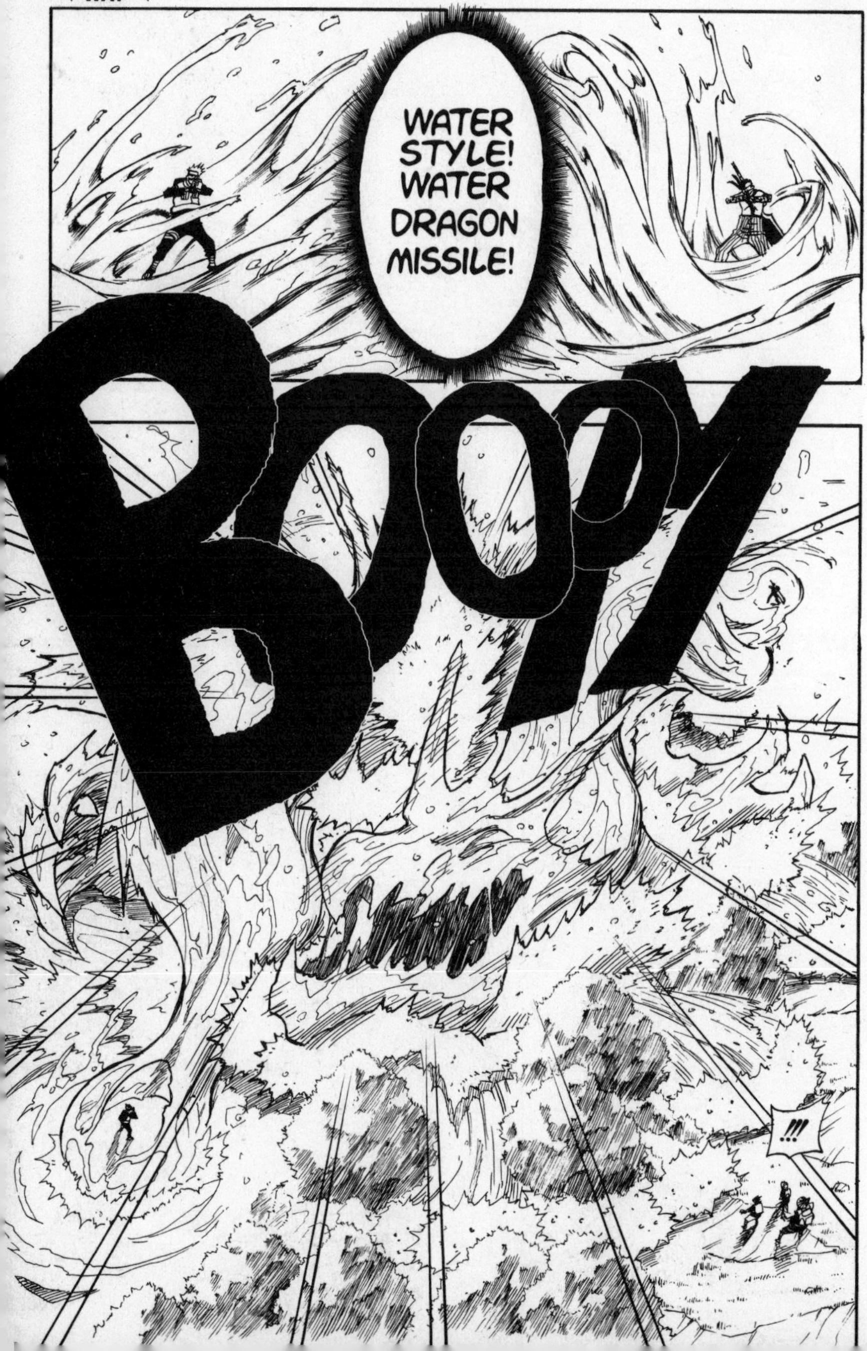
WATER STYLE! WATER DRAGON MISSILE!
BOOOM
!!!

READ THIS WAY

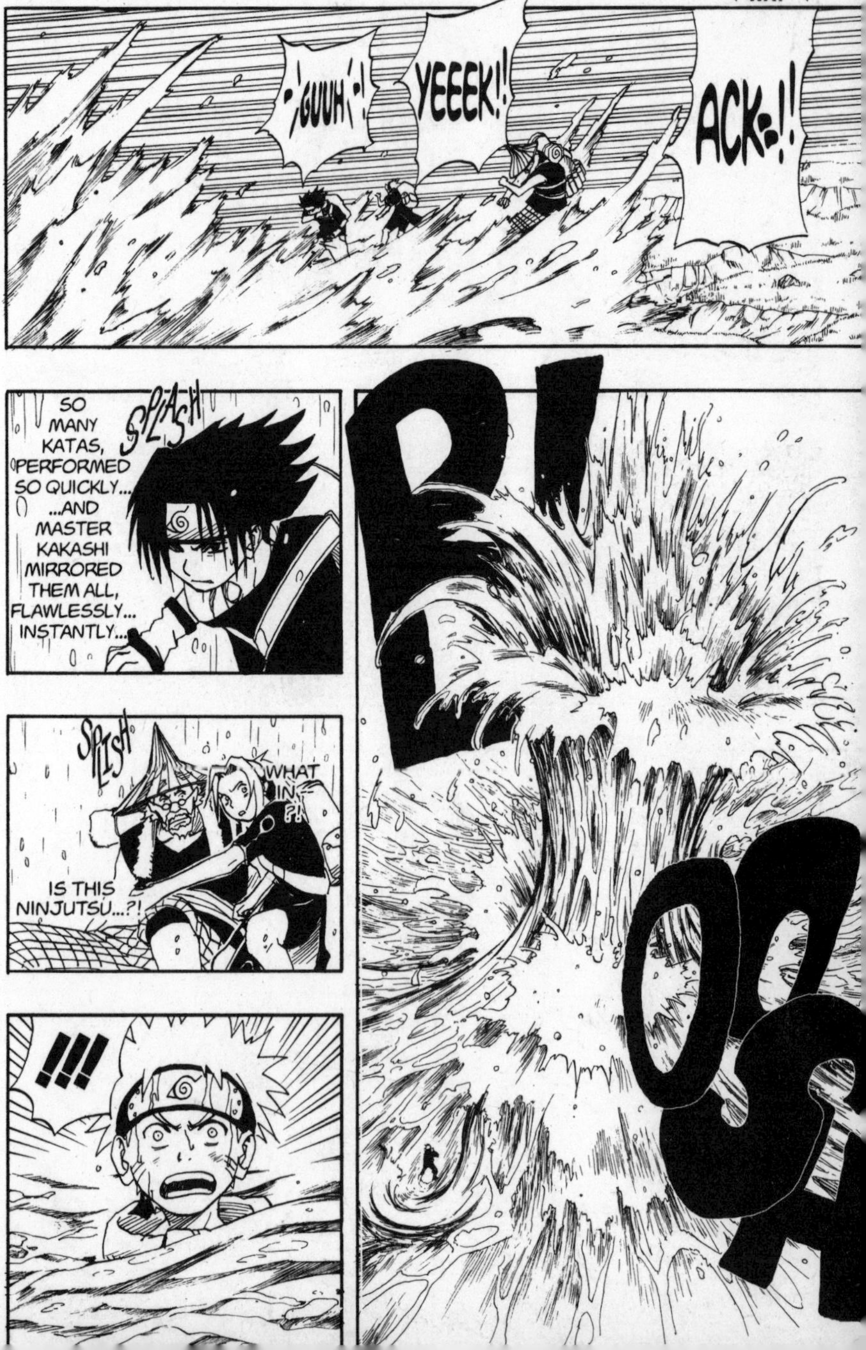
ACK..!!
YEEEK!!
GUUH..!
SPLASH
SO MANY KATAS, PERFORMED SO QUICKLY...
...AND MASTER KAKASHI MIRRORED THEM ALL, FLAWLESSLY... INSTANTLY...
SPLISH
WHAT IN--?!
IS THIS NINJUTSU...?!
!!!

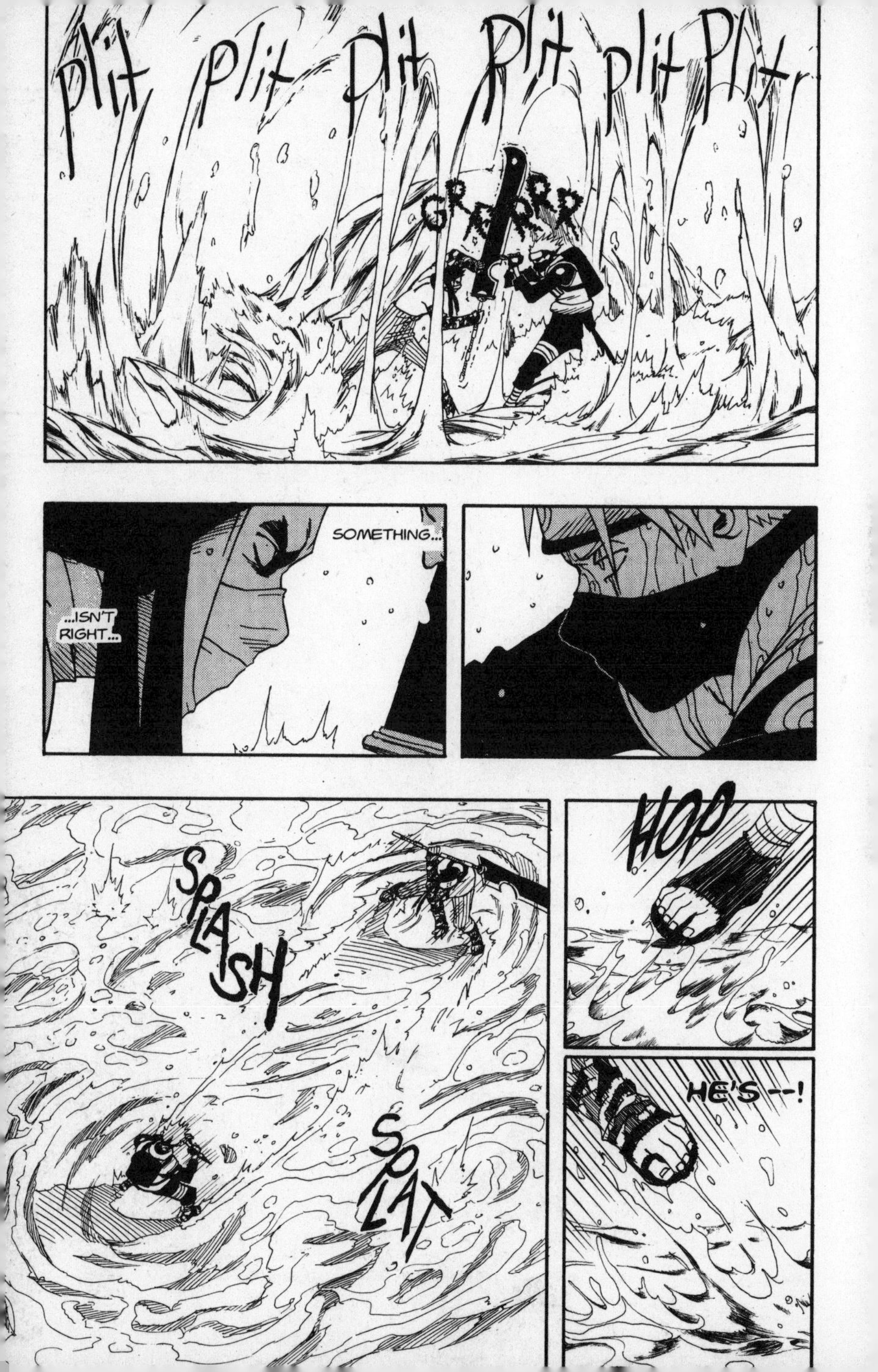
plit plit plit plit plit plit
GRARRR
SOMETHING...
...ISN'T RIGHT...
HOP
HE'S --!
SPLASH
SPLAT

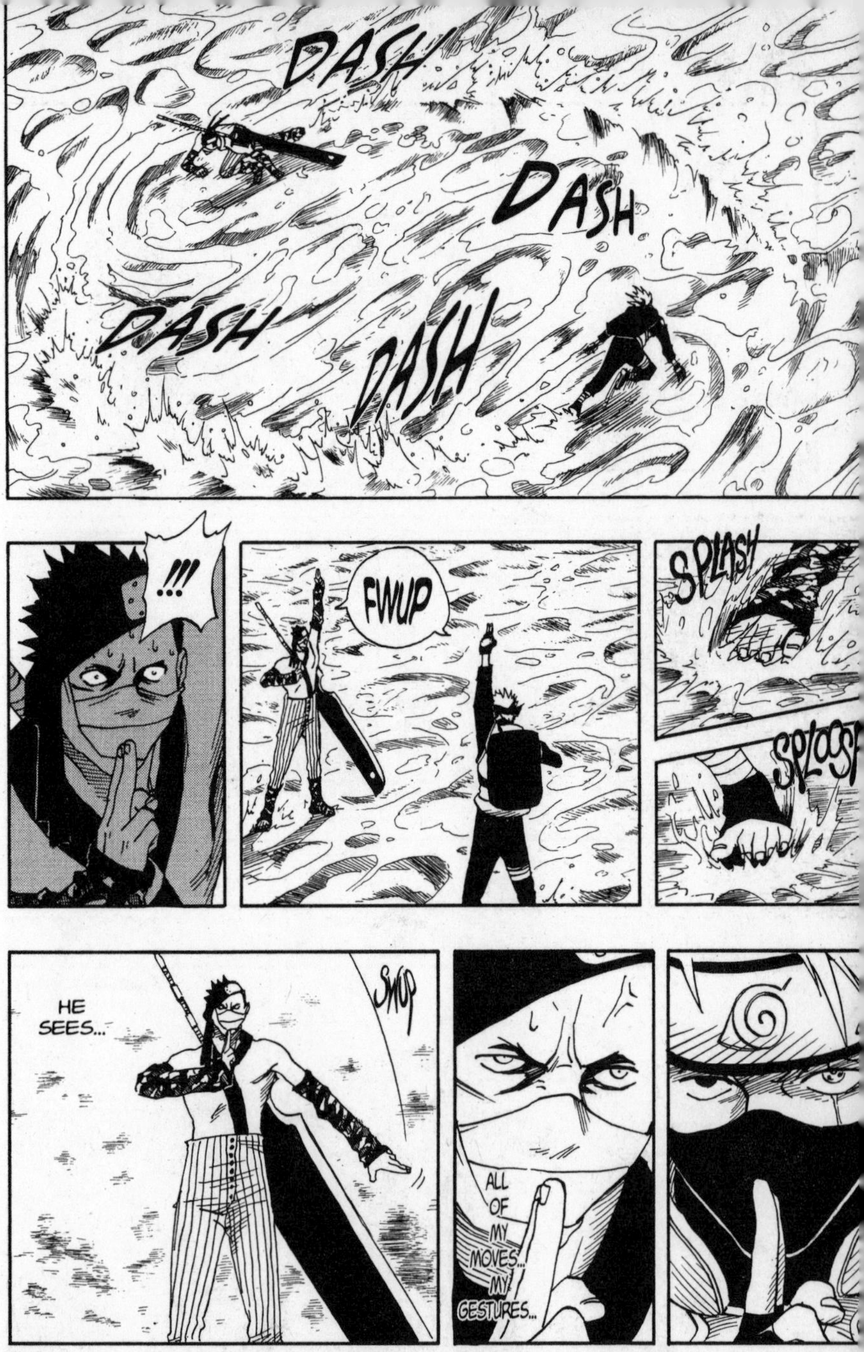
DASH
DASH
DASH
DASH
SPLASH
FWUP
!!!
ALL OF MY MOVES... MY GESTURES...
SWUP
HE SEES...

READ THIS WAY

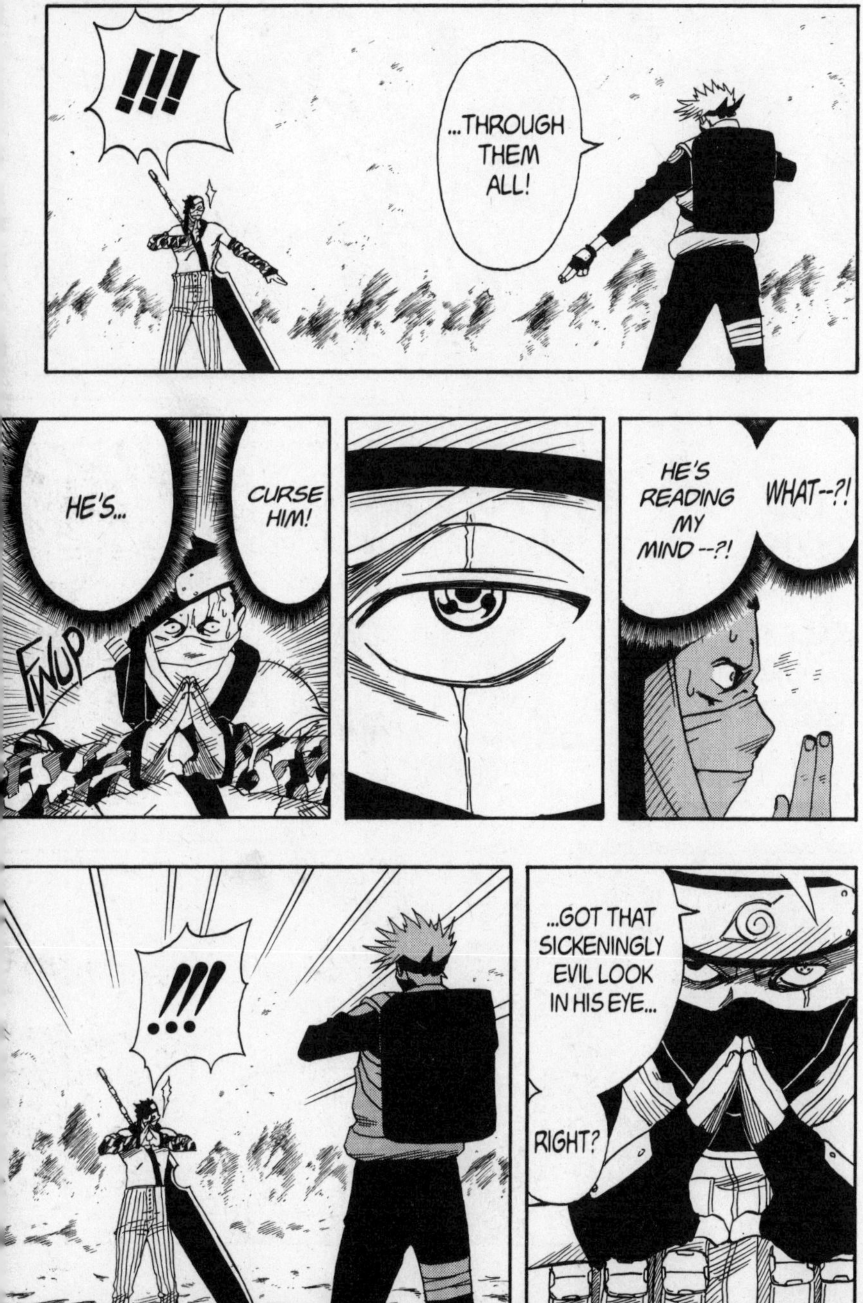
...THROUGH THEM ALL!
!!!
WHAT--?!
HE'S READING MY MIND--?!
CURSE HIM!
HE'S...
FWUP
...GOT THAT SICKENINGLY EVIL LOOK IN HIS EYE...
RIGHT?
...!!!

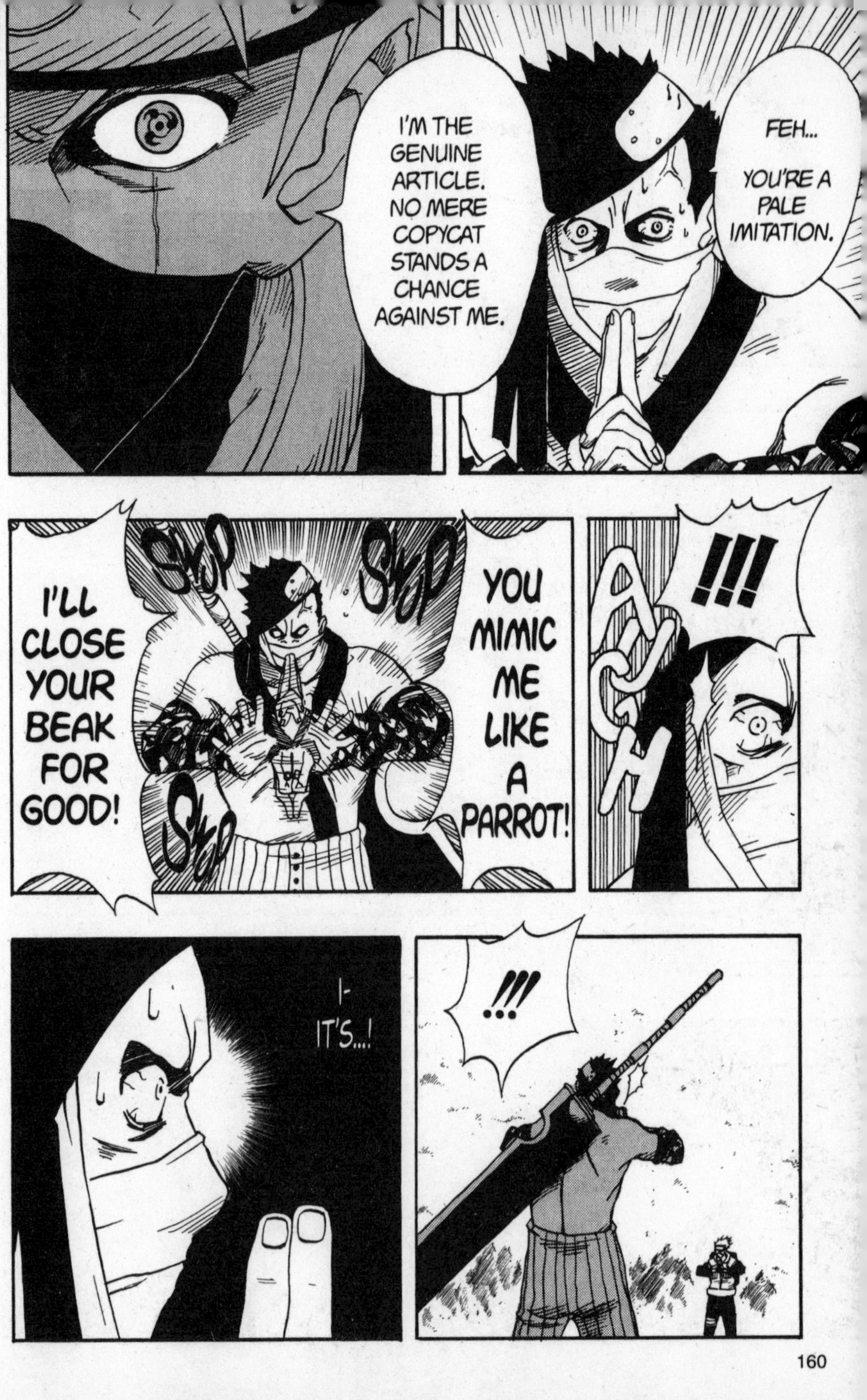
FEH...
YOU'RE A PALE IMITATION.
I'M THE GENUINE ARTICLE. NO MERE COPYCAT STANDS A CHANCE AGAINST ME.
!!!
YOU MIMIC ME LIKE A PARROT!
I'LL CLOSE YOUR BEAK FOR GOOD!
!!!
I- IT'S...!

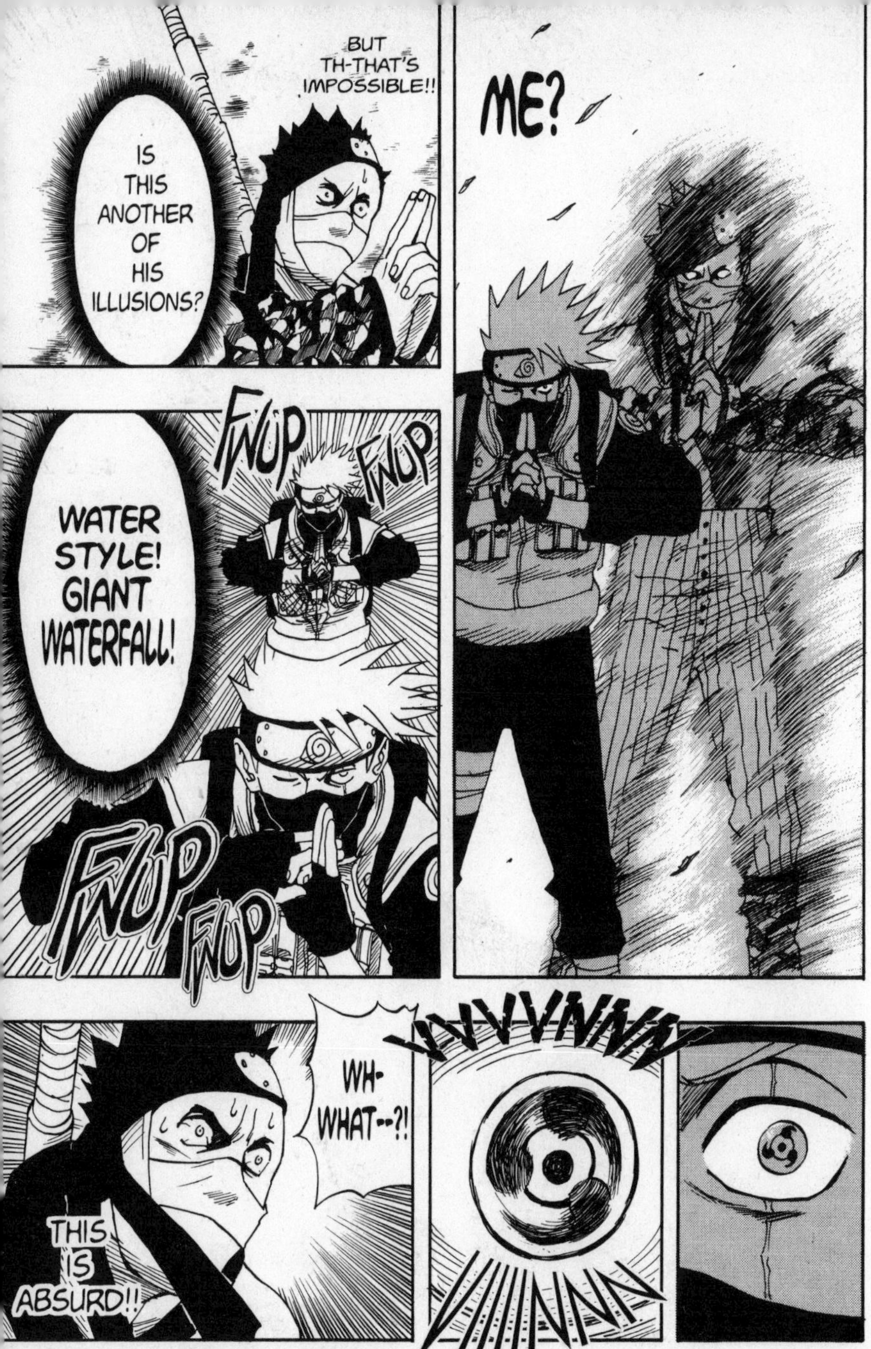
ME?
BUT TH-THAT'S IMPOSSIBLE!!
IS THIS ANOTHER OF HIS ILLUSIONS?
FWUP
FWUP
WATER STYLE! GIANT WATERFALL!
FWUP
FWUP
VVVVNNN
VVVVNNN
WH- WHAT--?!
THIS IS ABSURD!!

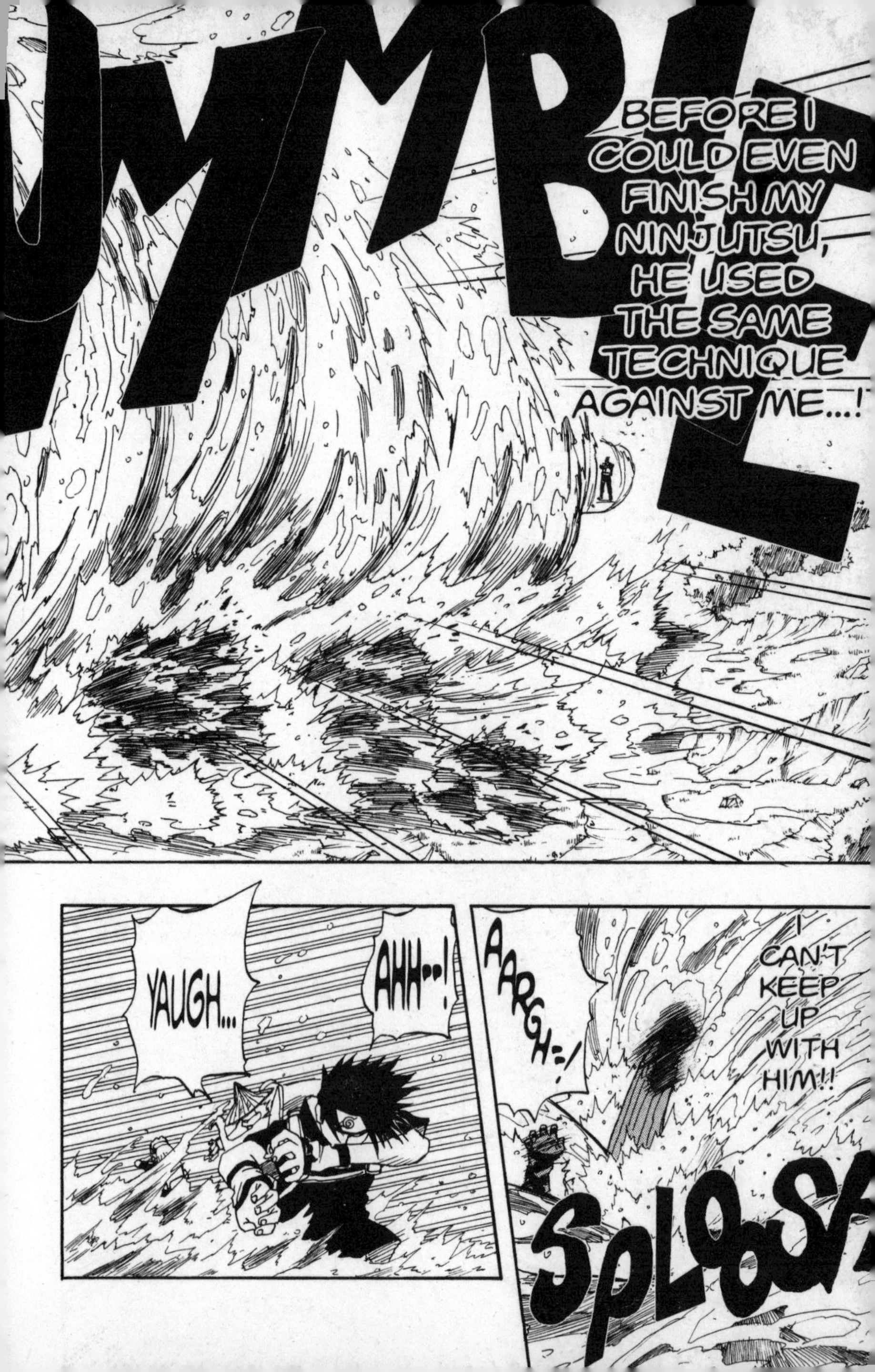
UMBLE
BEFORE I COULD EVEN FINISH MY NINJUTSU, HE USED THE SAME TECHNIQUE AGAINST ME...!
I CAN'T KEEP UP WITH HIM!!
AARGH..!
SPLOOS
AHH..!
YAUGH...

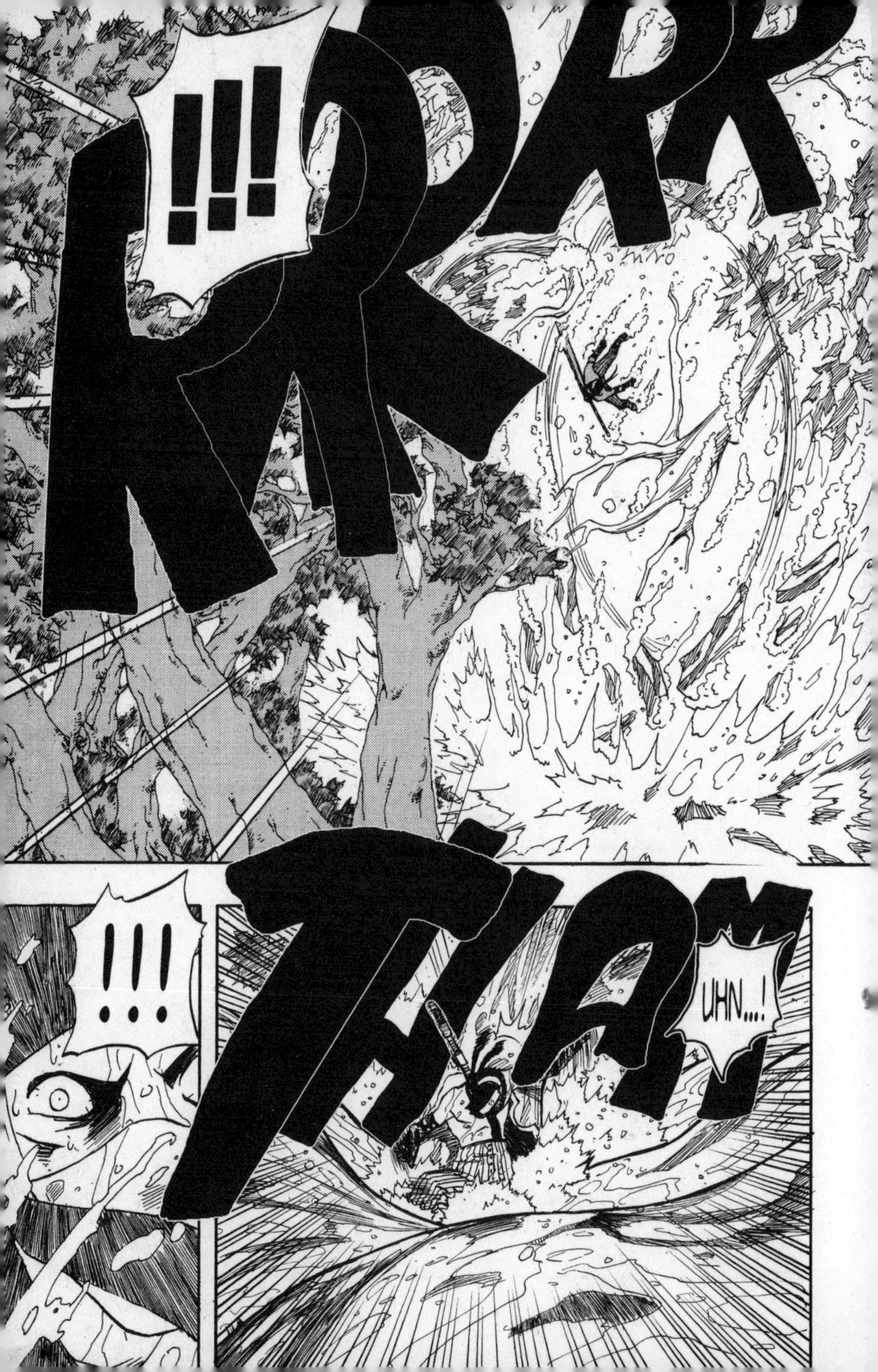
!!!!
UHN...!
!!!

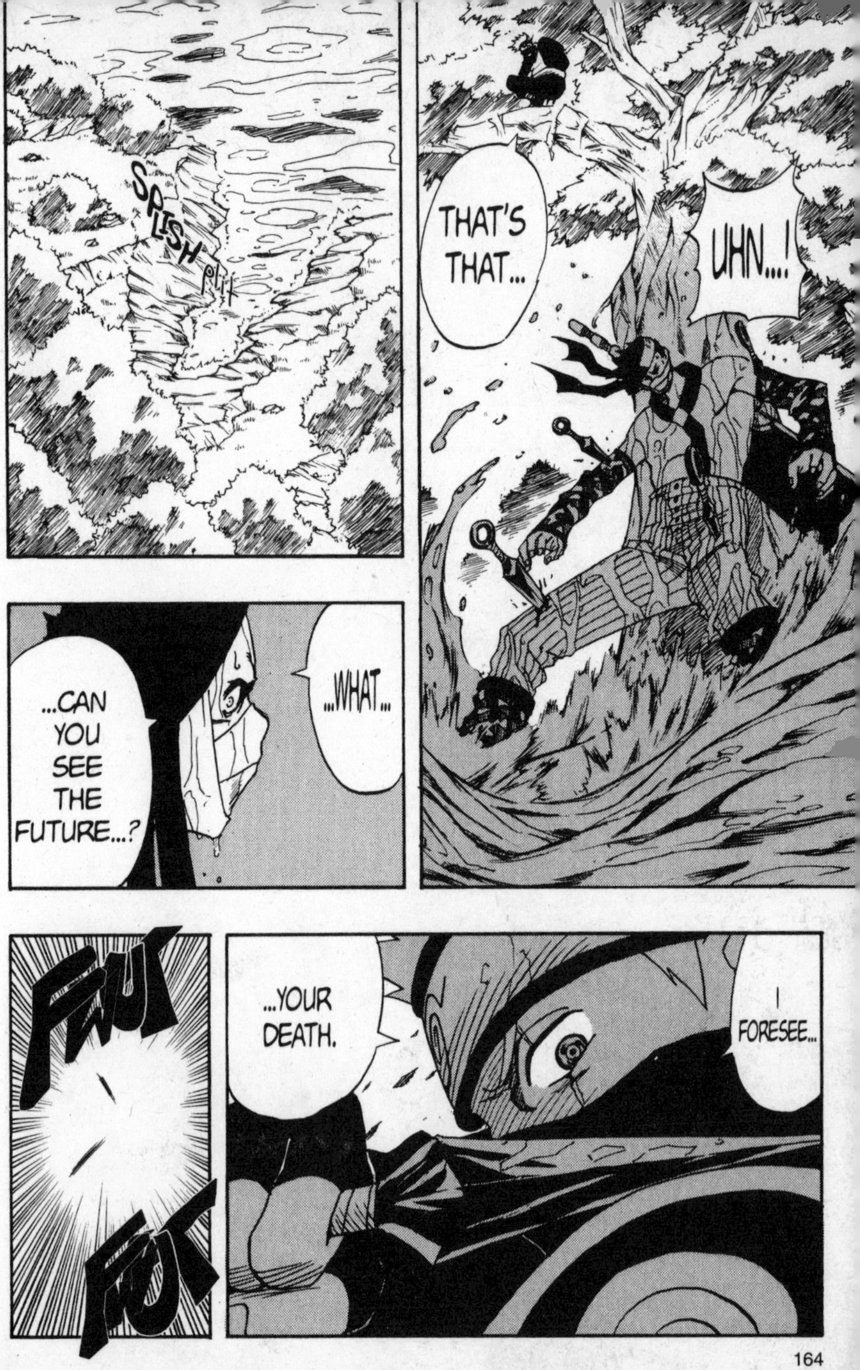
UHN...!
THAT'S THAT...
SPLISH
plit
...WHAT...
...CAN YOU SEE THE FUTURE...?
I FORESEE...
...YOUR DEATH.
FWUT
FWUT

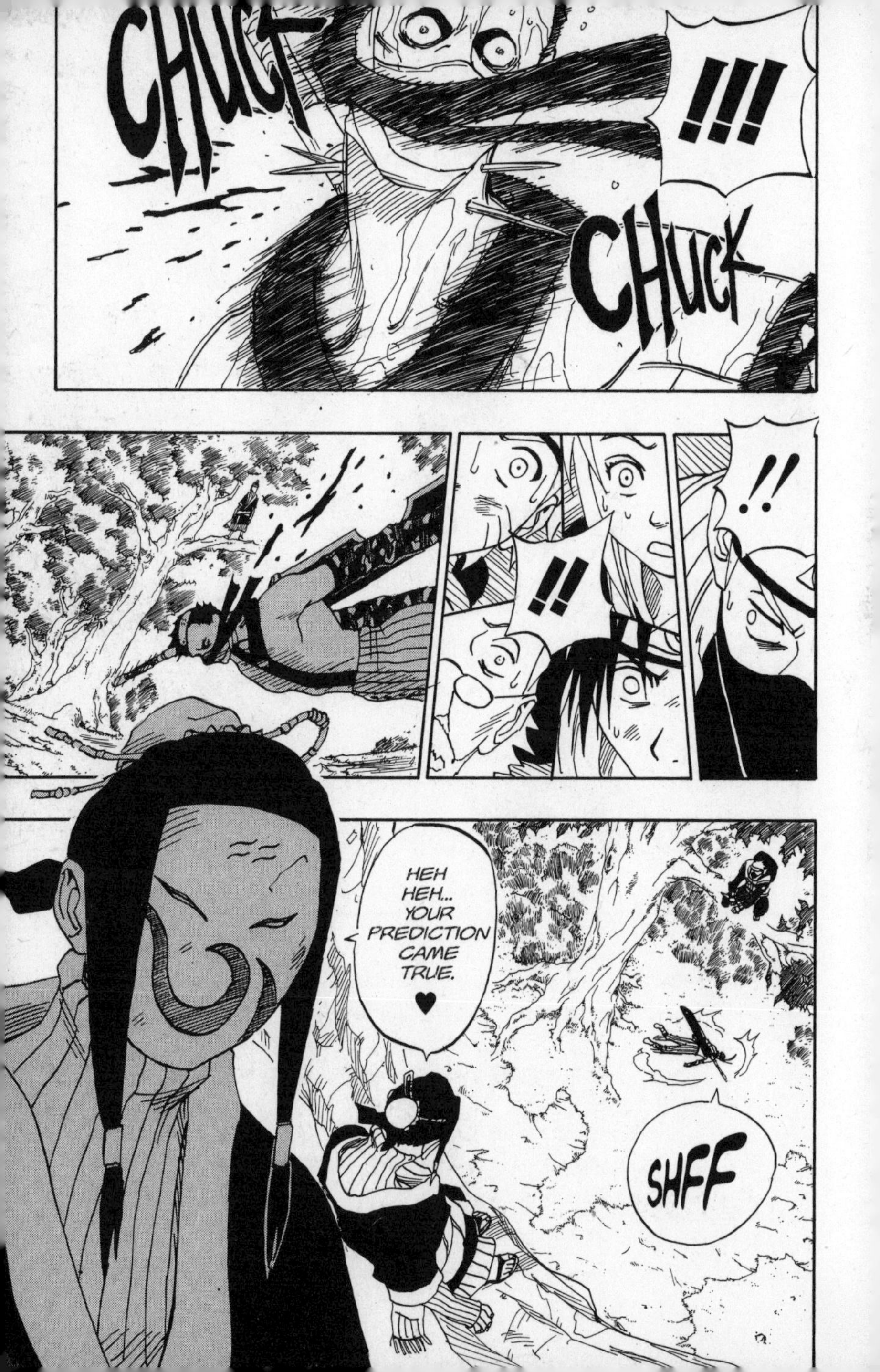
!!!
CHUCK
CHUCK
!!
!!
HEH HEH... YOUR PREDICTION CAME TRUE. ♥
SHFF

MAKE-OUT PARADISE

I've gotten a number of letters asking me to tell more about **Make-Out Paradise**, the books Kakashi is always reading. Therefore, I've decided to write a little bit about it.

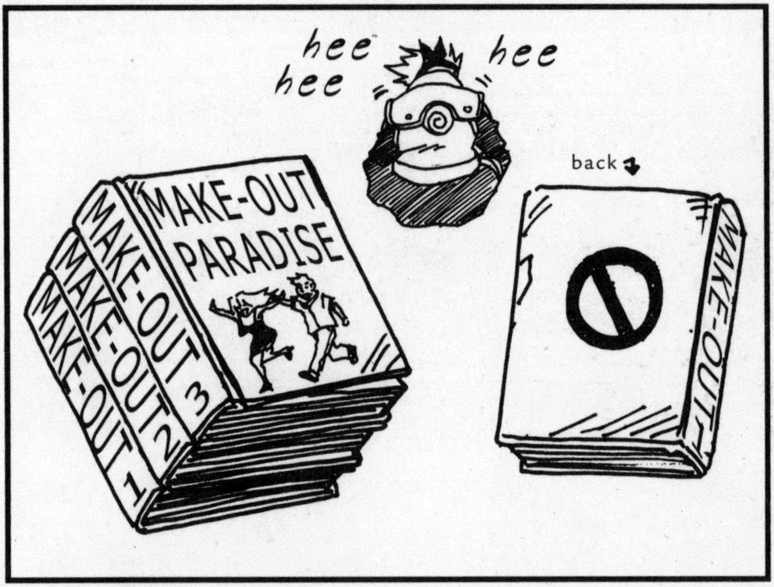
hee
hee
hee
back
MAKE-OUT PARADISE
MAKE-OUT 3
MAKE-OUT 2
MAKE-OUT 1
MAKE-OUT

Make-Out Paradise (a three-volume series) is Kakashi's favorite reading material! The plot involves.....................

....

......Umm...unfortunately, even though **Naruto** is "recommended for ages 13 and up," it's not *quite* "adult" enough to explain the story of **Make-Out Paradise**. Sorry! But I will say that if Kakashi gets his wish, **Make-Out Paradise** Vol. 1 may yet be published in English!

READ THIS WAY

Number 16: Who Are You?!

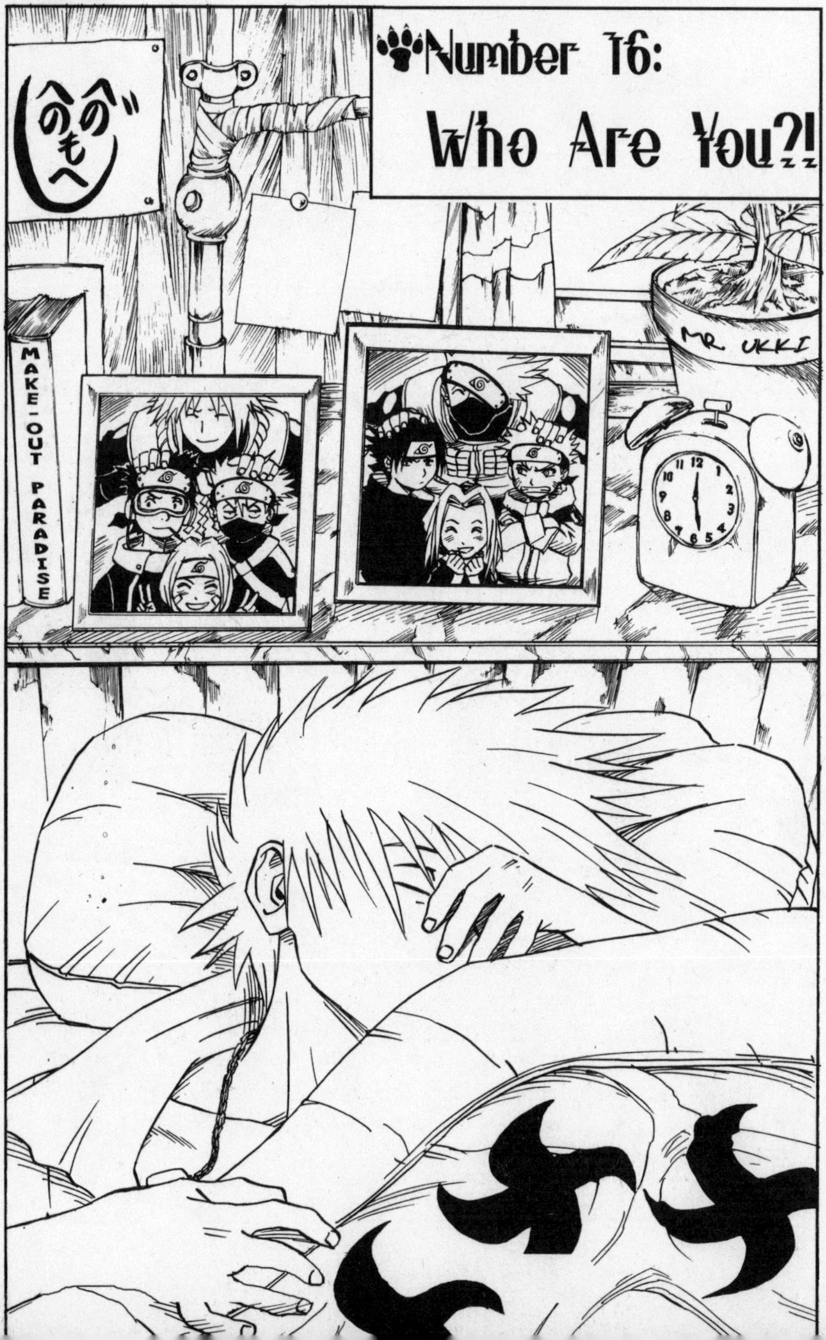
へのへのもへじ
MAKE-OUT PARADISE
MR. UKKI

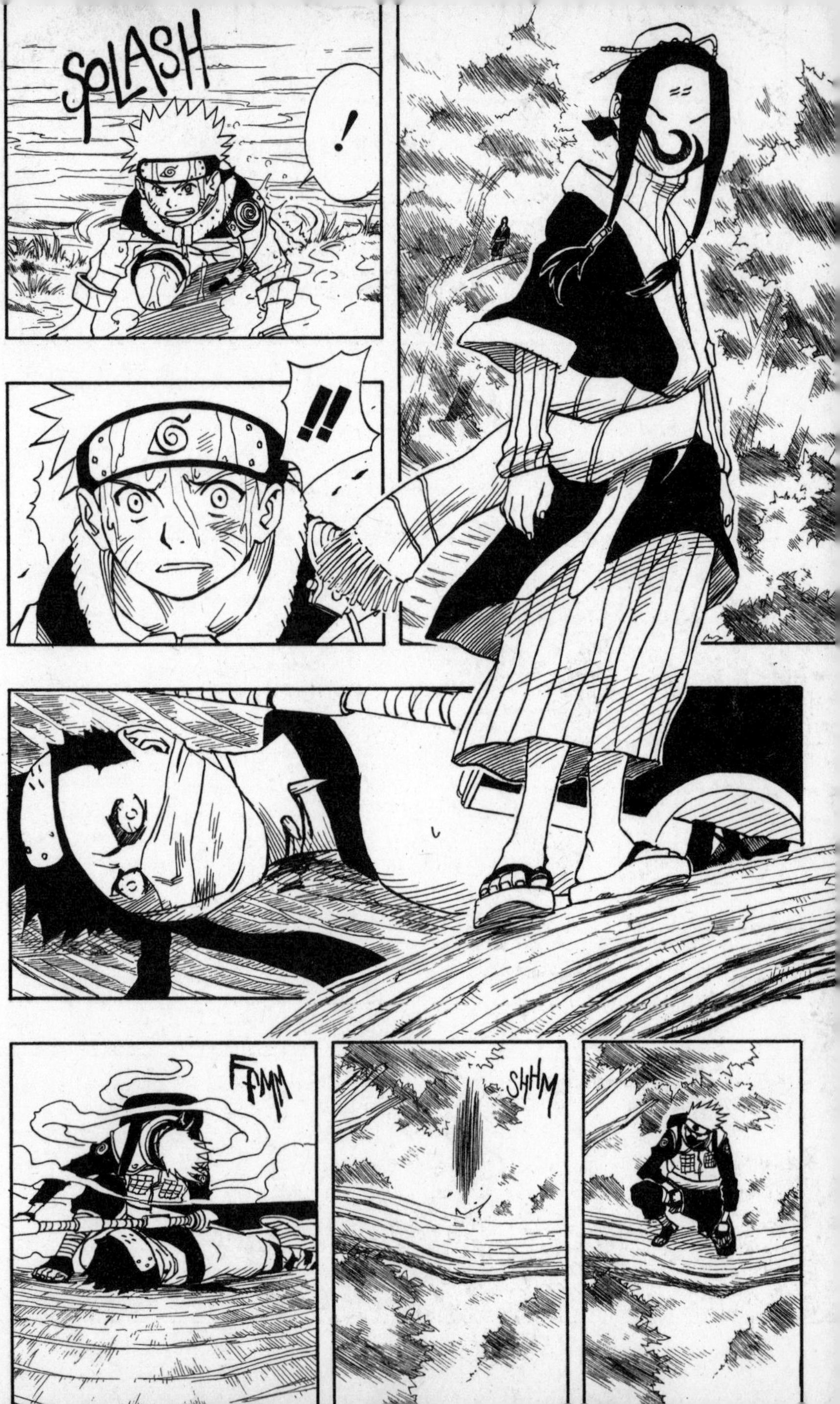
SPLASH
!
!!
SHHM
FFMM

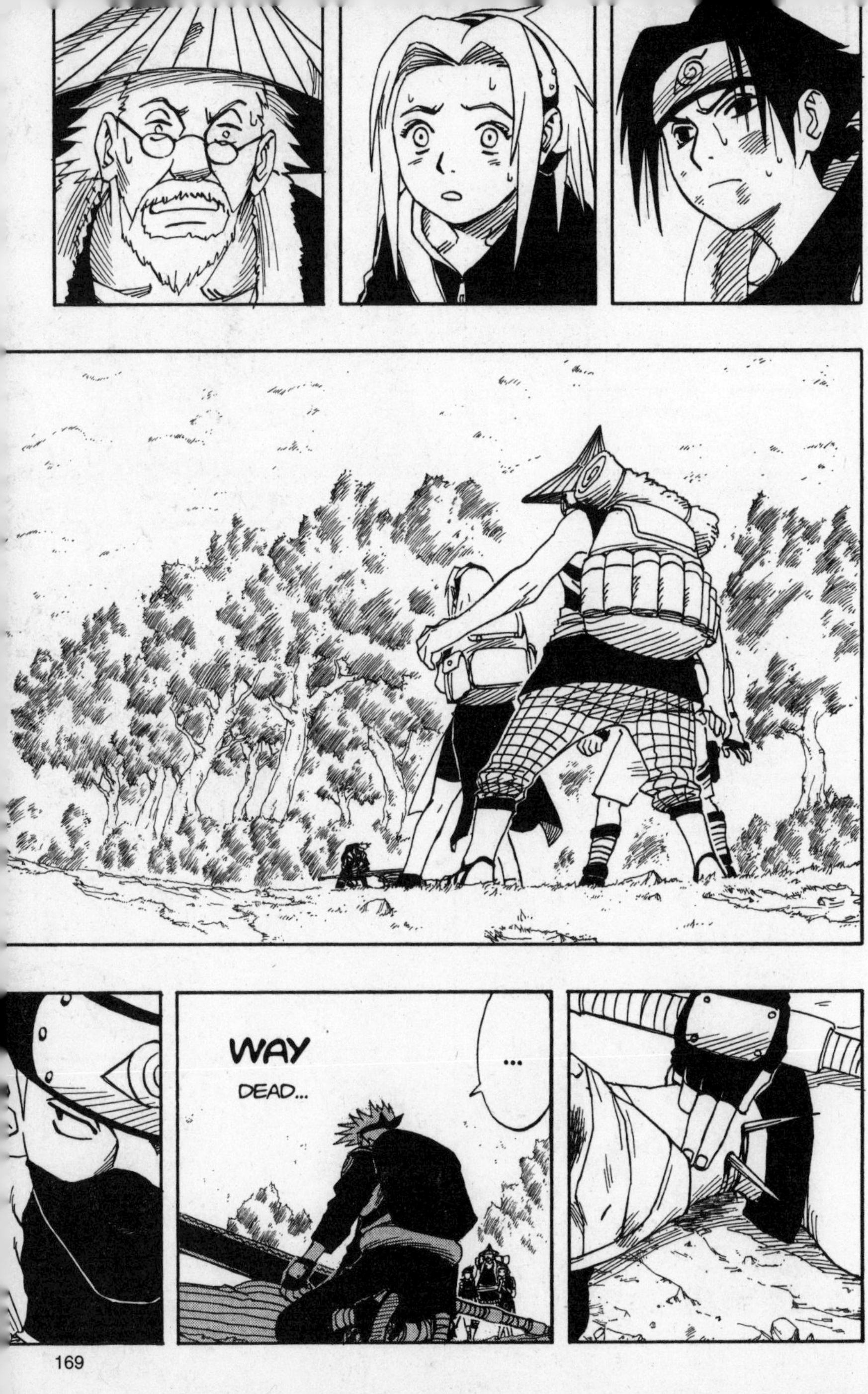
...
WAY
DEAD...

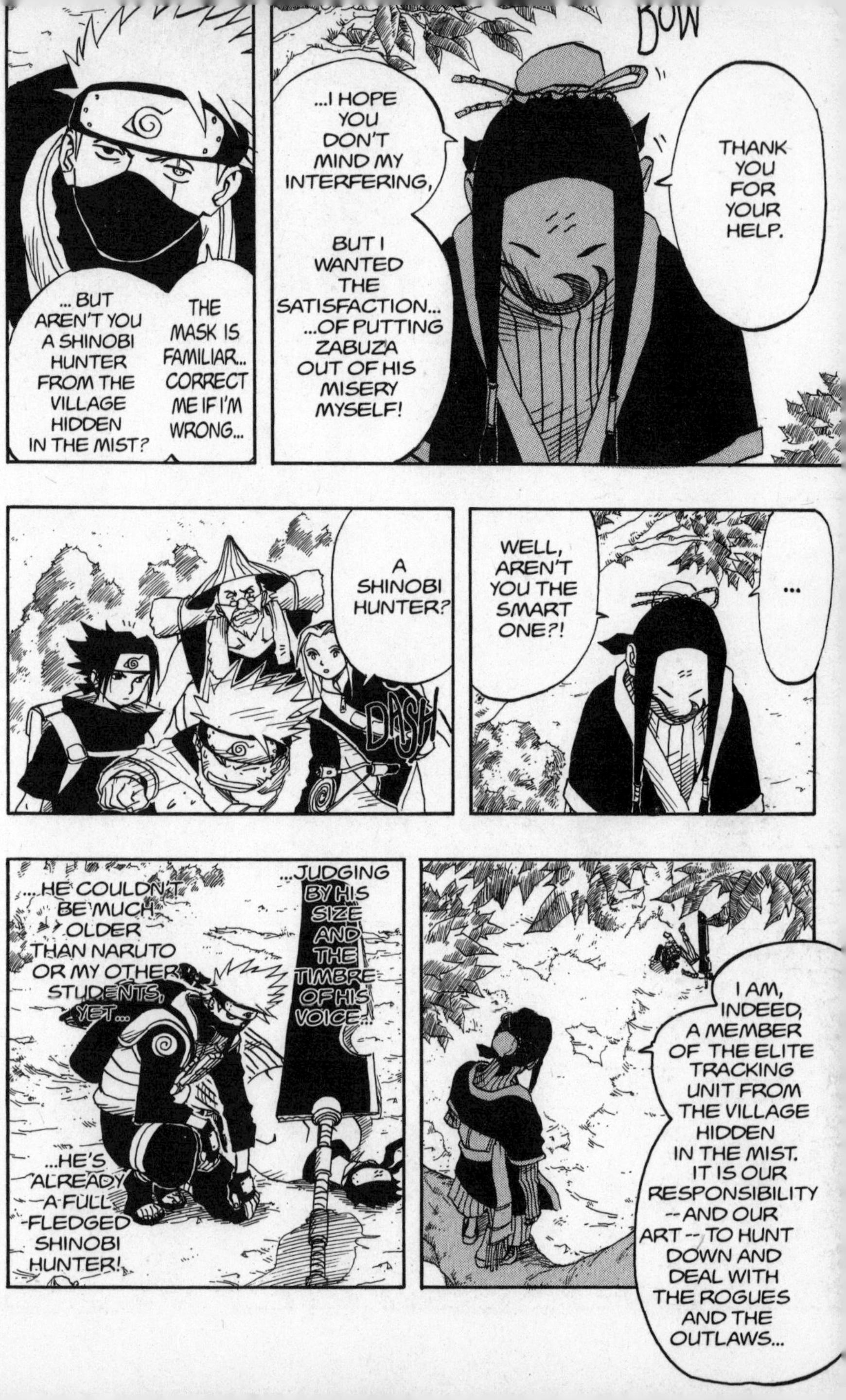
BOW
THANK YOU FOR YOUR HELP.
...I HOPE YOU DON'T MIND MY INTERFERING,
BUT I WANTED THE SATISFACTION...
...OF PUTTING ZABUZA OUT OF HIS MISERY MYSELF!
THE MASK IS FAMILIAR... CORRECT ME IF I'M WRONG...
... BUT AREN'T YOU A SHINOBI HUNTER FROM THE VILLAGE HIDDEN IN THE MIST?
...
WELL, AREN'T YOU THE SMART ONE?!
A SHINOBI HUNTER?
DASH
I AM, INDEED, A MEMBER OF THE ELITE TRACKING UNIT FROM THE VILLAGE HIDDEN IN THE MIST. IT IS OUR RESPONSIBILITY -- AND OUR ART -- TO HUNT DOWN AND DEAL WITH THE ROGUES AND THE OUTLAWS...
...JUDGING BY HIS SIZE AND THE TIMBRE OF HIS VOICE...
...HE COULDN'T BE MUCH OLDER THAN NARUTO OR MY OTHER STUDENTS, YET...
...HE'S ALREADY A FULL-FLEDGED SHINOBI HUNTER!

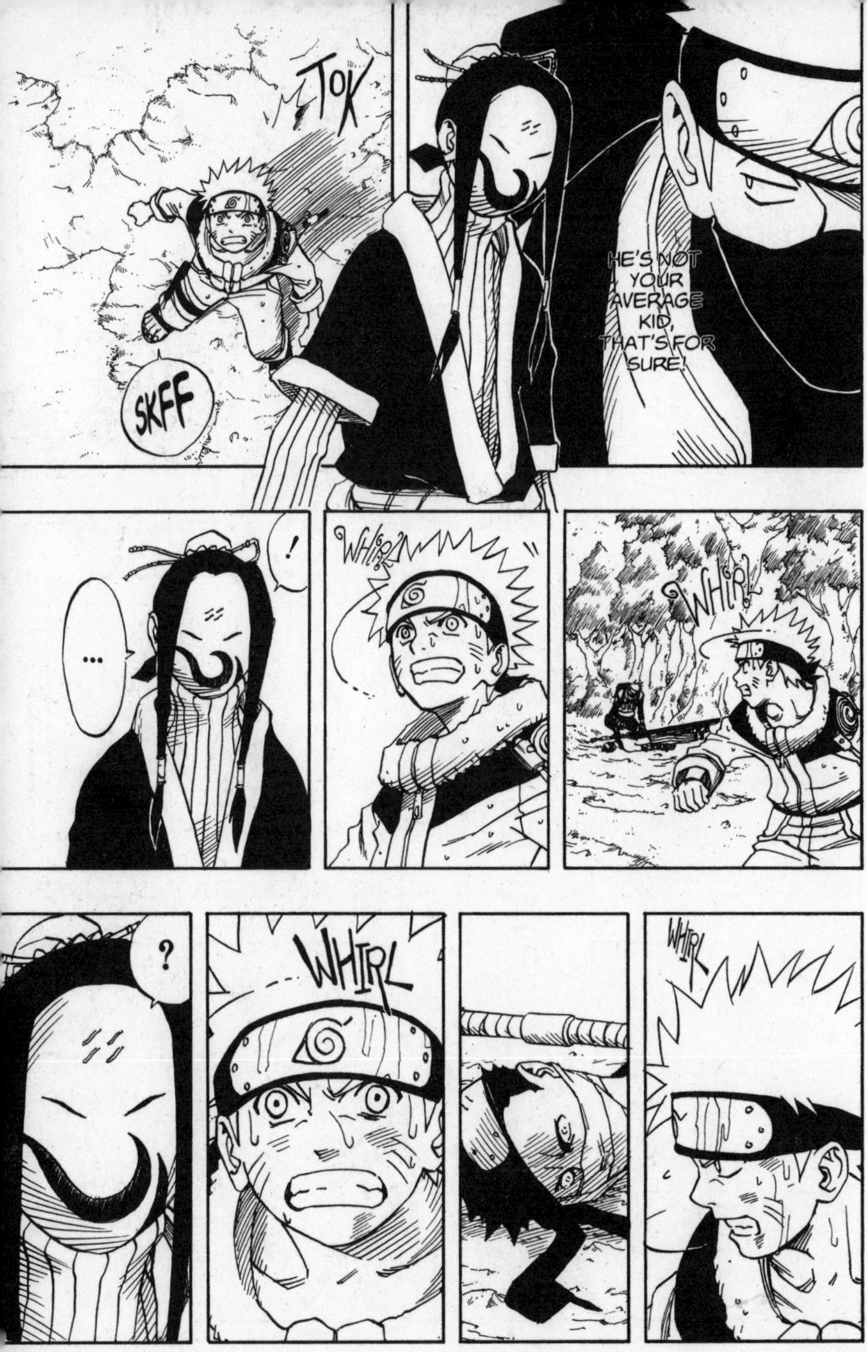
HE'S NOT YOUR AVERAGE KID, THAT'S FOR SURE!
TOK
SKFF
WHIRL
WHIRL
!
...
WHIRL
WHIRL
?

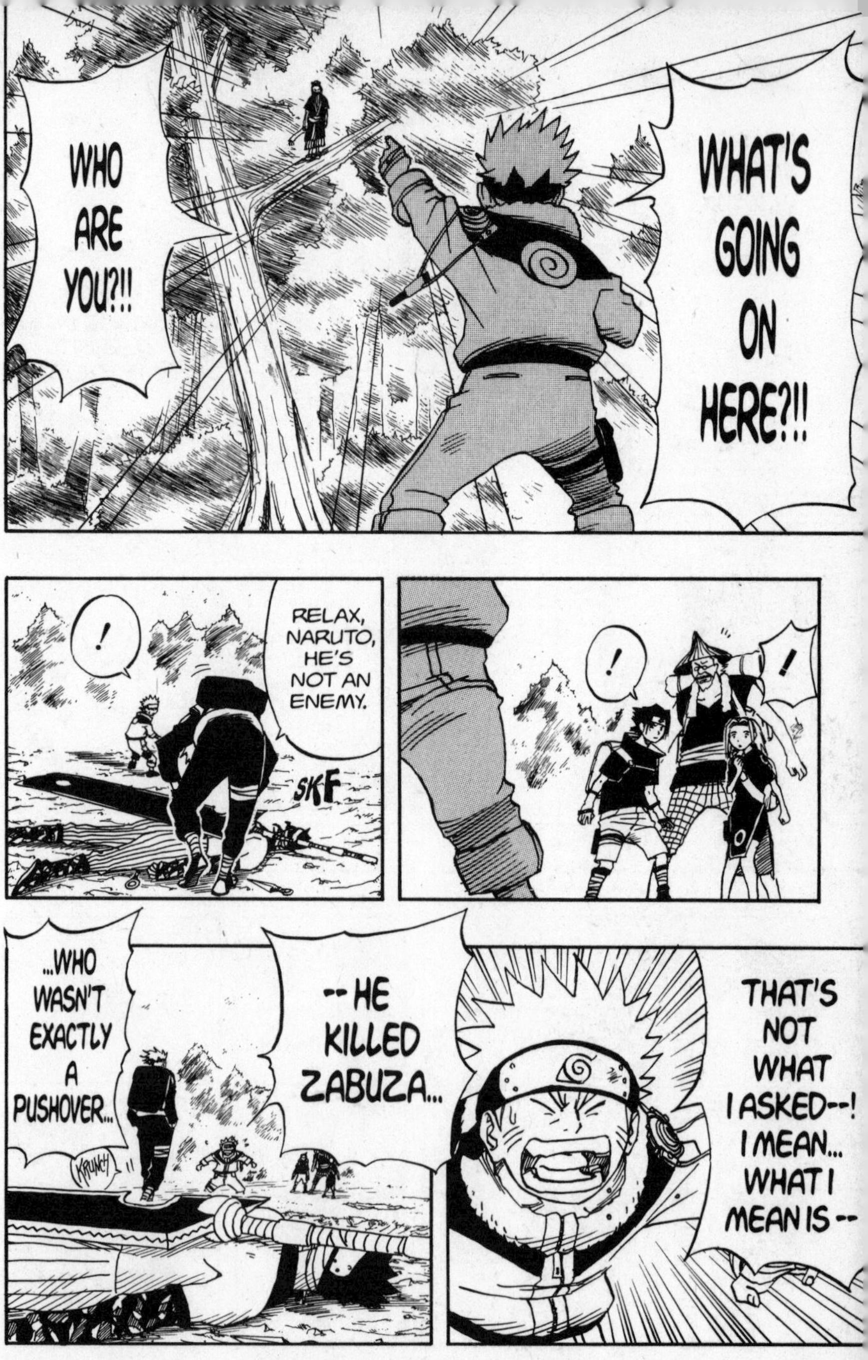
WHAT'S GOING ON HERE?!!
WHO ARE YOU?!!
!
!
!
RELAX, NARUTO, HE'S NOT AN ENEMY.
SKF
THAT'S NOT WHAT I ASKED--! I MEAN... WHAT I MEAN IS --
-- HE KILLED ZABUZA...
...WHO WASN'T EXACTLY A PUSHOVER...
KRUNCH

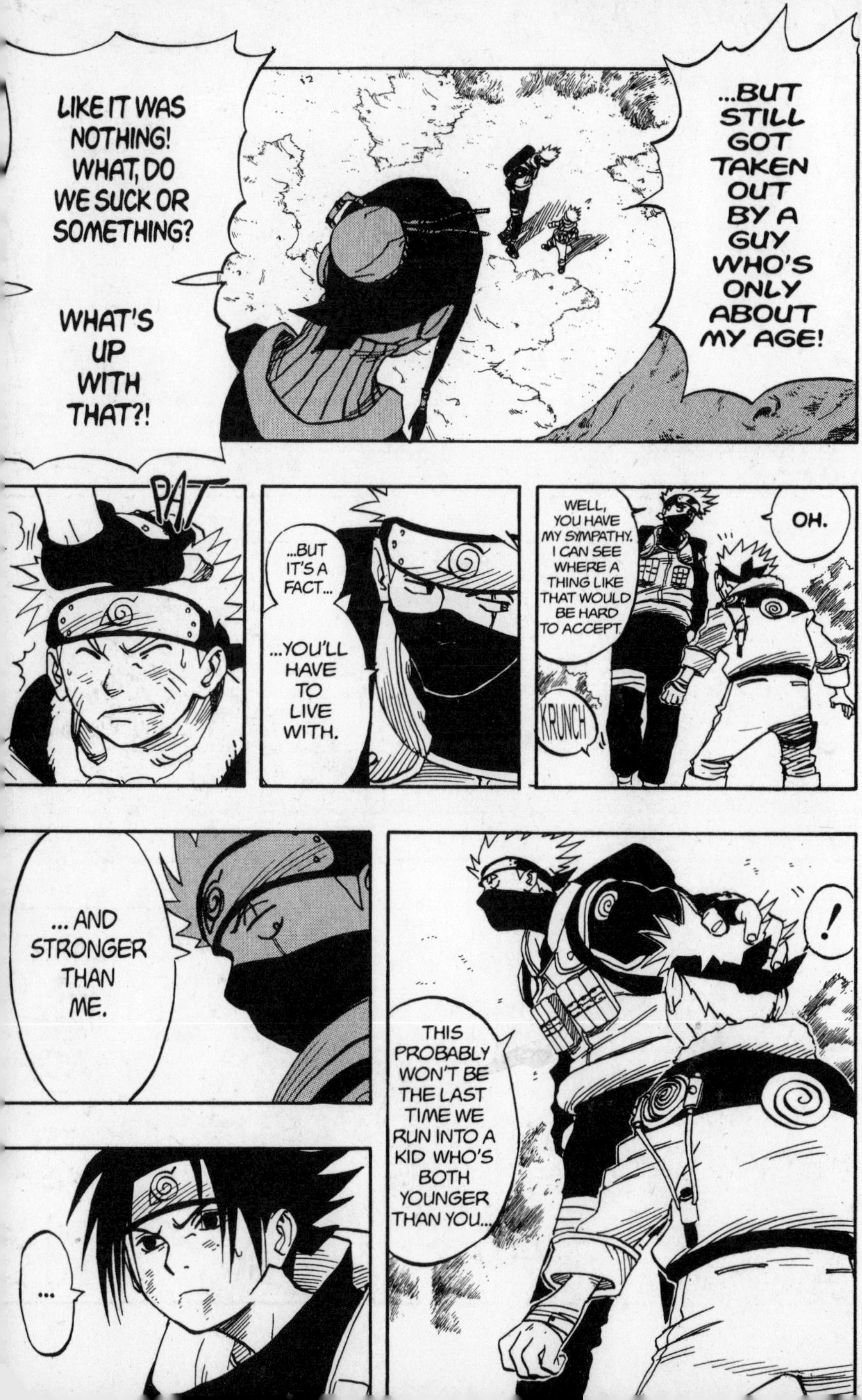
...BUT STILL GOT TAKEN OUT BY A GUY WHO'S ONLY ABOUT MY AGE!
LIKE IT WAS NOTHING! WHAT, DO WE SUCK OR SOMETHING?
WHAT'S UP WITH THAT?!
OH.
WELL, YOU HAVE MY SYMPATHY. I CAN SEE WHERE A THING LIKE THAT WOULD BE HARD TO ACCEPT.
KRUNCH
...BUT IT'S A FACT...
...YOU'LL HAVE TO LIVE WITH.
PAT
!
THIS PROBABLY WON'T BE THE LAST TIME WE RUN INTO A KID WHO'S BOTH YOUNGER THAN YOU...
... AND STRONGER THAN ME.
...

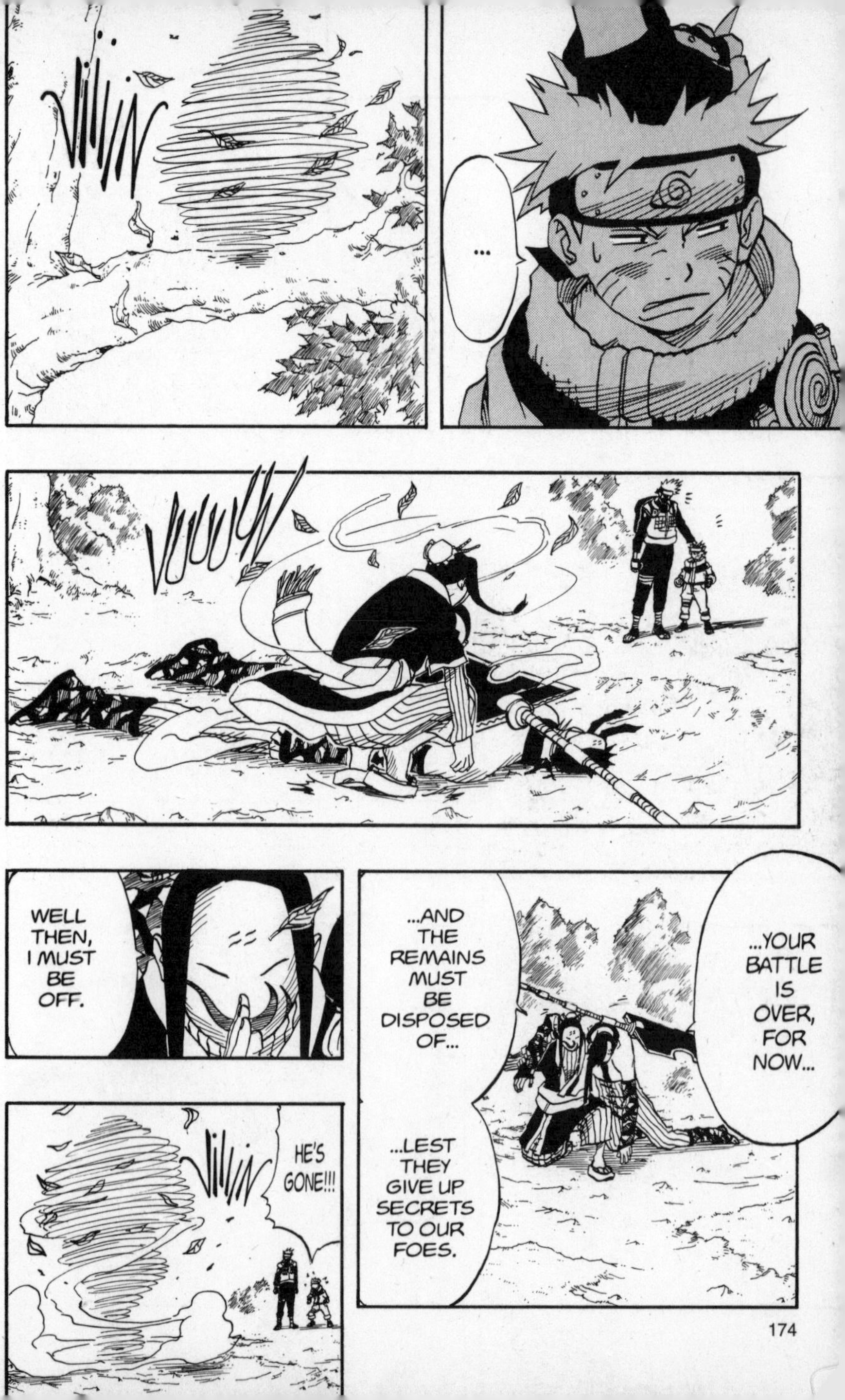
...
VIIIIN
VUUUUN
...YOUR BATTLE IS OVER, FOR NOW...
...AND THE REMAINS MUST BE DISPOSED OF...
...LEST THEY GIVE UP SECRETS TO OUR FOES.
WELL THEN, I MUST BE OFF.
VIIIIN
HE'S GONE!!!

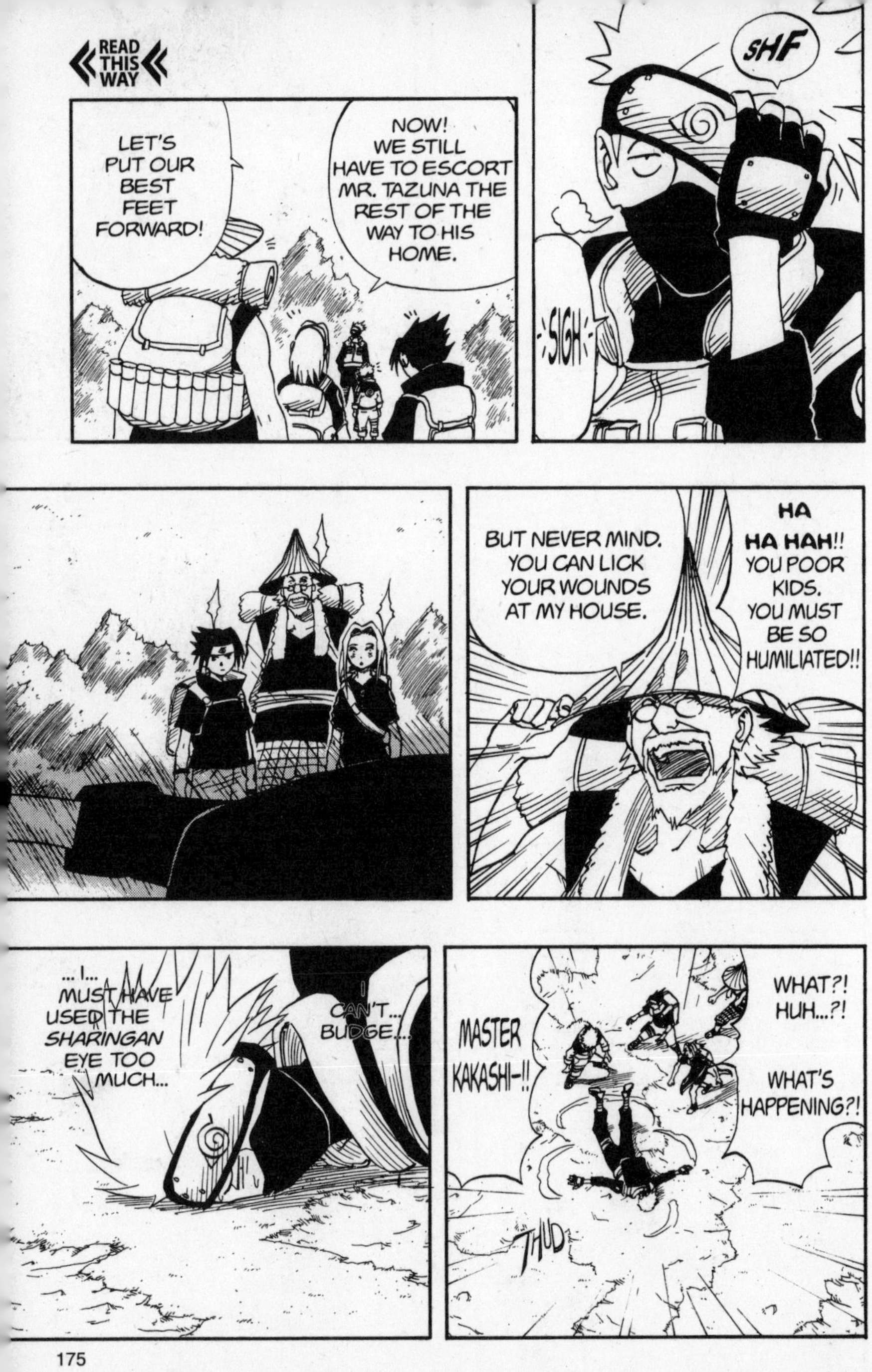
READ THIS WAY
SHF
SIGH
NOW! WE STILL HAVE TO ESCORT MR. TAZUNA THE REST OF THE WAY TO HIS HOME.
LET'S PUT OUR BEST FEET FORWARD!
HA HA HAH!! YOU POOR KIDS. YOU MUST BE SO HUMILIATED!!
BUT NEVER MIND. YOU CAN LICK YOUR WOUNDS AT MY HOUSE.
WHAT?! HUH...?!
WHAT'S HAPPENING?!
MASTER KAKASHI-!!
THUD
I CAN'T... BUDGE...
...I... MUST HAVE USED THE SHARINGAN EYE TOO MUCH...

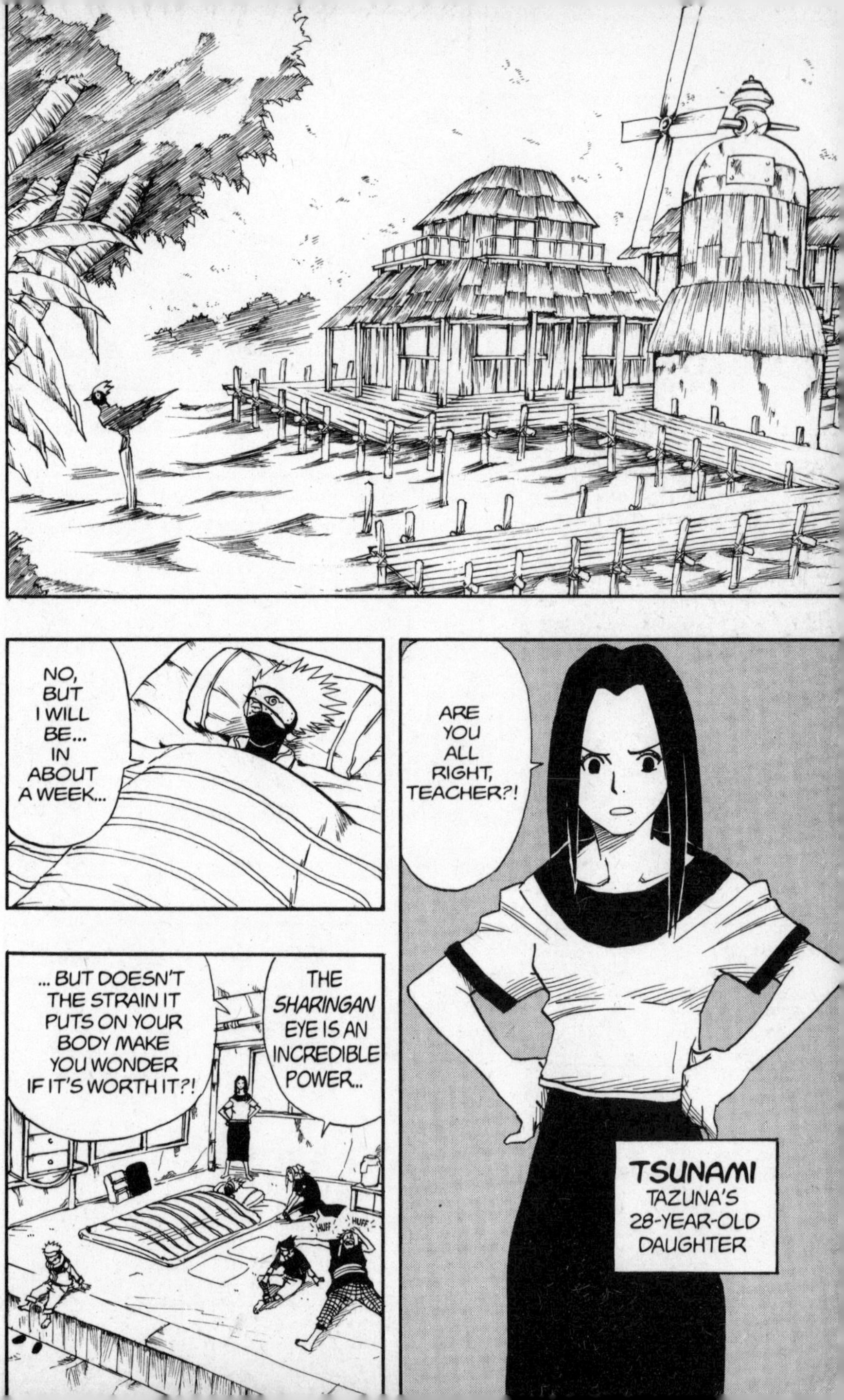
ARE YOU ALL RIGHT, TEACHER?!
TSUNAMI
TAZUNA'S 28-YEAR-OLD DAUGHTER
NO, BUT I WILL BE... IN ABOUT A WEEK...
THE SHARINGAN EYE IS AN INCREDIBLE POWER..
... BUT DOESN'T THE STRAIN IT PUTS ON YOUR BODY MAKE YOU WONDER IF IT'S WORTH IT?!
HUFF
HUFF

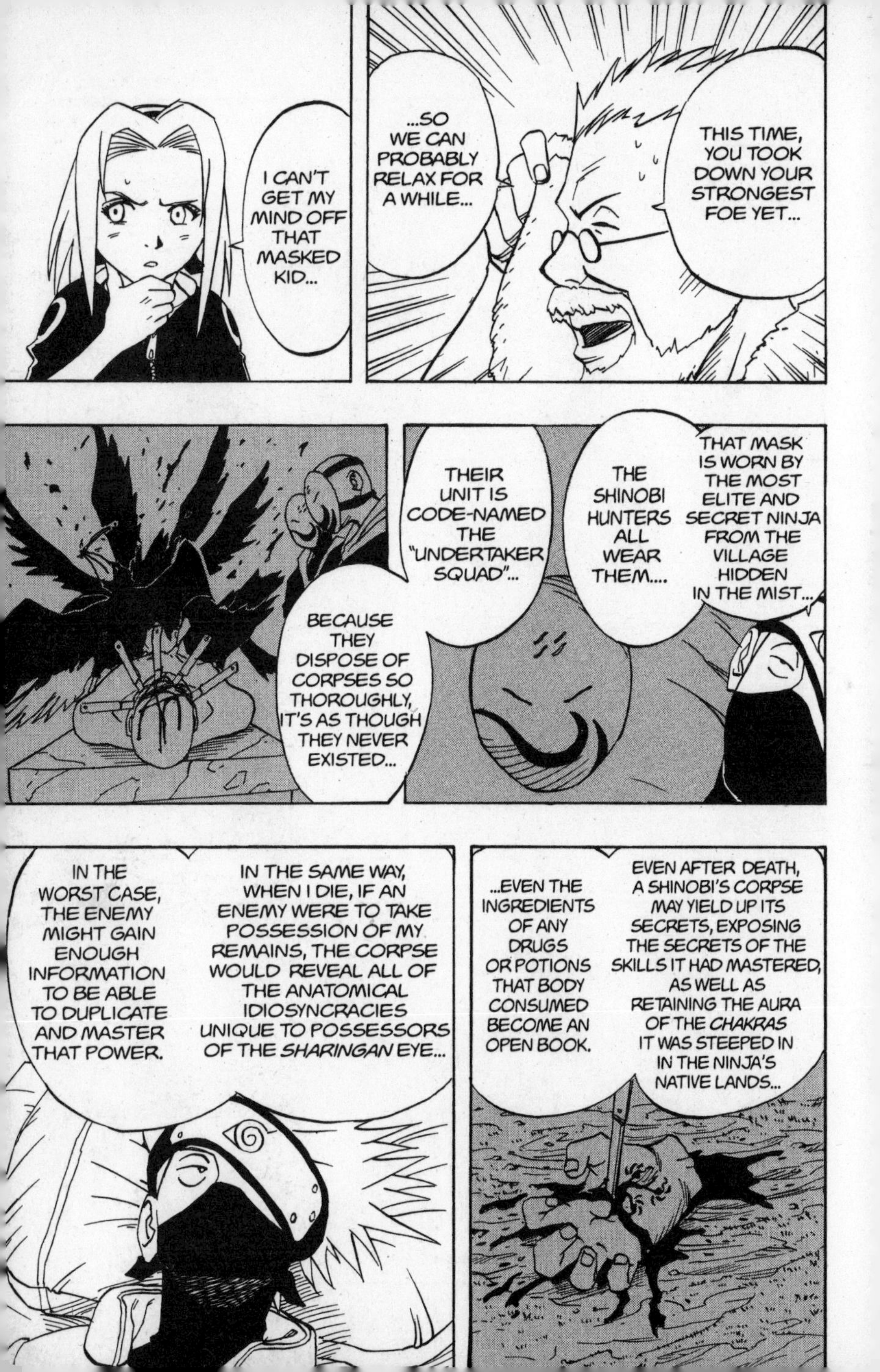
THIS TIME, YOU TOOK DOWN YOUR STRONGEST FOE YET...
...SO WE CAN PROBABLY RELAX FOR A WHILE...
I CAN'T GET MY MIND OFF THAT MASKED KID...
THAT MASK IS WORN BY THE MOST ELITE AND SECRET NINJA FROM THE VILLAGE HIDDEN IN THE MIST...
THE SHINOBI HUNTERS ALL WEAR THEM....
THEIR UNIT IS CODE-NAMED THE "UNDERTAKER SQUAD"...
BECAUSE THEY DISPOSE OF CORPSES SO THOROUGHLY, IT'S AS THOUGH THEY NEVER EXISTED...
EVEN AFTER DEATH, A SHINOBI'S CORPSE MAY YIELD UP ITS SECRETS, EXPOSING THE SECRETS OF THE SKILLS IT HAD MASTERED, AS WELL AS RETAINING THE AURA OF THE *CHAKRAS* IT WAS STEEPED IN IN THE NINJA'S NATIVE LANDS...
...EVEN THE INGREDIENTS OF ANY DRUGS OR POTIONS THAT BODY CONSUMED BECOME AN OPEN BOOK.
IN THE SAME WAY, WHEN I DIE, IF AN ENEMY WERE TO TAKE POSSESSION OF MY REMAINS, THE CORPSE WOULD REVEAL ALL OF THE ANATOMICAL IDIOSYNCRACIES UNIQUE TO POSSESSORS OF THE *SHARINGAN* EYE...
IN THE WORST CASE, THE ENEMY MIGHT GAIN ENOUGH INFORMATION TO BE ABLE TO DUPLICATE AND MASTER THAT POWER.

READ THIS WAY

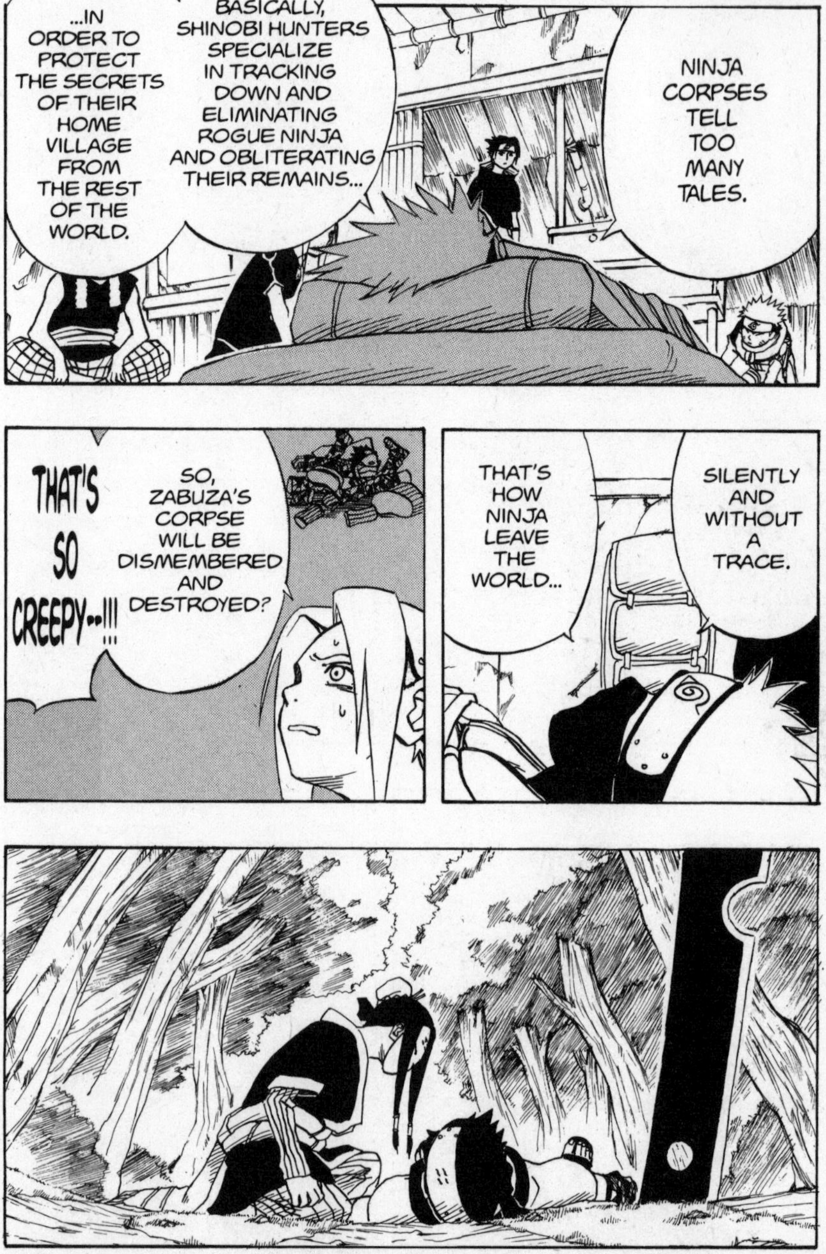
NINJA CORPSES TELL TOO MANY TALES.
BASICALLY, SHINOBI HUNTERS SPECIALIZE IN TRACKING DOWN AND ELIMINATING ROGUE NINJA AND OBLITERATING THEIR REMAINS...
...IN ORDER TO PROTECT THE SECRETS OF THEIR HOME VILLAGE FROM THE REST OF THE WORLD.
SILENTLY AND WITHOUT A TRACE.
THAT'S HOW NINJA LEAVE THE WORLD...
SO, ZABUZA'S CORPSE WILL BE DISMEMBERED AND DESTROYED?
THAT'S SO CREEPY--!!!

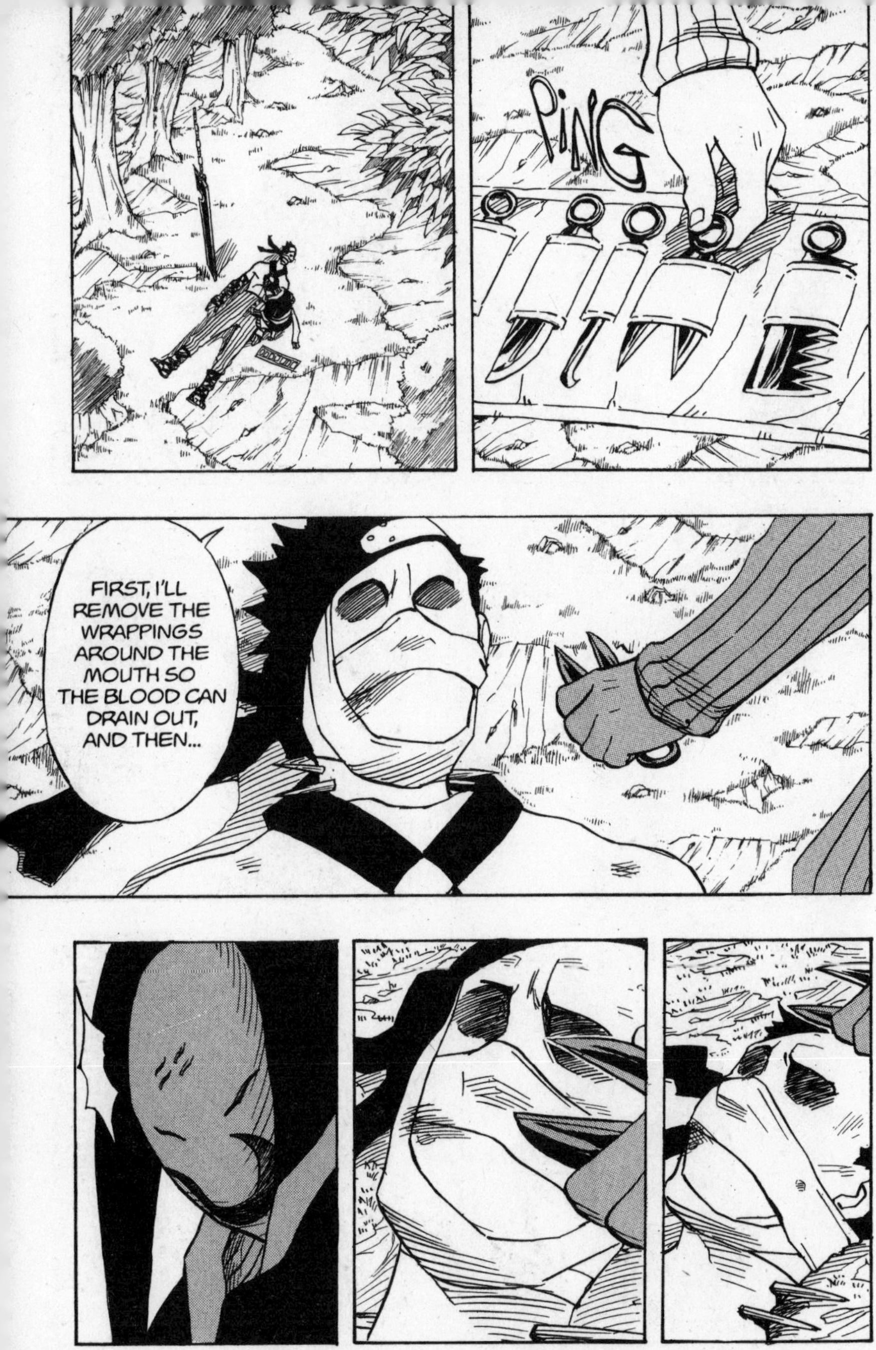
PING
FIRST, I'LL REMOVE THE WRAPPINGS AROUND THE MOUTH SO THE BLOOD CAN DRAIN OUT, AND THEN...

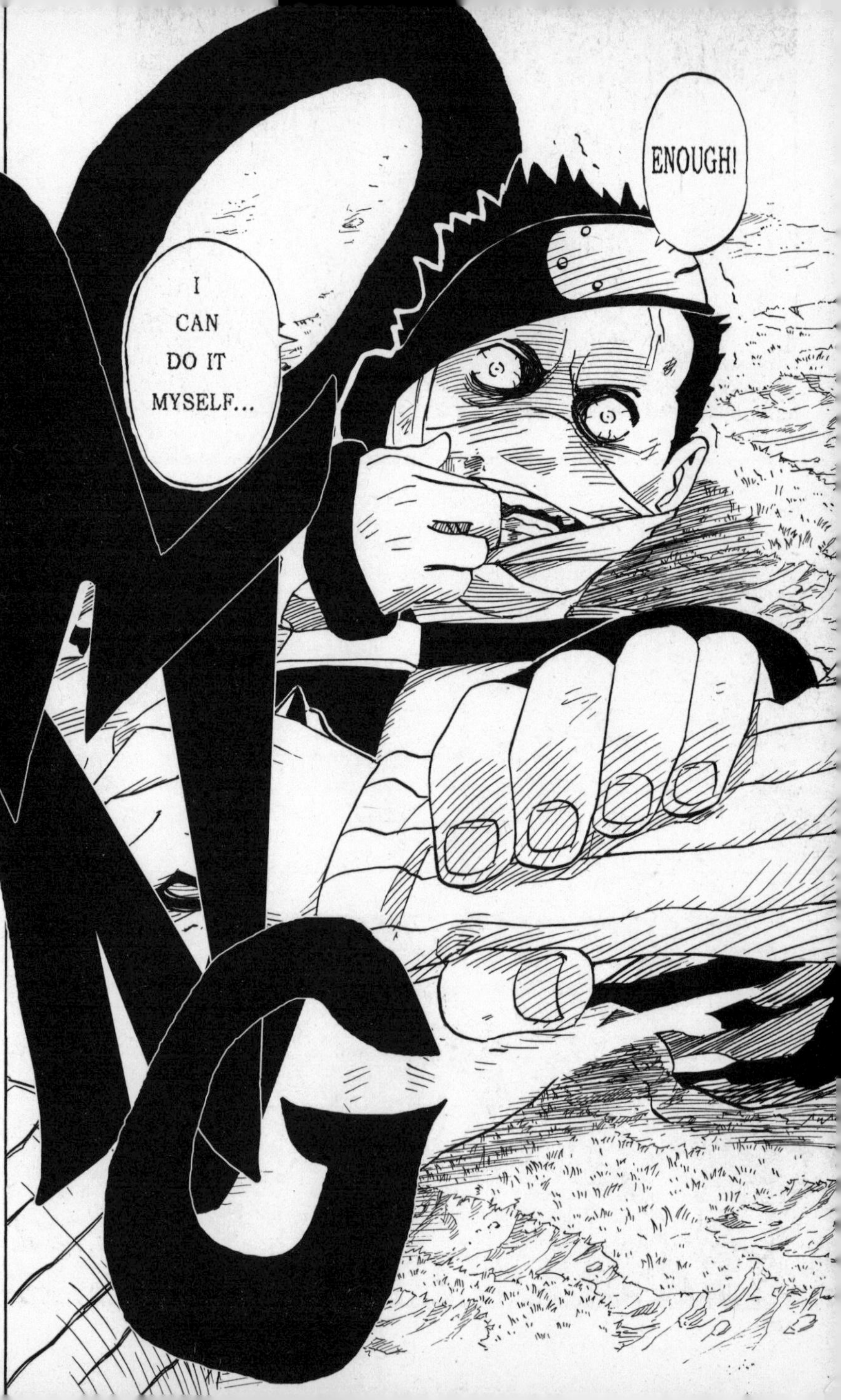
ENOUGH!
I CAN DO IT MYSELF...

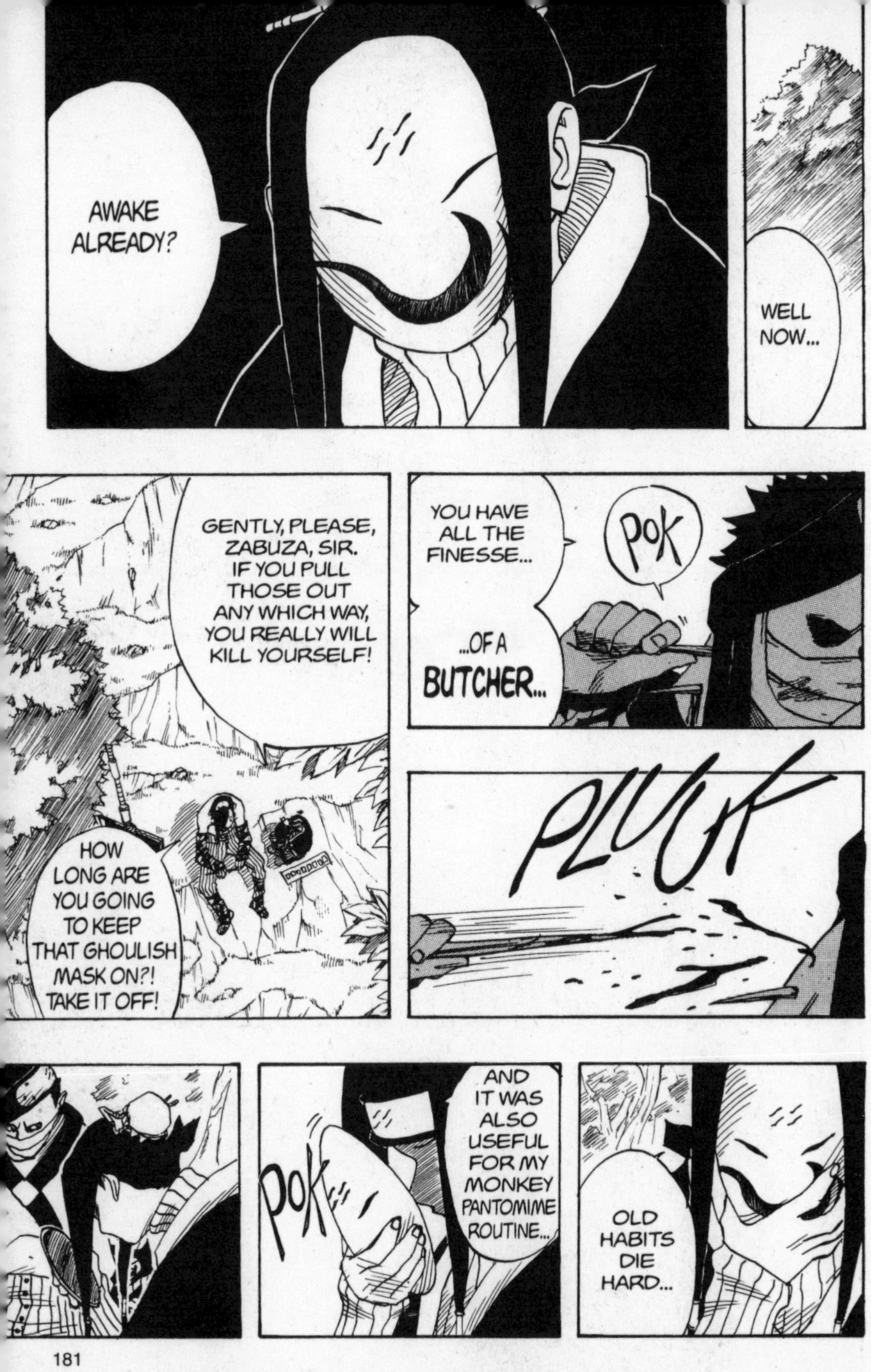

WELL NOW...
AWAKE ALREADY?
POK
YOU HAVE ALL THE FINESSE...
...OF A BUTCHER...
PLUCK
GENTLY, PLEASE, ZABUZA, SIR. IF YOU PULL THOSE OUT ANY WHICH WAY, YOU REALLY WILL KILL YOURSELF!
HOW LONG ARE YOU GOING TO KEEP THAT GHOULISH MASK ON?! TAKE IT OFF!
OLD HABITS DIE HARD...
AND IT WAS ALSO USEFUL FOR MY MONKEY PANTOMIME ROUTINE...
POK

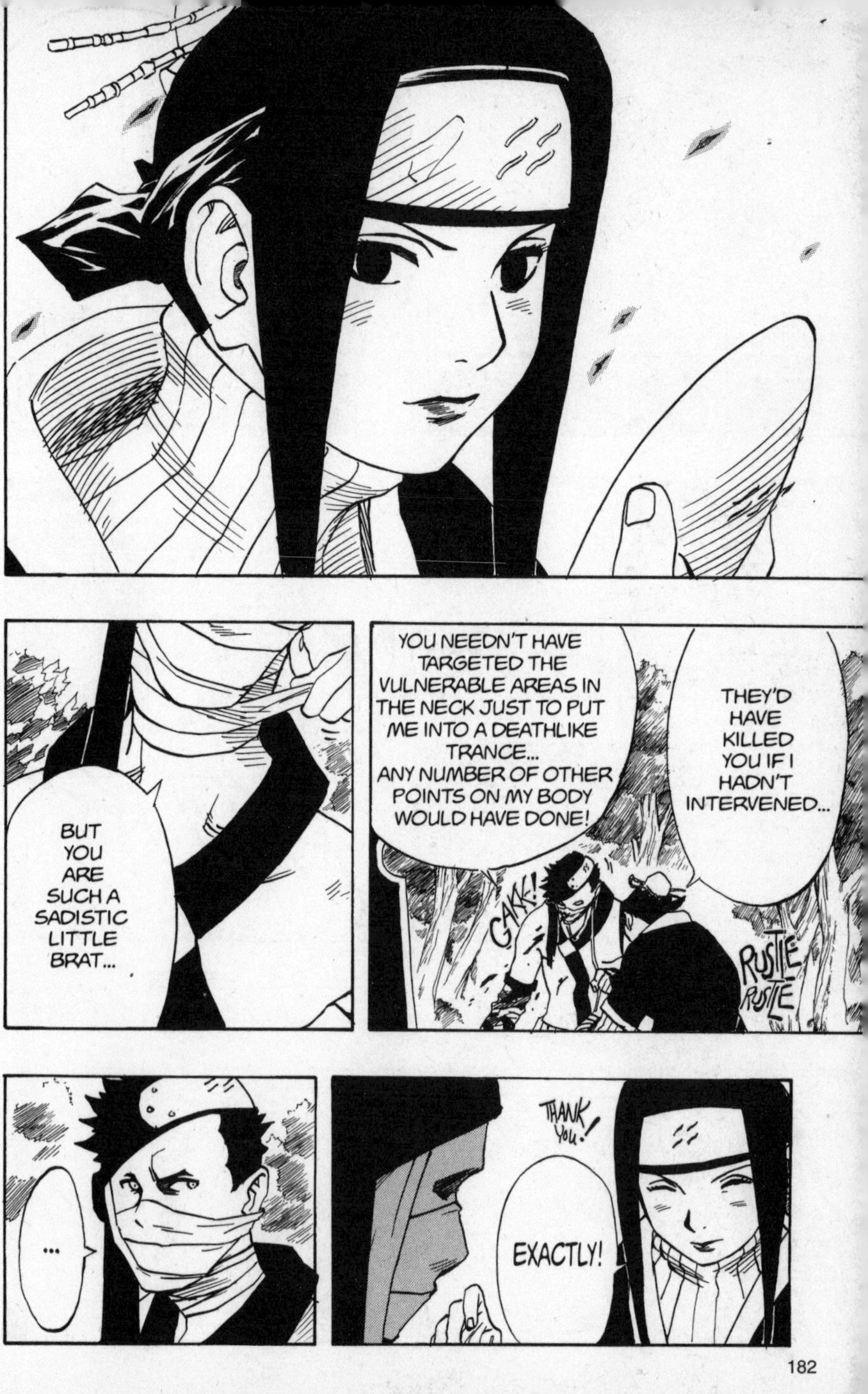
THEY'D HAVE KILLED YOU IF I HADN'T INTERVENED...
YOU NEEDN'T HAVE TARGETED THE VULNERABLE AREAS IN THE NECK JUST TO PUT ME INTO A DEATHLIKE TRANCE... ANY NUMBER OF OTHER POINTS ON MY BODY WOULD HAVE DONE!
RUSTLE RUSTLE
GAKK!
BUT YOU ARE SUCH A SADISTIC LITTLE BRAT...
THANK YOU!
EXACTLY!
...

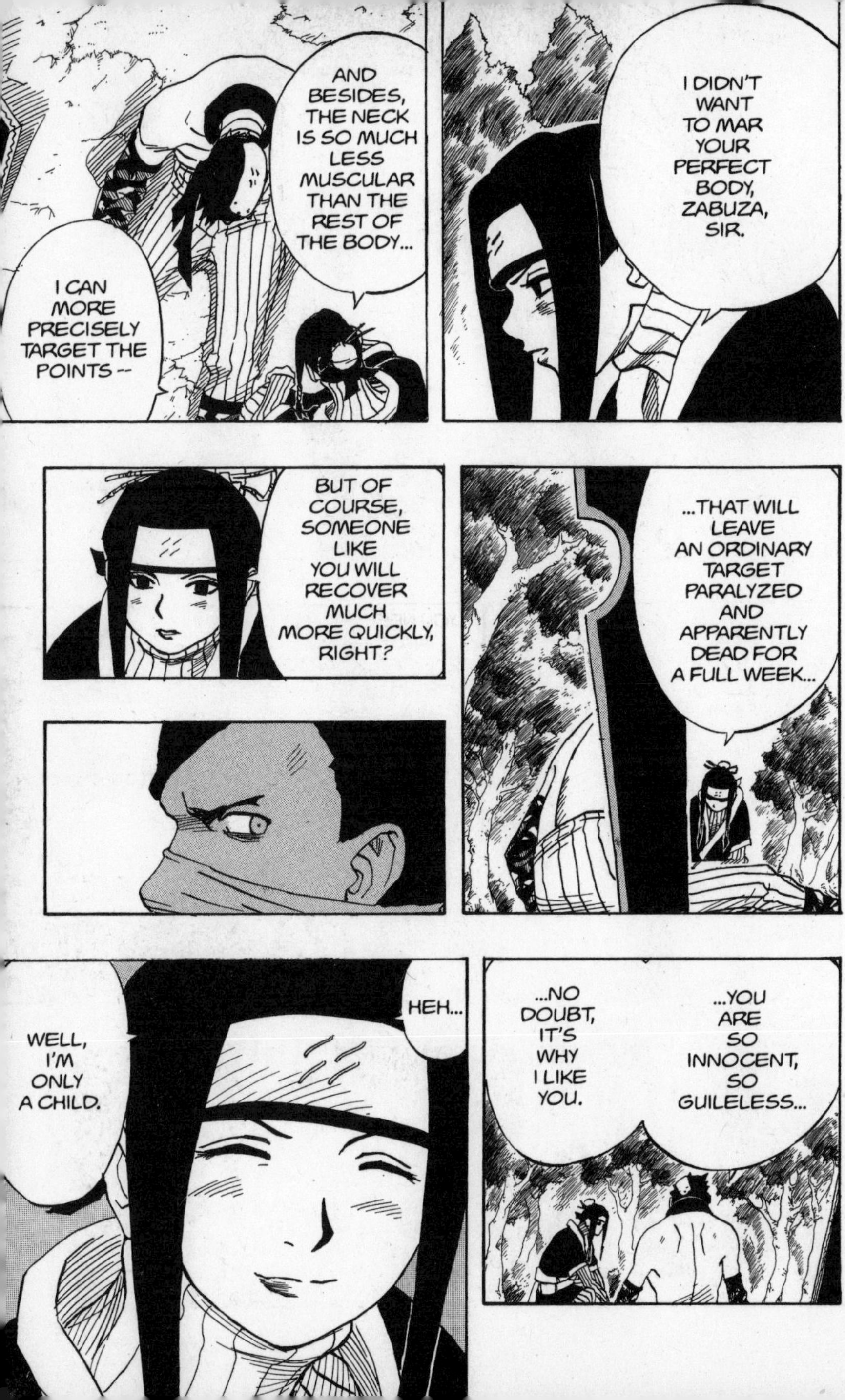
I DIDN'T WANT TO MAR YOUR PERFECT BODY, ZABUZA, SIR.
AND BESIDES, THE NECK IS SO MUCH LESS MUSCULAR THAN THE REST OF THE BODY...
I CAN MORE PRECISELY TARGET THE POINTS --
...THAT WILL LEAVE AN ORDINARY TARGET PARALYZED AND APPARENTLY DEAD FOR A FULL WEEK...
BUT OF COURSE, SOMEONE LIKE YOU WILL RECOVER MUCH MORE QUICKLY, RIGHT?
...YOU ARE SO INNOCENT, SO GUILELESS...
...NO DOUBT, IT'S WHY I LIKE YOU.
HEH...
WELL, I'M ONLY A CHILD.

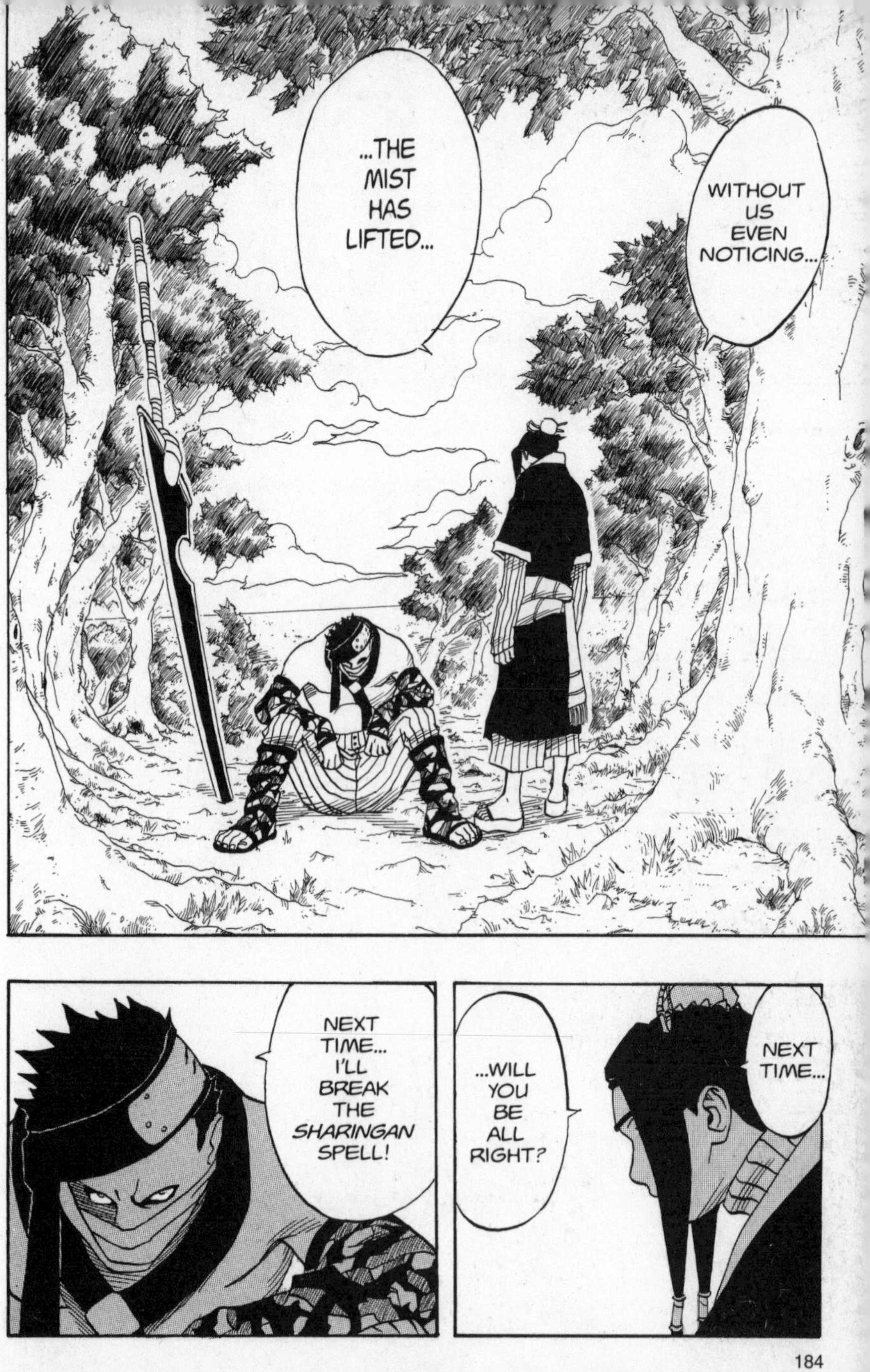

WITHOUT US EVEN NOTICING...
...THE MIST HAS LIFTED...
NEXT TIME...
...WILL YOU BE ALL RIGHT?
NEXT TIME... I'LL BREAK THE *SHARINGAN* SPELL!

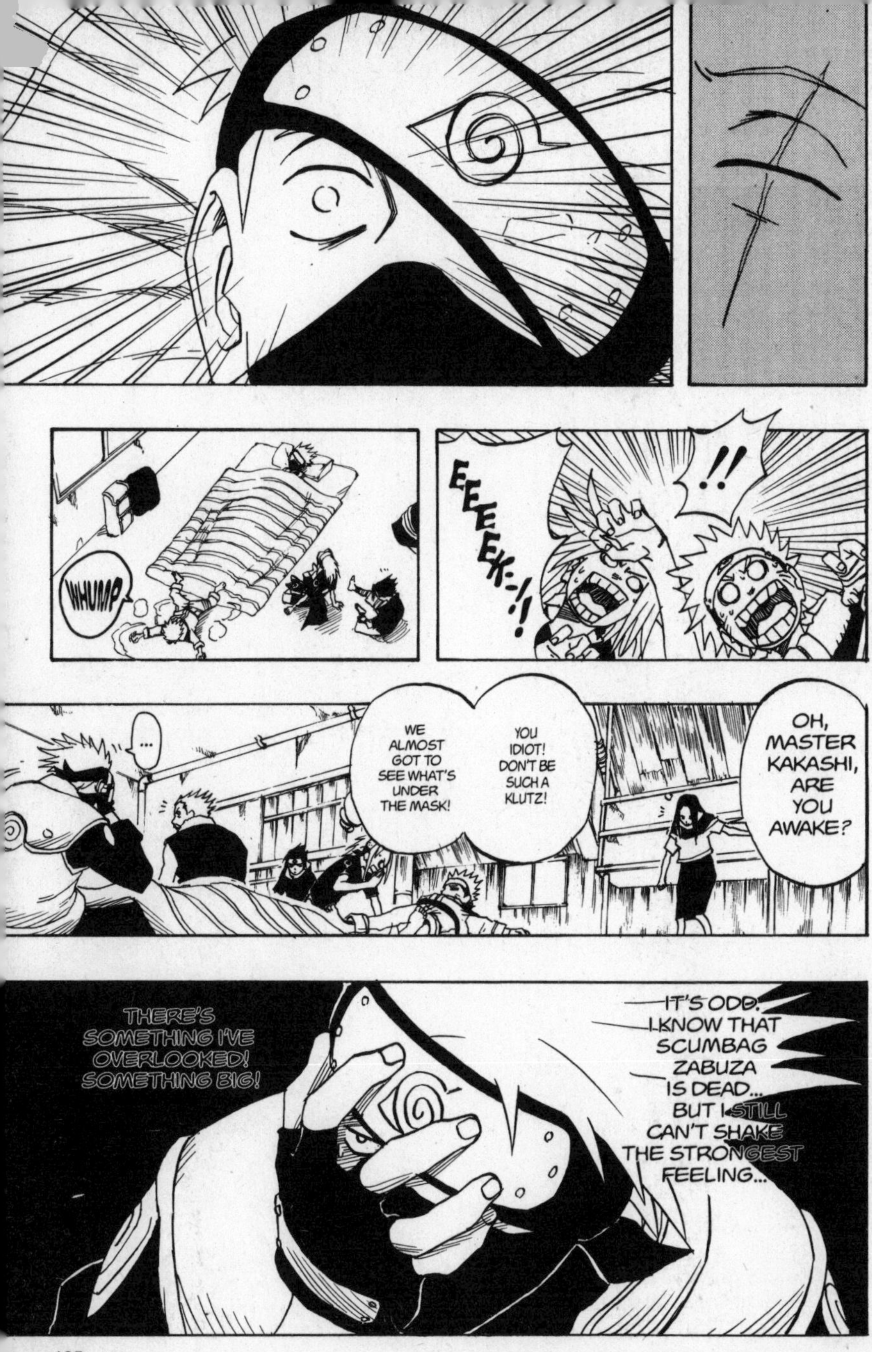
!!
EEEEK-!!
WHUMP
OH, MASTER KAKASHI, ARE YOU AWAKE?
YOU IDIOT! DON'T BE SUCH A KLUTZ!
WE ALMOST GOT TO SEE WHAT'S UNDER THE MASK!
...
IT'S ODD. I KNOW THAT SCUMBAG ZABUZA IS DEAD... BUT I STILL CAN'T SHAKE THE STRONGEST FEELING...
THERE'S SOMETHING I'VE OVERLOOKED! SOMETHING BIG!

Number 17: Preparations for Battle

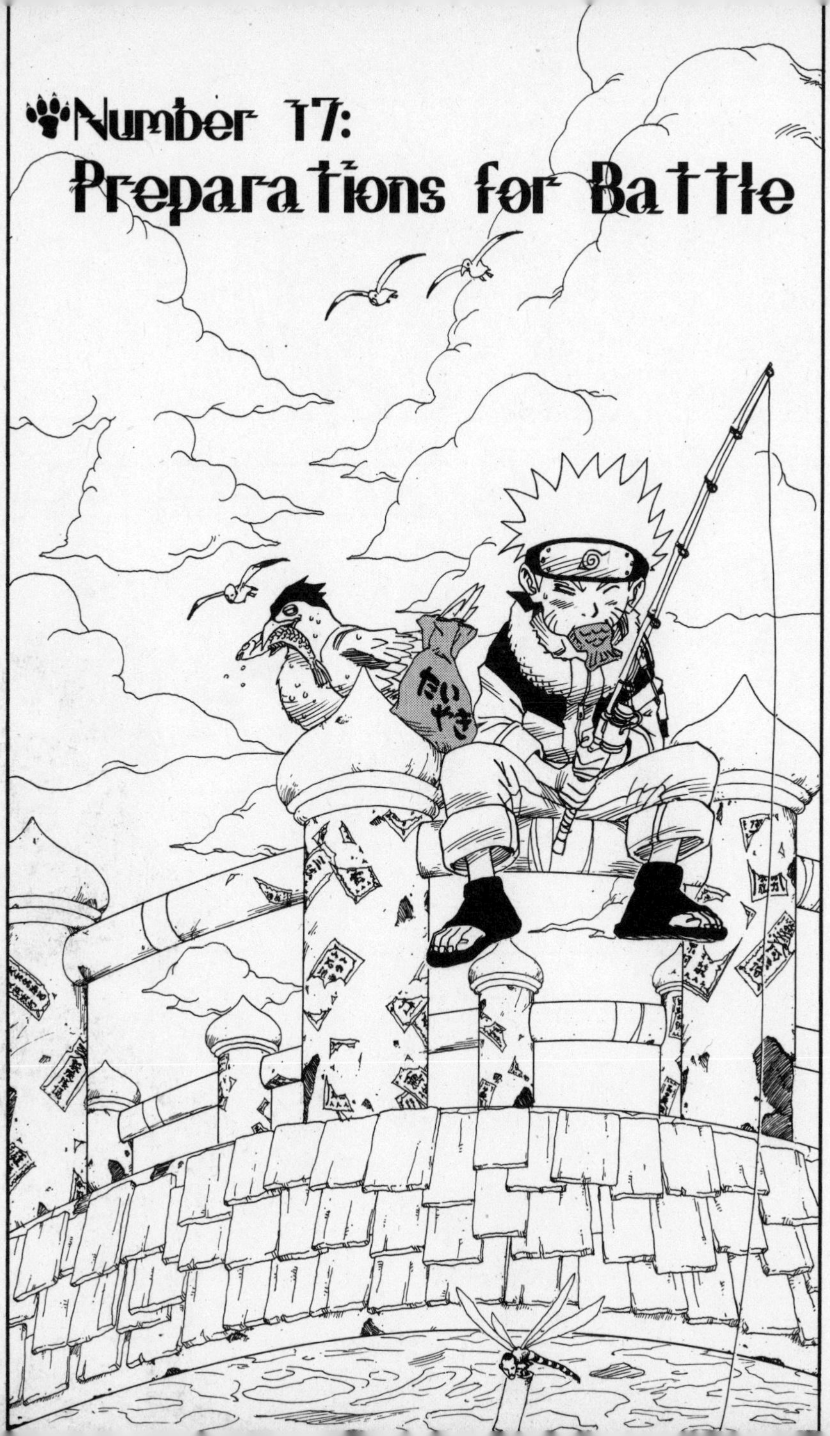
たいやき

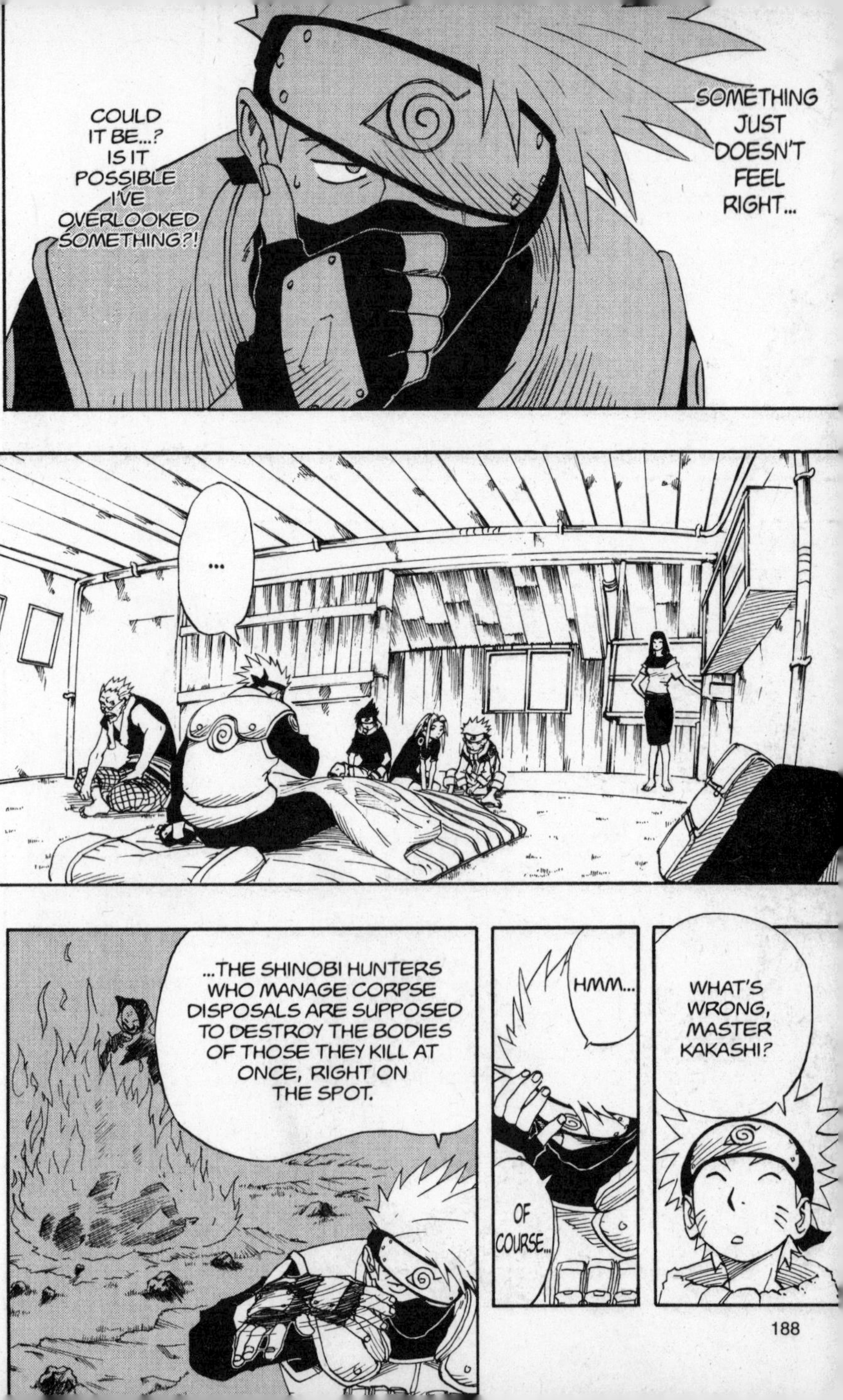

SOMETHING JUST DOESN'T FEEL RIGHT...
COULD IT BE...? IS IT POSSIBLE I'VE OVERLOOKED SOMETHING?!
...
WHAT'S WRONG, MASTER KAKASHI?
HMM...
OF COURSE...
...THE SHINOBI HUNTERS WHO MANAGE CORPSE DISPOSALS ARE SUPPOSED TO DESTROY THE BODIES OF THOSE THEY KILL AT ONCE, RIGHT ON THE SPOT.

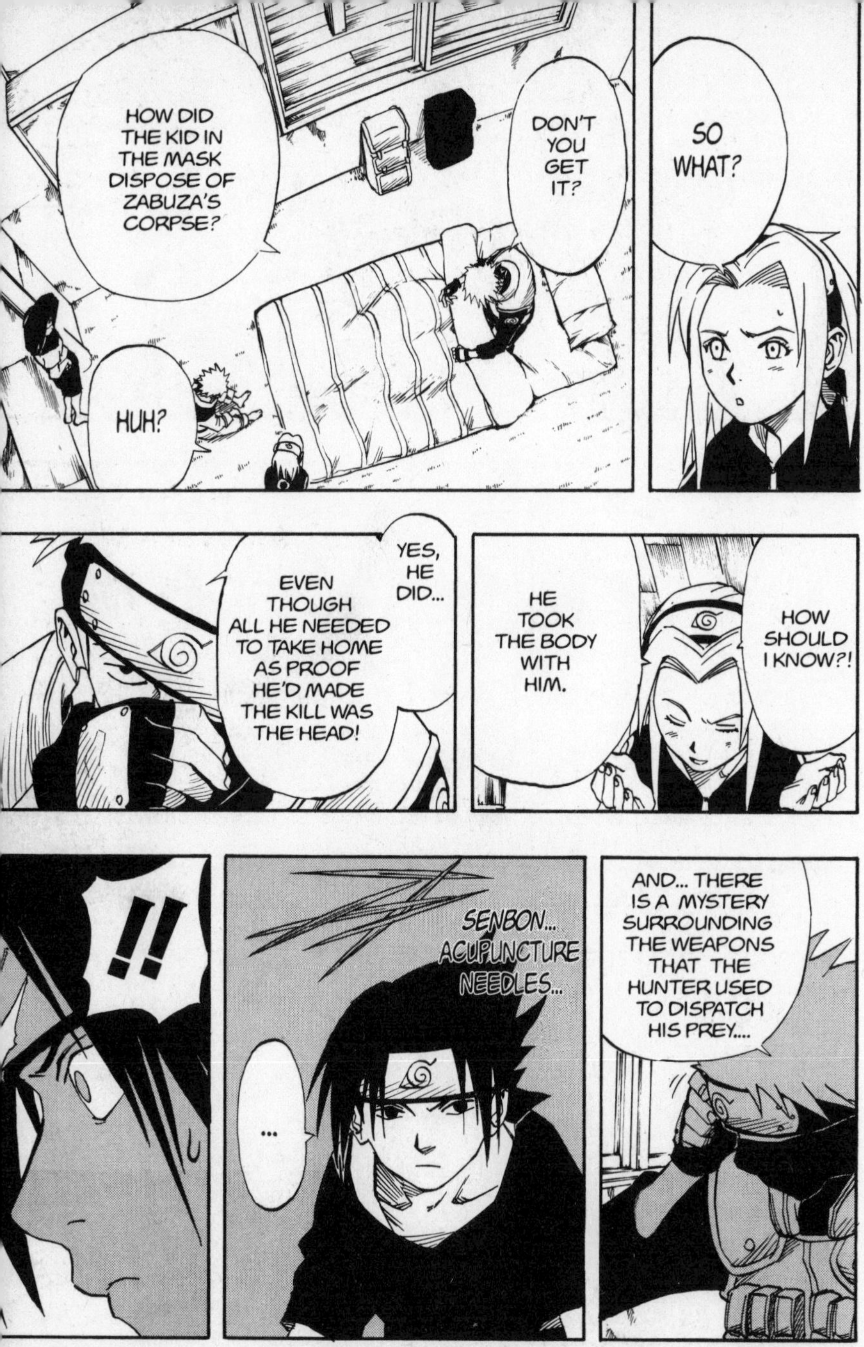
SO WHAT?
DON'T YOU GET IT?
HOW DID THE KID IN THE MASK DISPOSE OF ZABUZA'S CORPSE?
HUH?
HOW SHOULD I KNOW?!
HE TOOK THE BODY WITH HIM.
YES, HE DID...
EVEN THOUGH ALL HE NEEDED TO TAKE HOME AS PROOF HE'D MADE THE KILL WAS THE HEAD!
AND... THERE IS A MYSTERY SURROUNDING THE WEAPONS THAT THE HUNTER USED TO DISPATCH HIS PREY....
SENBON... ACUPUNCTURE NEEDLES...
...
!!

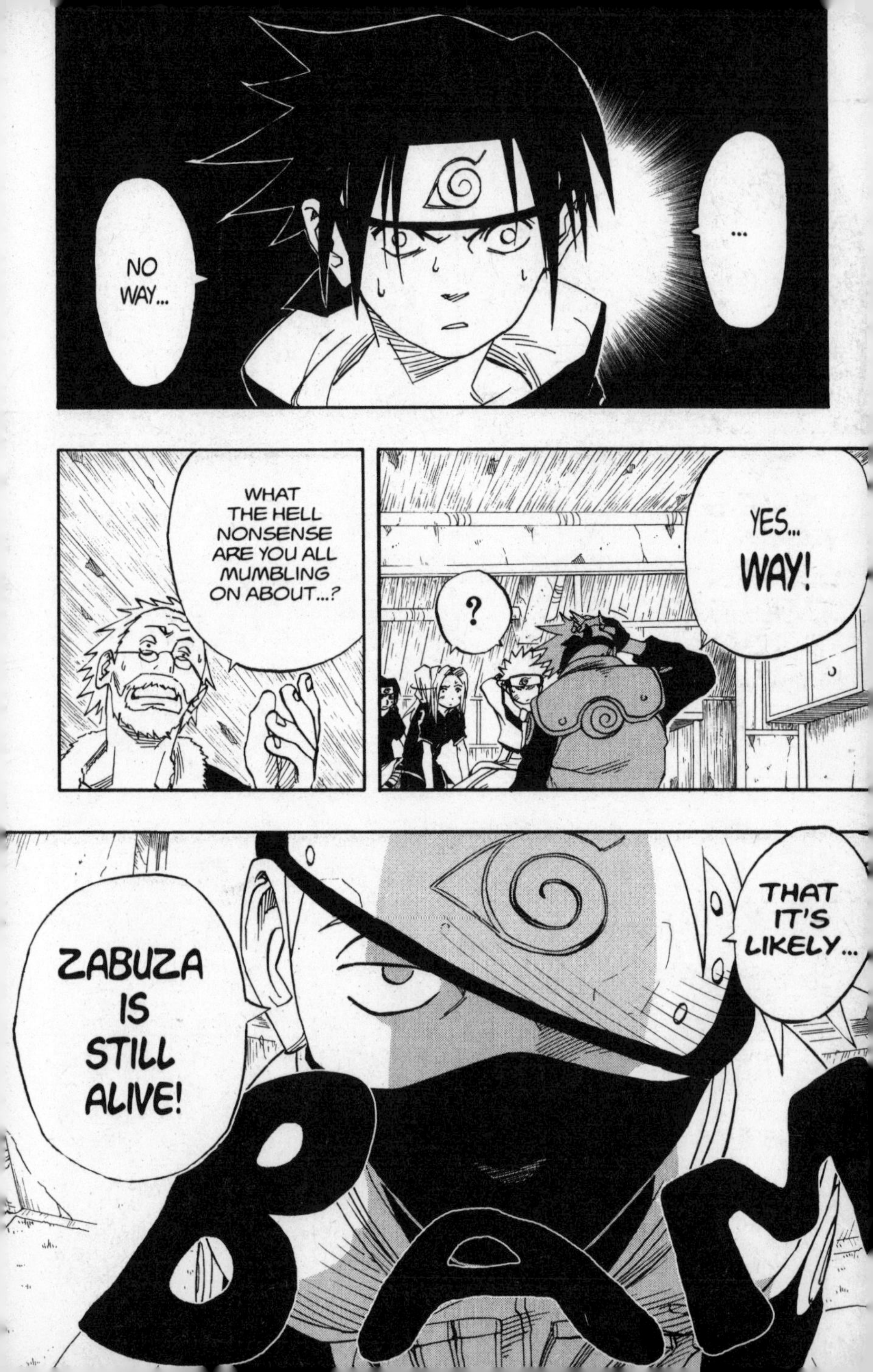
...
NO WAY...
YES... WAY!
?
WHAT THE HELL NONSENSE ARE YOU ALL MUMBLING ON ABOUT...?
THAT IT'S LIKELY...
ZABUZA IS STILL ALIVE!

READ THIS WAY

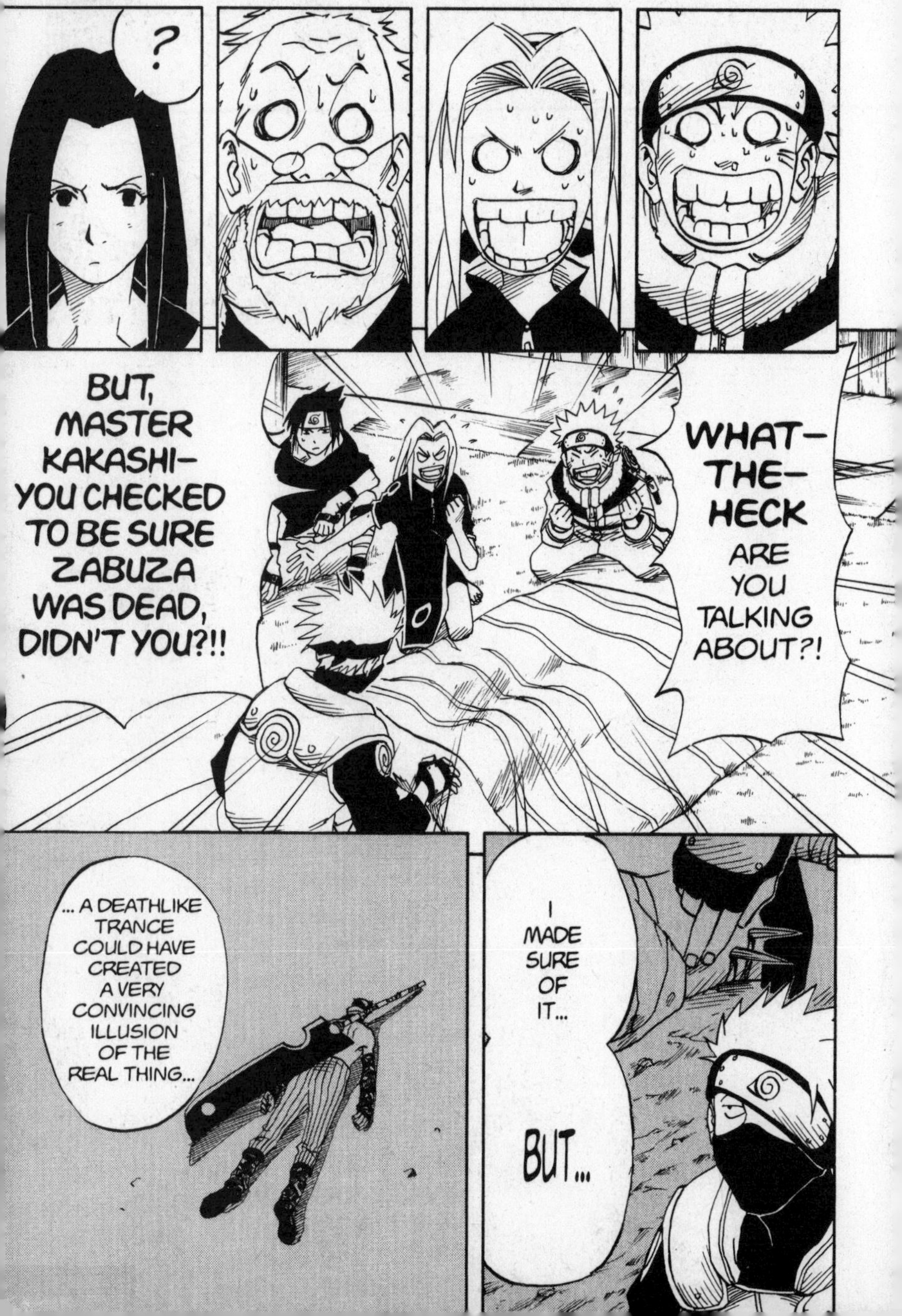
?
WHAT-THE-HECK ARE YOU TALKING ABOUT?!
BUT, MASTER KAKASHI- YOU CHECKED TO BE SURE ZABUZA WAS DEAD, DIDN'T YOU?!!
I MADE SURE OF IT...
BUT...
... A DEATHLIKE TRANCE COULD HAVE CREATED A VERY CONVINCING ILLUSION OF THE REAL THING...

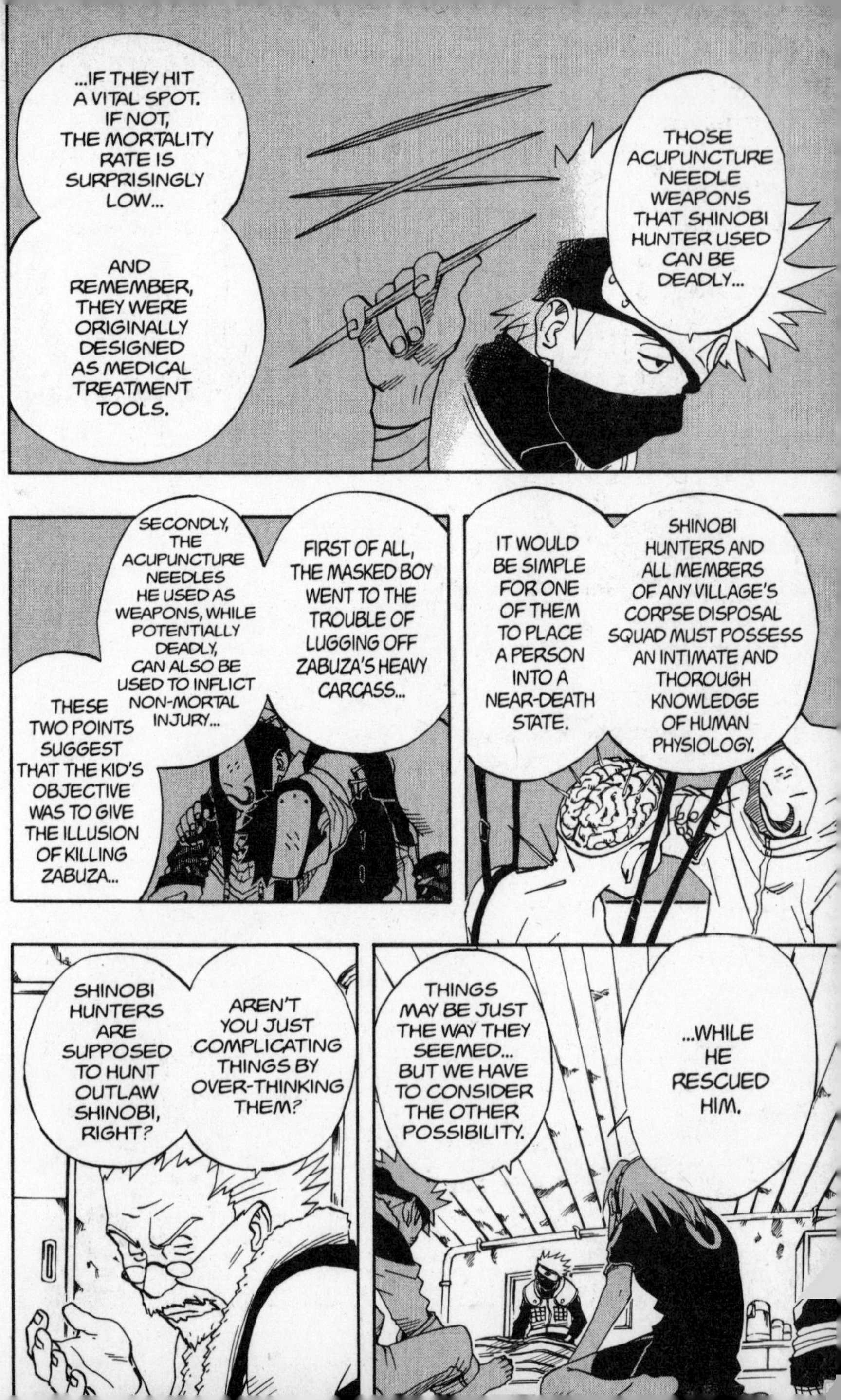
THOSE ACUPUNCTURE NEEDLE WEAPONS THAT SHINOBI HUNTER USED CAN BE DEADLY...
...IF THEY HIT A VITAL SPOT. IF NOT, THE MORTALITY RATE IS SURPRISINGLY LOW...
AND REMEMBER, THEY WERE ORIGINALLY DESIGNED AS MEDICAL TREATMENT TOOLS.
SHINOBI HUNTERS AND ALL MEMBERS OF ANY VILLAGE'S CORPSE DISPOSAL SQUAD MUST POSSESS AN INTIMATE AND THOROUGH KNOWLEDGE OF HUMAN PHYSIOLOGY.
IT WOULD BE SIMPLE FOR ONE OF THEM TO PLACE A PERSON INTO A NEAR-DEATH STATE.
FIRST OF ALL, THE MASKED BOY WENT TO THE TROUBLE OF LUGGING OFF ZABUZA'S HEAVY CARCASS...
SECONDLY, THE ACUPUNCTURE NEEDLES HE USED AS WEAPONS, WHILE POTENTIALLY DEADLY, CAN ALSO BE USED TO INFLICT NON-MORTAL INJURY...
THESE TWO POINTS SUGGEST THAT THE KID'S OBJECTIVE WAS TO GIVE THE ILLUSION OF KILLING ZABUZA...
...WHILE HE RESCUED HIM.
THINGS MAY BE JUST THE WAY THEY SEEMED... BUT WE HAVE TO CONSIDER THE OTHER POSSIBILITY.
AREN'T YOU JUST COMPLICATING THINGS BY OVER-THINKING THEM?
SHINOBI HUNTERS ARE SUPPOSED TO HUNT OUTLAW SHINOBI, RIGHT?

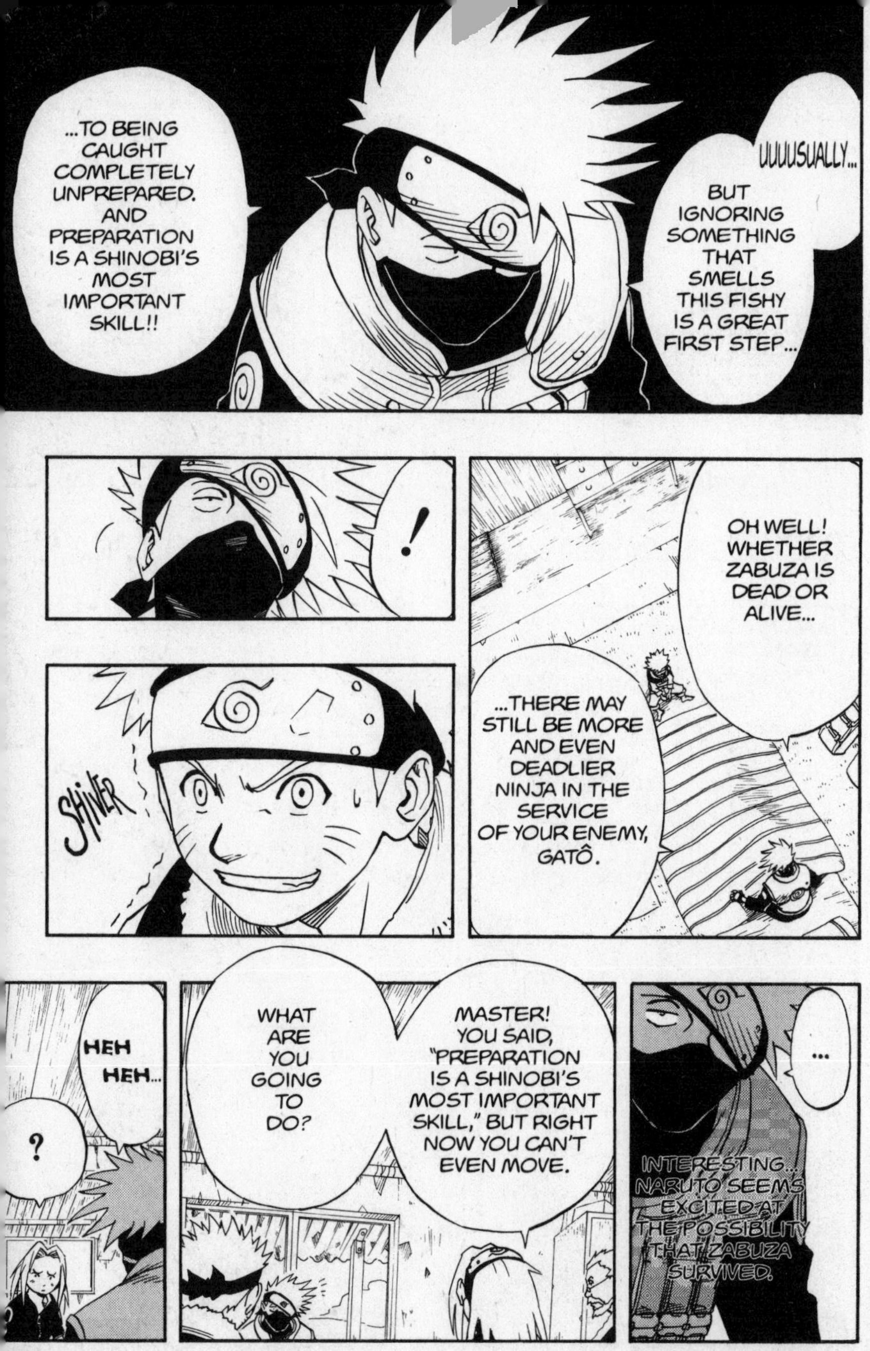
UUUUSUALLY...
BUT IGNORING SOMETHING THAT SMELLS THIS FISHY IS A GREAT FIRST STEP...
...TO BEING CAUGHT COMPLETELY UNPREPARED. AND PREPARATION IS A SHINOBI'S MOST IMPORTANT SKILL!!
OH WELL! WHETHER ZABUZA IS DEAD OR ALIVE...
...THERE MAY STILL BE MORE AND EVEN DEADLIER NINJA IN THE SERVICE OF YOUR ENEMY, GATÔ.
!
SHIVER
...
INTERESTING... NARUTO SEEMS EXCITED AT THE POSSIBILITY THAT ZABUZA SURVIVED.
MASTER! YOU SAID, "PREPARATION IS A SHINOBI'S MOST IMPORTANT SKILL," BUT RIGHT NOW YOU CAN'T EVEN MOVE.
WHAT ARE YOU GOING TO DO?
HEH HEH...
?

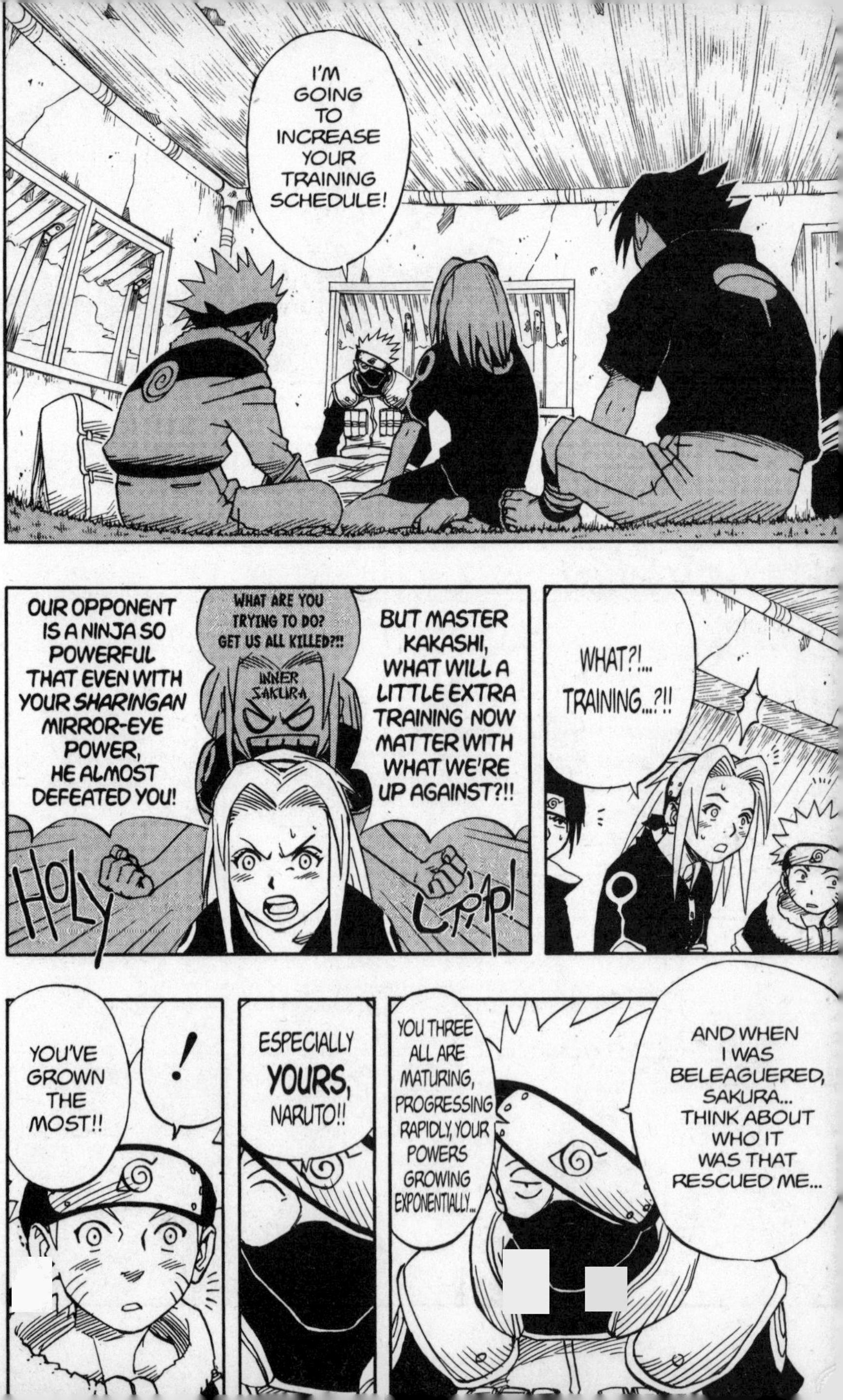
I'M GOING TO INCREASE YOUR TRAINING SCHEDULE!
WHAT?!... TRAINING...?!!
BUT MASTER KAKASHI, WHAT WILL A LITTLE EXTRA TRAINING NOW MATTER WITH WHAT WE'RE UP AGAINST?!!
WHAT ARE YOU TRYING TO DO? GET US ALL KILLED?!!
INNER SAKURA
OUR OPPONENT IS A NINJA SO POWERFUL THAT EVEN WITH YOUR SHARINGAN MIRROR-EYE POWER, HE ALMOST DEFEATED YOU!
HOLY CRAP!
AND WHEN I WAS BELEAGUERED, SAKURA... THINK ABOUT WHO IT WAS THAT RESCUED ME...
YOU THREE ALL ARE MATURING, PROGRESSING RAPIDLY, YOUR POWERS GROWING EXPONENTIALLY...
ESPECIALLY YOURS, NARUTO!!
!
YOU'VE GROWN THE MOST!!

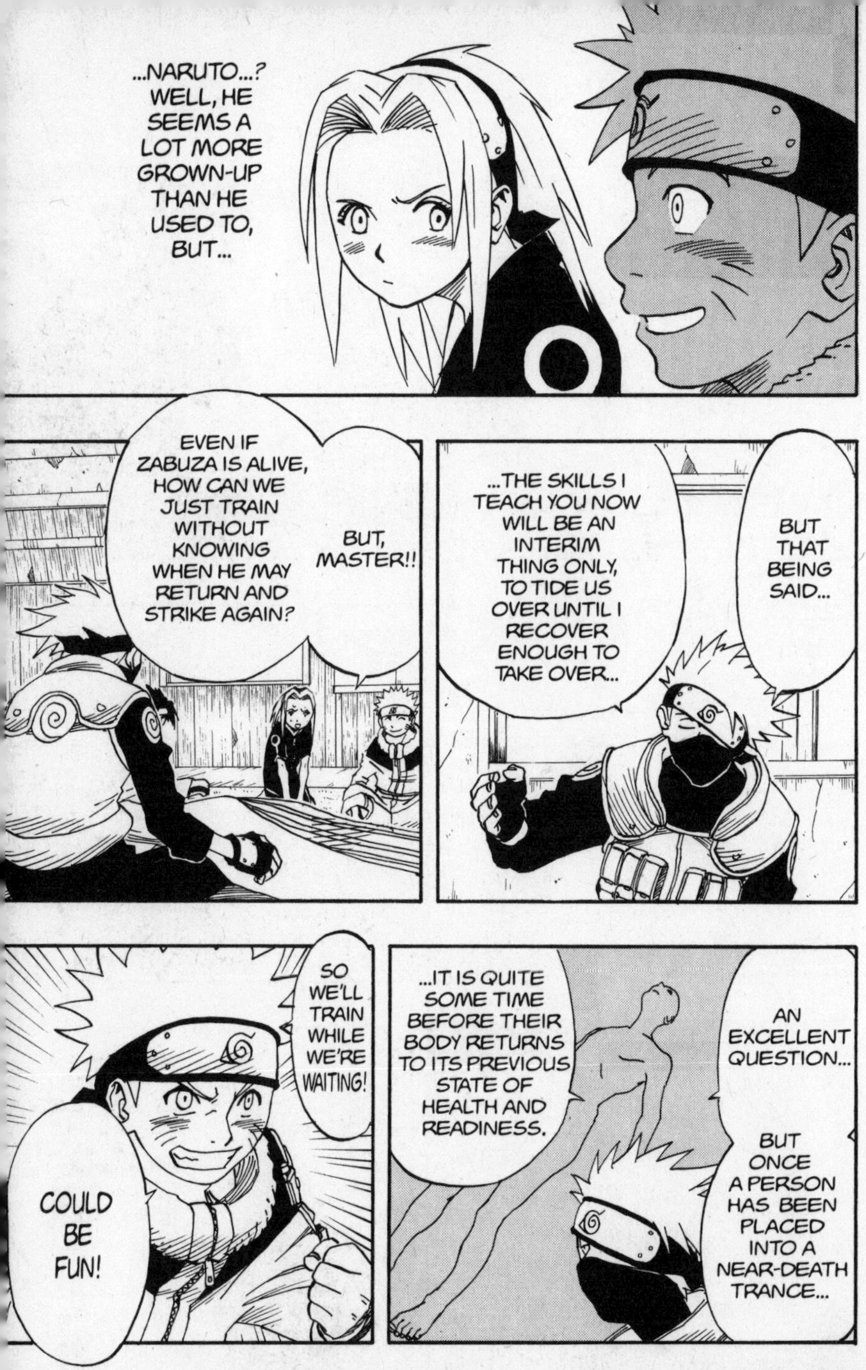
...NARUTO...? WELL, HE SEEMS A LOT MORE GROWN-UP THAN HE USED TO, BUT...
BUT THAT BEING SAID...
...THE SKILLS I TEACH YOU NOW WILL BE AN INTERIM THING ONLY, TO TIDE US OVER UNTIL I RECOVER ENOUGH TO TAKE OVER...
BUT, MASTER!!
EVEN IF ZABUZA IS ALIVE, HOW CAN WE JUST TRAIN WITHOUT KNOWING WHEN HE MAY RETURN AND STRIKE AGAIN?
AN EXCELLENT QUESTION...
BUT ONCE A PERSON HAS BEEN PLACED INTO A NEAR-DEATH TRANCE...
...IT IS QUITE SOME TIME BEFORE THEIR BODY RETURNS TO ITS PREVIOUS STATE OF HEALTH AND READINESS.
SO WE'LL TRAIN WHILE WE'RE WAITING!
COULD BE FUN!

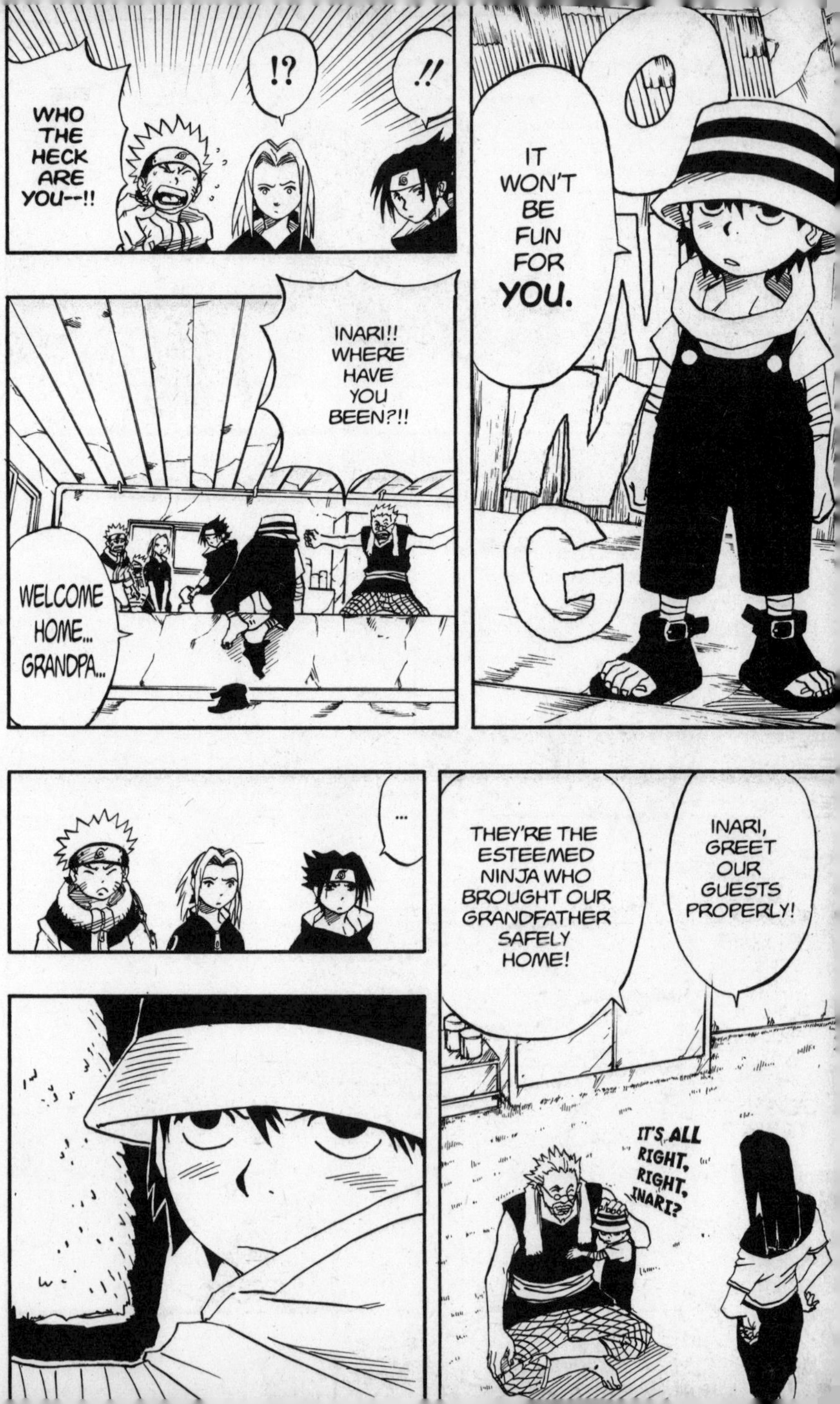
IT WON'T BE FUN FOR YOU.
!!
!?
WHO THE HECK ARE YOU--!!
INARI!! WHERE HAVE YOU BEEN?!!
WELCOME HOME... GRANDPA...
INARI, GREET OUR GUESTS PROPERLY!
THEY'RE THE ESTEEMED NINJA WHO BROUGHT OUR GRANDFATHER SAFELY HOME!
IT'S ALL RIGHT, RIGHT, INARI?
...

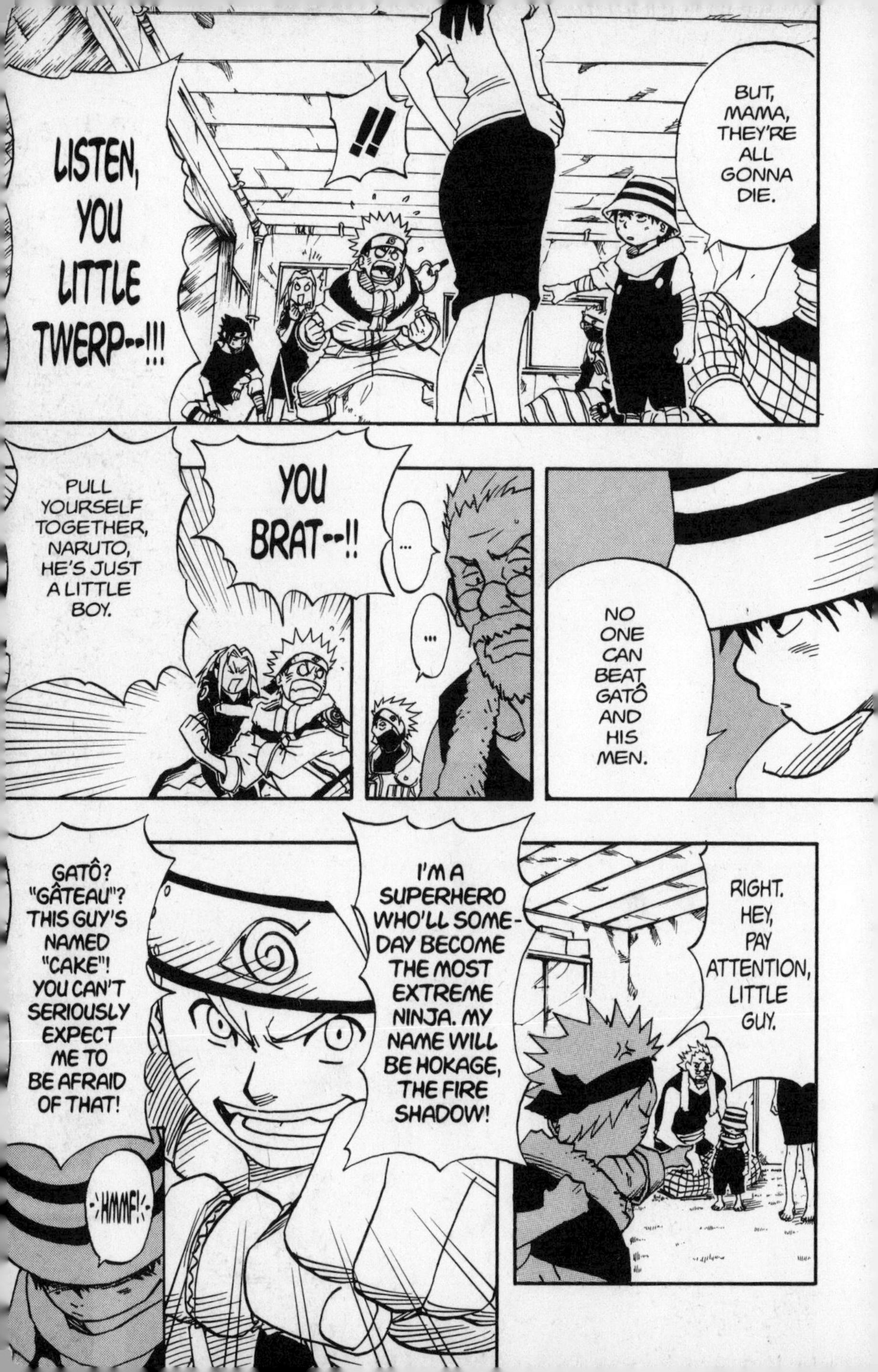
BUT, MAMA, THEY'RE ALL GONNA DIE.
!!
LISTEN, YOU LITTLE TWERP--!!!
NO ONE CAN BEAT GATÔ AND HIS MEN.
...
...
YOU BRAT--!!
PULL YOURSELF TOGETHER, NARUTO, HE'S JUST A LITTLE BOY.
RIGHT. HEY, PAY ATTENTION, LITTLE GUY.
I'M A SUPERHERO WHO'LL SOME-DAY BECOME THE MOST EXTREME NINJA. MY NAME WILL BE HOKAGE, THE FIRE SHADOW!
GATÔ? "GÂTEAU"? THIS GUY'S NAMED "CAKE"! YOU CAN'T SERIOUSLY EXPECT ME TO BE AFRAID OF THAT!
HMMF!

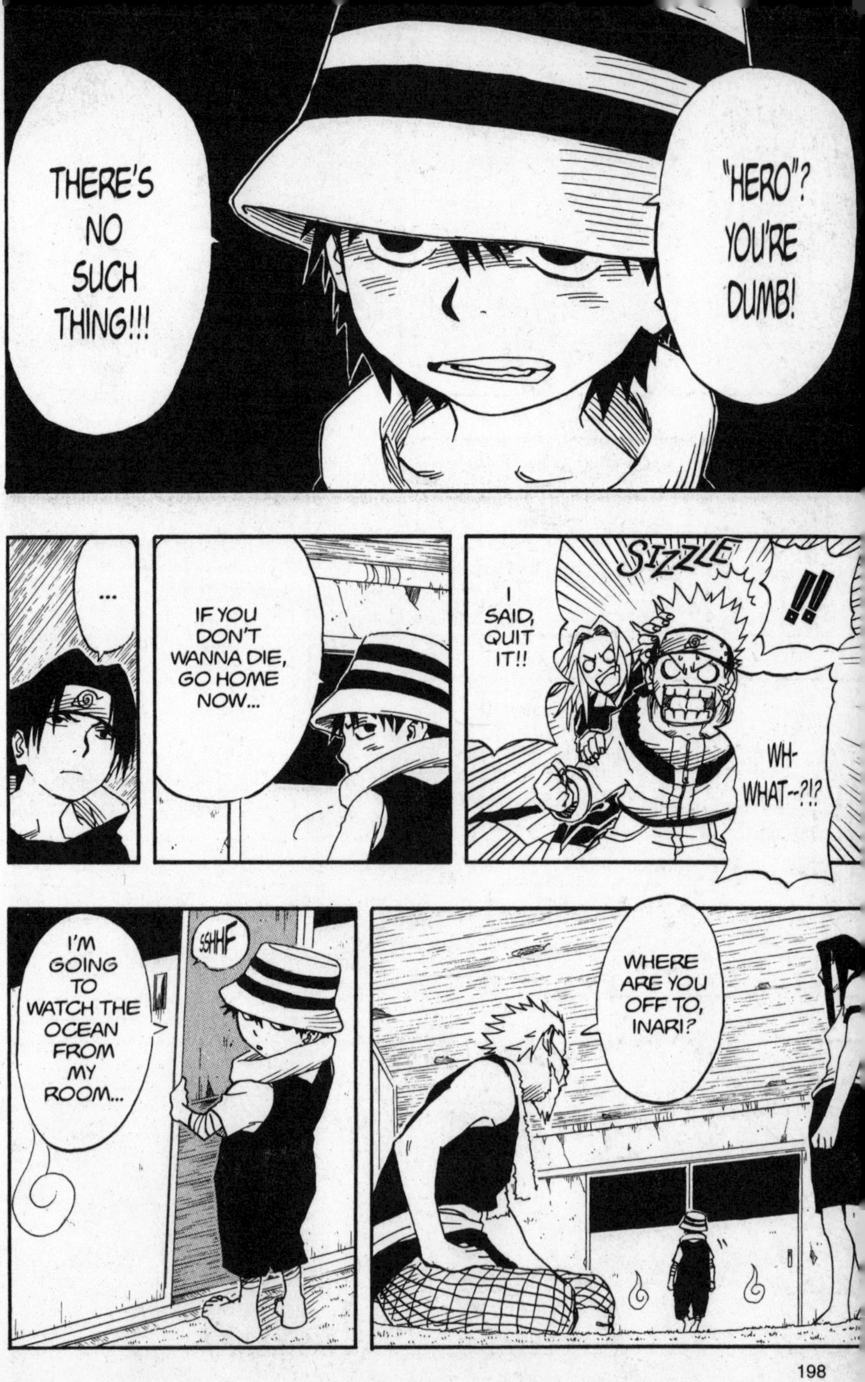
"HERO"? YOU'RE DUMB!
THERE'S NO SUCH THING!!!
SIZZLE
!!
I SAID, QUIT IT!!
WH-WHAT--?!?
IF YOU DON'T WANNA DIE, GO HOME NOW...
...
WHERE ARE YOU OFF TO, INARI?
SSHHF
I'M GOING TO WATCH THE OCEAN FROM MY ROOM...

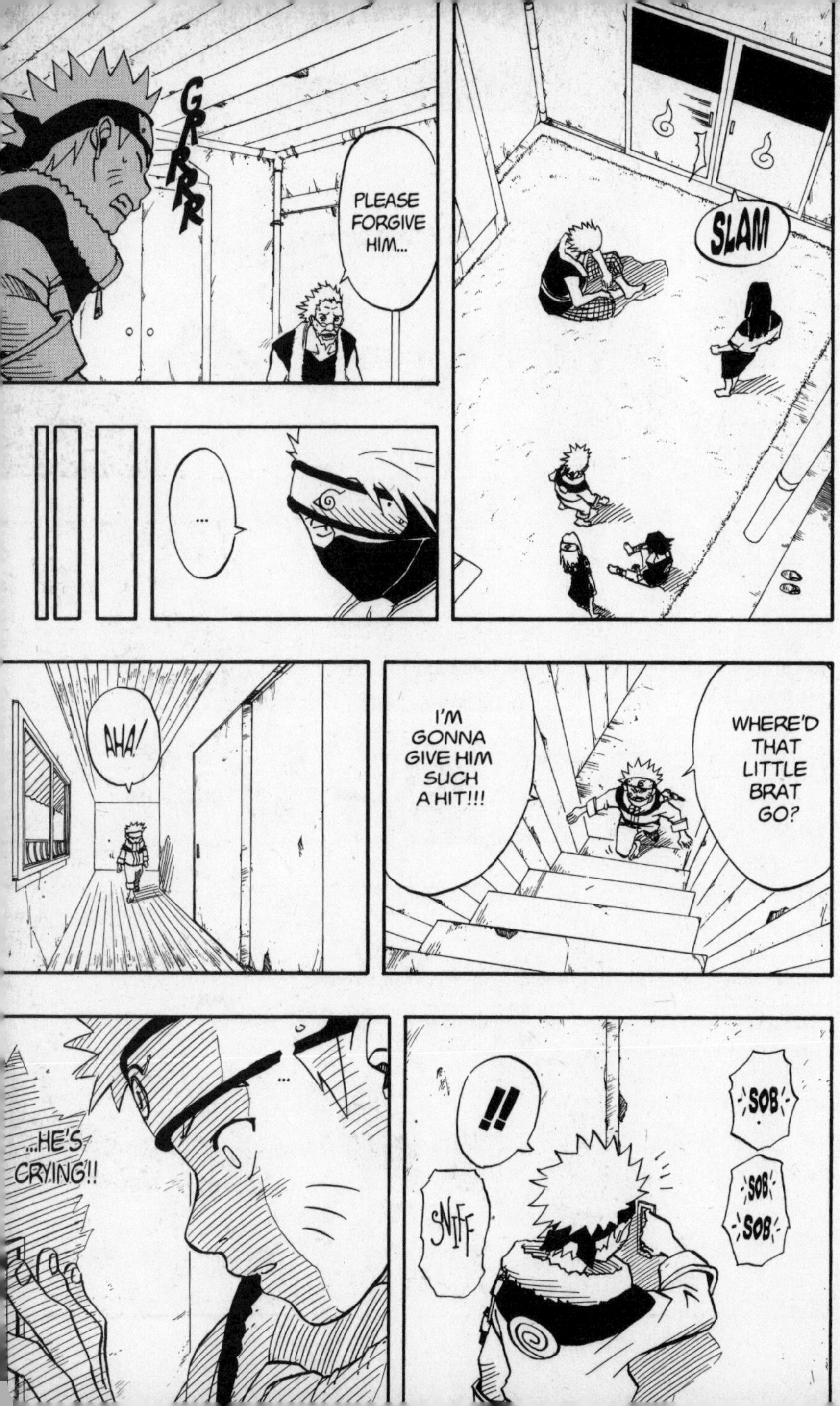
SLAM
PLEASE FORGIVE HIM...
GRRR
...
WHERE'D THAT LITTLE BRAT GO?
I'M GONNA GIVE HIM SUCH A HIT!!!
AHA!
SOB
SOB SOB
!!
SNIFF
...
...HE'S CRYING!!

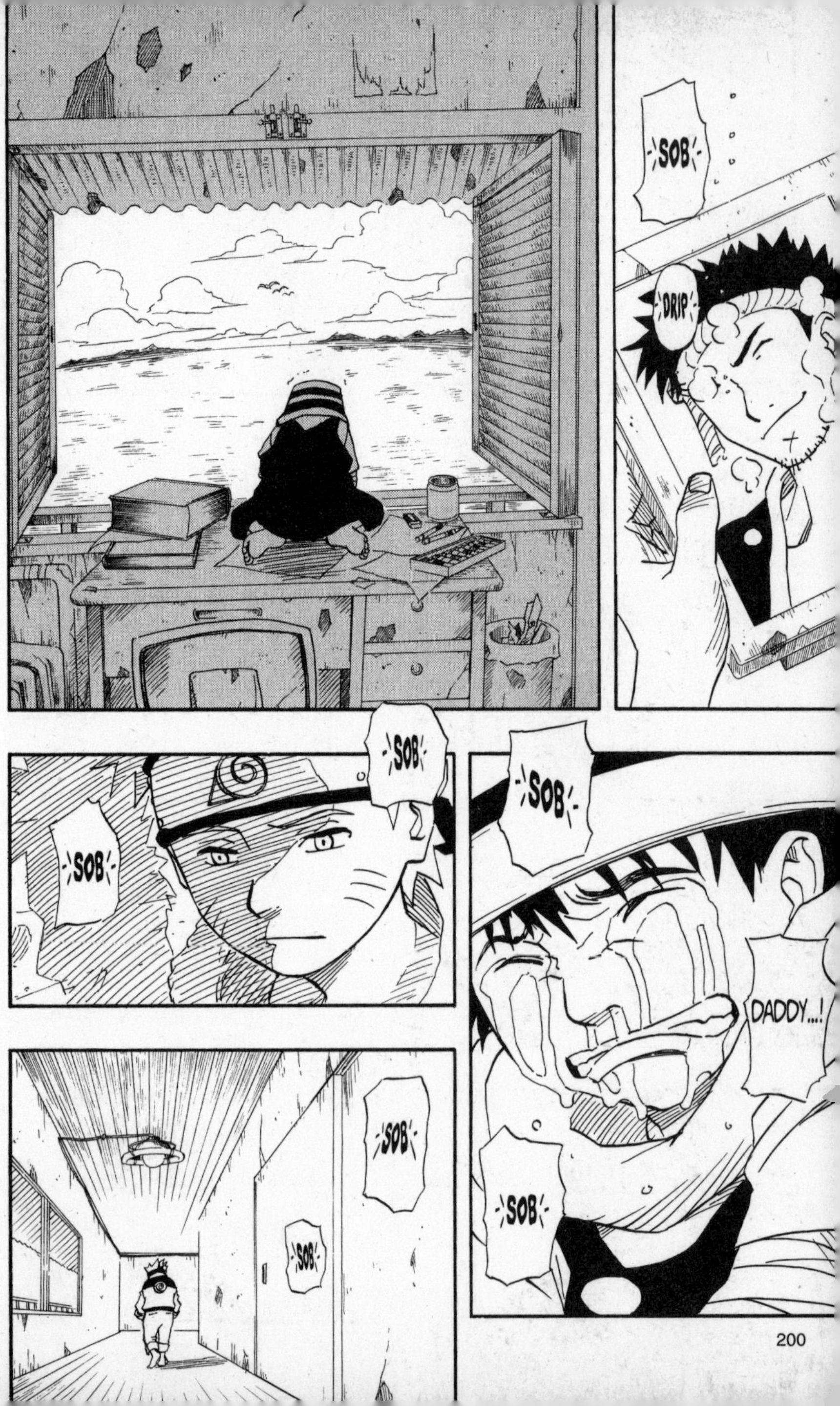
SOB
DRIP
SOB
DADDY...!
SOB
SOB
SOB
SOB
SOB

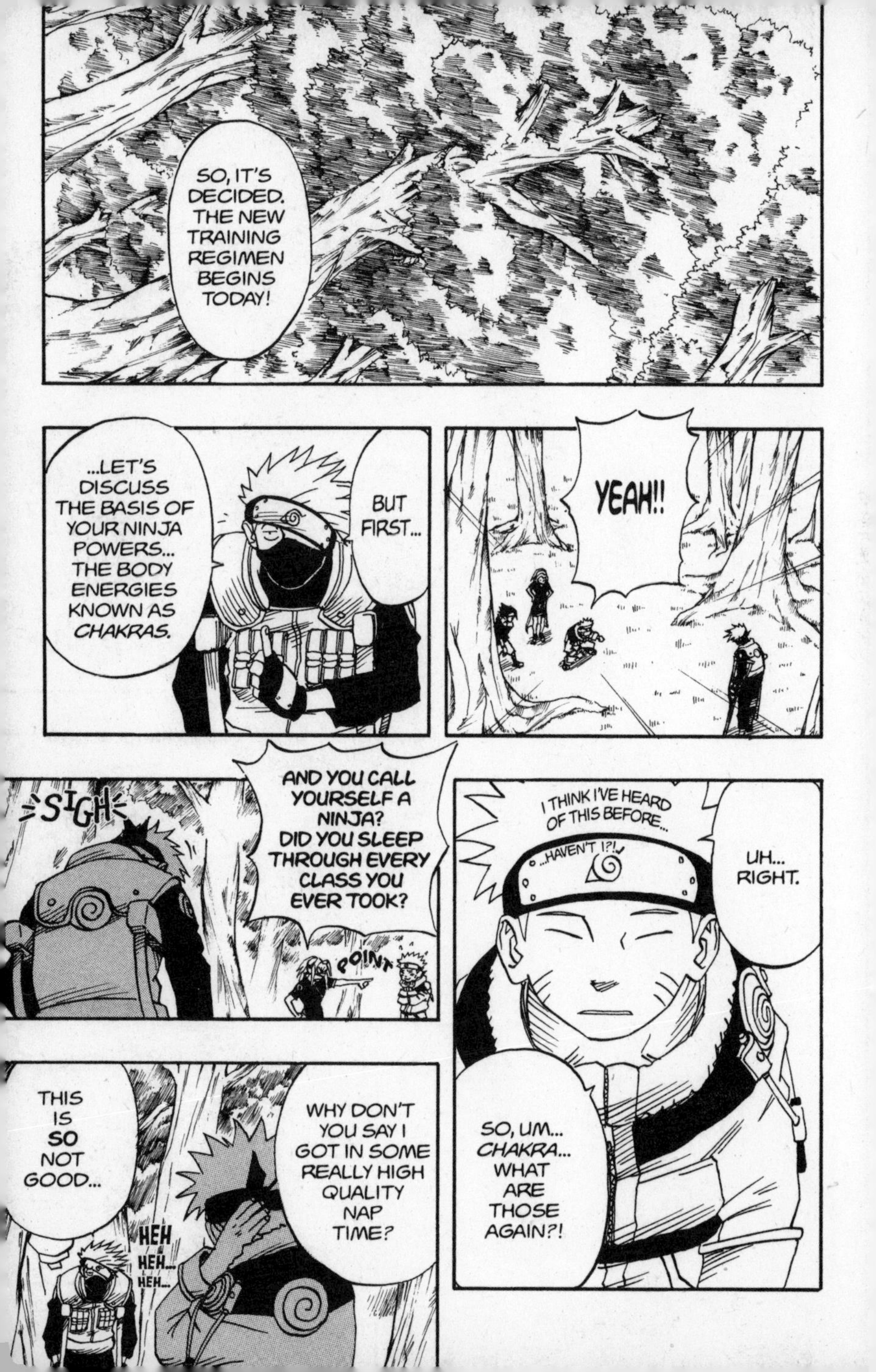
SO, IT'S DECIDED. THE NEW TRAINING REGIMEN BEGINS TODAY!
YEAH!!
BUT FIRST...
...LET'S DISCUSS THE BASIS OF YOUR NINJA POWERS... THE BODY ENERGIES KNOWN AS *CHAKRAS.*
UH... RIGHT.
I THINK I'VE HEARD OF THIS BEFORE...
...HAVEN'T I?!
SO, UM... *CHAKRA*... WHAT ARE THOSE AGAIN?!
AND YOU CALL YOURSELF A NINJA? DID YOU SLEEP THROUGH EVERY CLASS YOU EVER TOOK?
SIGH
POINT
WHY DON'T YOU SAY I GOT IN SOME REALLY HIGH QUALITY NAP TIME?
THIS IS **SO** NOT GOOD...
HEH HEH... HEH...

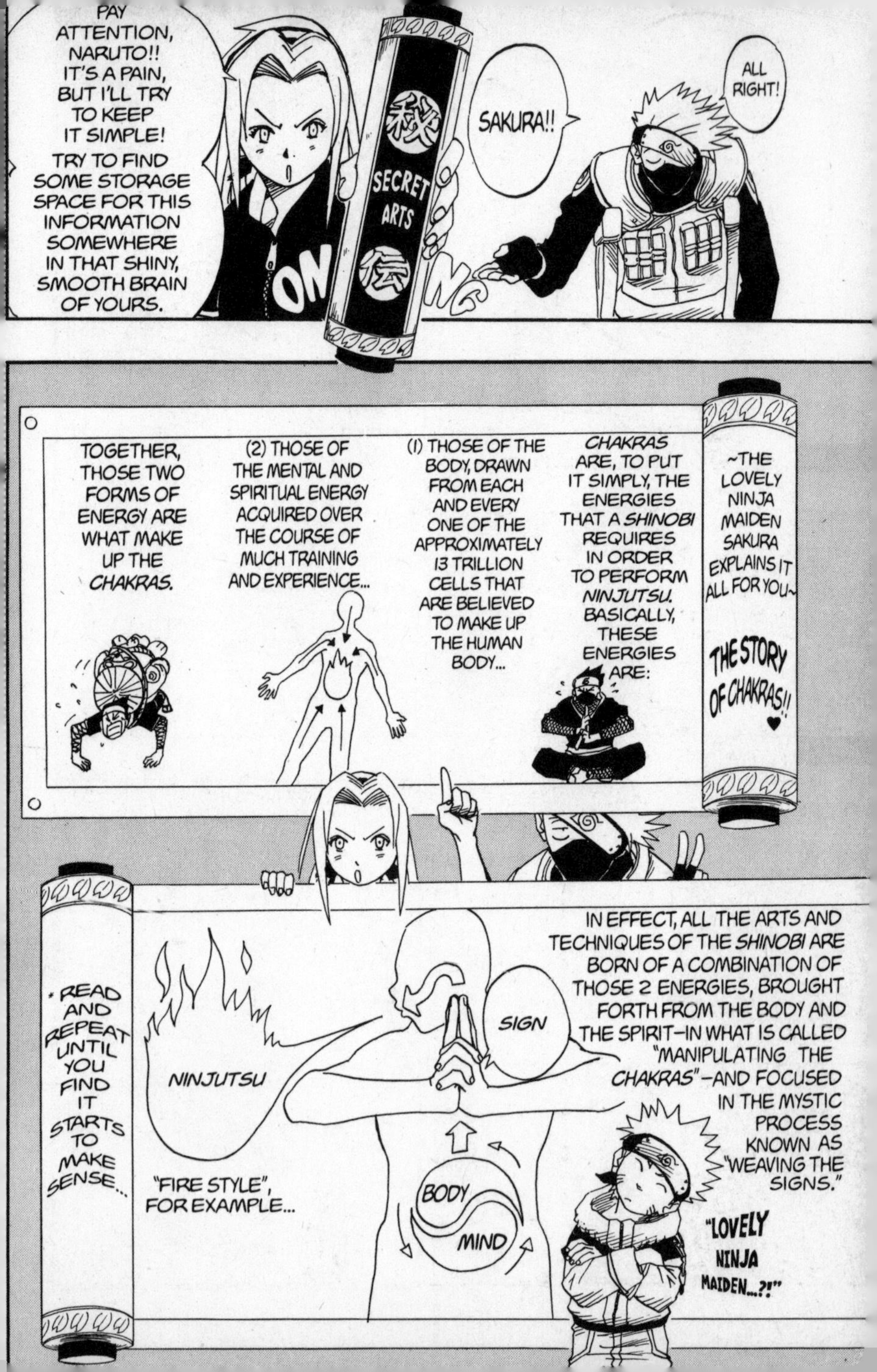
ALL RIGHT!
SAKURA!!
PAY ATTENTION, NARUTO!! IT'S A PAIN, BUT I'LL TRY TO KEEP IT SIMPLE!
TRY TO FIND SOME STORAGE SPACE FOR THIS INFORMATION SOMEWHERE IN THAT SHINY, SMOOTH BRAIN OF YOURS.
秘 SECRET ARTS 伝
~THE LOVELY NINJA MAIDEN SAKURA EXPLAINS IT ALL FOR YOU~
THE STORY OF CHAKRAS!! ♥
CHAKRAS ARE, TO PUT IT SIMPLY, THE ENERGIES THAT A *SHINOBI* REQUIRES IN ORDER TO PERFORM *NINJUTSU*. BASICALLY, THESE ENERGIES ARE:
(1) THOSE OF THE BODY, DRAWN FROM EACH AND EVERY ONE OF THE APPROXIMATELY 13 TRILLION CELLS THAT ARE BELIEVED TO MAKE UP THE HUMAN BODY...
(2) THOSE OF THE MENTAL AND SPIRITUAL ENERGY ACQUIRED OVER THE COURSE OF MUCH TRAINING AND EXPERIENCE...
TOGETHER, THOSE TWO FORMS OF ENERGY ARE WHAT MAKE UP THE *CHAKRAS*.
IN EFFECT, ALL THE ARTS AND TECHNIQUES OF THE *SHINOBI* ARE BORN OF A COMBINATION OF THOSE 2 ENERGIES, BROUGHT FORTH FROM THE BODY AND THE SPIRIT—IN WHAT IS CALLED "MANIPULATING THE *CHAKRAS*"—AND FOCUSED IN THE MYSTIC PROCESS KNOWN AS "WEAVING THE SIGNS."
"LOVELY NINJA MAIDEN...?!"
SIGN
NINJUTSU
BODY
MIND
"FIRE STYLE", FOR EXAMPLE...
*READ AND REPEAT UNTIL YOU FIND IT STARTS TO MAKE SENSE...

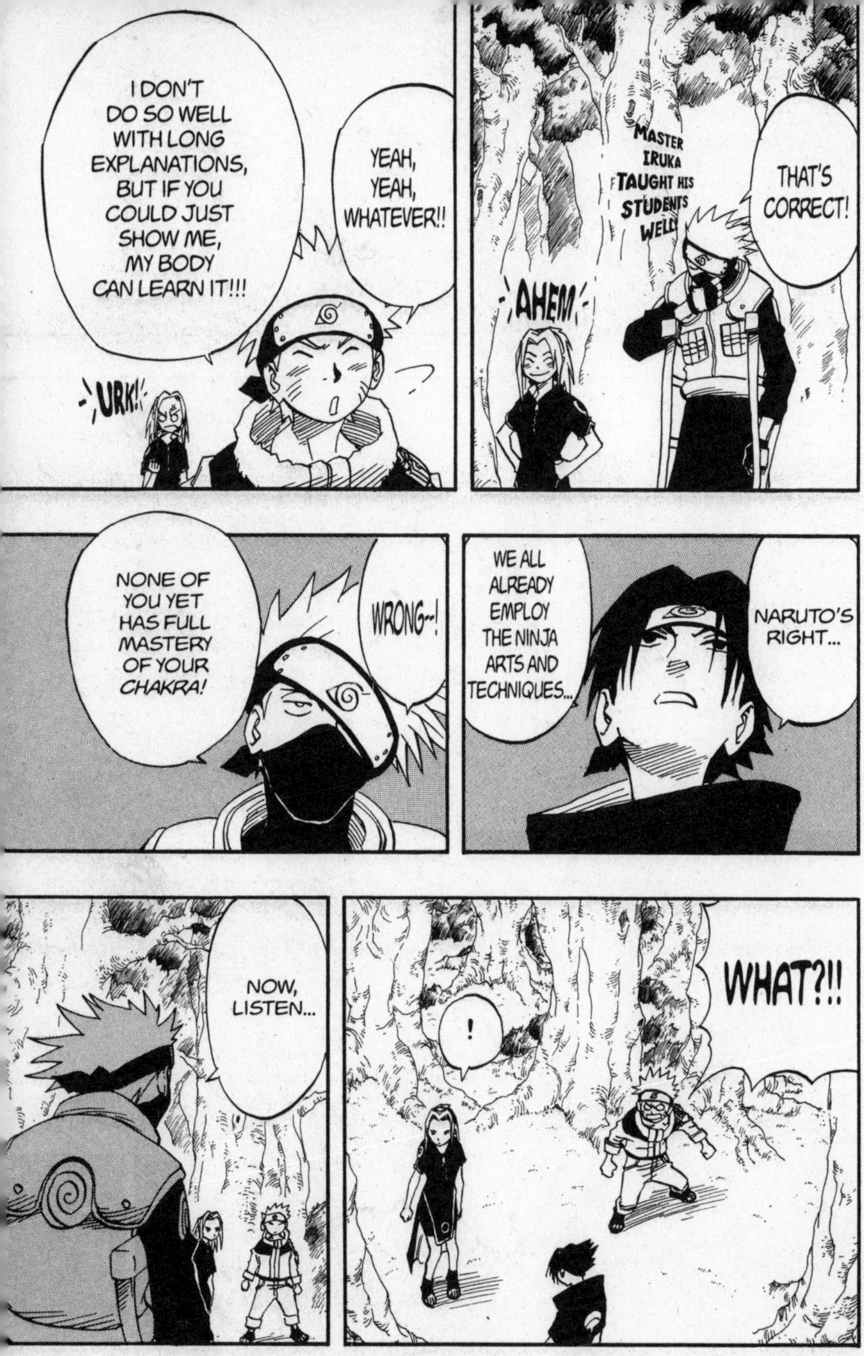
THAT'S CORRECT!
MASTER IRUKA TAUGHT HIS STUDENTS WELL
AHEM
YEAH, YEAH, WHATEVER!!
I DON'T DO SO WELL WITH LONG EXPLANATIONS, BUT IF YOU COULD JUST SHOW ME, MY BODY CAN LEARN IT!!!
URK!
NARUTO'S RIGHT...
WE ALL ALREADY EMPLOY THE NINJA ARTS AND TECHNIQUES...
WRONG--!
NONE OF YOU YET HAS FULL MASTERY OF YOUR CHAKRA!
WHAT?!!
!
NOW, LISTEN...

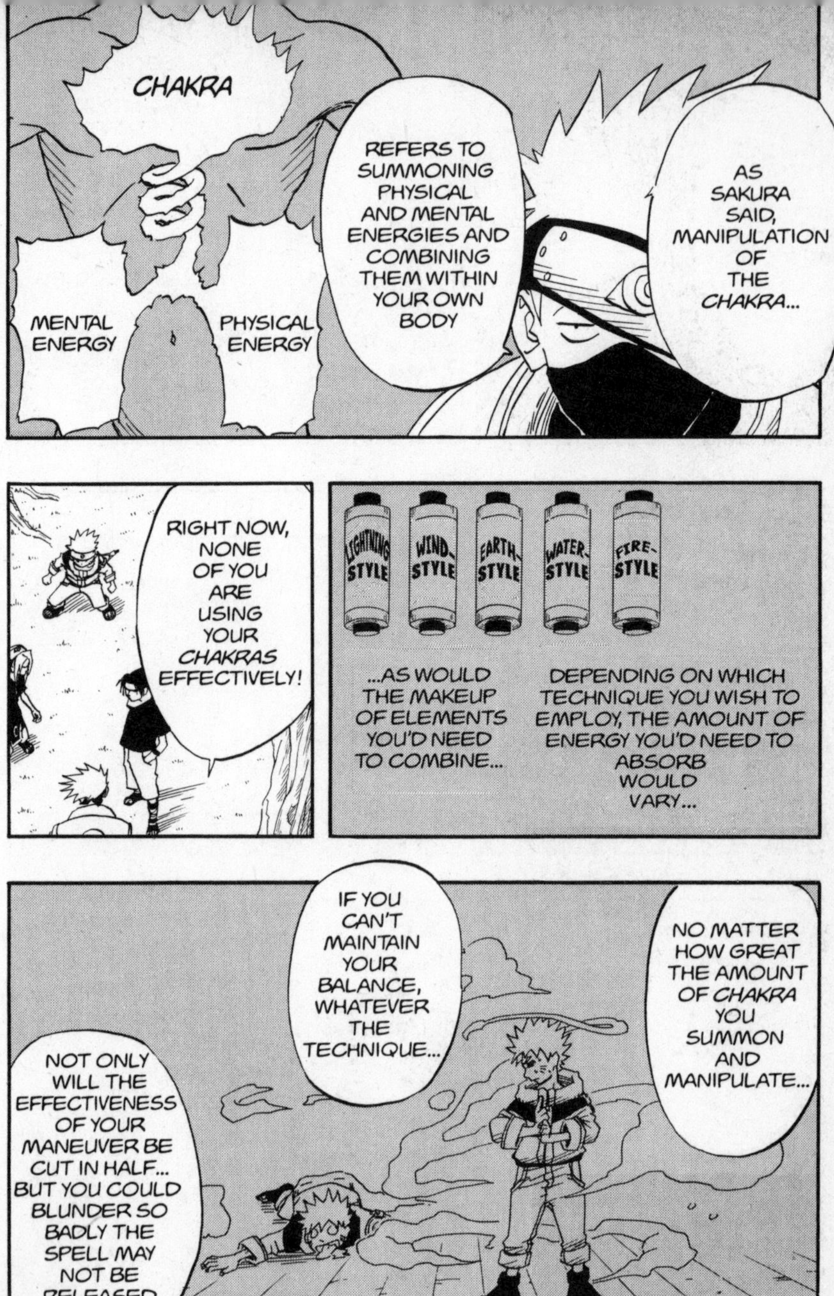
AS SAKURA SAID, MANIPULATION OF THE *CHAKRA*...
REFERS TO SUMMONING PHYSICAL AND MENTAL ENERGIES AND COMBINING THEM WITHIN YOUR OWN BODY
CHAKRA
PHYSICAL ENERGY
MENTAL ENERGY
FIRE-STYLE
WATER-STYLE
EARTH-STYLE
WIND-STYLE
LIGHTNING STYLE
DEPENDING ON WHICH TECHNIQUE YOU WISH TO EMPLOY, THE AMOUNT OF ENERGY YOU'D NEED TO ABSORB WOULD VARY...
...AS WOULD THE MAKEUP OF ELEMENTS YOU'D NEED TO COMBINE...
RIGHT NOW, NONE OF YOU ARE USING YOUR *CHAKRAS* EFFECTIVELY!
NO MATTER HOW GREAT THE AMOUNT OF *CHAKRA* YOU SUMMON AND MANIPULATE...
IF YOU CAN'T MAINTAIN YOUR BALANCE, WHATEVER THE TECHNIQUE...
NOT ONLY WILL THE EFFECTIVENESS OF YOUR MANEUVER BE CUT IN HALF... BUT YOU COULD BLUNDER SO BADLY THE SPELL MAY NOT BE RELEASED AT ALL.

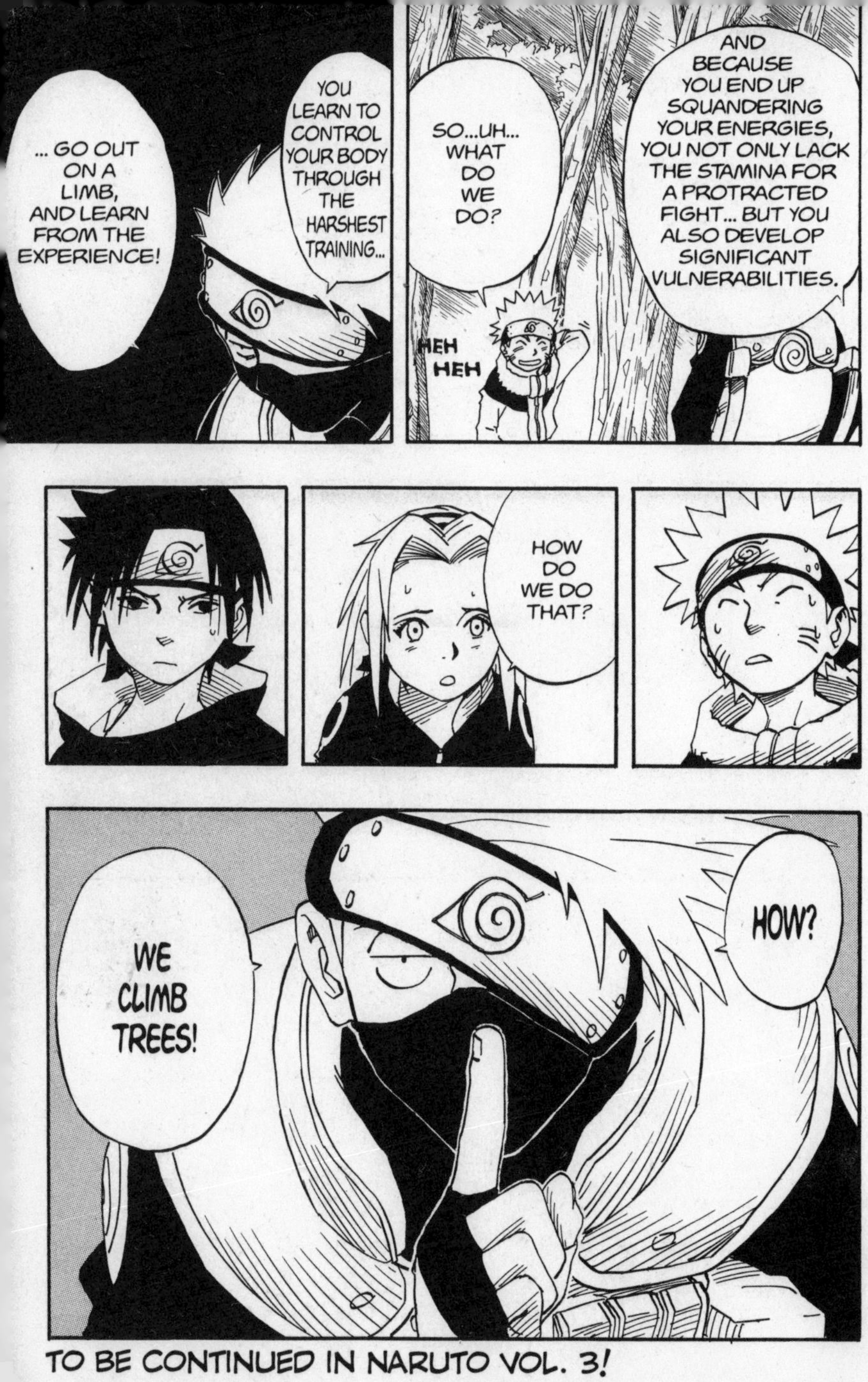
AND BECAUSE YOU END UP SQUANDERING YOUR ENERGIES, YOU NOT ONLY LACK THE STAMINA FOR A PROTRACTED FIGHT... BUT YOU ALSO DEVELOP SIGNIFICANT VULNERABILITIES.
SO...UH... WHAT DO WE DO?
HEH HEH
YOU LEARN TO CONTROL YOUR BODY THROUGH THE HARSHEST TRAINING...
... GO OUT ON A LIMB, AND LEARN FROM THE EXPERIENCE!
HOW DO WE DO THAT?
HOW?
WE CLIMB TREES!

TO BE CONTINUED IN NARUTO VOL. 3!

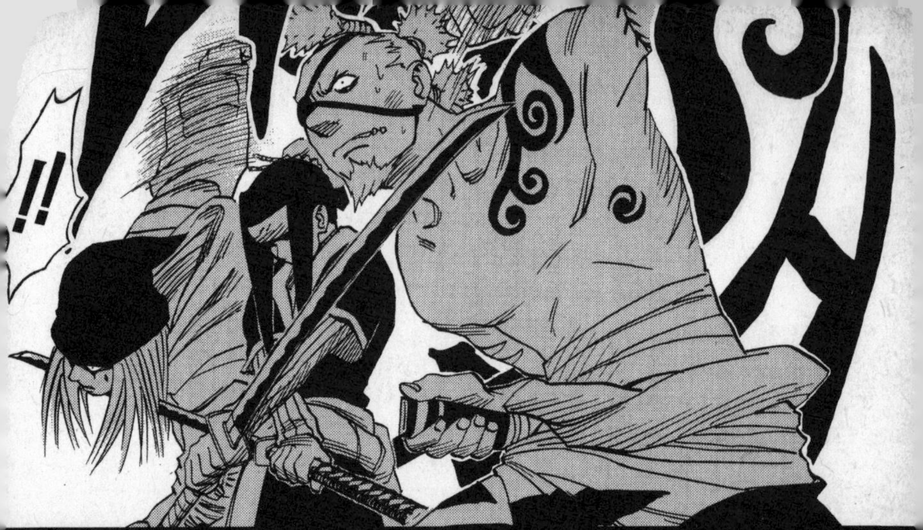
!!

IN THE NEXT VOLUME...
While Naruto, Sasuke and Sakura practice their skills with Kakashi's special kind of tree climbing, their enemies are healing up—and getting stronger! As soon as Zabuza recovers from his wounds, he's coming back to finish the job and kill Tazuna. Meanwhile, the heroes discover the true story of Inari's father; Gatô sends his samurai henchmen, Zouri and Waraji, to take a hostage; and the stage is set for a rematch! But this time, which side will Haku be on?
AVAILABLE NOW!

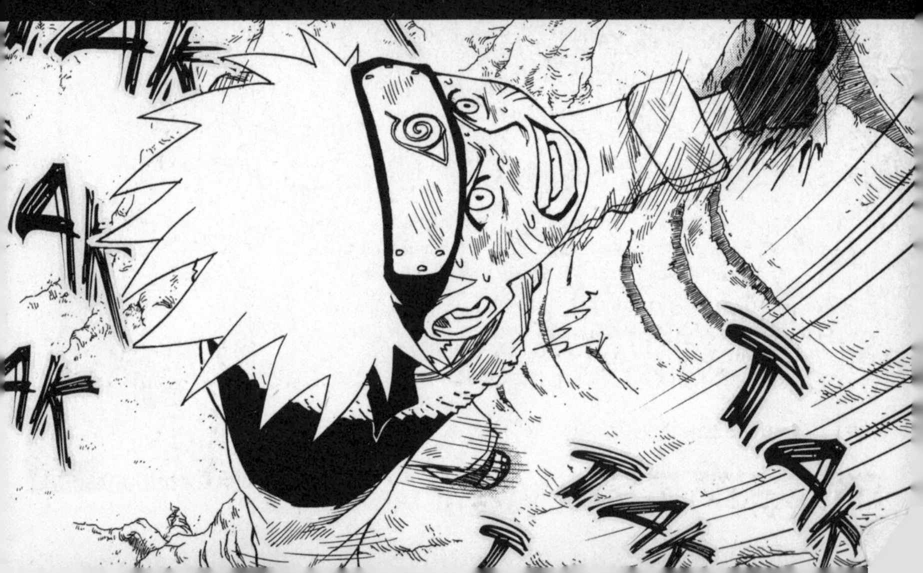

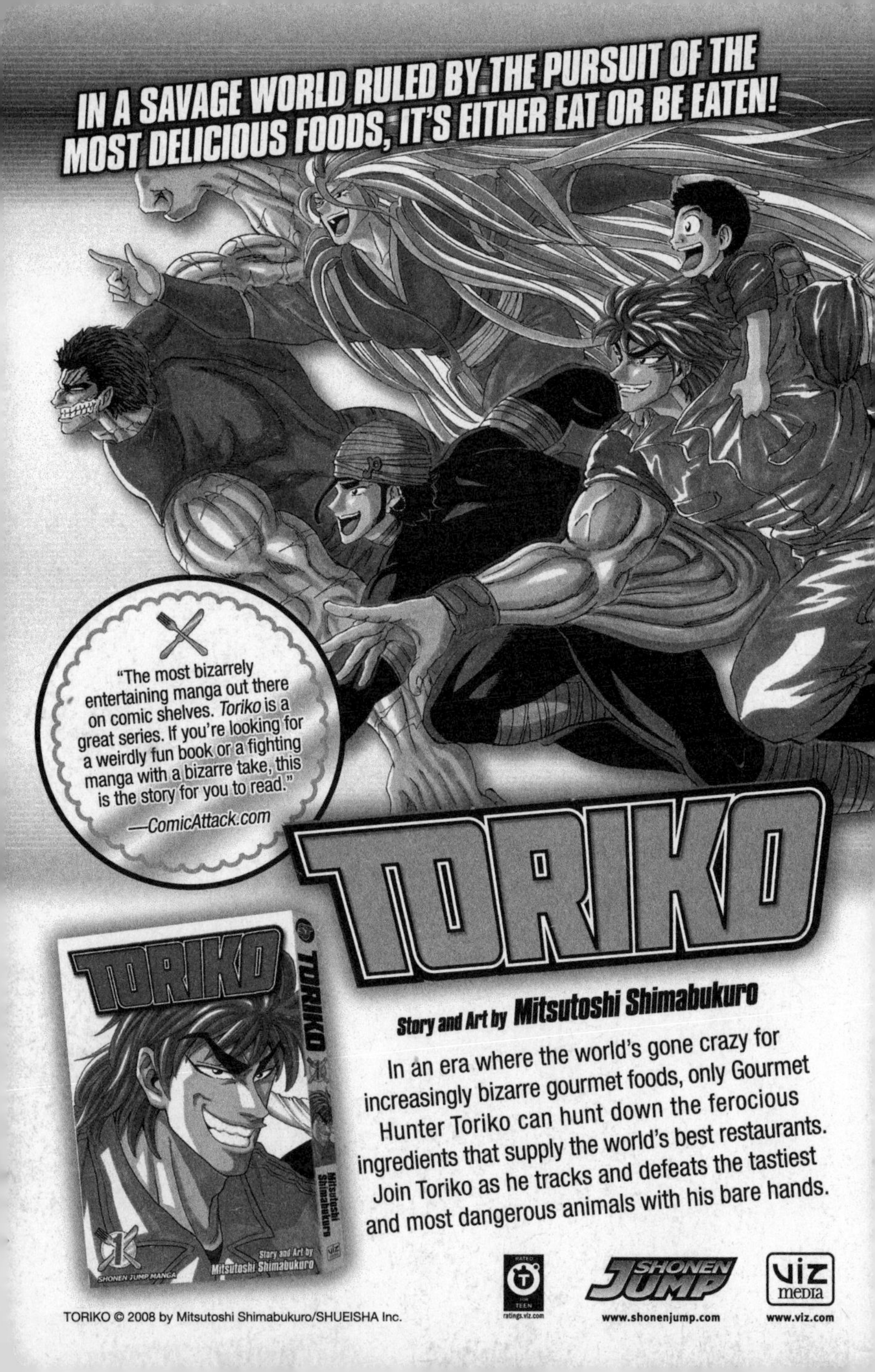
IN A SAVAGE WORLD RULED BY THE PURSUIT OF THE MOST DELICIOUS FOODS, IT'S EITHER EAT OR BE EATEN!
"The most bizarrely entertaining manga out there on comic shelves. Toriko is a great series. If you're looking for a weirdly fun book or a fighting manga with a bizarre take, this is the story for you to read."
—ComicAttack.com
TORIKO
TORIKO
Story and Art by Mitsutoshi Shimabukuro
SHONEN JUMP MANGA
Story and Art by Mitsutoshi Shimabukuro
Story and Art by Mitsutoshi Shimabukuro
In an era where the world's gone crazy for increasingly bizarre gourmet foods, only Gourmet Hunter Toriko can hunt down the ferocious ingredients that supply the world's best restaurants. Join Toriko as he tracks and defeats the tastiest and most dangerous animals with his bare hands.
RATED T FOR TEEN
ratings.viz.com
SHONEN JUMP
www.shonenjump.com
VIZ media
www.viz.com
TORIKO © 2008 by Mitsutoshi Shimabukuro/SHUEISHA Inc.

SEE INTO THE SOUL
OF *BLEACH*
WITH THE MANGA,
PROFILES AND ART BOOKS

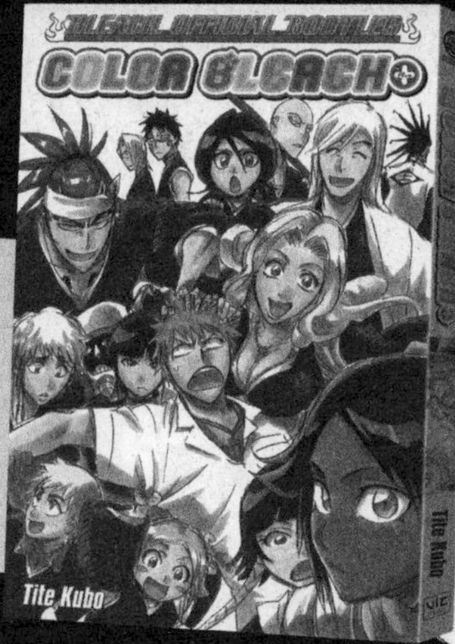

BLEACH OFFICIAL BOOKLET
COLOR BLEACH+
Tite Kubo

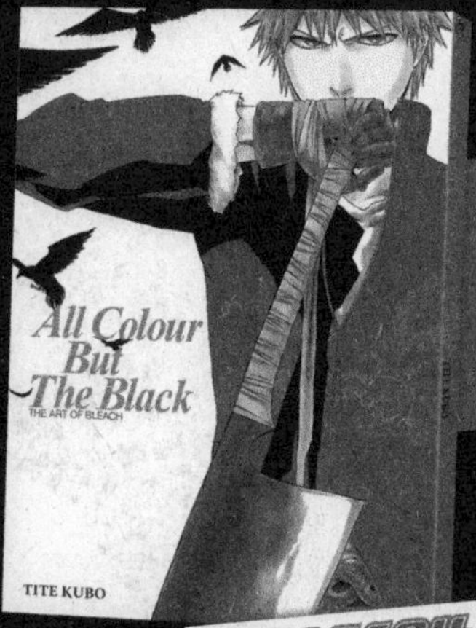

All Colour But The Black
THE ART OF BLEACH
TITE KUBO

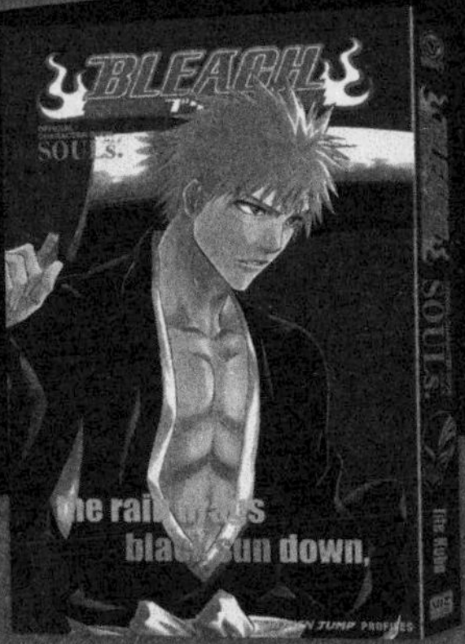

BLEACH
SOULS.

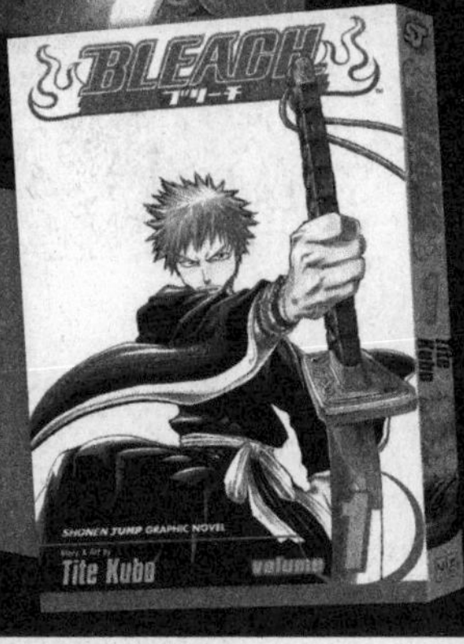

BLEACH
ブリーチ
SHONEN JUMP GRAPHIC NOVEL
Tite Kubo
volume

THE BEST SELLING MANGA SERIES IN THE WORLD!

ONE PIECE

Story & Art by EIICHIRO ODA

As a child, **Monkey D. Luffy** was inspired to become a pirate by listening to the tales of the buccaneer "Red-Haired" Shanks. But Luffy's life changed when he accidentally ate the Gum-Gum Devil Fruit and gained the power to stretch like rubber...at the cost of never being able to swim again! Years later, still vowing to become the king of the pirates, Luffy sets out on his adventure in search of the legendary "One Piece," said to be the greatest treasure in the world...

A PREMIUM BOX SET OF THE
FIRST TWO STORY ARCS OF ONE PIECE!
A PIRATE'S TREASURE FOR ANY MANGA FAN!

STORY AND ART BY EIICHIRO ODA

As a child, Monkey D. Luffy dreamed of becoming King of the Pirates.
But his life changed when he accidentally gained the power to stretch like
rubber...at the cost of never being able to swim again! Years later, Luffy sets off
in search of the "One Piece," said to be the greatest treasure in the world...

This box set includes VOLUMES 1-23, which comprise
the EAST BLUE and BAROQUE WORKS story arcs.

EXCLUSIVE PREMIUMS and GREAT SAVINGS
over buying the individual volumes!

BAKUMAN.

STORY BY TSUGUMI OHBA
ART BY TAKESHI OBATA

From the creators of *Death Note*

The mystery behind manga making REVEALED!

Average student Moritaka Mashiro enjoys drawing for fun. When his classmate and aspiring writer Akito Takagi discovers his talent, he begs to team up. But what exactly does it take to make it in the manga-publishing world?

Bakuman. Vol. 1
ISBN: 978-1-4215-3513-5
$9.99 US / $12.99 CAN *

The mystery behind *manga-making* revealed!

BAKUMAN

Story by **TSUGUMI OHBA** ✒ *Art by* **TAKESHI OBATA**

From the creators of **Death Note**

Comes with a *two-sided poster* and the *Otter No. 11* mini-comic!

Average student Moritaka Mashiro enjoys drawing for fun. When his classmate and aspiring writer Akito Takagi discovers his talent, he begs Moritaka to team up with him as a manga-creating duo. But what exactly does it take to make it in the manga-publishing world?

This *bestselling series* is now available in a COMPLETE BOX SET!

A 20% SAVINGS OVER BUYING THE INDIVIDUAL VOLUMES!

You're Reading in the Wrong Direction!!

Whoops! Guess what? You're starting at the wrong end of the comic!

...It's true! In keeping with the original Japanese format, **Naruto** is meant to be read from right to left, starting in the upper-right corner.

Unlike English, which is read from left to right, Japanese is read from right to left, meaning that action, sound effects and word-balloon order are completely reversed...something which can make readers unfamiliar with Japanese feel pretty backwards themselves. For this reason, manga or Japanese comics published in the U.S. in English have sometimes been published "flopped"—that is, printed in exact reverse order, as though seen from the other side of a mirror.

By flopping pages, U.S. publishers can avoid confusing readers, but the compromise is not without its downside. For one thing, a character in a flopped manga series who once wore in the original Japanese version a T-shirt emblazoned with "M A Y" (as in "the merry month of") now wears one which reads "Y A M"! Additionally, many manga creators in Japan are themselves unhappy with the process, as some feel the mirror-imaging of their art alters their original intentions.

We are proud to bring you Masashi Kishimoto's **Naruto** in the original unflopped format. For now, though, turn to the other side of the book and let the ninjutsu begin...!

—Editor

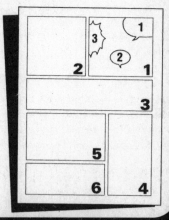